THE SEVEN MEN OF SPANDAU

Jack Fishman

THE SEVEN MEN OF SPANDAU

Published by Sapere Books.
24 Trafalgar Road, Ilkley, LS29 8HH
United Kingdom

saperebooks.com

Copyright © JHP Ltd, 1986, 1989.
First published under the title Long Knives and Short Memories, 1986.
JHP Ltd has asserted its right to be identified as the author of this work.
All rights reserved.

No part of this publication may be reproduced, stored in any retrieval system, or transmitted, in any form, or by any means, electronic, mechanical, photocopying, recording, or otherwise, without the prior written permission of the publishers.

ISBN: 978-0-85495-157-4.

TABLE OF CONTENTS

DEDICATION	7
1: SHORT MEMORIES	10
2: THE LAST OF THE HITLER GANG	22
3: SHOOT THE LOT!	46
4: RUDOLF HESS'S GREATEST FEAR	66
5: THE CLOWN PRINCE	100
6: A FIGHT FOR LIFE IN THE DEATH CELL	122
7: THE RICHEST MAN IN GAOL	145
8: THE GARDEN OF EDEN	165
9: A NAVAL ENCOUNTER	193
10: HITLER'S SUCCESSOR	211
11: THE WOMEN OF SPANDAU	230
12: EMERGENCY	285
13: SPANDAU LETTERS	306
14: TOUCHING IS NOT ALLOWED	331
15: THE PUNCHING BAG	345
16: FORBIDDEN WORDS	386
17: THE EIGHTH MAN OF SPANDAU	411
18: THE QUALITY OF MERCY	428
19: THE GOLDEN DILEMMA	459
20: ORDERS ARE ORDERS	481
21: AND THEN THERE WERE THREE	496
22: AND THEN THERE WAS ONE	518
23: SUMMING UP	562
AUTHOR'S NOTES AND ACKNOWLEDGEMENTS	575
BIBLIOGRAPHY	580
A NOTE TO THE READER	582

DEDICATION

I was seven years old when I first stood outside Spandau Prison and stared at its forbidding walls. My mother pointed it out to me on one of our many visits to Germany to see her relations. I learned to speak German through playing with children in the streets of Berlin and Hanover. I even met Adolf Hitler in Hanover when I was ten. I regret to say that, mistaking me for a German boy, he patted me on the head. In later years, when I became a newspaper reporter, the knowledge of Germany and its people that I had gained as a child proved invaluable.

I dedicate this book to my mother, who was alive when I began it and who encouraged me so much. When I started researching the Spandau story, well over thirty years ago, I typed the initial book I wrote on the subject on the little portable Underwood machine — my first typewriter — that my mother bought me when I was sixteen. I carried that machine with me throughout my early Spandau investigations in Germany, France, Britain, and the United States. Nostalgically, I typed this dedication to my mother on that same typewriter.

Jack Fishman

INTRODUCTION

The Seven Men of Spandau was my father's first book. Published in 1954 by W H Allen, nine years after the end of the war, a year before his mother died and I was born.

During and after the war, Jack worked as a journalist for *The Empire News*, one of the country's national newspapers owned by the Thompson organisation. Eventually he became the editor but in 1961 left to write the acclaimed biography of Lady Clementine Churchill, *My Darling Clementine.*

As a child Jack had been with his mother to Berlin to stay with her brother. Following the death of his father, they lived there for a while during which time Jack witnessed the rise of the Nazis and Adolf Hitler. For many reasons it left a deep impression on him. One day on his way home from school, a brief but bizarre encounter occurred as a result of a large crowd gathered outside the Town Hall. Forcing his way to the front to see what was happening, at the top of the steps stood Adolf Hitler, Speer and other leading Nazis, who then slowly descended to great the crowd. Seeing a child with blond hair and blue eyes, Hitler stood in front of Jack, smiled and patted him on the head, unaware that he was not of German descent but Jewish. Later he recounted the story, much to his mother's disbelief and horror.

Jack would not return to Berlin until after the war when he visited to research and take photographs for this book. By then the world was a very different place, as much of Germany and Europe had been devasted. The book concerns the seven Nazis who after the Nuremberg trial were imprisoned at

Spandau. Little was known about the most notorious criminals of the 20th century.

Who were these people who had been responsible for committing such appalling crimes against humanity?

Paul Fishman

1: SHORT MEMORIES

This book took more than thirty years to complete.

It began a few days after a unit of British soldiers arrived at Spandau gaol, in Berlin, to take over guard duties. The unit consisted entirely of National Service conscripts — boys who had grown up during World War II. They were marched to the briefing room to receive instructions from their commanding officer, who stood on a platform to address them.

'Do you know whom you are guarding in this prison?' he asked.

Nobody replied.

Turning to the blackboard behind him, the officer picked up a piece of chalk and wrote in big white letters:

HESS
FUNK
SPEER
SCHIRACH
NEURATH
DÖNITZ
RAEDER

Pointing to the first name, the officer inquired: 'Does anyone know who this man is?'

There was a silence, and then a hand shot up.

'Yes?' queried the officer.

'A black marketeer, sir?' came the naïve answer.

Not one among the soldiers — children of the war — had heard of the seven men of Spandau or knew the reasons for their imprisonment. So there was more than a modicum of truth in the comment made inside the gaol by Hitler's Minister of Production, Albert Speer:

'Most people in the world have forgotten what we are in for.'

The young soldiers were ignorant of the background of the men they were about to guard. They were unaware that the seven had been tried and found guilty for their complicity in what a distinguished German lawyer had described as

> a despotism which pressed for war by enslaving justice and freedom through terror, corruption, faithlessness, lies, and disregard for the most sacred human rights; which initiated war against the mightiest nations, violating international agreements, waged it with numberless and unparalleled cruelties, and by this criminal madness delivered the German people into inexpressible misery and its beautiful country into horrible devastation.

Two of the men in the prison had been chosen to carry on where Hitler left off. One, claiming 'a right inherited from Hitler's will', asserted that he would be entitled to place himself at the head of the German State when freed after his ten-year sentence. The other, imprisoned for the rest of his life, saw himself as a 'mystical spiritual leader' of the German nation, destined to restore the creed of his Führer.

Karl Dönitz, commander of the Nazi U-boats, who had announced himself President of the Third Reich after Hitler's suicide in the Berlin bunker; and Rudolf Hess, the Deputy Führer, who had parachuted into Britain in 1941 on a mission of 'peace': these were two of the seven men held in the world's most fantastic fortress.

In Berlin's Spandau Prison, the seven men, sentenced by the Nuremberg Tribunal for crimes against humanity, were surrounded by every conceivable escape-proof precaution.

They had formerly been among the most powerful men on earth, but the world soon forgot Grand Admiral Karl Dönitz, Deputy Führer Rudolf Hess, Hitler Youth Leader Baldur von Schirach, Reichsbank Minister Walther Funk, Grand Admiral Erich Raeder, Minister of War Production Albert Speer, and Foreign Minister and 'Protector of Bohemia and Moravia' Baron Konstantin von Neurath.

They had sat in the Nuremberg dock alongside Göring, Streicher, and Ribbentrop for attempting to enslave the world. In Spandau they now became numbers in an extraordinary prison tomb. Napoleon's banishment to the island of Elba wrote an unforgettable page in history; the exile of the seven Nazi Napoleons fashioned even more fantastic history after 1945, when three were sentenced to imprisonment for the rest of their natural life, two for twenty years, one for fifteen years and one for ten years. Millions with short memories swiftly forgot them, what they had done, and what they had tried to do. New generations, like the young British soldiers assigned to guard them, had little or no idea of their significance, or the symbolism of the gaol in which they were imprisoned.

Disturbed by the realization that so much of the evil that men do does not live on, I felt compelled to write the Spandau story. In 1954 I published the first edition of *The Seven Men of Spandau* — the first book on the subject — and was almost imprisoned myself for doing so. Much of the book's contents involved breaches of Britain's Official Secrets Acts, for the gaol was enveloped in total security.

Although everything about the prison was secret and its inmates were guarded by unprecedented security measures, I set out to pierce the screen around the seven. What were their lives like in the bizarre gaol? What did they discuss? What did they write in their letters home? What could I discover about their families and their past? I had to cut through secrecy, propaganda, lies, exaggerations and endless rumours. I received no authorized assistance for my 1954 book, but this time it has been a very different story. I was given official help in Washington, London, Paris, Bonn and Berlin, and had access to a mass of hitherto confidential documents and correspondence.

Within days of the publication of my first book on the subject, I was notified that the Secretary of State for Foreign Affairs, Selwyn Lloyd, wished to interview me regarding my disclosures; I was requested to meet him in his private room at the House of Commons. I replied that I would agree to discuss the matter only in the presence of an independent witness, and proposed that Evelyn Walkden, MP, a former deputy Government Minister, should accompany me. The condition was accepted. On arrival at the Foreign Secretary's Parliamentary room, we found him awaiting us with two companions — one from the Foreign Office German Division, and another from MI6 — the Secret Service.

Selwyn Lloyd opened the conversation by pointing out that a substantial proportion of the material in my book constituted breaches of official secrets, laying me, and others who must have co-operated, open to possible prosecution and imprisonment. I answered that instead of being threatened I should be thanked for exposing the gaol's serious security deficiencies. In support of this contention I handed the Minister a photocopy of a pencil-written letter smuggled out of the gaol by Dönitz. The letter instructed friends to prepare for his release and intended re-emergence in politics. This was clear evidence that the Grand Admiral had not forsaken his ambition to be recognized as Hitler's lawful successor.

That letter and other documents — including forbidden, private and secret official correspondence I had obtained — had for security reasons to remain unpublished at the time. But I have included them, and many others discovered since, in this book. The evidence I produced for the Foreign Secretary was irrefutable and valuable. No official proceedings were taken against me. The importance of the smuggled Dönitz letter, more than anything else, saved me from prosecution and possible imprisonment.

Twelve years later, Albert Speer published his illegally kept Spandau diaries. He noted that one of his warders, after reading newspaper-serialized extracts from my book, remarked to him: 'The ship has a hole in it. News leaks out and in.'

Speer added in his diary: 'Suppose Hawker [the guard] suspected that I have already smuggled many hundreds of pages out of the "best-guarded prison in the world"!'

Speer, Hess, and Dönitz discussed some of my disclosures in the gaol. Writing about this in his diary, Speer records:

> Hess is concerned about the report that he is the future leader of a German nationalist party. In a troubled tone, he says, 'That puts a heavy obstacle in the way of my release, coming as it does right during the foreign ministers' conference.'
>
> I ask innocently, 'Would you rather be represented as a repentant sinner, like me?'
>
> Hess hesitates. After some consideration he replies, downcast, 'At the moment, yes. I'd like to get out. How and why, I don't care.'
>
> In the library in the evening Dönitz, too, shows concern over the ambitions ascribed to him to become the Chief of State after his release. 'But the newspaper also wrote that I would like to establish a children's home,' he says, trying to comfort himself. 'My wife is trying to dissuade me from it because I'm too old. She may be right.'

> Hess assumes a false kindly tone. 'Well, well! Too old for a children's home, but young enough for Chief of State. Is that the idea?'

After my 1954 account of the prison had been published, I continued to collect information about Spandau Prison and the seven inmates. One day the complete story would need to be told. Speer could only draw back the curtain and reveal what he was able to see from his restricted viewpoint. He never saw fellow prisoners' letters home; he had no knowledge of their personal affairs and diplomatic manoeuvres to win possible earlier freedom. Nor did he have access to official documents concerning the gaol and the internal and external political, legal, and medical battles over the prisoners.

With the onset of the Cold War soon after World War II, the gaol was the last place over which the four Powers — the United States, Britain, France, and the USSR — were still joined in quadripartite control and required to act together. Nevertheless, behind the scenes a secret ceaseless war over the seven men raged for years between the four nations. When six were finally freed, either because of illness, or after serving their sentences in full, war continued over the solitary remaining inmate — Rudolf Hess.

In the 1960s, when political pressures mounted for the remission of sentences and earlier release of Hess, Speer, and Schirach, I decided to ask the men who had put them in the gaol to reconsider the verdicts they had reached at Nuremberg. The Tribunal had met the requirements of utmost impartiality, loyalty and sense of justice with consideration and dignity. Nobody dares to doubt that those who prosecuted and those who sat in judgement were guided by the search for truth and justice from the first to the last day. So how would these same men, years afterwards, view reasons so strongly tendered for showing leniency and mercy to the remaining convicted men in Spandau? I sought the opinions of the judges and prosecutors of Nuremberg, and obtained answers from the United States, Britain, France, and the Soviet Union.

From wives, relatives, lawyers, friends and enemies, I added to my picture of the seven and their characters, and began to understand, even more completely, what they meant to themselves and to others. I obtained information from neo-Nazi and anti-Nazi organizations. In Berlin and in Bonn, the seat of the West German Government, I examined official and unofficial records on Spandau and its prisoners; I visited their confiscated estates and former homes; I travelled with prisoners' wives to Berlin for their prison visits. I had access to documents revealing political and diplomatic activities to free the prisoners or alter conditions of the sentences; I spoke to people who had worked closely with the seven during their Hitler heyday, and took extracts from hundreds of letters written by the seven in their cells — both official and smuggled letters.

My quotations from conversations within the gaol are the prisoners' *actual translated words*. Their discussions and comments were extracted or assembled by drawing on the aforementioned sources, plus reports obtained from prison personnel. Only in a few instances — mainly for security reasons — have I altered circumstances relating to discussions, and on some occasions introduced relevant additional material obtained subsequently from inmates or others involved. Many of the photographs illustrating this book were secretly taken *inside* the gaol.

When I first saw the wives and families of the seven I plainly told them that my aim was to get at the truth about Spandau and its prisoners. Several wanted me to submit chapters for their approval before publication. I refused to accept this as a compulsory condition of interviews, pointing out that only the investigator could weigh facts, decide which were true, and be the ultimate arbiter. I assured them that I would quote whatever they told me without cuts or alterations on my part. In fact, because of their particularly controversial nature, I did voluntarily send a complete transcript of my discussions with the wives of Dönitz and Raeder to Dr Otto Kranzbühler — their lawyer, a former judge advocate of the German Navy, and the man who outstandingly defended both men at their trial. But for him, Dönitz would almost certainly have been hanged instead of escaping with the lightest sentence of all. Dr Kranzbühler acknowledged the transcripts I sent him and made no objections or amendments to any of the statements within them. Despite this, I was viciously attacked in Germany.

The Ruhr weekly newspaper *Fortschritt* (Progress) accused me of using 'gangster methods' to get the wives of the Spandau prisoners to talk. It alleged that words put into the mouth of Frau Dönitz were 'pure invention with the intention of stirring up the British people against the release of the supreme commander of the German Navy and keeping him in prison for life'.

Those behind this attack were particularly angry because I revealed Dönitz's intention, when he left gaol, to bid for the office of Supreme Head of State. Men who secretly supported neo-Nazi leader Dr Werner Naumann, arrested by the British for trying to overthrow the West German Government, were reported to be backing *Fortschritt*, with the intention of making it the official mouthpiece of powerful ex-Nazi Party members who were again holding influential positions all over the country.

The *Fortschritt* attack on me claimed:

Fishman has cold-bloodedly put into the mouths of Frau Dönitz and Frau Raeder the statements he reproduces, and makes a whole series of further statements of anti-British and anti-Jewish character in order to stir up anti-German feeling in his English readers.

We have been able to fully convince ourselves that not one of the statements which Fishman has published in direct or indirect speech was ever actually made by Frau Dönitz or Frau Raeder.

Fortschritt clearly did not check with Dr Kranzbühler, the Dönitz and Raeder families' lawyer. He would have honourably confirmed that interview transcripts had been vetted by him prior to publication and in no way faulted or rejected. I promised to let the wives defend their husbands and themselves, and kept the promise — which was more justice than was ever shown by Nazis to the millions they slaughtered. The Nazi underground, who engineered the *Fortschritt* newspaper attack on me, knew this.

The almost universal attitude shown and explanation given by the war crimes defendants was that they were caught in Hitler's web, unable to extricate themselves. They said they were obliged under coercion of orders — without any alternative but execution or suicide — to carry out their assignments. Only a few defendants, exhibiting courage and character, somehow managed to remove themselves from those infamous assignments. Nothing too serious happened to them, proving that escape was possible for those who really had the character and desire to put humanity and decency above personal security at any price. The seven sentenced to imprisonment in Spandau gaol were not among the courageous few.

Elaborate legal attacks were made upon the jurisdiction of the war crimes Tribunals on the grounds that the law being applied was *ex post facto* law and that the defendants had not known that they would be held accountable under such law when they were acting under German law. But there was nothing *ex post facto* about the law applied in these cases. Rudimentary laws of humanity, including elementary laws of war such as those relating to the treatment of prisoners, reprisals, and hostages, were old and international long before the Nazi war machine went into action. They were as much a part of German military and civil law as they were of international law. Hitler's Third Reich violated and suspended honest German law as well as international and natural law. The truth was that the war criminals observed and permitted themselves to be ruled only by the lawlessness of Nazi ideology. Their legal defence was simply 'superior orders'. In other words, officers of the fighting forces and officers of the State were entitled to do whatever their Führer decreed, regardless of whether it was contrary to all respected legal concepts and the dictates of humanity.

The final chapter of this book is a summing up of the significance of Spandau and the Nuremberg sentences from the man who presided over and summed up for the Tribunal: Lord Justice Lawrence. Years afterwards, he made a fresh assessment of the verdicts and the trial; his widow, Marjorie, Lady Oaksey, permitted me to conclude the book with it.

The judgements that sent these men to gaol were reached by a Tribunal whose main purpose was to illustrate emphatically that war that leads mankind into deadly ruin is to be regarded as the greatest crime against it. This crime cannot be justified by anyone who claims to be a human being. The verdicts of Nuremberg were as follows:

Deputy Führer Rudolf Hess — 'For wholeheartedly supporting all Germany's aggressive actions and taking part in war crimes and crimes against humanity': *life imprisonment.*

Minister of War Production Albert Speer (with Goebbels, Himmler and Dönitz one of the Nazis' 'big four') — 'For urging the extension of the slave labour programme, using concentration camp and prisoner-of-war labour, and conscripting a labour force of fourteen million workers': *twenty years' imprisonment.*

German Minister of Economics and Reichsbank President Walther Funk — 'For participating in the economic preparation for aggressive war and crimes against humanity including persons and property in occupied territories': *life imprisonment.*

Hitler Youth Leader Baldur von Schirach — 'For polluting the minds of children, establishing the Hitler Youth as a source of replacement for the Nazi Party, participating in policies against Jews in Austria, and being responsible for the sufferings of foreign workers': *twenty years' imprisonment.*

Grand Admiral Erich Raeder — 'For planning and waging aggressive war and carrying out unrestricted submarine warfare including the sinking of unarmed neutral merchant ships': *life imprisonment.*

Former Foreign Minister and Protector of Bohemia and Moravia, Baron Konstantin von Neurath — 'For carrying out and assuming responsibility' for the execution of the foreign policy of the Nazi conspirators, and authorizing, directing and taking part in war crimes and crimes against humanity': *fifteen years' imprisonment.*

Grand Admiral Karl Dönitz — 'For his participation in the war conspiracy, for permitting the order to shoot Allied commandos taken prisoner to remain in force, and, as Head of the State after Hitler's death, ordering continuation of the war': *ten years' imprisonment.*

Those were the seven men of Spandau.

2: THE LAST OF THE HITLER GANG

Three cell doors opened in the Palace of Justice in Nuremberg, Germany, on the afternoon of 17 October 1946. Three prisoners were handed brooms and mops and ordered to accompany armed United States Army guards. As they strode along the corridors, the silence suddenly gave way to the monotonous beat, beat, beat of hammers and the sound grew even louder. The noise reached a crescendo as the men entered a glaringly lit room and perceived, through eyes that smarted from the pungent fumes of chloride of lime rising from the washed floor, the stark timber of dismantled gibbets. Three gallows had just implemented the world's sentences on Hitler's Foreign Minister, Joachim von Ribbentrop; Jew-baiter Julius Streicher; Austrian quisling and tyrant of the occupied Netherlands, Seyss-Inquart; Kaltenbrunner; Frank; Jodl; Frick; Keitel; Sauckel; Rosenberg: names that had brought suffering and death to millions. All had died here for their crimes against humanity.

The three prisoners — Deputy Führer Rudolf Hess, Germany's Minister of War Production Albert Speer, and Hitler Youth Leader and former Governor of Austria Baldur von Schirach — knew, as they set to work with the brooms and mops, that only Reichsmarschall Hermann Göring, with a secret phial of cyanide, and Labour Front leader Robert Ley, who strangled himself with a handkerchief (torn into strips and soaked in water to make it taut), had cheated the executioners.

Göring had tried to use the Nuremberg trial as an initial propaganda step in creating a Third Reich legend. He had shouted at fellow prisoners: 'You can take your morality and your repentance and your democracy and stick it up my arse! When it is a question of the interests of the nation, morality stops.'

Hess, who had owed his exalted position to his unquestioning loyalty, and to the circumstance of his having been with Hitler from the earliest days of the Nazi movement, momentarily stopped sweeping the floor to stand beside a dark stain that could have been a bloodstain. He raised his arm in Nazi salute. Hess loved calling attention to himself by creating moments of drama. In the years that followed he often accused prison personnel of attempting to poison his food; he handed written diet requirements to the officer in charge of Nuremberg prisoners, imperiously demanding:

1. I request that I be given minced meat every other day (a small quantity) and more vegetables.
2. Vegetable soup on the days that I don't have minced meat. If possible, neither should be made with rotten meat, nor smelling of either petroleum or carbolic. No condiments (salt or pepper) to be used.
3. For the evening meal I should like fish and vegetables.

Hess was one of the few survivors of the Third Reich's hierarchy left. Three were cleaning the execution chamber under the watchful eyes of guards, and four others were in Palace of Justice cells. The seven — members of the Führer's inner circle — were described by Winston Churchill as callous gangsters with political trappings. They were the last of the Hitler gang.

'They will hang us all,' Baldur von Schirach had said.

Having escaped the scaffold, the remaining guilty men, whose lust for power had enslaved millions and turned Europe into a vast cemetery of nameless dead, awaited a future that, as months went by, could not have been entirely without hope. There was every reason for encouragement. Their guardians — the United States, Britain, France, and the USSR — not only could not agree as to the manner in which the sentences should be carried out, but in the wrangling that ensued began to show signs of mutual recrimination. Marked differences between the legal and penal codes of the four nations were already creating problems.

The Russian viewpoint was that the prisoners should serve their sentences in 'complete solitary confinement', without benefit of visitors or the privilege of being able to read books. The French endorsed this in so far as solitary confinement was suggested, but not otherwise. Both Britain and the United States asserted that such treatment constituted punishment that went beyond the Nuremberg Tribunal's meaning of confinement. Throughout these acrimonious discussions the prisoners remained in Nuremberg, and seven months slipped by until at last the Russians agreed that the sentences should be served under the German prison code.

Even this concession did not end the argument. There was still the question to be resolved of the choice of prison. General Clay, for the US, thought that the men should remain in Nuremberg. On behalf of Britain, Air Marshal Sir Sholto Douglas suggested a moated gaol in the British zone. But Marshal Rokossovsky said the Soviets preferred the old Berlin Prison of Plötzensee. Bogged down once more, the proponents went on talking, and this deadlock dragged on into the early summer of 1947 until the discussions dried up like an exhausted well, and agreement was reached. The decisions were, to put it mildly, top secret.

At 4 a.m. on the 18 July 1947 the seven were awakened and told for the first time that they were to be moved. They were ordered to pack their belongings into army kitbags. Having done this, each was handcuffed to an American military policeman and hustled outside. There, under an escort of armoured cars and truckloads of soldiers, the prisoners and their guards were transported in two ambulances to a nearby airfield. Once aboard the waiting Dakota plane, their handcuffs were removed. Two and a half hours later the plane circled low over Berlin, giving its cargo of war criminals a close-up aerial view of the great capital city they had helped bring to ruin. The aircraft descended at the Gatow bomber base built in a forest by the Luftwaffe and then occupied by the RAF.

Black-curtained cars swiftly took them on the final stage of their journey to the Spandau district of Berlin, where, at exactly 11 a.m., they arrived at their destination. The prisoners stepped from the cars and saw they were at No. 24 Wilhelmstrasse, the postal address of the notorious Spandau Prison.

Each of the seven knew the sprawling, red-brick fortress prison well. Its choice was poetic justice, for from 1933 it had been used as a collecting point for Nazi political prisoners *en route* to concentration camps. It had been the scene of the sufferings of thousands of Hitler's victims and still held the iron hooks upon which prisoners were strung up to die of strangulation by the 'short rope' method favoured by the Gestapo. The seven, each walking a little ahead of a guard on either side, passed the military guardhouse and then the warders' administration offices where keys for the first section of the prison were kept and where the telephone exchange operated. The warders' office was staffed by four prison officers, each representing one of the Allies, and administrative personnel from the four countries.

Beyond the guardhouse, which was part of the main encircling wall, the seven crossed the cobbled courtyard between the twenty-foot-high entrance doors and the cell block to a steel door, then walked up twelve curling stone steps into the central building. On the left, at the top of the steps, was a door marked 'Kommandatura'. This opened into the office of the four Allied Prison Directors who, in turn, governed the gaol each month. Opposite was the four-Power conference room, the meeting place of those who would henceforth control every living moment of the seven inmates.

A corner of Spandau Prison wall, with the notice 'WARNING — DANGER: Do not approach this fence. Guards have orders to shoot. By Order.' The watch-tower in the centre is manned by guards with machine-guns.

An American warder, Harvey Fowler, received them on their arrival.

The prisoners moved on past the visitors' room, through yet another massive steel door, the strongest in the prison, and along a stone-floored corridor that echoed only to the sound of their footsteps and those of their guards. At last they entered the office of the Chief Warder. Once inside, they were ordered to strip; they were then led naked across the corridor to the surgery, where they were weighed and examined by four doctors, one from each controlling nation. All seven, it was seen, had grown fat in the American-administered prison at Nuremberg, where food, cigarettes, and pipe tobacco were plentiful.

In the course of the medical examination the prisoners were also bodily searched for any possible secret phial of poison that might have been smuggled into their possession during the journey. Göring's sensational suicide was not forgotten. The first entries were made on the Spandau Prison medical records, and the men were then led back into the Chief Warders' room. In perfect German, Wally Chisholm, the Aberdeen-born chief British warder, said to them:

'From now on, you will be known only by numbers. These —' indicating seven heaps of clothing on the table '— are your clothes. They are numbered from one to seven. Number One!...'

Rudolf Hess, with his dark skin, wavy black hair, and thick shaggy eyebrows, looked more of an Irishman than a Nazi Aryan. Automatically, the former Deputy Führer, who had astonished the world by parachuting into Britain with a 'peace proposal', stepped forward to receive the No. 1 Spandau uniform. Ignoring his silent claim to leadership, Chief Warder

Chisholm handed the first pile of clothes to the blond, blue-eyed Hitler Youth Leader Baldur von Schirach, who immediately began to put on the underwear, grey shirt, brown corduroy trousers, and single-breasted jacket. A black-dyed US Army overcoat, grey skull-cap, and straw sandals completed the outfit. Later, the sandals were exchanged for wooden clogs so that the guards could always hear the prisoners whenever they moved about. On the back of the jacket and on both trouser kneecaps, the prisoner's number — his name, so to speak, until the day of release, or death — was painted in glaring white. They had been measured for the uniforms at Nuremberg.

'You're getting the same kind of clothing that you gave to concentration camp convicts,' they were told.

Spandau Prison uniform No. 2 was handed to tall, lean, Grand Admiral Karl Dönitz, who stepped forward, clicked his bare heels from force of habit, and took the pile of clothes.

Baron Konstantin von Neurath changed his clothes and identity to that of prisoner No. 3.

Short, stocky, Grand Admiral Erich Raeder, always a martinet for neatness, began to dress himself in the baggy uniform of No. 4.

No. 5 went to Albert Speer.

For No. 6 Walther Funk shuffled forward, fear in his every movement.

Last of all, No. 7, was the allotted prison number for Hess. He took the clothes, his face sullen, resentful that his right as Deputy Führer to the No. 1 uniform had not been recognized.

The prisoners were next ordered to empty their kitbags, and all their personal belongings, except family photographs, were taken away. From Dönitz the authorities took charge of a silver wrist-watch, a silver alarm clock, two fountain pens, a diamond-studded Grand Admiral's baton, a second naval baton (made by the famous Berlin Friedrichstraße jeweller Wilms), and 15,000 gold marks.

Among the general pile of belongings French examining officers discovered American cigars and cigarettes. They were regular prisoner-of-war issue in Nuremberg. 'We never get any decent imported tobacco, so why should these lousy Nazis have any?' exclaimed one of the Frenchmen. The Russians, Americans, and British agreed. It was unanimously decided to confiscate the Nazis' tobacco stocks. The seven were then read sections of the Internal Security Regulations:

> Prisoners will work daily, except Sunday, depending on their state of health. Work will include cleaning the prison, and other tasks to be decided by the directors...
>
> When not working, prisoners will exercise in a courtyard or inside the cell sections, depending upon weather conditions, for a total period of not less than one hour daily, divided into two periods, for morning and afternoon...
>
> Prisoners are permitted to receive spiritual guidance, and take walks communally, but [and then came the regulation the seven were to hate and fear most] prisoners are forbidden to speak to each other, or their guards, other than a Chief Warder, without special permission.

The silence rule, at first rigidly enforced, later became a major four-Power tension point; it further declared:

> Prisoners are allowed to address themselves to the Chief Warders with questions which concern their work, sickness, or other personal requests. In the absence of the Chief Warders the prisoners may address themselves to the warders in exceptional cases, and the latter [the warders] report it at once to the Chief Warders without having spoken themselves to the prisoners.

Punishment for prison offences may consist of cancellation of privileges, cutting off of lighting in the cell for a period of up to four weeks; reduction of food which will be replaced by bread and water; deprivation of furniture and clothing, and in special circumstances, fettering.

The initial daily routine announced was:

06.00 hours — Prisoners rise, dress and proceed two at a time to wash.
06.45-07.30 — Breakfast.
07.30-08.00 — Beds made; cells cleaned.
08.00-11.45 — Cell corridor cleaned and any other necessary work performed, the physical condition of each prisoner being considered when assigning work.
12.00-12.30 — Midday meal, to be eaten in the cells.
12.30-13.00 — Prisoners permitted to rest in cells when performing light work. When performing strenuous outside work, permitted cell rest from 12.30-14.00.
13.00 or 14.00-16.45 — Routine work.
17.00 — Supper.
22.00 — Lights out.

Mondays, Wednesdays and Fridays, prisoners will be shaved and have their hair cut, if needed, between 13.00 and 14.00 hours.

The prisoners were required to salute Prison Directors and were subjected to a personal search twice daily. On washday Mondays, Dönitz and Schirach had to wash all the socks in a cast-iron cauldron, while Hess and Speer laundered underwear and bedding in the bathroom.

The daily schedule was interpreted differently by each of the controlling nations during their respective turns as governors of the gaol. The Directors were answerable to the Legal

Committee of the Allied Kommandatura, the controlling body of Berlin's Occupation Powers. The four Directors conferred every Thursday morning, accompanied by interpreters and stenographers. The prison's daily routine was to stay the same for some time until, weather permitting, from approximately 10.30 every morning, the seven were allowed to work in and enjoy the prison garden. There, each tended his own group of allotments, growing whatever he wished — as long as the produce was of value to the gaol's kitchens. The cultivation of flowers was a subsequently added privilege, although they were forbidden to take any of the blossoms to the cells. On Sundays they were allowed a 'lie-in' with no corridor — or cell — cleaning duties to perform until it was time for their garden outing. On bad weather mornings they read in the cells.

When the induction procedure was over, the seven were marched from the Chief Warders' room to pass through yet another steel door a few steps along the corridor. The door opened, and the seven went into what was the inner cell block of Spandau, an escape-proof 90-foot inner corridor containing thirty-two cells. Hess was led to the cell on the far right. He walked in; the door clanged and was then locked with a large iron key. Hess faced what was intended to be his home for the rest of his natural life. The freshly painted cell with yellow walls and whitewashed ceiling was approximately 3 metres long, 2.7 metres wide, and 4 metres high, and furnished with a black iron-frame bed equipped with headrest and a white, linen-covered, American Army-issue mattress supported by metal strips. Hess had requested, and been given, a thick wooden base for the bed to help his back. The heavy grey synthetic-fibre blankets were not particularly warm, but the seven could hardly complain about them as the blankets were stamped in black letters 'GBI', which denoted that they had come from

Albert Speer's own slave labour camps. GBI was the origin mark of the *Generalbauinspektor* (Inspector-general of buildings), one of the sections that had been administered by Speer. The cell also contained a small open cupboard with shelves and hooks for clothes and towels, a wooden chair, and a brown-varnished wooden table. The bed faced the steel door to enable guards to check through a square spy-grille. The cell doors were always double-locked and barred.

As Hess spread out books and his own stock of medicines on the shelves and table, he was informed that in an emergency he could summon a warder by pressing a red button in the cell, which would release a flapped red disc in the corridor outside. To minimize the risk of suicide, the cell had been stripped of all protruding objects on the walls; lighting cables had been sunk out of sight; heating pipes were protected by ventilated covers; and the glass pane of the high barred window, which could be reached and opened, had been replaced with thick celluloid.

Hess looked up at the glaring light above a bare bulb protected by an iron grille to prevent anyone removing it and attempting to electrocute themselves. There was a 150-watt lamp for reading, and a 40-watt lamp for checking sleeping prisoners at night. Even the porcelain toilet bowl inside the cell had been taken into account as a potential suicide hazard; but Hess surely realized that the prison's Directors must have been confident that the noise of a basin being smashed by someone in order to cut himself suicidally would be as ear-shattering in the gaol's silence as the sound of a bomb exploding — despite the 23-inch-thick stone walls.

The three-storey red-brick building with the large smoke stack rising from the mess hall was enclosed by a wall 732 yards long and 15 feet high. The outer wall rose to 30 feet, and as a further discouragement to hopeful inmates the 10-foot-high barbed wire around the entire prison was reinforced by a deep 6-foot-high electrified barrier bearing a 4,000-volt charge. Berliners made a habit of scavenging for stray rabbits that were always electrocuting themselves on the high-voltage wire at night. The gaol had its own power station servicing the wire defence, to ensure independence of domestic Berlin supplies — which were vulnerable to sabotage.

On twenty-four-hour watch over the prison were well over a hundred soldiers armed with automatic rifles and tear-gas bombs. Nine look-out towers served as the eyes of the area. Every ten minutes guards in the searchlight towers pressed a button to register electrically a periodic time-check on an indicator in the Commandant's office. This electronic check continued twenty-four hours a day, every day. Guard-tower sentries reached their vantage points by ascending a ladder and pulling the ladder up afterwards. The spotlight-equipped high wooden towers, later replaced with concrete towers, efficiently covered every part of the gaol and the surrounding grounds outside. Military orders stated that the use of firearms was permitted only if outsiders penetrated the prison by force or other illegal means; in self-defence, and then only if a prisoner and accomplices threatened a soldier's life and limb; and in case of an attempted escape, only if there was no other way to frustrate it. Even if it became necessary to direct shots at a prisoner, they were to be aimed to immobilize, not kill.

Outside the cell block, each duty unit of soldiers provided by the Power in charge for the month comprised 2 officers, 2 sergeants, 6 corporals, and 44 privates. Guard rotas were on a 50-per-cent on/50-per-cent off basis.

There was no way into the gaol except through the main entrance; and no other way out. Not even a helicopter daring to try to pick up prisoners on outdoor exercise could have survived the criss-crossing gun defences.

The inner cell block, manned by professional prison warders only, changed teams every eight hours. In the beginning, all warders carried truncheons, but the practice was soon discontinued. The men wore RAF-type uniforms with the insignia 'CCG' (Control Commission for Germany), and the teams consisted of a Chief Warder and Deputy Chief Warder representing the nation in control at the time, plus one warder from each of the other three nations. To prevent prisoners tapping out messages to each other, there was an empty cell on each side of every occupied cell. Anti-suicide checks were made every fifteen minutes, night and day, through the spy-grilles. After lights out, surveillance was carried out with the aid of a lamp that hung outside the door of each cell.

The suicidal tendencies or potentialities of the seven imprisoned Nazis received intense medical study. In cells and interview rooms their personalities were prodded and probed by psychologists and psychiatrists. Psychologist Dr G. M. Gilbert recorded Hess as having an IQ of 120. He was classified as 'Passive, suggestible, naïve, not very brilliant, suffering from hysterical amnesia, incapable of facing reality and avoiding frustration by developing functional disorders and stomach pains'.

A thick file of evidence already corroborated this assessment. For example, during the years he was imprisoned in Britain, Hess even wrote to King George VI alleging maltreatment and persistent attempts to poison him. A five-page letter accompanied an even lengthier document he compiled headed 'Statement and Protest'. The letter was cleared for delivery to Buckingham Palace, and in it Hess complained:

> I still believe in the fairness of the English people, therefore I feel certain that the treatment I have suffered is not in accordance with their wishes. I have no doubt that only a few people are responsible for it.

Later he again wrote to the King, withdrawing accusations previously made against staff guarding him, admitting that one officer had, in response to a challenge, eaten some of his food and swallowed tablets Hess had also assumed to be harmful. In a second letter, he confessed to King George: 'The incident forced me to the conclusion that my complaints are the result of auto-suggestion brought on by my captivity.'

Dönitz, who continued to play the Grand Admiral even in prison, remaining aloof from his compatriots, was recorded by psychologist Dr Gilbert as having an IQ of 138. He was classified as 'Very intelligent but politically naïve, feeling he was kicked upstairs to answer for crimes he knew nothing about.'

The American psychiatrist Lt Col William H. Dunn considered Dönitz 'Poised, affable, pleasant-spoken, with more humour than most of the others but,' added Dr Dunn,

> at times it becomes barbed — particularly in speaking of the trial, which he considered dominated by politicians. Has very little in the way of dejection and suicidal ideas. Felt that if he had been before a military tribunal he would have been cleared in three hours. His conscience is clear. Felt he had fought cleanly for his country and the government in power. Demonstrates rather strikingly the attitude of the 'good' German who feels he was only discharging his duty to the nation and was not involved in the common guilt and shame of his people.

To Walther Funk, one-time Bavarian gadabout, who had become a forlorn hypochondriac, constantly whimpering and lolling about as though without the strength to sit erect, Dr Gilbert gave an IQ of 124. In Funk's report, the psychologist noted: 'Feels roped in, betrayed and rather depressed.'

Also on Funk, psychiatrist Dr Dunn recorded:

> Talked at length of his various physical ailments. Discussed his Party activities and his opportunistic transition into Party affairs. It is to be expected that he will develop some depressive reaction to a severe sentence but will probably not be a serious suicidal risk.

Dr Gilbert found Neurath 'A bewildered conservative of the Hindenburg school; finds consolation in the fact that he resigned when things began to get too hot; generally apathetic. IQ: 125.'

Dr Dunn's tests listed Neurath as

> A quiet, soft-spoken professional diplomat whose manner is most correct and polished. Appears to be in excellent health and in fact has no complaints in spite of his age and hypertension. Evades gracefully his assignments in Bohemia and Moravia and betrays little evidence of guilt feeling. Does not impress as a serious suicidal risk or as being potentially psychotic in reaction to sentencing.

Dr Gilbert found Speer 'Matter-of-fact and straightforward. Recognized Hitler's destructive force and admitted guilt in supporting him. Reconciled to his fate and showed little anxiety. IQ: 128.'

> Talks at length of the mistakes and crimes of the Hitler Government, and talks of it with apparent sincerity. Shows very much less in the way of rationalization than any of the others. Apparently flattered at first by the interest of Hitler in his architectural ideas. As he was given more work as a

government official, his insight and disillusionment grew, but this was countered for a long period by rationalizations. Has given expression to his repudiation of Hitlerism.

Erich Raeder was, Dr Gilbert found, 'An irritable old man with a practical, unimaginative mentality, but academically intelligent. IQ: 134.'

Dr Dunn registered Raeder as an alert man who appeared almost as much concerned about his hernia and ill-fitting truss as the war crime charges made against him. Dunn's impression was that Raeder, who was anxious for a hernia operation, hoped to die during the operation. The doctor also noted:

> Throughout the discussion one gained the impression of deep distress over his present position and that he felt very keenly the shame of it, and of the kind of death he might face. No psychiatric disorder, but a reactive depression must be considered as potentially present with a possible suicidal attempt.

The medical specialists were in total agreement regarding Schirach, whom they decided was 'Sufficiently introverted to be able to provide himself with escape through thought or poetry if pressures became too great.' Schirach, who felt he had to vindicate the role of German youth to the end, had a positive desire to face his sentence.

Almost before the keys turned in the locks of Spandau's cell doors, the opening salvoes were fired in what was to develop into an incessant campaign to ease gaol conditions and decrease sentences. The first attempts made were those of Baroness von Neurath. As a result, the Control Commission for Germany sent the following report to the Foreign Office in London:

Subject: *Imprisonment conditions of Von Neurath.*

The following are extracts from the Prison Regulations for Spandau Allied Prison.

1. The Prisoners will be kept in solitary confinement (separate, isolated cells) though work, religious services and walks shall be communally conducted. Prisoners shall neither talk with one another nor communicate with each other or others unless specially authorized by the Governorate.

All kinds of non-official intercourse between prison staff or employees on the one hand and prisoners on the other is strictly forbidden.

2. The supreme executive authority over Spandau Allied Prison for the confinement of War Criminals sentenced to imprisonment by the International Military Tribunal is vested in the Allied Kommandatura Berlin.

The Governorate is responsible for the direction and supervision of the entire service routine, and its members are superior to prison staff, employees and workers engaged in duties or work connected with the institution.

Disciplinary staff shall consist of civilian warders belonging to the Four Allied Powers and their numbers shall be fixed on a numerical quadripartite basis.

Office and domestic staff employed inside the institution shall consist of male persons of the United Nations.

3. A prisoner will be permitted to write and receive not more than one letter every four weeks, unless the Governorate, for sufficient reason, withdraws this privilege. In exceptional cases the Governorate may allow the writing of one additional letter.

Letters shall not consist of more than one official sheet of note paper of four pages.

A prisoner may at the discretion of the Governorate be allowed to receive letters at the same intervals at which he may write them.

4. A prisoner will be permitted to receive one visitor in each period of two calendar months unless the Governorate

withdraws this privilege for sufficient reason. The Governorate shall determine which persons shall be permitted to visit a prisoner.

Not more than one visitor or one visitor accompanied by one child under the age of 16 years will be permitted to visit a prisoner at one time.

Additional private visits in connection with urgent family affairs may be authorized by the Governorate without observing the fixed intervals.

5. For religious welfare the Higher Executive Authority (The Legal Committee of the Allied Kommandatura Berlin) shall appoint suitable clergymen of the Allied or United Nations.

Religious books will be made available for the use of prisoners, and a prisoner may, if he wishes, receive the ministrations of a priest of his faith. The Governorate will make reasonable provision for the prisoners to practise suitable religious rites within the prison.

The Institution will be provided with a suitable library, and in the distribution of books the character and aims of the prisoner, and his reasonable preferences and wishes will be taken into consideration.

In the opinion of this Division there is no prospect of securing Quadripartite agreement for the conditions of imprisonment to be relaxed. Neither the French nor the Russians would agree to this. They consider that the present conditions are not severe enough and were opposed to the prisoners being permitted to work and hold religious services together. It must be remembered that the conditions in Spandau Prison compare very favourably with conditions in other German prisons.

Hitler had named Göring as his successor should anything happen to him. Hess, he had added, would be next in line. 'Should anything happen to Hess,' Hitler had declared in a speech, 'then by law the Senate will be called and will choose from its midst the most worthy — that is to say, the bravest — successor.' There was in fact no law governing such circumstances; nor was there a Senate. In his first message home from Spandau, Hess wrote:

> This is my first letter from our new quarters. They are not basically different from the old ones. In some minor respects, as always after a change of abode, they are not so agreeable, but on the other hand, they have advantages. In the former category is the fact that we are not permitted to send this kind of letter more than once in 28 days. I realized in Nuremberg that I would not be permitted to continue writing so often and felt that the fact that I was able to do so indicated some imminent change. In each 28 days we may receive only one letter, but at the moment there is no limit to its length. Conditions: it must be written clearly in Latin characters!... My number is now the lucky seven!
>
> There is a positive side, however: The 'rooms' are newly painted and fresher and cleaner. And imagine, I have a pillow with a pillow case, and a mattress covered with white linen — the first I have seen since leaving England! Also, I have a chair and no longer have to pretend that the edge of the bed is a sofa. One drawback is that the white linen covering of the mattress means more trouble washing — and we must do that ourselves! vvvvv.[1]
>
> Yesterday for the first time I was in the washing queue with Dönitz. I pictured myself as Gudrun by the shores of the North Sea, although she, I am sure, breathed air with more ozone in it. How we scrubbed, rinsed and wrung out! We did our best, but I am afraid that good housewife would cast despairing and pitying glances on seeing our methods...

---

[1] According to his wife, Hess used little wavy lines — vvvvv — in his letters to indicate a pause for laughter. She called it the Hess 'laughter-line'.

Our removal here was sudden. Very early in the morning at the first cockcrow we were awakened with the interesting news — exactly as I had told my comrades it would happen although none of them believed me! As we are not burdened with the kind of valuables that can be eaten by moths or corrupted by rust, it did not take us long to pack...

Now we will calmly await what may happen to us — as we did before. Or at least I shall do so without necessarily going to the extent of the fakir who sees that his mission and happiness consist of holding one arm upright day and night. Mentally and spiritually I sometimes feel like that myself, but only sometimes — from that state I am far removed vvvvvvv.

Yours

Karl Dönitz also sat down at his cell table soon after his arrival in the gaol to write to his wife Inge:

Meine Ingeliebste,

We are in Spandau. I may write two letters in six weeks, and may receive the same number during the same period. I may receive parcels, but no food. Send me a hairbrush and soap, which seems to be short here. As far as I understand it, I can receive visits every two months for fifteen minutes. The Allies seem to have agreed about us. Direction and guarding is undertaken by all four nations simultaneously. To write more about this is unnecessary.

Notwithstanding the fairness and decency of the local Directors and guards, I must say I will never acknowledge my sentence as a just one or internationally sound. I am here as a political prisoner on orders from above to be treated as a common criminal.

Yours and my heart have now digested the move to here, and the ups and downs of life cannot change one's own values.

Dein Junge [Your boy]

The sprawling gaol, built in 1876, had 132 single cells, 5 punishment cells, and 10 outsize cells, each capable of holding 40 prisoners. Before the Allies requisitioned it in November 1946 for an expected hundred or more war criminals, it had housed 600 convicts. Dönitz knew all this. Who, then, was sharing the place with them? When a guard opened his cell door later, Dönitz decided, despite the no-talking rule, to ask the question that was on his mind.

'Who else is in here with us?' he asked. The guard hesitated, then feeling that this was one question he would be justified in breaking the rules to answer, replied:

'There are no other prisoners but you seven. It's all yours.'

On 11 August 1947, less than four weeks after they had arrived at the gaol, the prison's four Directors met to discuss a crucial issue. At the close of the discussion, a top secret memorandum was forwarded to the Legal Committee of the Allied Kommandatura Berlin. It was headed:

Subject: Death of a prisoner.
To: Chairman of the Legal Committee.
The following procedure to be adopted in case of the death of a prisoner is submitted for your attention. The proposal was accepted by the four medical officers and the four Directors of the prison.

In case of death of a prisoner, whatever the cause thereof, each nation will appoint a medical officer or a specialist to conduct the autopsy. This Committee of Medical Officers will prepare a document certifying the cause of the death. Thereafter, the body will be cremated.

For the Allied Directors,
Henry H. Frank
US Representative
Chairman

The Kommandatura's Legal Committee recommended approval of the proposal, and further recommended that after cremation the ashes should be scattered in secret. The final decision was up to the Deputy Commandants of Berlin, but they failed to reach agreement when they initially debated the matter. The French and British representatives asked for additional time to study the very sensitive question. The British stated that their delegation considered that the bodies of those Spandau prisoners who died in gaol should be treated like those of ordinary prisoners, namely that bodies should be handed over to relatives, if the latter so wished. He reminded his colleagues that certain of the Spandau prisoners might survive the termination dates of their sentences. Under these circumstances, the Allied Kommandatura would have no voice in the matter of the disposal of the bodies after death. He therefore saw no reason to draw a distinction between those Spandau prisoners who died while in prison and those who died after expiration of their sentences.

The chairman of the meeting pointed out that, if the bodies were released, the prisoners might come to be regarded as martyrs. He proposed that the report of the Kommandatura's Legal Committee be adopted.

The Soviet representative objected to the British view, recalling that the minimum sentence imposed by the International Military Tribunal was ten years' imprisonment. It was difficult to foresee, he said, what would happen in Germany during this period, but the British suggestion might well result in a very dangerous situation in which the graves of these criminals could be used by militaristic elements for every kind of Nazi demonstration. The acceptance of such a proposal would result in contravention of the procedure established by the International Military Tribunal. Insisting that the Allied Kommandatura had no right to do this, the Soviet spokesman recommended approval of the report already unanimously accepted by the Legal Committee.

Having heard the opinions of his colleagues, the British representative deferred to their wishes. The meeting agreed: to approve the report of the Legal Committee; to notify the Prison Directors accordingly; and to keep the decision totally secret — even from the prisoners' families.

The document setting out burial arrangements for the seven, which became Spandau's top secret, was consequently originally drawn up with the object of preventing former Nazis from discovering the remains and enshrining the war criminals as martyrs. There was certainly some basis for this possibility at the time; Hess contributed to this concern by asserting: 'Some day, honour guards will be stationed beside the graves of the eleven martyrs who were hung at Nuremberg until they can be put into one communal grave.' He wanted an honour guard for despicable Himmler's grave, and maintained that Göring's medals should be placed in his coffin.

It was therefore laid down that in the event of the death of a Spandau prisoner the body should be transported secretly to a crematorium where the coffin would be burned in the presence of the four Prison Directors. The ashes would then be removed to the prison where they would be retained under guard in the main office safe. No chances would be taken of ashes being stolen and used as a 'martyr relic' by underground Nazi followers. The most favoured means of disposing of any such ashes was from the cockpit of an aeroplane flying over the sea.

Cremation, the method favoured by Hitler's concentration camp administrators for disposal of their victims' bodies, was, the four-Powers decided, the only way to deal with the corpse of any Spandau inmate who died in gaol.

3: SHOOT THE LOT!

The Nuremberg trials had taken place within the same year as Germany's defeat. They had had to deal with new crimes for which there was no provision in national or international law. The seven imprisoned in Spandau never knew how close they were to being summarily shot by a firing squad, or hanged, soon after they were captured. Nor did the rest of the world. There almost never was a Nuremberg Tribunal.

The controlling decision affecting war criminals was reached during the winter 1943 Moscow Conference between President Roosevelt, Winston Churchill, and Marshal Stalin. They agreed two principles. The first was that those charged with atrocities in invaded countries should be sent back to the country where the crime was committed and there judged and punished under the laws of that country. The second covered major war criminals whose offences had no particular geographical localization, and they were to be punished by joint decision of the Governments of the Allies.

The problem of the arch criminals was the most important because what was to be done about them would have profound and far-reaching effect upon the law and morale of international society. The crucial question was whether or not they should be brought to trial before a judicial tribunal, or whether the Allies should follow the precedent set in 1815 for dealing with Napoleon. The Moscow discussions indicated that the Napoleonic precedent would be followed and that arch criminals would not be dealt with by judicial procedures but by joint decision of the Allies.

(On 2 August 1815 Austria, Russia, Prussia and Britain signed a convention declaring Napoleon to be their common prisoner. He was to be punished without trial in order not to give him, as the Prince Regent of England put it, 'any further opportunity of disturbing the peace of Europe'.)

Legal proceedings instituted under judicial process in which there was no law under which a court could convict for the real crimes would result in arguments for generations to come that the accused were judicially murdered. The Napoleonic precedent was not open to such objections, however. The Allies could state reasons for condemning the arch criminals, and these reasons would then become a doctrine that could by legislation be incorporated into international law.

At first it seemed that justice demanded a trial, on the grounds either that no man should be punished without due process of law, or that only a trial could make the verdict sufficiently impressive, or on both grounds. But would it satisfy justice to convict such men of specific crimes of murder and robbery when in fact they were guilty of the infinitely greater offence of attempting to conquer and enslave the civilized world?

The object could not be vengeance but justice. To do justice these men had to be judged for their total offences against mankind, not merely for some offence that happened to come within the rules of evidence in a criminal court; for that would be like sentencing a gangster not for all his murders and racketeering, but because he defrauded the Government on his income tax return. Nor could anyone be permitted to escape through the defence that — although he signed, cosigned, executed, or administered measures that violated international law — he should be held innocent because he thought acquiescence would enable him to maintain and safeguard his department. Nobody who by his actions had condemned masses of people to persecution, mistreatment, brutality, imprisonment, deportation, and extermination could be allowed to avoid responsibility for his conduct.

On the other hand, it was by no means self-evident that prompt execution would be in all cases the most suitable judgement. As Churchill said: 'The grass grows quickly over the battlefield, but over the scaffold, never.'

Anticipating the possible debate concerning the war criminals at an imminent meeting between Britain, the United States, and the USSR, the lawyer Lord Simon — Britain's Lord Chancellor — wrote to Churchill on 24 January 1943. The letter, headed 'Punishment of Hitler', advised:

> If this subject comes up at the approaching meeting of the 'Big Three', I would very strongly urge that, whatever is decided upon, it should not be left to some tribunal of judges to determine the *penalty* to be imposed. That must be determined by the Allies themselves. But that is not to say that it is impossible that an international tribunal of judicial character should not report to the Allies the result of their consideration of a widely drawn indictment of Hitler & Co.
>
> The offence charges in the arraignment would be in substance the policy pursued of world conquest and the methods employed to achieve it. These would be the grounds on which the Allies would propose to base their action.

It was recognized that the accused would be likely to deny the court's authority and might even refuse to answer charges or use the court as a platform for making long propaganda speeches. Nevertheless, it was considered that after giving the accused the opportunity to be heard and calling witnesses, the tribunal would be able to report whether or not accusations had been adequately established.

Lord Simon cautioned Churchill against any description of charges as 'war crimes', as he felt this would lead to a wrangle over the definition of a war crime, but his letter concluded: 'Hitler's offence against mankind is none the less heinous and deserves the extreme penalty.'

When the matter arose for inter-Allied discussion at a Moscow conference of Foreign Ministers, Cordell Hull of the United States expressed forthrightly:

> If I had my way, I would take Hitler and Mussolini and Tojo and their accomplices and bring them before a drumhead court-martial and at sunrise on the following morning there would occur an historic incident.

Russia's Foreign Minister, Molotov, was also expectedly in favour of 'stern swift justice'. But Britain's Anthony Eden was of the opinion that 'All the legal forms should be observed', whatever that meant.

When Roosevelt, Churchill, and Stalin met at Teheran, and the question of war criminals first arose, Stalin said that at least 50,000 of the German General Staff must be physically and summarily liquidated. President Roosevelt, perhaps thinking the proposal was some kind of grim joke, countered in that spirit by saying that it should be only 49,000. Churchill, not considering the subject at all humorous, said the British would never stand for such mass murders.

'I would rather', he said, 'be taken out into the garden here and now and be shot myself than sully my own, and my country's, honour with such infamy.'

Months later, at the British War Cabinet's request, Lord Simon submitted proposals for dealing with the major war criminals. Expounding the principal considerations to be borne in mind, Simon advised:

In view of the progress made towards final victory over Germany, has not the time arrived to raise — with President Roosevelt, at any rate — certain questions connected with the carrying out of intended punishment? It is much to be hoped that the principal criminals may, before the end, be disposed of by the people whom they have led to destruction, or may take their own lives — but if they fall alive into the hands of the Allies what is to be done with them?

I am strongly of opinion that the method by trial, conviction, and judicial sentence is quite inappropriate for notorious ringleaders such as Hitler, Himmler, Göring, Goebbels and Ribbentrop. Apart from the formidable difficulties of constituting the Court, formulating the charge, and assembling the evidence, the question of their fate is *a political, not a judicial, question.* It could not rest with judges, however eminent or learned, to decide finally a matter like this, which is one of the widest and most vital public policy. The decision must be 'the joint decision of the Governments of the Allies'. The Moscow Declaration, indeed, has already said so.

I am equally clear that these leading and notorious criminals cannot be left untouched, while lesser people who have committed atrocities and war crimes under their orders and with their approval are tried and heavily punished. Such a course would be universally, and rightly, condemned. It may not be essential to make a precise public announcement of Allied intentions as regards the major criminals at present — the Moscow Declaration is itself a general indication, and a new statement might evoke reprisals against Allied individuals in German hands — but it seems to me most desirable to open confidential consultations on the subject with some of our Allies, and to get a decision now as to what is to be done. Otherwise, when the time comes, there may be a disastrous difference of view.

The list of war criminals who might be dealt with without trial, which was prepared by the Foreign Secretary, was criticized in some quarters for its omissions, but I am disposed to think that this method will only be considered appropriate and justified in the case of the small group of leaders who are known to have been responsible for the conduct of the war, and who have at headquarters authorized, approved or acquiesced in the horrible atrocities that have been committed.

A formula which might meet the Prime Minister's suggested views would be as follows:-

The Moscow Tri-partite Declaration of November 1st, 1943, had announced that the Allies intended to arrange for the trial and punishment of enemy war criminals who had already been captured or who fell into their hands, but the Moscow Declaration was stated to be made 'without prejudice to the case of the major criminals, whose offences have no particular geographical localisation, and who will be punished by the joint decision of the Governments of the Allies'. The time has come to announce that among these major criminals are Hitler, Göring, Goebbels and Ribbentrop, but the Allies reserve the right to add to their number. Upon any of these major criminals falling into Allied hands, the Allies will decide how they are to be disposed of, and the execution of this decision will be carried out immediately.

After giving considerable thought to Lord Simon's report, Churchill made a startling proposition. The Allies would issue a 'wanted' list of fifty to a hundred major war criminals, who would be hunted down as world outlaws. On their arrest, the Allies would decide their fate and put it into effect forthwith. Or, upon irrefutably identifying them, the nearest general would be empowered to shoot them within six hours without reference to anyone else.

Drawing on Lord Simon's report, Churchill personally drafted the following telegram, which he forwarded to

Roosevelt, suggesting that it be sent by the President and himself to Marshal Stalin:

1. In the Moscow Conference of Foreign Ministers before Teheran, the Prime Minister of Great Britain submitted a draft proposing the local punishment of war criminals in the countries and, if possible, at the scenes where their atrocities had been committed. With some small amendments this document was approved and has been published to the world with general acceptance and approval. This document, however, did not attempt to deal with the cases of the major war criminals 'whose offences have no particular geographical localisation'. This matter was touched on in conversation at Teheran without any definite conclusion being reached. It has now become important for us to reach agreement about the treatment of these major criminals. Would you consider whether a list could not be prepared of say 50 to 100 persons whose responsibilities for directing or impelling the whole process of crime and atrocity is established by the fact of their holding certain high offices. Such a list would not of course be exhaustive. New names could be added at any time. It is proposed that these persons should be declared, on the authority of the United Nations, to be world outlaws and that upon any of them falling into Allied hands the Allies will 'decide how they are to be disposed of and the execution of this decision will be carried out immediately'. Or, alternatively, 'the nearest General Officer will convene a Court for the sole purpose of establishing their identity, and when this has been done will have them shot within six hours without reference to higher authority'.

2. It would seem that the method of trial, conviction and judicial sentence is quite inappropriate for notorious ringleaders such as Hitler, Himmler, Göring, Goebbels and Ribbentrop. Apart from the formidable difficulties of constituting the Court, formulating the charge and assembling the evidence, the question of their fate is a political and not a

judicial one. It could not rest with judges however eminent or learned to decide finally a matter like this which is of the widest and most vital public policy. The decision must be 'the joint decision of the Governments of the Allies'. This in fact was expressed in the Moscow Declaration.

3. There would seem to be advantages in publishing a list of names. At the present time, Hitler and his leading associates know that their fate will be sealed when the Germany Army and people cease to resist. It therefore costs them nothing to go on giving orders to fight to the last man, die in the last ditch, etc. As long as they can persuade the German people to do this, they continue to live on the fat of the land and have exalted employments. They represent themselves and the German people as sharing the same rights and fate. Once however their names are published and they are isolated, the mass of the German people will infer rightly that there is a difference between these major criminals and themselves. A divergence of interests between the notorious leaders and their dupes will become apparent. This may lead to undermining the authority of the doomed leaders and to settling their own people against them, and thus may help the break-up of Germany.

4. We should be very glad to have your views upon this proposal at your earliest convenience. It is, of course, without prejudice to the great mass of German war criminals, who will be handed over for the judgement of the countries where their crimes have been committed.

W.S.C.
17.9.44

Churchill's 'wanted' list and summary execution suggestion received a mixed reception in Washington. The State Department favoured it. The War Department didn't. The military recommended trial by an international court, principally because they believed that, so far as Hitler and company were concerned, a trial would create a better impression for posterity. Their unexpected ally was Marshal Stalin. 'There should be no executions without trial, otherwise the world will say that we were afraid to try the major criminals,' he said, taking the line that the maximum penalty that could be imposed without trial was lifelong imprisonment.

This original Stalin thinking was largely responsible for influencing the USSR's attitude throughout the Spandau seven's years of imprisonment, and the Soviet hard line towards premature release. The Soviets wanted it never to be forgotten that it was for the sake of justice, for the vindication of the underlying sense of difference between right and wrong, that these criminals received their punishment. And it was so that their punishment should be a deterrent for future generations, and that mankind should know that civilized nations will never tolerate this kind of crime, and that punishment is bound to follow.

Curiously Stalin and the Soviet State were anxious to convince world opinion, including Germany, that the appalling crimes perpetrated were the result of that pernicious body of doctrine that the Pope aptly described as 'State idolatry'. Stalin felt that through means of a trial it could be shown that criminal war acts represent a degradation of international standards taking civilization centuries back, and popularizing behaviour thought to have been ruled out of all human action.

United States Attorney-General Francis Biddle discussed the advisability of a trial with President Roosevelt and Secretary of War Henry L. Stimson, and, in greater detail, with the Assistant Secretary, John M. McCloy. Biddle was of the view that there should be no execution of leaders out of hand, or after a drumhead court-martial, but that there should be a serious and fair trial. All departments concerned agreed on a general procedure outline, which was approved by the President and which he took to the Yalta Conference for discussion with Churchill and Stalin.

On 26 January 1945, only days before the historic Yalta 'Big Three' meeting, Lord Simon updated his brief on major war criminals for the War Cabinet and for Churchill to take to the conference. It was headed: 'Punishment of Hitler and his Chief Associates'.

Simon considered that the advantage of the proposals he had submitted to Churchill was that the judicial body, however composed, would not be required to determine the sentence. 'That', he explained in his memorandum, 'must be for the chief heads of governments to decide.' He continued:

> The essence of the plan is that the Allies should draw up an 'arraignment' of Hitler and others in broad and general terms, confining themselves to matters which really are beyond dispute and which, in themselves, are quite enough to justify the extreme penalty. A Judicial Committee appointed by the Allies could then undertake the task of deciding whether this 'arraignment' was adequately proved, and for this purpose they would have Hitler, Mussolini, etc. before them and give them full opportunity of giving evidence, or cross-examining, and of making speeches through themselves or their advocates. The contents of *Mein Kampf* might well provide some material; the public declarations of the accused will also be relevant.
>
> I do not see why the abominable maltreatment of the Jews in Germany should not be included, for the object would be to charge Hitler with the main features of his conduct which have made him *hostis humani generis*.
>
> I would strongly urge that the matters charged in the proposed 'arraignment' should not be described by the technical phrase 'war crimes'. The maltreatment of Jews in

Germany is plainly not a war crime, and if it is suggested that Hitler's policy in supporting the war was a war crime, this will at once raise a technical controversy on which opinions will be divided and much time wasted in argument if he seeks to defend himself.

Lord Simon warned that there remained questions that would present themselves as soon as it was decided that Hitler, and others who were most prominent, should be specially treated. He asked: 'Where is the line to be drawn between them and the general body of war criminals who are going to be dealt with by military tribunals or by the courts [of the countries] in which their crimes were committed?' He concluded:

I do not think that the list of leaders to be dealt with by special treatment should include men, however important and however wicked, whose names as the principal enemy leaders are not known to the public. The righteous demand for exemplary punishment administered to the authors of the war will be met by taking a shorter list.

Despite these discussions the war criminals issue was never reached on the Yalta Conference agenda in February 1945; and on 13 April President Roosevelt died. That very day, Britain's War Cabinet held a special meeting and again decided formally that they favoured summary execution of top Nazis. The issue was raised by President Truman at the San Francisco Conference of nations in April.

Churchill commented: 'The only test by which human beings can judge war responsibility is Aggression; and the supreme proof of Aggression is Invasion.'

On 7 August 1945 the United States, Britain, the USSR and France signed the agreement and charter in London providing for the trial, formulating the law, and establishing the practice. On appointing Francis Biddle as the American member of the Tribunal, President Truman confided to Biddle that he was particularly anxious that this first serious attempt to try those leaders who had been responsible for launching the war, and who were the prime cause of the appalling atrocities that followed in the wake of that war, should not run into disagreements between the four nations that might prevent or obstruct this significant experiment in the field of international justice. It was Truman's hope, he told Biddle, that Nuremberg might serve as a working example for the world of how four nations could achieve results in a specific field of endeavour. Recalling the failures in trying war criminals after World War I, he assured Biddle that he was fully aware of the difficulties that would be encountered. There were four different systems of law to be reconciled, with their varying points of view and procedures. International law — the law and practice of nations — was indeed a base and a background, but it had in its practical application become sterile and academic. There were language difficulties and the whole thing was in a tentative and uncertain state.

The Nuremberg judges set out to define a standard of conduct of responsibility which could be reasonably and properly applied to all men and women, including officials of every State and nation — the victors as well as the vanquished.

Thus events led to the Nuremberg court-room. Rudolf Hess, Albert Speer, Karl Dönitz, Erich Raeder, Baron Konstantin von Neurath, Walther Funk and Baldur von Schirach were given the right to fight publicly for their lives and freedom before the eyes of the world, in the city where their Führer's fanatical hate-filled oratory had transformed normally decent people into savage mobs screaming for conquest and blood.

Nuremberg had in 1938 given its name to what Hitler termed 'a new creed for the masses' — anti-Semitic laws by which Jews were deprived of their rights as citizens and forbidden to marry Aryans.

Only the trial Stalin insisted on staging from the start saved the seven who ended up in Spandau prison from summary execution on arrest. Francis Biddle also wanted a properly constituted hearing, but more than any other single factor it was Stalin's weight that tipped the scales in favour of the Tribunal.

After more than ten months of almost uninterrupted proceedings, the Nuremberg trial sentenced twelve of the defendants (including the absent Martin Bormann) to hanging, three to life imprisonment, four to lesser terms of imprisonment, and acquitted three. The Tribunal also declared the Leadership Corps of the Nazi Party, the SS, the SD, and the Gestapo to be criminal organizations, with certain restrictions. International law, as such, binds every citizen just as ordinary municipal law does; acts adjudged criminal when committed by an officer of the Government are criminal also when done by a private individual. The guilt differs only in magnitude, not in quality.

Dean Robert G. Storey, who during the trial served as deputy to United States Chief Prosecutor Robert H. Jackson, admitted afterwards: 'The Russians favoured the death penalty for all of them.'

Never before in history had there been on such a scale the organized cruelty that was witnessed during World War II. The Allies were saying: 'We are prepared before the bar of history to take upon ourselves the responsibility that a man who has been guilty of high crimes and misdemeanours should be punished in his own person.'

US Chief Prosecutor Jackson commented: 'If you are determined to execute a man in any case, there is no occasion for trial; the world yields no respect to courts that are merely organized to convict.'

Opinions were expressed that Ministers such as Hess, Speer, Schirach, Neurath and Funk, and war leaders like Dönitz and Raeder, could not be held accountable for their countless crimes before a court of law. The common-sense answer was that if there was no existing law to try these men, then such a law should be created. If that was impracticable, then they must be brought to trial by political action. Nuremberg was not a court of law in a technical sense, but it could be truly described as a court of justice. And all the defendants received justice. Arguments for and against them frequently raged almost as fiercely in the privacy of the judges' chambers as they did in open court.

In a letter Judge Biddle wrote to President Truman on 9 November 1946, he said:

> It was interesting to feel — what all of us so keenly felt — the change in the point of view of the defendants and their lawyers as the trial progressed. At first they were indifferent, sceptical, hostile. But very soon, as the tribunal ruled on the merits of motions that arose, frequently against the prosecution, and went to great pains to obtain witnesses and documents even remotely relevant to the defendant's case, this attitude changed; the defendants began to fight for their lives. And what had threatened to be a sounding board for propaganda or a stage for martyrdom turned into a searching analysis of the years that felt Hitler's rise to power and his ultimate destruction — the objective reading of this terrible chapter of history. This change was in itself an instinctive tribute to our concept of justice.

During the trial, Funk and Schirach showed expedient repentance. Funk was constantly tearful. Speer appeared to be sincere about his repentance. Dönitz considered the indictment to be 'a bad joke', and Hess claimed to have lost his memory. Admitting later to his companions that he had been faking, Hess boasted: 'It was a great effort for me to remain expressionless.'

The unanimous decisions that despatched Hess, Speer, Schirach, Neurath, Funk, Dönitz and Raeder to Spandau, instead of to the gallows, were not easily reached by the judges. In his letter to the President, Judge Biddle admitted:

> This unity resulted from a willingness by all four nations to compromise on inevitable and desirable differences in points of view. This give and take, the essence of democratic process, could not have been accomplished overnight. Many weeks went by before mutual confidence between the members, an essential condition to prompt and effective work, was established. And this stability, this day-to-day relationship, made easier the development of a habit of co-operation. The comments I have made about the unanimity are not affected by the dissent on certain individual defendants, as indeed, the judges of the USRR were careful to point out. The dissent did not express any disagreement with the fundamental principles of international law, in which General Nikitchenko fully joined; in fact it was on those principles that he based the reasoning for his dissent. The dissent, in a word, was over the inferences which should be drawn from conflicting evidence. I personally believe that this difference — on the facts and not on the law — was extremely healthy.

Consciously or unconsciously, Albert Speer repudiated the Third Reich in a manner that made a good impression on judges and prosecutors. Deeply thoughtful, he appeared with shoulders bowed under the shame of his people and the moral degradation to which he had helped lead them. He made it plain that he despised Göring, seated in the defendants' box with him, because Göring stood for all the brutal ambitions that had brought the Fatherland to misery. His frankness and contrition at the trial were impressive. Within the judges' chambers, away from the eyes and ears of the world, the question that had to be answered was whether he was simply letting fate and the court work their will, or whether he had tried to nudge them away from the hangman's noose.

Speer proved to be the first seriously controversial case considered by the Tribunal. He had taken at least 30,000 concentration camp labourers from Himmler, and although he had recommended fair treatment for conscripted labourers, he undoubtedly had been informed about the harsh conditions that prevailed. The problem presented by his case was not of guilt or innocence, because he was clearly guilty. The main issue was how to evaluate a number of factors that pointed towards mitigation. When it came to sentencing him, the divergent views of the judges quickly came to a head.

Both French judges, as well as Judge Lawrence of Britain and Judge Parker of the United States, wanted him imprisoned for a limited term of years. Lawrence proposed fifteen years, and France's Donnedieu de Vabres agreed But Judge Biddle voted against this, recommending that Speer be sentenced to death, and Nikitchenko, of Russia, agreed. The court was consequently locked in a two-two tie. In the middle of this, Britain's alternate judge, the hawk-like, towering, six-foot-three-inch Sir Norman Birkett, arrived and suggested a ten-year sentence. The deadlocked judges adjourned. The following morning, Biddle ended his advocacy of the death penalty but persuaded Lawrence and Donnedieu de Vabres to back a longer term of imprisonment. The Soviets were outvoted three to one, and Speer received twenty years.

Judge Lawrence had strength and an understanding of men that came from a human friendliness rather than any turn of shrewdness. Short, stout Henri Donnedieu de Vabres was seconded from the Sorbonne University because the French felt that an international law specialist would be required. He was Professor of the Law School in Paris and also in Montpellier.

Major-General of Jurisprudence I. T. Nikitchenko, grave and dignified, still only in his forties, was the youngest member of the Tribunal. Vice-President of the Supreme Court of the Soviet Union, he was also Deputy to the Supreme Council of the Russian Socialist Federated Republics. Apart from his Tribunal deputy, Wolkhoff, he was accompanied by Professor A. L. Trainin, recognized as Soviet Russia's outstanding consultant on international crime.

Francis Biddle, the senior American judge at the trials, who was fifty-nine at the time, had been private secretary to Oliver Wendell Holmes, one of the most distinguished judges of the United States Supreme Court. He had also held several Government posts in the Roosevelt administration. He became Solicitor-General and remained in this office until 1941. Thereafter, until June 1945, he was US Attorney-General. Biddle supported Lawrence's appointment as President of the Tribunal.

The first judges' vote on Baron Konstantin von Neurath indicated that the Soviets, the British, and Judge Falco of France wished to convict him on all charges, whilst Donnedieu de Vabres wanted to hold him on two counts. As usual, the Soviets voted for death. Judge Lawrence favoured a life sentence. Judge Birkett, Donnedieu de Vabres, and Biddle preferred fifteen years. Judge Parker felt it should be only five. Neurath was finally convicted on all counts and sentenced to fifteen years — a relatively merciful sentence considering he was convicted on all four charges.

Judge Biddle dismissed Baldur von Schirach's defence image of himself as a virtuous young idealist as 'hogwash'. Emotionally, the court plainly detested Schirach. Only the complexities of his case saved him from execution. The Soviets and Judge Lawrence voted for the death penalty. The French initially hovered between a life sentence and death, then switched to twenty years or life. Judges Biddle and Donnedieu de Vabres finally agreed with Sir Norman Birkett and swung the voting so that Schirach received a twenty-year sentence.

By challenging every prosecution assertion, large and small, Grand Admiral Erich Raeder made a bad impression on the Tribunal. Judge Biddle thought Raeder deserved to be shot, but his American colleague, Judge Parker, opposed the death penalty. The Soviets also wanted him executed. Judges Lawrence and Biddle recommended life, and Donnedieu de Vabres, twenty years. The deadlock was broken by unanimously convicting Raeder on all three counts and sentencing him to life imprisonment.

The proceedings against Grand Admiral Karl Dönitz almost overshadowed those against the other defendants who were convicted, because his unusual career produced intense divisions. The court could not help comparing Allied and German submarine policies, and Dönitz's brilliant lawyer, Dr Otto Kranzbühler, argued that in the battle of the Atlantic Dönitz used precisely the same tactics as Admiral Nimitz (Commander-in-Chief of the US Pacific Fleet) in the Pacific.

The case of Dönitz, proud and stiff, with a temper he found hard to control, came up for consideration by the court on four different occasions. In the judges' chambers, Biddle called for the Admiral's complete acquittal. All the others dissented. France's Robert Falco suggested ten years 'because his guilt was much less than Raeder's'. Birkett wanted twenty years, and the Soviets acknowledged that they would accept a lesser penalty than the one given to Raeder. Judge Nikitchenko approved ten years. Donnedieu de Vabres suggested five to ten. Biddle compromised on the basis that he would write the final opinion on the case to enable him to record reservations. It was solely Biddle's advocacy that eventually wore down the other judges until they consented to a relatively mild sentence, convicting Dönitz on two counts and giving him ten years.

Walther Funk almost certainly escaped the death penalty only because he was the tenth defendant considered by the Tribunal, and because he was regarded as a weak man. His appearance of unimportance was his trademark. Funk was connected with every type of crime covered by the indictment, yet he managed to avoid the gallows. He was a man who simply 'went along' with the Nazis for the ride.

The British and Soviet judges, as well as America's Judge Parker and France's Judge Falco, held that Funk was guilty of all charges. Donnedieu de Vabres and Judge Biddle determined he was guilty on three counts and were therefore doubtful about the death penalty proposed by the others. By a three-to-four vote (the Soviets still wanted him hanged) Funk received a life sentence.

The judges deadlocked on the issue of an appropriate sentence for Rudolf Hess, although all agreed that he should be found guilty. Judge Falco recommended that they first vote on whether to impose death, then on life imprisonment, and finally on a term of years, with the understanding that the first sentence to receive three votes by senior members of the Tribunal would be final. The suggestion was adopted. Judge Nikitchenko's death penalty proposal was outvoted by three to one in favour of a life sentence. Then, by switching his support to life imprisonment, Nikitchenko forestalled the possibility of a lesser sentence. It was his deciding vote that determined that Rudolf Hess should remain in Spandau prison for the rest of his life. And only Soviet determination that the sentence should mean what it said — for life — kept Hess in his Spandau cell long after Britain, America, and France were prepared to free him on mercy grounds.

4: RUDOLF HESS'S GREATEST FEAR

'Give me a hundred reliable men and two planes, and I can get Hess and the other six out of Spandau. In the event of unexpected difficulties, Hess will be given escape priority.' This boast to smash through the security defences of the world's most jealously guarded prison was made by SS General Otto 'Scarface' Skorzeny, the man who rescued Mussolini from the Allies after Italy's defeat in the war.

The Spandau escape plot was said to have been discovered by British Intelligence investigators during the interrogation in January 1953 of six Nazis after their arrest on charges of scheming to overthrow the Government of Western Germany. Leader of the plot was Dr Werner Naumann, onetime assistant to Goebbels in Hitler's Propaganda Ministry. West Germany's Chancellor Konrad Adenauer subsequently claimed that it was a false alarm. Otto Skorzeny kept silent and declined to discuss the matter.

Years later, on 26 August 1970, an anonymous caller threatened to bomb the prison, the US consulate, and other official Berlin buildings if Hess was not freed by 1 September. The prison guard was reinforced; the police investigated, and there were no September bombs. In April 1973 a warning that extremists planned to hijack a British Airways aircraft flying to Berlin unless Hess was freed led to massive precautions at several German airfields. Police attention was centred mainly on Stuttgart, where investigators sought nine people reported to have made bookings for the British plane. Their names were supplied to the airline by the police, and a British official at

Stuttgart confirmed that the airline had been given details of the alleged plot, including its objective.

Hitler greeting his deputy, Rudolf Hess, at party ceremonies just four months before war was declared in September, 1939

According to information on which West German police and US and British Intelligence acted, extremists intended to snatch the aircraft while it was *en route* to West Berlin's Tempelhof aerodrome. The pilot was to have been forced to overfly Berlin, refuel at Warsaw, then continue to Moscow. The reasoning behind the scheme was that, since Russia was the solitary power still insisting on Hess's imprisonment, a threat to blow up the aircraft would be most effective at Moscow.

Extra security was instituted on all British Airways flights to Berlin, including special baggage and body searches, stricter police checks on all passengers' passports, and more detailed examination of aircraft. It was later admitted that the hijack had been cancelled or postponed at the last moment following the defection of a member of the group — a twenty-nine-year-old local-government employee in the Munich area — who confessed to having originated the action. He alleged that he opted out because he had arranged for the hijack to be carried out without violence, but other plotters decided to smuggle nearly 40 lb of explosives on to the aircraft and detonate it, if necessary.

Although police did not rule out the possibility that it was a flamboyant hoax to publicize the 'Free Hess' movement, they nevertheless interviewed Professor Berthold Rubin, a lecturer on Byzantine history at Cologne University, who had been involved previously in a number of operations for the campaign. On 10 May 1966, on the anniversary of Hess's flight to Scotland, the professor parachuted on to the Duke of Hamilton's estate where Hess had landed his plane in 1941. Rubin admitted that he was aware of the Easter 1973 hijack plot, and had advised strongly against it. He asserted: 'I'm sure that Hess, if he knew, would also be against any such lunacy.' Police evidence indicated that the hijacking idea also appeared to have been motivated by an imminent visit by Mr Brezhnev to Bonn. The extremist group felt that because of improved relations between Russia and West Germany the Soviet leader would be more inclined to free Hess.

It was not difficult to understand why former SS General Skorzeny and remnants among the old-time Nazi hierarchy, as well as younger Hess freedom campaigners, professed such regard for Hitler's Deputy Führer — the lackey who had done everything but wag his tail when the Führer was around. Six-footer Hess, bearer of an 'honourable' Nazi scar in the shape of a hairless patch on the scalp (collected in one of the early beer-cellar battles), would have been at home among dangerous reactionaries. Not only did he consider himself first in the Nazi line of succession, but to practitioners old in the art of creating false gods and national myths he was a natural for a build-up as an enigma and an arbiter of destiny. Usually silent and moody, his personality puzzled plenty of Germans, who could not decide whether he was uncannily brilliant or just a zealous fool; nevertheless his self-created mysticism made him a perfect focus for the ambitions of a new Party imbued with the diabolism of Hitler's old ideas.

Whatever the truth about the Skorzeny rescue story, or the intended hijack of a British passenger aircraft to pressure four Governments into releasing Hess, no such doubts surrounded a terrorist plot to free Hess that was shattered by West German police in March 1978. That month they arrested a dozen members of a neo-Nazi organization that had fashioned itself on parallel lines to the extreme left-wing Red Army Faction. These right-wing Hess followers were also held responsible for a series of bank robberies and weapons thefts. Security measures at Spandau Prison were immediately increased.

Police discovered the escape organization whilst probing an incident in which armed men raided a Dutch camp in the NATO exercise area at Bergen, Lower Saxony, and stole four submachine guns. It was assumed that the attack had been engineered by left-wing terrorists until detectives found that a neo-Nazi group in Lüneburg was responsible. More cells, operating under the camouflage of a 'sports association', were located in Hamburg, Nuremberg, Cologne, and areas of Schleswig-Holstein. The 'sports' cover was utilized to train unit members in the handling of arms and in assault tactics. Impressed by the success of left-wing terrorists in obtaining funds and munitions, the neo-Nazis decided to imitate their methods and were preparing further actions, including hostage-taking aimed at compelling the release of other war criminals held in West German prisons.

Whilst neo-Nazis valued Hess as an outstanding symbol of the past, within Spandau he left only an impression of fanatical mediocrity. Sentenced to imprisonment for the rest of his natural life, he believed that destiny had chosen him for a greater role than any he had yet played, and that his day of freedom would come.

Let us, however, look at him as British warder Belson saw him one day through the spy window of No. 7 cell. The prisoner was not on his bed or seated at the table. He lay on the floor of the cell, flat and inert, eyes tightly shut, hands clasped behind the head. Sharply etched was the high, slightly receding forehead, enlarged at the top and overhanging the eyes that were bushy-browed. Beneath was a wide-ridged nose and its broad 'pug' tip. It was the face of a man living in the strange silent world of unreality. For five minutes he lay like this, his body wholly still. Then the tightly shut eyes suddenly blazed open, so that their vivid blueness appeared even bluer.

Hess had completed his yoga relaxation, the exercise he had learned as a boy from watching Arabs slide from their camels to the floor of the desert and its somnolent, burning sands, to relax without seeming to breathe. The guard eyed Hess a moment or two longer and then turned away, leaving the prisoner alone once more.

Much had happened to Hess both before and after that astonishing flight to Scotland that was intended to achieve agreement between Germany and Britain. He had been born in Alexandria on 26 April 1894, the family having settled there when the future Deputy Führer's grandfather took a fancy to Egypt and left Germany to set up there as a merchant. The old man did well and, ultimately, was able to hand over a flourishing business to Hess's father, who in turn consolidated the family gains. However, when it came to Rudolf perpetuating the father-to-son tradition he demurred. Raw cotton and lentils were not for his speculative eyes; he was a merchant of a different commodity and felt his business lay in Germany. He went there as a student at Munich University and almost at once came under the influence of Professor Karl Haushofer, who was to dominate much of his future philosophy and thought. It was, in fact, the learned professor who really inspired Hess's wartime flight. Haushofer's theory of geopolitics (geographical facts determining political relationships) was to become part of Nazi doctrine, and it was hardly surprising that Hess became devoutly attached to his tutor.

Hess's great political exemplar, however, was Adolf Hitler himself. Hearing the future Führer harangue and rave in a Munich beer cellar in 1923, he was at once inspired to throw in his lot with the National Socialists, the movement that spawned Nazism. Shortly after their first meeting Hitler and

Hess were picked up and tossed into a Landsberg fortress for attempting to overthrow the Bavarian Government. It was there Hitler, aided and abetted by Hess, wrote *Mein Kampf* the testament of hate that became the Nazi Bible. In those days Hitler was No. 7 in the movement and Hess No. 16, but they were very much closer than these ratings indicated. When it came to murder and ruthlessness they were inseparable.

Hess aped Hitler in every possible way: interest in astrology, vegetarian diets, belief in herbal remedies, even usually standing — like Hitler — with hands folded across his genitals. He bestowed the Führer's favourite name on his son; Wolf was the name of Hitler's best-loved dog.

Because he was the most retiring of the Nazi leaders and his public image was therefore less bloodthirsty, Hitler chose Hess as the perfect person to present public justification for the infamous 'Night of the Long Knives'. On this night Hitler decided to liquidate Ernst Röhm, his oldest comrade-in-arms, stoutest supporter and leader of the notorious Stormtroopers. Röhm and his gangs of thugs, whose fists and weapons battered a path of power for Hitler, alienated the middle classes by ignorantly ridiculing intellectual and spiritual preoccupations, particularly religion. Hess, Göring and Goebbels made broadcasts threatening 'the ridiculous scamps'; but they realized that comparatively mild public condemnation would not make the problem go away. Something more was required, perhaps proof that Röhm was preparing to acquire greater personal power through a coup.

From the earliest days of the Nazi movement, Hitler had insisted that the Stormtroopers were to be a political and not a military force. They were to furnish the physical violence and terror by which the Party could smash its way to political dominance. Röhm disagreed with Hitler over this interpretation of his Stormtroopers' role, seeing them as the backbone of the National Socialist revolution and the nucleus of a future army. They would be for Hitler what the French conscript armies were to Napoleon after the French Revolution. Realizing that he could not grab control without the support, or at least the toleration, of the old army generals, as well as the backing and loyalty of the armed forces, which still possessed the physical clout to remove him, Hitler had to admit that his two and a half million bullying, brawling, brownshirted, jackbooted Stormtroopers had also developed into a threat — to him. Men who had contributed towards his attainment of power in February 1933 were a liability by June 1934. They had to be removed.

It was arranged for the Gestapo to provide 'documentary evidence' confirming to Hitler that, if he did not comply with Röhm's ambitions, his friend intended to overthrow, or, if necessary, assassinate him. On 30 June 1934 what became known as the 'Night of the Long Knives' took place.

Hitler and his entourage, accompanied by SS members of the Gestapo, drove to the little Bavarian lakeside town of Bad Wiessee and the hotel where Röhm and Stormtrooper comrades were staying. Some of the Stormtroopers were killed on the spot. Röhm and others were arrested as 'prisoners of State'. Arrests based on Gestapo-prepared lists were also under way in Munich, and then continued in north Germany. How many were slaughtered in the purge was never definitely established. To the Reichstag Hitler said that 61 were shot, including 19 'higher SA (Stormtroop) leaders'; that 13 more died 'resisting arrest', and 3 'committed suicide' — a total of 77. But there were actually hundreds of victims. At the Nuremberg trials, it was stated that many were eliminated merely because they were 'just not very popular', and a figure of more than 1,000 was indicated.

Hitler rose to power by murdering anyone who seriously opposed or endangered him. Through it all Hess was right there by his side. This was the manner in which they 'broke with friends' who embarrassingly reminded them of the methods that had achieved power. Hess's role was generally underrated or understated.

One of the Nazi Party's most influential financial backers, the multi-millionaire industrialist Fritz Thyssen, openly admitted: 'Rudolf Hess was instrumental in bringing about a closer relationship between the Nazis and myself.'

As Deputy Führer, Hess, by Hitler's decree of 21 April 1933, was granted full power to decide, in the name of the Führer, all matters concerning Party leadership. From 1933 the Nazi Party and the State became increasingly integrated, and Hess concerned himself with such diverse aspects as foreign and racial policies, technological development, and education. He became the author and co-signatory of many of Hitler's policies. He was also a Reich Minister without Portfolio. In fact Hess and his office became the channel through which all legislation or decrees of the Reich had to pass, except certain matters concerning the armed forces, police, and Foreign Office.

On 27 April 1941, shortly before his flight to Britain, the *Nazional Zeitung* newspaper made the following statement:

> Rudolf Hess was once called the 'Conscience of the Party'. If we ask why the Führer's Deputy was given this undoubtedly honourable title, the reason for this is plain to see. There is no phenomenon of our public life which is not the concern of the Führer's Deputy. So enormously many-sided and diverse is his work and sphere of duty that it cannot be outlined in a

few words; and it lies in the nature of the obligation laid upon the Führer's Deputy that wide publicity hears little of the activity of Rudolf Hess. Few know that many Government measures taken, especially in the sphere of war economy and the Party, which meet with such hearty approbation when they are notified publicly, can be traced back to the direct initiation of die Führer's Deputy.

Eventually, defeated, Hitler went to an inglorious Valhalla, and Hess was imprisoned for life for everything he did before flying to Britain.

When Hess pulled his gaunt 11-stone body up from his Spandau cell floor it was 6 a.m. The gaol's day had begun. Seven cell doors opened, and in single file the prisoners were led through the inner cell block door down a corridor on the right, to the washroom. This stone-floored retreat consisted of three sinks, two baths opposite each other, with wooden duckboards beside them, six shower stalls, and a laundry wringer. Two at a time, the prisoners went to wash. That morning, Baldur von Schirach edged over to the sink nearest the door. Hess moved to the same sink and pushed Schirach aside.

'This is my sink!' he said.

'They are all sinks, so what does it matter who uses which?' Schirach exclaimed angrily. The other five prisoners watched and said nothing.

'This is the sink I shall always use, and as Deputy Führer, and senior among us, I have the first right and first choice of everything — even in prison!' Hess shouted. 'That is what I wish and that is what it is going to be!'

When Hess was angry, the old Nazi arrogance and haughtiness quickly appeared. On one occasion when the seven were working in the prison garden, a group of Allied inspecting officers noticed Hess standing apart from the others and sent a guard to discover the reason. The guard returned to inform the officers: 'Herr Hess feels, as Deputy Führer, that deputations should go to him and not him to them.'

The guards were about to intervene in the washroom row when Schirach moved aside; Hess, using the perfumed soap his wife had been permitted to send him, began washing himself. After drying with the army-type towel, he removed his ill-fitting set of yellow-stained false teeth, rinsed them, then put them back in his mouth.

It was to this washroom that three times a week the seven came, one at a time, to be shaved by the prison barber. And it was here that they came, two at a time, every Friday at 9 a.m., for a bath, and to do their laundry; only Grand Admiral Raeder, bow-legged and crippled with arthritis, declined the bath — he was a shower man. The baths were prepared by the two prison staff male nurses. The 'Friday bath forum' was a favourite conversational opportunity for the prisoners and they took advantage of it even in the days when talking was forbidden. Almost from the very beginning, the seven defied this rule.

Albert Speer manoeuvred his six feet three inches into one bath, while Hess, more narrow-chested and round-shouldered than he used to be, got into the one opposite.

'My wife tells me my boy is now very good at figures,' said Hess, opening the conversation. 'He's just like his father, although I could never really be bothered with figures. Perhaps Wolferl [his pet name for his son Wolf] will become an accountant, or go into business. Or maybe he will become an engineer. I would like that because I nearly became one myself.'

Not to be outdone in this mention of family accomplishments, Speer referred to the cello playing of his fifteen-year-old son Fritz.

'I think Wolferl will be musical too,' countered Hess. 'When I was twelve years old in Alexandria, I and my brother had piano lessons from a German *Fräulein*. She was flabbergasted with my talent, which just goes to show that I should have become a composer. I ought to have done, then I might not now be sitting here. But maybe it wouldn't have come to anything anyway, because my brain didn't co-ordinate too well with my fingers, the distance from my brain to my fingers was too great.'

This was no sudden flash of Hess humour. He was devoid of any real sense of humour. As Schirach said, 'Hess had been known to make only one joke in his life, when he compared Germany with a hedgehog and her enemies as foxes. But even this touch of Teutonic humour was not his own; it originated from one of Wilhelm Busch's fables.'

The bathroom talk of home seemed to silence the men for a moment, until Hess remarked, 'I spent half my life in the mountains, and it is no wonder that the mountains and I are one. That is where I would go back if I were free. I realized at Nuremberg that I had to take every possibility into account: death, imprisonment, or a mad-house. I am still surprised, though, that I didn't receive a death sentence.'

Each morning, except Sundays, after their washroom visit, the seven returned to clean their own cells and the prison corridors. Even the cleaning implements came under the prison's anti-suicide regulations. Nothing was permitted to be used that could be remotely lethal. The rims of buckets had bevelled edges; soap had to be non-carbolic. A bar of carbolic soap issued in error one morning was found in Raeder's cell.

An immediate inquiry was ordered and the offending guard was disciplined.

Cleaning duty completed, Hess awaited the twice-daily security search of his cell and person; ten minutes after it was over the cell door opened again to admit the prison medical officer. Shoulders hunched, Hess shuffled towards his visitor.

'You don't look much like a Deputy Führer nowadays,' said the doctor. Hess instantly straightened up, clicked his heels, and bowed. Unintentionally, the doctor next committed a breach of the Spandau regulations by offering his hand to the prisoner. Hess, wary as always, hesitated, and made no response to the gesture. It would have been different with the others.

'And how are you?' the doctor asked, knowing full well the approximate pattern of the reply.

'Pains! Pains in my belly. Bellyache!' Hess croaked. 'I can't go on. Don't you see how much I'm suffering?'

The doctor was certain he was malingering. Every test — and Hess became the most examined prisoner in the world — showed no sign of any physical ailment. A British psychiatrist who visited him in the gaol reported: 'His pains are probably hysterical. No psychiatric treatment necessary. To be treated gently, but firmly.' Another neuro-psychiatrist, Dr Hans Lowenbach, diagnosed after a two-hour check 'negative attitudes' and 'passive obstructionism', noting that Hess clearly enjoyed the attention achieved through his misbehaviour. Psychiatrists were forever examining him, and he revelled in the idea of being 'unfathomable'. Only when threatened with disciplinary punishment did he stop playing up. Then the deep-set eyes blazed alternately with hatred or disdainful contempt.

When US Army psychiatrist Dr Robert Levy asked: 'How do you get on with the other prisoners?' he replied: 'Well, we are all comrades.'

The doctor looked around the whitewashed cell walls. They were completely bare.

The prisoners were permitted to keep eleven family photographs at a time in their cell. No one in Spandau seemed to know why this figure was decided upon. But eleven it was and, on receipt of any new photographs, prisoners had to surrender others in exchange. All photographs removed on exchange were filed, numbered, and available to prisoners for further viewing on request.

'Why haven't you any pictures of your family on the wall?' inquired the doctor.

'No photographs,' said Hess shortly.

Ignoring the denial, the doctor began a thorough search of the room. Under the mattresses of the prisoner's bed he found two photographs of Hess's wife and son.

'Why don't you put them on the wall?' he suggested.

'No.'

The doctor was prying into the mind of Hess. 'You are to fix these photographs on the wall and that is an immediate order! And they are to stay there.'

Reluctantly, and sullenly, Hess obeyed. The doctor had not finished probing. 'Why don't you ever see your wife and son?' he began again. Hess did not allow them to visit him for many years.

The prisoner looked down at his clothes, held open his jacket, and replied, 'Not like this.'

During his incarceration Hess tried, in some ways successfully, to keep the truth from the doctors and psychiatrists who probed the secret recesses of his mind. In a

1946 Nuremberg letter to his wife he wrote: 'I strictly refuse, under the circumstances arranged here for visiting, to come together with you or anybody else under conditions which I consider undignified.' That was the reason he always gave the Spandau authorities, but there was more to it than this simple excuse.

Hess had refused to see his wife or son since the day he flew to Britain. Although he invited her to visit Nuremberg on many occasions, he asked her to come on days when visits were not permitted. Hess was tortured and racked by a deadly fear and his nightmare was self-induced. He was afraid of himself and saw himself as his own executioner. I learned of this secret fear from the first person to realize what had happened to him — his wife. In an unguarded moment, the truth came out:

> Rudolf built a mental wall about himself as a protection against the strain he was under, but I knew and he knew it was only a very thin wall. That was why he avoided me visiting him in Spandau. I might cry. The strain and emotion could have proven too much for both of us — we hadn't seen each other for a long, long time — and Rudolf was afraid that my presence would smash his defences.
>
> Once breached, a wall so thin would be beyond repair, and then God knows what would have happened. His mind might have gone completely. And so he wouldn't see me, nor our son. He couldn't bear the thought of our boy seeing his father as a felon.

It was not only the sight of his wife or son that Hess feared. Anything evocative that reminded of the past, such as the simple beauty of music and flowers, was an assault on his plaster-cast defences. He was gravely disturbed even by the music that on Saturday afternoons came from the chapel at the far end of the Spandau inner cell block. The chapel was a double-sized cell, furnished with seven chairs, three religious pictures, and an old harmonium. The altar was simply a table upon which stood a bronze cross, a Bible, and two candles. Every Saturday it echoed for almost an hour with the playing and raucous singing of Funk, Speer's light baritone, and the voices of the other four. Hess was always absent, nor did he ever attend the services conducted by the French prison chaplain. When asked why, he just gave an empty wave of the hand. Only hymns or religious music were permitted, but sometimes while Funk played a Bach prelude — and he played brilliantly — he suddenly switched the melody to a German folk song or some ditty suggested by the others. Hess feared these too-familiar tunes.

On special occasions, such as Christmas or Easter, the chaplain was permitted to give the prisoners a gramophone recital in the chapel. On 4 April 1953 Hess wrote to his wife:

> This afternoon we had an Easter concert. A Haydn symphony, a Schubert quartet, a Mozart quartet, and another symphony — I don't know its name, yet it was familiar to me and pierced the armour with which I surrounded my soul and heart in the same way as cosmic rays cut through thick lead walls. Had it been possible I would have run away. But I was saved from being overcome by the noise of transport planes continually passing over the prison. The disturbance they caused interrupted my mood, and annoyed me, which perhaps was strange for a former pilot.

Hess had always been perverse, often childishly so. Frau Hess freely admitted that 'Rudolf was awkward sometimes because he loved teasing people.' This 'awkwardness' was often manifested by his pretending to be a victim of amnesia. From the time of his imprisonment in England he resisted any thorough medical examination of his mental state with the plea, 'I cannot remember.'

He boastfully admitted one day to one of the medical officers at Spandau: 'I hoped by faking mental trouble to be sent home from Britain in the prisoners-of-war exchanges that were then taking place. I tried hard enough, but it just didn't come off. To try to fool the doctors I became the "victim" of mental blackouts. It was like grand opera — all pretence. I made out that I couldn't recollect who I was, and this would go on for as long as I wanted it to. When I grew tired of the "attack" I then remembered my name and gazed around with astonished eyes in the realization that I had returned to the world from which I had retreated. It was a great game every time I played it.'

According to Hess this histrionic gift, first tried out during his incarceration in Britain, saved him from the gallows at Nuremberg. He confessed: 'During the trials I realized that my ability to fool everybody by simulating attacks of amnesia could be used in my defence. I am certain but for this — my acting ability — I would have been sentenced to death.'

To try to jog Hess's apparently lost memory, he was provided with a film show twelve days before the Nuremberg trial started. Handcuffed to a guard, he was taken to a small theatre to witness newsreels of himself and many of his prison colleagues. Lights were installed to partly illuminate Hess's face when the theatre lights dimmed, to enable his reactions to be watched by a team of psychiatrists. Justice Robert Jackson, the United States prosecutor for the Nuremberg trials, and General William J. Donovan, head of America's Office of Strategic Services, were also present.

Hess saw himself strutting about with Hitler and other members of the Nazi hierarchy, declaiming speeches in praise of the Führer. When the screening ended he was asked: 'Do you remember?'

'I recognize Hitler and Göring,' he said, 'and recognize the others, but only because I heard their names mentioned and have seen their names on cell blocks in this gaol.'

'Don't you remember being there?'

'I don't remember. I must have been there because obviously I was there. But I don't remember.'

Even on a copy of his indictment Hess scrawled in English: 'I can't remember — Rudolf Hess.'

An international psychiatric team was summoned to examine him further. Dr Nolan D. C. Lewis, Professor of Psychiatry at Columbia University and Director of the New York State Psychiatric Institute and Hospital, was joined by Dr Donald E. Cameron, Professor of Psychiatry at the University of Illinois; and with the fluent German-speaking Dr Gilbert they worked on him for hours, then continued to study him from the opening of the trial. Their report stated:

> Our examination revealed that Hess is not insane, has no disorder of consciousness, understands the nature of the proceedings against him. He asserted that he had suffered a loss of memory for the past, but it was the definite impression that what he interpreted as depending on memory was not available to an examiner, but what he did not understand as depending on memory as such was reproduced.
>
> He claimed that he had no recollection or mental image of his parents yet he answered some other questions about his family without utilizing his usual phrase, 'I don't know'. Moreover he carried on the various mental and physical activities of his daily life despite the alleged loss of memory for the time when he learned them. The titles of some of the books he has been reading indicate that he must have, in order to understand their significance, retained some of the

background of his education and training, although he says he does not remember what studies he undertook in his early years and has no memory of his tutors. However, when asked if he had ever studied astrology he replied emphatically, 'No', instead of 'I don't remember'.

These among other phenomena suggest that a part of the memory loss is simulated and it is probable that the hysterical or unconscious part is rather superficial. He adhered quite consistently to the pattern of saying 'I don't know', 'I don't remember' to questions relating to his past life. It is probable that this type of response was originally developed consciously as a protective measure during a period of stress; that it has become habitual and has therefore become unconscious in part.

Detailed studies by means of special techniques that could have been made to determine the extent of the unconscious elements in his memory loss were resisted by him. His refusal was explained in such phrases as 'My memory has nothing to do with my responsibility'... 'I can get my memory back by experiments after the trial'... 'There is no possibility of doing it in a natural way.' He obviously wanted to retain the amnesia.

His behaviour was dissimilar to that of the usual amnesic as evidenced by the lack of any attempt to recover his memory. His behaviour during the early sessions of the trial, his apparent inattention to the proceedings and books which should have been of great vital interest to him that were under discussion, must be interpreted as abnormal reactions.

It is now the consensus among psychiatrists that only an unstable person can or does use this method of dealing with major issues of life, and there is a sufficient amount of evidence in his personal history to indicate that he has been an unstable personality and has a neurotic character which has expressed itself in hysterical symptoms from time to time. His present claim to loss of memory is one of these hysterical reactions developed in connection with the dilemma in which he found himself in England.

The British record states that he had a loss of memory from November 1943 to June 1944, at which time it was recovered. His present amnesia started in February 1945 and now serves the psychological purpose of complicating the examination proceedings.

He therefore has a selective amnesia, hysterical in type, utilizing defence mechanisms of an emotional neurotic nature. He has no brain disease as such and his capacity for thinking is basically intact. His difficulty being emotionally determined, he is not wholly aware or entirely conscious of the significance of his symptoms and although his ability is unimpaired he does not use it in the examinations and may not during the trial proceedings.

Ten outstanding international medical specialists studied Hess to decide whether he was fit to stand trial and understand the proceedings. The second afternoon session on the ninth day of the Nuremberg trials was exclusively occupied with discussion of Hess. All the other defendants were in their cells, and Hess alone remained in the dock. Suddenly, in the midst of protracted arguments concerning his mental state and fitness to plead, Hess stood up and indicated that he wished to speak.

Staring at the judges, he said: 'Mr President, I would like to say this. At the start of the proceedings this afternoon I gave my defence a note in which I expressed my opinion that the proceedings could be curtailed if I were allowed to speak.

'In order that I may be allowed to continue attendance at the trial and receive judgement along with my comrades, as I wish to do, and in order that I be not declared unfit for trial, I offer the following statement to the court — a declaration which I had not originally intended to present until a later point in the course of the trial.

'From this time on my memory is again at the disposal of the outside world. The reasons for the simulated amnesia are of a tactical nature. Actually only my ability to concentrate is somewhat impaired. On the other hand, my ability to follow the trial, to defend myself, to question witnesses, and to answer questions myself is not impaired.

'I emphasize that I assume full responsibility for everything that I have done, everything that I have signed, and everything I have co-signed. My deep-seated conviction that the court is not a legitimate one is not altered by the above statement. I have successfully maintained the illusion of "amnesia" with my official defence counsel; he has acted accordingly in good faith.'

Hess sat down, and for an instant there was utter silence. Then Justice Lawrence announced: 'The proceedings are adjourned.'

The following morning the President declared: 'The Court has carefully considered the petition of the defending counsel of the defendant Hess and has also had the opportunity to discuss it in detail both with the defence and with the prosecution. The Court has also taken into account the detailed medical report which has been made on the condition of the defendant Hess, and has come to the conclusion that no reasons exist to order a further examination of the defendant. Since the defendant Hess has made a statement to the Court, and in view of the existing evidence, the Court is of the opinion that he is at present capable of pleading. The petition of defending counsel is therefore rejected, and the trial will proceed.'

The psychiatrist Dr Douglas M. Kelley and Dr Gilbert visited Hess in his cell after the statement to the Tribunal. Hess immediately asked Kelley: 'How did I do? Good, wasn't I? I really surprised everybody, don't you think?'

Hess continued to enjoy bouts of amnesia in Spandau gaol. On one occasion when the American Prison Director, Lt Col Smith, made one of his frequent visits to the prison garden, Hess went over to Funk to ask who 'the strange man' was.

'You know very well who he is,' replied Funk.

A few moments later Hess complained to Schirach, 'Funk is trying to tease me. He says the man here is the American Director of the prison. Tell me the truth — who is he?' So it went on from one to the other until, angrily, Hess strode away. For months afterwards, during which time he was examined by an American Army psychiatrist, Hess persisted that Lt Col Smith was a stranger to him.

In the prison garden one morning during this 'amnesia' period, Speer recommended Hess to read a book by the personal physician of Germany's 'Iron Chancellor', Bismarck.

'Who in the world is Bismarck?' Hess asked.

Unsure whether this blackout on German history was feigned or not, Speer obliged by explaining some of Bismarck's exploits in world politics.

Overhearing the conversation, Schirach interjected, 'No! no! You've got it all wrong. The Bismarck referred to in this book is the man who invented the Bismarck herring and earned a fortune by making it the most popular pickled herring in Europe.'

Speer, with a twinkle in his eye, insisted that Schirach's explanation was right, but Hess was not the man to have fun poked at him. Abruptly he got up and stalked away without another word.

One fine spring morning of that same year, on 13 April 1950, the Deputy Führer's errant memory returned from its overdue flight and he approached Speer with the dignified request that he be asked a number of general knowledge questions. Not averse to playing schoolmaster, Speer obliged, and Hess responded with the correct answers. The same performance was enacted with the help of Schirach, to whom he explained that his memory had returned the previous night at exactly eleven o'clock. The prisoners were not allowed to possess watches, and Hess did not explain how he had arrived at the precise hour of his recovery.

Of the seven prisoners Hess was always the most troublesome. Because he forever tried to attract attention, always endeavouring to assert himself, it was not in the least surprising that he received more punishment than any of his fellow criminals. Spandau's daily log-book told the story of his insolence and insubordination. Whenever Frau Hess failed to receive a letter from her husband she knew that for the time being he would be unable to send or receive one, and was being disciplined. One such incident started one morning when the guard entered Hess's cell to find him still in bed and apparently determined to stay there.

'Come on, get up.'

'No, I can't. I'm ill.'

'Get up, Number Seven.'

The order was repeated three times but Hess made no attempt to rise and lay there determinedly, until at last the guard called for assistance. The prisoner was hauled out of bed and marched out of his cell at a smart pace. The incident was reported immediately to the four Prison Directors, and as a result a punishment order was issued against Hess for wilful disobedience. For the following three days his bed was removed from the cell from first thing in the morning until lights out, so that the prisoner was deprived of any rest period.

Only the wooden chair was allowed to remain. Reading was forbidden, and all books were taken away.

A few days later Hess repeated the performance, complaining that he had become worse and was unable to get out of bed to wash or get his meals. As a doctor had declared that there was nothing physically amiss with him, Hess soon found that no one would bring his meals to him. Somehow, he 'managed' to get his food. He was still full of woe, asserting that he was unfit to leave his bed. This malingering cost fourteen days' solitary confinement and the removal of all reading and writing materials.

One morning he refused to wash, explaining: 'I washed last night.' When the guard pointed out, 'People normally wash three times a day', Hess replied: 'I'm normal and I wash only once.'

Hess and his periodic 'ailments' caused endless trouble. He was a chronic hypochondriac with a mania for 'nature' cures. Like many complex contradictory characters, his moral outlook and philosophical beliefs were based on time and circumstance. For instance, when he heard that a child had been born on the wrong side of the blanket to a friend of the family, who had been left in the lurch, he was full of indignation and censure. His sanctimonious attitude on the subject caused Funk to remind him of an offer he had made in the winter of 1939. Then, as Deputy Führer, he had said that he was prepared to be the godfather to the illegitimate children of soldiers killed in the war, and had declared: 'We are no longer concerned with antiquated man-made traditions and principles of morality.' Hess wrote to his wife on the subject of delinquent lovers and pre-marital chastity:

> If my son Wolf would do what this young man did, and produce offspring without my knowing it, so to speak behind

my back, and not tell me because of pure cowardice, there would be a hell of a lot of trouble. If the said son however came and confessed, I obviously would put on a stem face and say, 'Couldn't you wait a little?' and 'Couldn't you consider the traditional sequence, marry first and then produce children, you son-of-a-gun? However, now that it has happened, I demand gentlemanly behaviour, also an immediate wedding.' And I couldn't imagine why he shouldn't, from a purely financial point.

What is the difference between marriage or no marriage? If the man responsible is not financially able, mother and child have to be looked after by either the family on the father's side or the mother's side, or by both. However, the father, the one really responsible, is always the seducer. One cannot demand that a girl resist a man for ever, it's against nature, based on the fact that manhood is the active element.

With a man, the will is dominating. He can therefore be master of himself far better than the female who is more emotional. In this particular case, the only excuse one can make is that it was the month of May and so again it's nature. Not for nothing do the statistics of birth prove that more people are born in February.

As regards the reputation of the little father, he will suffer nowadays far less in the eyes of decent-thinking people, if he takes the consequences of what he has done very quickly, rather than if he leaves the poor thing.

From the day British security officers had clapped Hess into the Tower of London, along with his precious peace proposals, he never ceased to be fascinated by the miracle of his failure. It was unexplainable to him and remained an obsession; an absorbing subject upon which to ponder, speculate, and argue.

When he landed in Scotland the authorities behaved as though he was a dangerous Trojan Horse dumped in their midst. The chance to exploit the affair, as Hitler feared Britain would, was bungled. Even Intelligence departments failed to apply to the interrogation of 'Captain Horn', as Hess first called himself, the ingenuity that they applied so successfully to other prisoners.

Hess was still a member of the special Defence Council, a trusted confidant of the Führer, and the repository of valuable political, economic, and strategic information, yet he was handled amateurishly. Winston Churchill mistakenly assigned the Cabinet Minister Lord Simon to interview Hess in the rambling Victorian country house near Aldershot called Mytchett Place, where Hess was kept for a time. Lord Simon's personality — brilliant in law, but cold — was a bad choice for prying open Hess, who declared that he had come to cut through red tape and 'bring the two Nordic brother peoples together'. He was anxious to make known 'the moderation of the Führer's peace terms', as he had learned them in the course of many conversations with his leader.

Simon flatteringly addressed Hess as 'Herr Reichminister', but failed to handle him. Hess became more and more hostile and defiant, then finally resorted to making threats. 'If our terms are not accepted now, they will be much worse when Britain is defeated and brought to its knees!' he warned.

Accompanying Lord Simon at this interview was Ivone Kirkpatrick of the Foreign Office. Kirkpatrick had been First Secretary at the British Embassy in Berlin from 1933 to 1938 and had occasionally met Hess at functions. After Simon and Kirkpatrick departed, Hess collapsed in despair. All hopes of spectacular glory had crashed about him. He later admitted that he had come to make peace 'on any terms', provided Britain would join Germany in attacking Russia. That was the first time he mentioned the coming attack on the Soviet Union.

Hess was not the only Nazi who wished to make peace with Britain to avoid a two-front war with her and Russia. James Bond's creator, Ian Fleming, who served in World War II Intelligence, is credited with having initiated the idea of luring one of the Nazi leaders to Britain with the aid of astrology. Hitler, Hess, and others in the Nazi hierarchy were avid astrology followers. Fleming's idea was to try to convince Hess, who he knew was strongly influenced by astrology, that an influential group of pro-German Britons were ready to receive him and that, as Hitler's deputy, he could pave the way to a negotiated peace and the overthrow of the Churchill Government.

Fleming is said to have passed the idea to two associates, one in another branch of British Intelligence, and the other a contact in Switzerland. All agreed that Hess was the likeliest candidate for the scheme. The Swiss contact arranged for loaded horoscopes to be supplied to Hess. They were slanted not only to point to the feasibility of peace moves in Britain, but to direct Hess's attention to specific people and to the most favourable date for action.

Because it was thought unwise to use too important a personage for Hess to contact in Britain, since neutral ambassadors could be used by the Germans to check the reliability of such rumours, the plotters are alleged to have selected the subtler ploy of using the Duke of Hamilton's name to mislead Hess. Both Hess and his principal adviser, Professor Karl Haushofer, were known to be romantics with a snobbish awe of titles and royalty. Furthermore, the Duke was in command of a fighter squadron in a fairly remote part of Scotland, which provided the opportunity of suggesting a landing place for Hess.

Captured German reports confirm that Hess conceived the notion of working through allegedly pro-German circles in Britain to induce the British to yield. Hitler's notorious Foreign Minister, Ribbentrop, said before he was executed at Nuremberg that Hess considered the Duke 'quite erroneously, to be a friend of Germany'.

According to Richard Deacon's *A History of British Secret Service*, Ernest Schulte-Strathaus, one of Hess's advisers on astrological matters, forecast in January 1941 that an unusual conjunction of the planets would take place on 10 May 1941. This was the day that Hess flew to Scotland. It was claimed that on that date six planets in the sign of Taurus coincided with the full moon.

After Hess's flight, Schulte-Strathaus denied emphatically that Hess chose the date through his advice. Nevertheless he was imprisoned by the Nazis because he was Hess's astrological adviser.

Hitler also blamed the influence of Professor Haushofer for the flight, and his son Albrecht was said to have been implicated, too. But as Albrecht was arrested for participation in the 20 July 1944 bomb plot to assassinate Hitler, and was shot in the final days of the war, any role he may have played in the Hess flight may never be known.[2]

Of all mishaps and lost causes, Hess felt the failure of that peace flight most poignantly and his mind clung to it tenaciously. He talked about it over and over again to anyone in Spandau who would listen to him.

---

[2] Hess first introduced Hitler to Professor Haushofer, a former general and founder of the theories of 'geopolitics'. His ideas heavily influenced Hitler's early style, but Haushofer did not agree with all aspects of Nazism. The professor committed suicide after his son was murdered by the Nazis in 1945.

'You know how conversation between friends can often bring out a startling idea,' Hess would say. 'Well, such a thing happened between Professor Haushofer and myself. I had known him from my student days and used to attend his lectures. Afterwards we never lost sight of each other. It is possible to recognize the influence of the professor in *Mein Kampf*.

'In the early days of the war we had a long discussion together. Haushofer spoke of the senselessness of air raids and, being a family man, I agreed with him. It was then that he told me he felt certain that there were people in Britain who realized the folly of the war and would be only too willing to help bring it to an end.'

In a further account of this conversation Hess explained that Haushofer mentioned the name of the Duke of Hamilton and suggested that he was influential and a person of common sense. Hess, it appeared, recollected that he had met the Duke at a dinner in Berlin during the occasion of the Olympic Games. He also knew that his friend Haushofer was supposed to possess second sight and that during World War I, in which he was a general, he claimed that by premonition he had on more than one occasion been able to escape death.

'It was this extraordinary faculty of Haushofer's,' Hess said, 'that decided me to undertake the flight to Britain. Haushofer had told me of three dreams he had experienced in which he had seen me piloting an aeroplane to an unknown destination. This revelation convinced me that I had to fly to this Duke of Hamilton who could take me to see the King with an offer of peace. I felt certain that the King would be able to get rid of the warmongers and replace them with a peace party.'

To Hess, reared on a totalitarian regimen, there was nothing fantastic in the notion of Britain's monarch overruling

Parliament and the constitution and dismissing Churchill and his Government in favour of one willing to arrange peace terms with Germany.

'In view of the military situation I was convinced that Britain could be persuaded to negotiate,' Hess told anyone willing to listen. 'Nevertheless, in deciding to undertake the mission I had to make the hardest decision of my life. I realized how easily my motives could be mistaken and that I should be accused of madness.

'I planned everything carefully and shared my secret only with my adjutant. The first move was to obtain a plane from Willi Messerschmitt. He gave me one when I explained that I needed it for long-range training flights and an occasional bit of sport. The machine was converted into a single-seater and auxiliary tanks were fitted in the wings. This gave me an additional three hundred gallons of fuel. It was necessary to postpone the flight on several occasions because of the weather before I finally took off from the Messerschmitt airfield at Augsburg. Before I left, my adjutant took charge of the letters I had written to my wife, parents, and my brother, and one of them contained my will. There were letters also for Himmler and Hitler. To the Führer I explained the reasons for my flight and expressed confidence in my ability to persuade Britain to accept the peace proposals I carried with me, and to start negotiations with Germany to end the war. I planned to remain away for a couple of days before returning to Germany.'

His letter to Hitler, dated 10 May 1941, had concluded: 'And if, my Führer, this project ends in failure ... simply say I was crazy.'

Hess never became more animated than when he was able to recall the physical facts of his exploit. He carried with him a letter of introduction to the Duke of Hamilton provided by Haushofer on a pretext that it would be required for a proposed meeting (which Hitler had supposedly approved) with the Duke in a neutral country:

'Göring was chief of the Luftwaffe, but he wouldn't have had the nerve to do what I did and fly to Scotland alone. When you consider how little flying practice I had had since World War I, I think I did extremely well. It was really wonderful flying alone over the North Sea. When I reached the coast I had to dive for cloud cover to avoid a Spitfire, but I crossed it at 450 miles an hour and flew over a little town just south of Holy Isle.'

Hess hedge-hopped across the countryside, but when he found himself near Dungavel, the Scottish seat of the Duke of Hamilton, he flew on to the West Coast to take bearings. Turning east once more he followed a railway track and then a road south of Dungavel and almost met with disaster. In parachuting from his machine, after shutting off the engine and setting it in a steep dive, he blacked out, but came to before landing. He hurt his ankle as he hit the ground.

It was 10.45 on the night of 10 May 1941.

'I landed only ten feet away from the door of a small farmhouse, and soon I was sitting by the fire drinking tea,' Hess recalled. 'A little later I was taken by car to Glasgow and put in the cells before being removed to hospital because of the injury I had sustained. Guards with fixed bayonets stood around my bed watching me. Eventually I was able to see the Duke of Hamilton, to whom I explained my mission, before being taken away.'

Hess was supremely confident that unless Britain negotiated she faced utter defeat and ruin: indeed, the terms of his peace proposals all pointed to this fact. The proposals, an extension of those brought to London on the eve of the war by an agent of Göring, were:

(1) Germany to be given a free hand in Europe.
(2) Britain to have a free hand in the Empire except for the surrender of former German colonies.
(3) Russia to be regarded as part of Asia as a basis for certain demands to be made to Stalin which would have to be satisfied either by negotiation or by war.
(4) Britain to evacuate Iraq.
(5) The peace agreement to provide for reciprocal indemnification of British and German nationals whose property had been confiscated as a result of the war.
(6) These proposals to be addressed to a British Government other than that of Mr Churchill, who had planned war since 1936, and his colleagues, who had lent themselves to his war policy.

In the Frimley and Camberley urban district of Surrey, a mile and a quarter east of Farnborough, in the locality called Mytchett, Hess was taken to the hospital, Mytchett Place, for an interview with Viscount Simon and Ivone Kirkpatrick, representing the Government. Lord Simon was supposed to be a 'Dr Guthrie' and his companion from the Foreign Office a 'Dr Mackenzie'. Hess immediately got into his stride with a Hitler-style of harangue on the wrongs that Germany had been forced to endure. When asked to come to the point he began to explain what the Luftwaffe would do to Britain unless his peace terms were accepted.

'Think of the rows of children's coffins and the weeping mothers. It is the Führer's desire to prevent this catastrophe before it is too late,' he said.

The Foreign Office dismissed the Hess affair with the comment that he had picked the wrong time and the wrong people. He had also let the cat out of the bag concerning Hitler's intentions towards Russia. Hess demanded accommodation at Buckingham Palace, but he had to be satisfied with the Tower of London. He did not much care for the sound of bagpipes that he heard outside his window but he thought the Tower 'enchanting'.

'You know what Hitler said about you?' inquired Speer after hearing Hess delve once again into the past.

'I don't know and I don't want to know,' was the angry retort.

He was well aware that the Führer had declared him insane and had forbidden any further mention of his name in newspapers or over the radio. All hospitals, streets, and squares named after him were ordered to be changed, and even his Nazi membership card (accepted 15 April 1925) was removed from the Reich index.

Yet Hess still kept a devoted regard for the memory of Hitler. 'My loyalty to the Führer was not impaired by the measures he took against me,' he said, 'and it is still as great as ever it was. I am sure that Hitler afterwards approved my action although I had failed to consult him about it. My wife in one of her letters to me told me that whenever any suggestion was made that I had been guilty of traitorous conduct Hitler became angry and said he was convinced of the purity of my motives.'

The British author A. P. Herbert satirized Hess's arrival in Scotland with a poem entitled 'Hess':

> He is insane. He is the Dove of Peace.
> He is Messiah. He is Hitler's niece.
> He is the one clean honest man they've got.
> He is the worst assassin of the lot.
> He has a mission to preserve mankind.

He's non-alcoholic. He was a 'blind'.
He has been dotty since the age of ten,
But all the time was top of Hitler's men...

In its judgement on Hess the Nuremberg Tribunal brought his 'peace attempt' into its proper perspective by declaring:

> Hess was responsible for handling all Party matters and had authority to make decisions in Hitler's name. Until his flight to Britain, he was Hitler's closest personal confidant. Their relations were such that Hess must have been informed of Hitler's aggressive plans, and indeed took action to carry them out. In conversations after his arrival in Britain, Hess wholeheartedly supported all Germany's aggressive actions up to that time, personally agitated for war against Poland, and helped to frame laws dealing with the Poles and Jews. He knew Hitler's war aims but never opposed them.

In Spandau, Hess declared that he had come to realize how mistaken was the whole idea of Nazi racial ideology, that the Nazis in attempting to destroy class barriers succeeded only in substituting a system of racial discrimination that was far worse. 'But despite our mistakes,' he promised, 'Germany will be reborn in all its power and glory and fulfil the destiny of our race.'

The memory of Germany's vanished 'glory' stayed cherished in many secret cells by countless Nazis. It was to Hess, regarded by the former British Ambassador to Germany, Sir Nevile Henderson, as 'the adopted son of Hitler', that this underground movement, powerful and threatening, looked for the swaggering rebirth of *Der Tag*.

5: THE CLOWN PRINCE

It was no ordinary trial. It could hardly be that with the court sitting in the prison visiting room at Spandau, and neither prisoner nor guards to be seen. In all there were ten people present: the judge and the counsel for the prosecution, who were American and looked it; Dr Hans Flächsner, eminent lawyer and advocate at the Nuremberg trials, appearing yet again for the defence; a court stenographer from the War Crimes Commission; and also an interpreter.

Separated from this little group by a wall of wire mesh, and arranged in a half-crescent, were all four Directors of the prison. A war crimes court was in session but there was no dock and no prisoner — only a witness chair. To the witness chair there came the man whose testimony the court wished to hear: Albert Speer, one of the seven men of Spandau and undergoing a sentence of twenty years' imprisonment. His evidence was of paramount importance to the trial of another merchant of death, Friedrich Flick, accused of the exploitation of slave labour.[3] Since the unalterable rules of Spandau

---

[3] Flick was sentenced at Nuremberg in December 1947 as a war criminal to seven years' imprisonment for exploitation of slave labour, plunder, and spoliation of property in occupied countries, and for membership of the Nazi SS. He was released in August 1950, and in 1952 the Allied Control Council agreed to him regaining control of part of his industrial empire. Two of his Ruhr coal companies and a steelworks with a total share capital of £25 million became independent, with Flick's two sons controlling 74 per cent of steel shares and Flick senior receiving approximately £11 million for the two coal-mines.

precluded Speer from attending the trial of Flick at Nuremberg, the court had transferred itself to Spandau.

All in the improvised court rose as Speer took the oath according to German law, with right arm raised: 'I swear to God the Omniscient, to tell the truth and omit nothing and add nothing.' There was a discreet rustle as the ten occupants of the court seated themselves on rough wooden chairs, and the proceedings began.

From ten in the morning until midday Speer was questioned and examined on the structure and conditions of the whole labour organization in Germany during the war. At first Speer believed this was yet another of the innumerable interrogations he had undergone regarding his own activities, but, on realizing that he was a witness at a properly constituted court of law, his attitude changed, and he answered both prosecution and defence fully and with complete frankness, explaining the operations of the German war economy.

When the court adjourned at twelve, two guards arrived and led Speer back to his cell. The judge and counsel were invited into the adjoining four-Power conference room as luncheon guests of the four Prison Directors. At 1 p.m. the court resumed for another three hours, and the cross-examination continued throughout the following day.

When the court finally completed its work in Spandau, Dr Flächsner, Speer's advocate at Nuremberg, asked the Prison Directors if he could have a brief personal conversation with his old client. Because of the exceptional circumstances, the Spandau 'family only' visiting rule was waived for fifteen minutes, and Speer, grasping the unexpected opportunity, discussed his domestic affairs.

'An important question going through my mind again and again, Hans,' he said to the lawyer, 'is the one concerning my children visiting me. Since Albert and Hilde are older than the others it is only to be expected that they should feel they are entitled to be the first here, and I have written to my wife and asked her to have a talk with them about it. She knows my point of view.'

Plainly worried, Speer continued: 'Because of the conditions and surroundings, the visit can be dangerous to all of us. I am afraid the children may look upon me as someone different from the father they have known and remember, and that in the short time at my disposal I would be unable to reach them in the way I want to.

'To be honest, such a visit — and this is the real reason for my hesitation — would stir me up too much. Nothing expresses our misfortune more, a misfortune not easily understood outside a prison, than the parting from my wife and children, now growing up into maturity without a father. But if the two big ones really want to come, I will submit.'

The minutes disappeared in swift flight. As Speer was signalled to end the conversation, his parting words were: 'Do your best to help my wife. I have the constant fear that she could be broken by life. Fate has distributed the burden unjustly between us. She has to carry all the load, all the worry of the children.'

As lawyer and former client said *auf Wiedersehen* — a handshake was forbidden by security regulations — Speer added: 'I am getting no more than I deserved for my colossal mistakes.'

Everything about the tall and powerfully built Speer, with his large scholastic head and massive hands, had been colossal. The slick careerist who fawned his way into high favour had always possessed colossal nerve, and made colossal use of the persuasive art of flattery.

A family album photograph of Speer with his Newfoundland "Illo," taken at the end of the war, just before his arrest. Speer tried to reorganise the chaotic German communications when Dönitz became head of State.

Typical of thousands of middle-class German youths of his generation, Speer saw his chance in 1932, and grabbed it. The

Nazis wanted their new Party headquarters in Berlin decorated. Speer got the job, and his work suited the flamboyant Nazi taste down to the ground. They were delighted, and so it was that with the growth of the new movement Speer won his place as Germany's 'Public Decorator No. 1'. Rallies, exhibitions, street displays — Speer handled them all, his shrewd showmanship satisfying Hitler's love of ostentation.

Speer's flamboyant mock-classic, mock-marble arches and platforms of painted plywood, his long swastika streamers fluttering from towering masts, his ever-changing illuminated patterns created by massed searchlights — all these added impressively to the Hitler style of razzamatazz. The young man was given control of the artistic and technical presentation of all major political demonstrations, and right of access to the Führer at any time.

Giant urns of fire blazing on the eerie walls of the Tannenberg memorial during the funeral there of President von Hindenburg were a characteristically imaginative Speer contribution.

By moulding his style to conform to Hitler's ideas, Speer became at the age of twenty-eight the Führer's personal adviser on architecture, or so-called architecture.

'I was given an office in the Unter den Linden, to which Hitler had a passage built from the Reich Chancellery,' he said, talking frankly, as he always did in Spandau, about his own rise and fall. 'Whenever he found the time, Hitler would come to my office to pencil in his own touches to my sketches for new buildings.'

The Hitler-Speer partnership produced an abundance of gigantic rectangular-shaped public buildings, with massive columns in front and eagles on top. Together they rebuilt cities. Speer was able to consolidate the position he had won because he knew how to handle Hitler. As a supreme egotist and a frustrated architect, the Führer eagerly adopted Speer's ideas as his own, and Speer had the wit to foster this kind of larceny.

Hitler's vast new Chancellery building, Göring's ostentatious Air Ministry and the colossal Nuremberg stadium — scene of the gigantic Nazi rallies — were all Speer's architectural reflections of the Führer's megalomania. Berlin was scheduled to be given a thousand-foot-high domed hall to hold audiences of one hundred thousand.

Hitler boasted, 'These buildings will be so gigantic and so solidly constructed that even the Pyramids will become insignificant in comparison with the colossus of stone which I shall erect.'

Speer conceived awe-inspiring settings for Hitler's speeches by ingeniously employing his knowledge of mass psychology. Within two years of joining the Nazis at the age of twenty-seven, he brilliantly organized the enormous Party rally at Berlin's Tempelhof airfield, creating overwhelmingly emotive pageantry. He curried favour with Hitler by translating the Führer's ego into buildings of incredible extravagance and vulgarity. By indulging Hitler's fantasies, Speer furthered his own ambitions.

This fawning courtier, who ceaselessly flattered the Führer's egotistical architectural 'suggestions', gave a rare glimpse of his true thoughts when he met the great orchestral conductor Wilhelm Furtwängler at a reception.

'It must be glorious to be able to build on such a grand scale according to one's own concepts,' said Furtwängler.

With a tinge of unmistakable irony, Speer answered: 'Imagine if somebody told you: It is my unalterable decision that from now on the Ninth Symphony shall be played only on the mouth organ.'

Inspector-General for the planning and building of the Reich capital; Inspector-General of Germany's roads and bridges; Inspector-General of water and electric power; membership of the Prussian State Council — these and a host of other plum jobs were tossed into Speer's lap before he was thirty-three. His family background and upbringing should have made him detest the policies of the master and regime he served, but Speer confessed:

'I sold my soul like Faust. Hitler was my Mephistopheles, although I didn't think at the time that I was selling my soul.'

Ambition and the temptations of power seduced and corrupted Speer. Telling himself, 'I am only a technician. I have no political task, no political responsibility', conveniently divorced his conscience from evils committed by his associates. On 8 February 1942, however, when Hitler elevated him to Cabinet rank by appointing him Minister for Armaments and Munitions, the excuse that political decisions were none of his business vanished.

This elevation took place when Germany's war production chief and Speer's greatest rival, Fritz Todt, was killed in a mysterious flying accident. Hitler immediately gave Speer the task of completing the work that had begun on the great fortifications set up against Allied plans for a second front; Hitler also gave him the appointments of Reich Minister for Armaments and Munitions, Commander-in-Chief of the Labour Organization, Inspector-General of the Highways, President of the Armaments Council, Inspector-General for Water and Fuel, and President of the Office of Reich Architecture — a suitably 'kolossal' job for a man of colossal ambition.

In the last week of 1943 the final 'glory' was donated. Speer was named as co-equal with Goebbels, Himmler and Dönitz among the top Nazis. The insignificant architect with big ideas, who produced the V1 and the V2 secret rocket weapons and Hitler's prefabricated U-boats, qualified for his place among the war criminals and a cell in Spandau.

Speer was the only one of the Spandau seven who unreservedly admitted guilt, but he continued working and planning for the future. Always on the table in his pastel-green-distempered cell, with its family pictures around the walls, lay a set-square, a drawing block, and an untidy pile of drawings and blueprints. The green-distempered walls were by special permission of the prison officials. Speer did the job himself. 'I would like to paint my cell in this colour,' he explained in his application, 'because it is easy on eyes strained after years of nightly inspection and weakened by the lighting conditions with which we have to contend.' The concession was agreed to on medical recommendation.

Cell lighting was a sore point with both Speer and Baldur von Schirach. The illumination was from the solitary light in the ceiling protected by the anti-suicide grille. The light was at first so poor that it was hardly possible to read by it, and Speer and Schirach complained of eye-strain. In answer to these objections, the lighting was changed from one extreme to another, but nothing was said by the prisoners that might encourage the authorities to revert to the old arrangement.

During the afternoon rest period, and every night after supper until lights out at ten o'clock, Speer busied himself with drawings and designs for industrial buildings, blocks of flats, houses, stadiums, and streets and highways for the Germany of tomorrow. He felt less inconvenienced by the absence of Hitler than by the lack of a compass (classified as dangerous because of its metal point), so that he had to draw circles and crescents freehand. When he needed a slide rule, he wrote to one of his old colleagues in the profession and asked that nothing but a celluloid one should be sent. From other friends he got supplies of drawing paper, every sheet of which was tested for secret writing before being given to him.

His one-time secretary, Frau Annemarie Kempf, described Speer as having a genius for untidiness. He continued true to form, but like most untidy people he had an aptitude for discovering without any seeming difficulty any document or drawing, and did this however littered his cell table. Only with respect to his handwriting did Spandau affect his old habits. It became much neater and more readable.

Once he had completed a set of drawings or blueprints they were removed and stored in a large cupboard in one of the administration offices. Speer said, 'I must keep on working and storing up ideas while my brain is still fertile so that I can earn something for my family as soon as I get out. America would be the best place for us to go. That's where the money is.' His architectural brain-children remained stacked away in a Spandau cupboard until he completed the punishment meted out at Nuremberg for 'crimes against humanity, including the abuse and exploitation of human beings for forced labour in the conduct of aggressive war'.

To the prison staff, Speer was not only the most intelligent, the most outstanding personality of the seven: he was also, so to speak, the 'clown prince'. Always ready for a laugh, he tried to extract humour from every possible situation. When the duty Director made his routine morning visit to the men, each cell was opened in turn; with Speer, inspection time was a social occasion. Immediately the visitor arrived, Speer stood up and, in his deep voice, announced slowly and distinctly:

'Do come into my office. Have a chair. I'm sorry there's no whisky and soda. Now what can I do for you today, dear chap?'

No one ever sat in response to his invitation, but this did not discourage him from making the offer.

When given a pair of army spectacles to ease the eye-strain of his work, he read the printed notice on the box giving advice on how to wear them with a respirator, and instantly called the guard, demanding a 'respirator for my spectacles'. So insistent did he become that he nearly had the harassed guard believing that such spectacles could be used only with a respirator.

One Sunday evening, the humourist of Spandau sat down at his table, lit his pipe, and began to write his family a description of his daily life:

Dear Mother,

After a good and sufficient supper, I have lit my large pipe, and looked into the blue clouds considering what I should write. First, I want to ask you something which will encourage you all, and that is to firmly convince yourselves that I am well. And as I am, physically, completely in order, my whole being circulates around a few simple points:

Sleeping: It comes often, with an especially long sleep on Sundays. That's why I slept for four hours today. But don't worry, I'll sleep again tonight. Sleeping is certainly a most sensible activity, and I only regret that I can't hibernate in winter like a bear. Many say that I have the qualifications of such an animal.

Garden: My rock garden gives me great pleasure as it is still in full blossom. The highlight of the garden 'show' is a single gladiolus, but besides that, I grow some nice plants and flowers. Pity my rock garden can't be packed and shipped to our home in Heidelberg just once. In spring, I will tell you a few names of the flowers you must get for your garden so that you may have something 'superior', too. I also double-trench a little in my part of the garden — especially under the nut trees. The children will prick up their ears now.

Eating: Unfortunately, I appear to be in danger of developing a paunch; in fact, to be truthful, I must admit that already it is clearly visible and so once again I have to face the old problem of weight. And by the way, mother, I have a confession to make while on this subject. I often tampered with the old scales at home and especially whenever I expected a bad report from school. By fiddling with the screw I could make it appear that I weighed more than I did, and that always put you in a good temper, which was so necessary whenever you heard from my schoolmaster. At the moment the British are in control, so I have on my table the familiar mixed pickles, tomato ketchup and English mustard.

Reading: During the last few weeks I have read rather less than usual having been somewhat surfeited by various works. Nevertheless, I find Ernest Hemingway's *For Whom the Bell Tolls* interesting and am reading it in English. After a meal I invariably take up a novel before turning to the study of more serious literature, which I feel it my duty to do. Most beautiful, however, is the last half-hour or so before I go to sleep at night, when I think of you all at home.

Using maps and geography books from the library, Speer decided to take an imaginary walk around the world — in the prison garden. As he averaged 215 paces to cover the garden path completely, he converted this to metres and kilometres and mentally travelled the route he had mapped out for the day's walk around the world. Then at night he recorded in a notebook progress, landmarks, and 'impressions' he had physically and mentally reached, as well as noting them on a world map with little flags.

Clandestine photograph of Speer working in the Spandau garden in his shorts. At Nuremberg he was termed 'one of the few men who had the courage to tell Hitler the war was lost.'

Only rarely did the normally easy-going Speer let off steam and shout at warders, risking punishment. Always apologetic, he would admit: 'If I didn't do this sometimes, I would go crazy.'

Despite his apparent high spirits Speer treated prison guards with respect, and this never failed to arouse the suspicions of the other six. His attitude was interpreted simply as a desire to crawl and pander to authority in the hope of securing favoured treatment. He was even accused by Funk of having become an informer for the Russians. This was untrue.

Nevertheless, Speer's buffoonery hid the real man, the unifier of Germany's great armament industries and the ruler of those slaves — millions of them — who were dragooned into labouring for the war effort. Sometimes the camouflage slid from his face as the loneliness of his life opened like an enormous wound; in anguish, he would turn to one of his fellow criminals and ask, 'Is it possible that they will let us out before our time? Life here is becoming endless agony.'

It was Speer who first defied the ban on talking and spoke freely both to his fellow prisoners and guards. He was discouraged neither by repeated warnings nor by threats of punishment. The truth was that this interdict was disliked by the prison staff, too, and eventually was abolished.

Occasionally, as in the autumn of 1952, a complaint by Speer rebounded like a boomerang. During a search of his cell by British guards, papers and drawings were moved and examined; Speer's usual composure disappeared. Scornfully he criticized the searchers for 'unjustifiably disrupting privacy'. This was no quip from the Spandau jester and, for his pains, he was confined to his cell for seven days as a punishment for impertinence and insubordination.

It was Speer, too, who, whenever Hess committed some indiscretion such as abusing a guard, went at once to his defence. He had his own ideas about the Deputy Führer and his physical disabilities. 'The odd feature about the cramps Hess is prone to,' explained Speer, 'is that Hitler suffered similarly, and particularly when the war was going the wrong way in the autumn of 1944. Hitler consulted one doctor after another, repeatedly complaining of stomach cramps and loss of voice. There's no question that both Hitler and Hess were in the same psychiatric category.'

What Speer did not know was that Hitler's indisposition during the period mentioned by him was traced later to his favourite doctor having prescribed a daily overdose of a drug compounded of strychnine and belladonna. It resulted in a condition of chronic poisoning that aggravated the very pains it was intended to relieve.

Though essentially a lone wolf, preferring his own company, Speer was nevertheless a good mixer, although he and Schirach never hit it off. When questioned about this hostility by a senior officer, Speer said, 'Sir, there are quarrels in the best of families' — a sly dig at the constant dissension that also existed between the Allied Directors of the prison.

Forthrightness was a characteristic Speer ought to have developed much earlier in his career, as he was only too well aware. 'I should have spoken my mind to Hitler years ago,' he confessed in a prison conversation. 'When I woke up and realized he was destroying the future, I ought to have kicked the bastard in the pants or killed him. But I did neither.'

Speer paused as the past came flooding back. The twitch of his bushy eyebrows, and the irritable manner in which he nibbled at his fingernails while carefully measuring every word, revealed the inner torment of a man who had gone down to defeat realizing only too keenly how and why he had failed. He went on almost dreamily:

'It is, perhaps, hard to understand, but Hitler really did have an almost hypnotic personality and mastery of the power of suggestion, although that is no excuse for the criminal blunders of myself and the others. After World War I, it was inevitable that some kind of Hitler would arise in Germany. The circumstances were ripe, and the country ready, for just such a person; and so this madman was able to determine the fate of the nation.

'I am not excusing myself. As a Minister of the Nationalist Socialist Government, I acknowledge responsibility for its broad policies. Even under an authoritarian regime, total responsibility cannot be evaded.'

Warming to his subject, he went on: 'Hitler played the old game of divide and conquer and by 1937 was already planning for the war that was to come. The Führer had always insisted that right or wrong did not enter into military calculations and that it was victory alone that counted. He was an incurable optimist, and so confident was he in 1941 that resistance to the German armies in Russia was at an end, and victory in sight, that he decided the aircraft industry should have priority over all others in view of his plans to mount an attack against Britain in the spring of the following year. The order was carried out and was not rescinded until January 1942, by which time reserves of materials for the army were almost exhausted. As one defeat followed another, the Führer's mind deteriorated still further. Even his handwriting began to look like that of an old man.'

Following the bomb plot against Hitler's life in 1944, Speer started to recognize his own political responsibility. His feelings towards the Führer changed, although he never denied his loyalty, even at his Nuremberg trial. It was in the spring of 1944 that misgivings about the war and doubts about Hitler deeply troubled him, because in April 1944 Speer fell seriously ill. Months in bed gave him time to think things clearly through. The realization that affected him most was the conclusion that, although Hitler knew the war was lost, he blamed the German people for 'letting him down' instead of accepting responsibility himself. It had become obvious that the Führer was ready to destroy the entire country and commit national suicide rather than concede defeat.

Speer wrote to the Führer that he could work only 'with a feeling of inner decency and with conviction and faith'. In another memorandum to Hitler, he bluntly forecast: 'The war is lost.'

As production chief, Speer's value to the war machine was incalculable. He was ruthless in his use of slave labour and abuse of human beings. He worked concentration camp inmates from 72 to 100 hours a week, even admitting that in some plants under Himmler's control there were 'no limits'. He was also unconcerned about his gross breach of international laws in employing prisoners of war in factories.

In the two and a half years following his appointment as Armaments Minister, he reorganized weapons production to such an extent that even the Allies were amazed at the speed with which supplies resumed after saturation bombing by Allied air forces. The recovery secret mainly lay in plants he established in old coal-pits and disused salt-mines. From the time he took over he startlingly increased output.

Between 1942 and 1944 annual output of aircraft was increased from 15,596 to 39,807, of tanks from 9,300 to 27,000, of heavy guns from 11,800 to 40,000, and of submarines from 191 to 233.

During the war's early years, he was convinced that Germany's fate was inextricably linked to Hitler; but when faced with the Führer's scorched-earth wishes, he could not, and would not, carry them out. He told Hitler that it was the Führer's duty to save the German people, not destroy their land. Hitler was furious, but Speer persisted in demanding withdrawal of the order for the demolition of factories, mines, roads and bridges to confront the Allies with total devastation. He refused to flood coal-mines in the Saar, Holland and Belgium, and, instead of blowing up French iron-ore mines and smelting works, kept them intact. Hitler accused him of defeatism, treason and sabotage, but could not bring himself to have his favourite protégé shot, although he deprived Speer of many powers.

Asked by Dönitz in Spandau gaol why he had failed to carry out the Führer's scorched-earth policy when Germany faced defeat, Speer answered:

'Because one maniac in the country was enough. After my brother was killed at Stalingrad, I felt more than ever that it was my duty to carry on the fight to the utmost, though I knew already the war was lost. On 30 January 1945 I sent a detailed report to Hitler suggesting that every effort should be made to end hostilities because the armament industry was practically in ruins and no longer capable of functioning for war.

'Knowing well enough that the politicians would not pass on my report to the militarists at the Führer's headquarters, I had several copies of the report distributed to the top generals. It was tossed aside and it was then that I decided I must destroy Hitler before he completed the destruction of what remained of Germany. The past had kicked up in my face and I knew it — I knew then how wrong I had been over the years.

'When Hitler sent for me I guessed what he wanted to scream about. He was beside himself as he accused me of spreading defeatism and ordered me publicly to declare that the war was not lost. I wasn't buying, and he looked at me and said, "I'll give you twenty-four hours to reconsider your decision. Talking defeat is traitorous and I still know how to deal with traitors." He glared at me, but for once that had no effect and I had my say with him. He had to listen, and he nodded when I told him more than once that whatever the differences between us he could rely on my continuing to carry out my duties. That offer he accepted and the ultimatum he had insisted upon first was conveniently forgotten.'

It is indisputable that Speer did countermand Hitler's order for the destruction of German industry after telling the Führer that his demands were those of a madman. 'I escaped his wrath,' said Speer, 'only because he knew, although he would not for a moment admit it, that the war was irretrievably lost. In the autumn of 1944 we had produced two new poison gases, which we named tabun and sarin, and they were capable of terrifying results. No respirator, or indeed any other form of protection, could withstand them, and three factories were engaged on full production. Goebbels and Ley were trying to persuade Hitler to use them, but there were those among us, and they included army commanders and generals, who were opposed to gas warfare. It was about that time that I decided to kill Hitler.'

According to Speer the liquidation of the Führer was to be accomplished by infiltrating poison gas through the air-conditioning plant of the underground bunker that he occupied in Berlin, and where he spent the last hours of his life. The plan was knocked sideways when a protective chimney was built around the ventilation funnel and no further opportunity presented itself.

That is Speer's story and he stuck to it, but even his closest friends remained sceptical whenever it was mentioned. They believed that although Hitler's assassination was a consummation greatly to be desired by Speer, he did not at any time ever get beyond the consideration stage.

At Nuremberg, Speer did not attempt to dispute the advantageous point in his favour that he had *contemplated* killing the Führer he had loved so devotedly for years — with a love that blinded him to so much that was happening around him. Only much later in Spandau did he amend the story slightly and admit: 'I *thought* of killing him once; very briefly, and too late for it to really matter. But I'm sure that I could never have done it. In some ways I do not regret not killing him because it was destiny that he had to die by his own hand at the last.'

On 29 March 1945, when he visited Hitler in the Berlin Chancellery bunker, Speer did not try to deny to him that he had chosen to sabotage scorched-earth instructions.

'Why do you go behind my back like this?' Hitler challenged. 'Any other man I would have shot.'

On 23 April, Speer flew back to a Berlin almost encircled by Russian troops to say goodbye to Hitler, who would be dead in days. Bluntly he told his Führer that he still had not carried out the destruction orders. Hitler, now already beaten, accepted the news almost matter-of-factly.

However, it was not moral revulsion over brutal crimes committed by the Nazis that made Speer rebel against his beloved Führer and deliberately wreck decrees. It was because Speer's conscience as a specialist technician was outraged. The focus of his life was construction, not destruction, and now Hitler wanted to bring everything crashing down with him — not only his Third Reich, but all of Germany. Only then did Speer, who was still only forty, turn against him.

At the start of the Nuremberg trial — which Speer described to his Spandau colleagues as 'necessary' — he was ready in himself to pay the death penalty for his contribution towards Hitler's Third Reich. He was anxious to admit responsibility, but only for those actions that he claimed had been within his realm of influence. 'I don't believe there can be any atonement in my lifetime for sins of such huge dimensions,' he said. 'But I am a much different man than I was in 1945. Any penalty would have been just for me — even death.'

Speer did not try to shield himself by suggesting he was innocent or at most ignorant of his enormities. He recognized his guilt as surely as he recognized the implacable face of justice. At that forward hour he became a realist, but it was too late.

In mitigation of the war crimes charged against him the Tribunal declared: 'He was one of the few men who had the courage to tell Hitler the war was lost.'

In Spandau, Speer dismissed as ludicrous claims that the mass extermination of Jews was not Hitler's idea. As for suggestions that Hitler was unaware of what people like Himmler and Heydrich were doing in the concentration camps, he contended:

'It is out of the question that these murders were committed without him giving the orders, because the issue of the Jews was one of the most important in his life. He frequently discussed the fate of the Jews in such a way as to leave no doubt about his intentions. I tolerated the persecution of Jews by depersonalizing them. If I had continued to see them as human beings, I could not have remained a Nazi. I did not hate them. I was indifferent to them.

'If I had known of the scale of his annihilation of Jews in concentration camps, I would have told him that killing them was insane, and that I needed them to work in our factories.

Killing them was a waste. I had no thought, other than oiling the war machine. Even with blood.

'In so far as Hitler gave me orders and I carried them out, I accept the responsibility for this. Of course, I did not carry out all his orders.

'My main guilt was my tacit acceptance of the persecution and murder of millions of Jews.'

Had Speer confessed this at Nuremberg, he probably would have hanged. He did not say it because he wanted to live, and because he could not accept the almost unbearable truth that he did know. The thought of what he had condoned by inaction and silence never ceased haunting him in Spandau, which became not so much a prison for him as a refuge.

In countless ways, by prostituting his talents and ethics, Speer, the most efficient and most intelligent of Hitler's aides, did more than almost anyone to build and sustain the Nazi dream. Without him, the war would have ended much sooner. In many respects his greatest crime was that he made Nazis acceptable to the arts and sciences. Despite a candid admission of guilt, he insisted that the concentration camps, persecution of minorities, and forced labour programme were 'political decisions' and therefore not within his control. Although one could easily be swayed by his frank regrets, one could never be completely certain of the true reasons for his confessions. Admission of responsibility in no way diminished his culpability.

Speer worked tirelessly ever after to persuade the world that he was 'different', and he was. His strong character, so graphically illustrated by his behaviour in gaol, as well as his intelligence and education, made him exceptional among the general run-of-the-mill Nazi mediocrity that surrounded Hitler. Was he a brilliant, ambitious man who finally faced facts and found enough courage to attempt to make some kind of genuine repentance and amends? Or was he, in truth, merely a polished intellectual hypocrite who openly admitted errors and guilt only when his career was already in ruins and when reality left him no choice?

6: A FIGHT FOR LIFE IN THE DEATH CELL

The noisy kitchen trolley laden with plates, dishes, bread, butter and steaming hot soup containers moved along the corridor pushed by a man wearing the white apron of a chef. It could have been any mobile staff canteen on its rounds, except that it was trundling along the corridors of Spandau.

It was lunch-time. The trolley stopped by a cell door, and the American guard, Owens, shouted in German, 'Number One!' as he unlocked the door. Tall, blond Baldur von Schirach immediately came out and went to the trolley. He picked up an unbreakable plate with a small pat of butter on it, a hunk of black bread, some soup in a bowl, and then went back into his cell and heard the key turn on him.

One by one, each of the other prisoners was called, and they in turn collected their food in the same manner. Meat, vegetables, everything was put into the soups to make a convenient-to-serve and sustaining meal.

Breakfast was at 6.45 a.m., consisting of porridge and milk, black coffee (always black), and, sometimes, an egg. There was a further issue of coffee (served in a mug) at 10 a.m., and supper was largely a repeat of the breakfast menu. After bread-and-soup lunch, the cell-opening routine began again for the second course: an apple — always an apple. There were never puddings, nor second helpings.

During Russian months, meals almost invariably included barley and noodle soup and ersatz coffee, salted herrings or herring roe, bread and butter, meat with boiled potatoes and carrots. When the Americans took over, breakfast comprised fried eggs with bacon, and apple jelly. Lunch included soup, meat cutlets, potato salad, pineapple slices, and half a litre of milk. A typical supper was roast turkey with beans, melon, cheese, white bread, and coffee with cream. From a dietary point of view, the seven had little cause for complaint during non-Russian months.

Spandau prisoner No. 6, Walther Funk, nervously shuffled out for his apple, then returned to his cell to finish his meal. Formerly the owner of a fabulously rich and fruitful farming estate, Funk had loved only the best food and wine. Now the outlook appeared to be mostly meat, soup and apple lunches for the rest of his life.

Born in 1890 at Trakehnen in East Prussia, Funk came from a substantial merchant family. He studied journalism at Berlin and Leipzig universities; after he married a wealthy manufacturer's daughter he speedily enlarged his acquaintanceship with the heavy industrialists. These, together with his own family connections, provided a wide and powerful circle of contacts. By 1926 Funk was editor-in-chief of the *Berliner Börsenzeitung* — the stock-market newspaper — and it was largely due to his efforts that Hitler obtained the funds to achieve his early election successes.

Fat, round, bald, and small, Funk wheedled his way into the Nazi hierarchy, becoming Hitler's Economic Minister and President of the Reichsbank. It was Funk who negotiated the tie-up between the Nazis and the great industrialists so that millions were poured into the Party funds; Funk who helped equip and victual Hitler's armies by dispossessing the conquered and blackmailing frightened neighbours into accepting German goods in payment for delivering essential war material.

Accused at Nuremberg of also having hoarded in the Reichsbank vaults tons of gold teeth taken from concentration camp victims, Funk pleaded: 'I have been mistaken in much. I was too credulous.'

In fact he had always carefully played along with the SS, especially with Otto Ohlendorf, head of the SS Security Service — and with good reason. Not only was collaboration with the SS instrumental in bringing him the stolen possessions of concentration camp victims, but Funk knew Ohlendorf had a very interesting file on his degenerate private life.

In February 1945 Funk instructed that 75 hundredweights of gold, packed into 150 sacks, together with diamonds and sackfuls of banknotes, should be transferred to a mountain fortress. When the Allies invaded Germany, they found in abandoned mines enough booty to fill three massive vaults in the Frankfurt branch of the Reichsbank. At the Nuremberg trial the notorious Oswald Pohl, chief of the Economic Office of the SS, who handled these transactions for his organization, explained in detail 'the business deals between Funk and the SS concerning the delivery of the valuables of dead Jews to the Reichsbank'. He emphasized that Funk knew very well the source of the goods they were turning into cash through pawnshops.

Funk's shifty-eyed, flabby, lugubrious face gave him the appearance of an insignificant, bald nobody of fifty-five. One of the American officers guarding him at Nuremberg described him as looking like a man 'incapable of running a gas station'. Yet he was party to the most cold-blooded of crimes and a man of huge influence in Nazi Germany, eventually becoming the 'plenipotentiary of the war economy'.

In the Nuremberg exercise yard, Funk said Göring had told him: 'Reconcile yourself to your fate and die a martyr's death.

Don't worry; some day — even if it takes fifty years — the German people will rise again and recognize us as heroes, and even move our bones to marble caskets in a national shrine.'

But Funk was not the martyr type. 'I don't have the stuff for heroism,' he admitted to Neurath. 'I didn't then and I don't now. I always came up to the door, but never entered.'

It was Funk who was responsible for 'Kristallnacht' (the 'Night of Broken Glass') — the name given to Nazi terror and destruction wrought on 11 November 1938. It was also Funk who informed Göring and the Austrian economist Dr Fischböck: 'I have prepared a law elaborating that from 1 January 1939 Jews shall be prohibited from operating retail stores and wholesale establishments, as well as independent workshops. They shall be further prohibited from keeping employees or offering any ready-made products on the market; from advertising or receiving orders. Wherever a Jewish shop is operated the police shall shut it down.'

The Spandau chapel organist, who had regularly played the piano for Hitler's pleasure, Funk required constant medical care and attention. Among the seven his health was much the poorest. Even in the old days he was an ailing man, but all his life he knew how to profit from it. If, for instance, he was visited by his crony Dr Ley, the Labour Front leader, and realized that Ley wanted some finance or signatures from him, he would sit moaning and groaning behind his desk giving Ley a long report on the state of his health until his visitor would finally say, 'Walther, it breaks my heart to trouble a sick man like you', and would go without obtaining what he had come for.

Funk continued to behave in the same way inside Spandau. He told a prison medical officer: 'My health troubles started when I contracted venereal disease at the age of thirteen in a low beer-house in East Prussia. There, schoolboys, and I was one at the time, seduced waitresses behind the curtains.'

Women, food, and drink remained the favourite topics of conversation of this old, self-pitying roué. He nevertheless professed to be deeply religious and played Bach, Beethoven, Mozart, and Schubert on the worn prison chapel harmonium with the touch of a concert pianist. Funk delighted in giving young Spandau guards and his fellow prisoners advice about women from his great fund of personal knowledge and experience; he would tell them about Berlin haunts and hot spots, and sing obscene songs, of which he had an extraordinary and seemingly inexhaustible repertoire.

Within the celibacy of Spandau he recounted erotic excursions in Casablanca. He had habitually visited Morocco to sample fresh sexual delights, revelling in taking vacations from Hitler's 'pure Aryanism' racial doctrines and experiencing sex with all races and colours.

'What wonderful parties I used to have,' he sometimes recalled, his thick sensuous lips smiling at the memories. 'Everybody who mattered came. We had the best wines, the finest champagne, nothing but the best. And they were real parties, they lasted all night. I used to eat too much, drink too much, and, of course, plenty of girls. They were the best, too. We had dancing girls, naked girls' — and Funk laughed with relish at his thoughts.

'I always did well with the women,' he boasted to the guards. 'French women, ah!' He threw a kiss in the air. 'But Egyptian women — perfect!'

Funk paid heavily for old depravities. His nerves were strung taut; he could not stand noise or the impact of too much light, and needed frequent morphia and cocaine injections to ease his suffering. To enable him to sleep at all he had to take a heavy dosage of sleeping tablets. Emotionally unstable, he consumed a vast quantity of aspirin, and of almost any type of medication given to him. He loved frequently administered pills, which strangely always had a psychologically favourable effect on him. This wretched caricature of a man, who suffered from persistent and maddening migraine headaches, frequently spent days and nights during which he was unable to find rest, cursing and screaming at the guards in German, French, English, and Russian.

A sinister character named Voitov — who came to the gaol as a warder, terrorized his colleagues, and eventually managed to get himself promoted to acting commandant of the Soviet unit — took special delight in baiting Funk. Voitov enjoyed provoking him until Funk furiously unleashed a torrent of abuse in Russian. If anyone was helpful to a prisoner, Voitov would shout in Russian: 'Stop! That is contrary to the Nuremberg agreement. No comfort!'

Funk hated the Russians, and they in turn despised the former financial juggler more than his fellows. They infuriated him by carrying out one particular regulation to the letter, which called for the duty guard to flash a light through the spy-hole of each cell throughout the night as a security measure. For Funk the light flicked on every fifteen minutes, every night, all night. He would storm, rage, and bang on the cell door, yelling, 'Dirty Russian pig! Dirty Russian pig!' but the lights continued to flash.

In the morning, when the prison doctor made his daily check-up, he would ask, 'How many times last night, Funk?'

The answer was invariably, 'Twenty-three, twenty-four times. It is terrible! Please help. Those swines of Ruskies!'

British, American and French medical officers were powerless to alter this security measure, which the Russians insisted on. The question of the lights was regularly raised at Spandau Directors' four-Power meetings, but the Russians always said, 'It is the rule to switch on.' The only alternative was to give Funk sufficient sleeping tablets to knock him out. But these did not work on some occasions, so the inevitable happened: one night, Funk's nerves cracked.

In his customary manner he had been yelling and complaining about the noise and the lights preventing him from sleeping, when the French guard on duty decided to go to his cell. All guards had been warned by the doctors not to interfere with the prisoner whenever it was apparent that he had become frantic, but unwisely this particular guard unlocked the door, and entered.

The fat body of Funk hurled itself at the rash visitor, knocking him to the floor. A raging, screaming animal grasped the guard's neck, striving to choke the life out of him. Gasping for breath, the Frenchman somehow managed to unlock the grip on his throat, but pint-sized Funk, with the strength of madness, lifted him up and threw him bodily from the cell. Other guards rushed to the rescue and pinioned Funk while aid was summoned. The crazy prisoner was then given a shot in the arm and quietened.

On 6 October, 1952, Funk wrote the following statement in his cell to the Directors of the prison:

> For years a paper, by special order of the Directorate, was fixed to the little barred window of my cell door so that, with every change of shift in the evening or the night, the guard starting his duty could see that I had been treated and must not be disturbed. The paper was thus fixed so that from the cell corridor the guard could look right through the cell any time he wished.

On Monday, September 29th, I was wakened out of my narcotic anaesthetic by loud talking close to my cell door window, which let through every noise from the cell corridor. There was also knocking and noisy touching of window and door. When, under great strain, I succeeded in getting up, I found that the paper with the Directorate order for my protection had been removed. Because of that I became terribly excited owing to the nature of my illness. This developed into a severe nerve and heart attack, when I realized that outside in the cell corridor they were laughing about my horrible suffering.

I obviously could not know that the Herr Russische Direktor was before my door and had instigated the incident. I then became afflicted with a gruesome attack of mad violence of a kind which had never come on me before. The American specialist who two and a half years ago diagnosed my inflammation of the nerves stated that in strong conditions of excitement I would have no clear consciousness nor control of will.

In the days that have passed since this incident, I still have severe nervous disorders and heart attacks. *I beg the Directors to protect my life, which is endangered through such incidents.* [Funk underlined this sentence.] I beg to request that after surgical treatment I am not disturbed by light or noise, and that on other nights, too, the constant disturbance of sleep through lighting of the cell, stops.

Walther Funk

Allied warders wore rubber-soled shoes to deaden the sound of their footsteps at night, but the Russians wore boots, until a 'boots crisis' put an end to this. The crisis was brought about through Soviet guard Taradankin, who deliberately fixed metal studs to the soles of his boots so that he could noisily march to and fro and disturb the prisoners. Eventually even his Russian comrades joined prisoners' and guards' protests about the metal-studded boots. The Russians, who meticulously reported every irregularity, including warders sleeping on duty on their chairs outside the cell doors, reported Taradankin's boots, too. He was replaced, and Soviet warders were also issued with rubber-soled shoes. There was a slight drawback to the prisoners' victory because the silent shoes made it difficult for them to hear approaching guards when they were writing letters for smuggling or making illegal diary notes.

In 1948 Funk had an operation in the prison hospital for hernia, and it was suggested at the weekly meeting of the Prison Directors that he should be allowed to rest for a day and a night without the routine disturbance. The proposal was turned down unanimously, the edict being that 'Under no circumstances were the seven to be mollycoddled in any way unless dangerously ill.' In the late summer of the following year Funk was responsible for Spandau's greatest medical dispute. Because of a disease that affected his bladder and prostate gland, it had become necessary to open the urinary tract every ten days and Funk was given morphia and atropine injections. Despite the drugs, the treatment invariably reduced him to a state of almost complete collapse. His medical chart read, 'Pain threshold low', but it was fear that induced his condition, for the treatment was not unduly painful. Then, one night, during a period when the British were responsible for cell surveillance, guards heard the prisoner banging on his cell door and crying out, 'Help me! Help me!' A glance inside the cell told its own story. The floor looked as if a beast had been slaughtered there. Funk had suffered a haemorrhage.

An emergency call went out for the duty medical officer, and Funk, after being given an injection, was carried to the casualty room and given an immediate blood transfusion — British blood from the army blood bank.

After further examination and a conference of all four doctors, it was agreed that an operation on the prostate was imperative in order to save Funk's life. The Chief American Medical Officer in Berlin offered his services on condition that the patient was transferred to the US Army hospital in Berlin, but this stipulation was not acceptable for reasons of security. Finally it was agreed that Major Guinchard, Chief Surgeon and Urologist at the French hospital at Reinickendorf, in the French sector of Berlin, should perform the operation inside Spandau.

When Funk's wife heard of these arrangements she telegraphed the following message to the American High Commissioner for Germany: 'I beg of you to permit the operation on my husband to be performed in a hospital outside the prison where there are better surgical facilities and he can be given better attention.' But the decision had been made. Neither Funk nor any of the seven were permitted under any circumstances to leave Spandau, not even for the length of time required for an operation.

Spandau had no operating theatre so one was set up — inside the execution cell, which was deemed the most suitable place for conversion. An operating table and complete theatre surgical equipment were brought from the US Army hospital in Berlin, and the operation date was fixed for 15 October 1949.

When told of the arrangements by the duty medical officer, Funk's spirit broke. Weeping and shaking with nerves, all he could say was, 'I want to die.' Every night until the eve of the operation, on the verge of yet another collapse, he was given heavy doses of sleeping pills, and guards were ordered to avoid disturbing him. However, before Funk reached the operating table he managed to fool the doctors by not taking his sleeping pills. There was something he had to do. Aware that the guards were not as watchful as usual, he sat down at his cell table one night with a sheet of notepaper that bore the official stamp of the prison. Nobody knows how he got hold of it, because every sheet issued was counted and recorded. He wrote:

My Will Testament. Para 1. (One paragraph only.)

I leave everything I possess to Luise Funk, née Schmidt, at present living at Gasthaus Zoehr, Hechenberg. My possessions are the house of Berghof, on the hill in the district of Kirchbichl and in the borough of Bad Tolz, and all the estate that goes with it including the farms later added which are officially listed.

Also the furniture of the house, two life insurances of the Allianz Versicherung; plus the remunerations from my directorship of the Controlling Board of Directors of the Bank für Internationalen Zahlungsausgleich at Basle, Switzerland, which have not been paid to me since the beginning of the war.

Also, my personal valuables for which I received a deposit ticket at Nuremberg and which is now, together with the valuables, in safe keeping in Spandau. They are:

A golden wedding ring; one wrist-watch; one golden tie-clip with the initials 'W. F.' set in rubies; two golden cuff-links with eight stones each setting the initials 'W. F.'; two golden buttons.

Written and signed before my operation.
Spandau — 11.10.49.

Walther Funk

This illicit last will and testament of Walther Funk was smuggled out of Spandau. It was not, of course, witnessed.

On the morning of 15 October the surgeon, Major Guinchard, arrived, accompanied by an assistant nurse from the French hospital. Thus it was that dark-complexioned, auburn-haired Mademoiselle Asiglio, a pleasant-faced woman in her mid-thirties, became the first and only woman ever to enter the forbidden inner cell block of Spandau. With the assistance of the prison's two Dutch medical orderlies, Boon and Prost, Mademoiselle Asiglio completed the final preparations for the surgery that was to take place.

There was a full muster of prison officials and doctors on the morning of the operation, and everybody's nerves were more than somewhat edgy. The first major operation ever to take place in Spandau was about to be performed; should it end in Funk's death, the repercussions could well be imagined. There would always be someone ready to whisper, 'Murder!' on the score that the surgery had not taken place in a hospital, particularly since it was the task of both prison and medical staff to maintain the health of the seven so that they could serve to the fullest extent the sentences passed upon them at Nuremberg. No such doubts, however, beset the British doctor. Bluntly he expressed his opinion: 'These men are prisoners, and prison rules are laid down to be obeyed. We tend to get soft.'

At that moment on the operating table Funk began to breathe in the anaesthetic, and so the fight for his life began in an execution cell under which lay a room that contained a coffin of plain wood made to his measurements. When the operation was over and Funk drowsily opened his eyes, it was to see Nurse Asiglio sitting at his bedside watching him. He realized he was in a strange room, although back again in the inner prison block, in a white-walled retreat that had been specially adapted to serve as a convalescent bay. Now began the days of crisis for the patient for his heart was weak and his life was at a dangerously low ebb. Nurse Asiglio was always there, except for the few rest periods she took while male nursing orderlies came in as reliefs. In the meantime Frau Luise Funk received a letter postmarked from the prison that read:

> Your husband has been operated on. You may come and see him the first half of December.
>
> The Directors,
Allied Prison, Spandau

With the help of his 'saviour angel', as he called Nurse Asiglio, Funk recovered. On the seventh morning, as she tended him, he told the nurse of a dream he had had during the night: 'I dreamt that my wife and I were visiting my dead parents. My wife was in the garden walking along the path to the river where the little steps are, and where a boat was always tied up, and I was on the other side.

'I called to her to row the boat across to fetch me, and as usual she came very quick for she has a lively temperament. The boat, however, capsized. She fell into the water and I lost sight of her. It gave me a terrible shock and I jumped into the river and managed to get her out. There she was, wet in my arms, and we were both shedding tears over her being saved.'

Funk asked whether the nurse could interpret his dream.

'Maybe it means that I could rescue my wife from a terrible happening through the agency of a good deed. Perhaps it means I could rescue her by getting healthy again? I'm doing everything I can to do so,' he added.

Nurse Asiglio could not interpret the dream, but when Funk's wife heard of it she explained: 'It was intended to convey to me his original intention to die or commit suicide in order that I, whom he visualized as living in very poor circumstances, would benefit by his death through getting the very heavy life-insurance as well as the pension to which I would be entitled as a widow of a high civil servant.'

However, Funk did not die; nor did he commit suicide. Mademoiselle Asiglio nursed him for eight days, and for two days his condition was critical. When a warder approached his bed to see how he was progressing, Funk flung a bottle of urine at him, shouting:

'I am not a spectacle for inquisitive people!'

The operation was as successful as it could be in view of his general condition, but the trouble had been eased, not cured. Funk had to receive treatment every few days for his old problem, urinary retention. His medical record was really formidable. His diabetes was cleared early in 1952, the same year that he underwent yet another operation, this time for appendicitis.

In December 1953 Funk and Erich Raeder were informed that surgery on the prostate gland was necessary for both of them. The decision to operate was taken after consultation between a four-Power medical commission and the Allied Commandants of the prison. The operations were fixed for Boxing Day, and Major Guinchard, the French surgeon who had performed the previous prostate operation on Funk, was scheduled to undertake the task.

Once again Funk decided, this time in association with Raeder, to lodge official protest against the medical arrangements, with a plea that surgery and treatment take place outside Spandau in a Berlin hospital — 'to ensure the best possible facilities for survival and recovery'.

It was decided to refer the request to the higher authority of all four Governments. Meanwhile, postponement of the operations was ordered. Funk then said he would refuse the operation until the authorities considered an application for his immediate release.

'Since the Nuremberg judges did not sentence me to death but to life imprisonment, they obviously did not intend for me to die,' he declared in his petition. 'Yet to allow me to remain in gaol any longer will result in my death.'

It was months before the operations were carried out. Four jeeps filled with soldiers escorted the ambulance when Funk was transferred to the British military hospital. The prison's four Directors followed in their individual cars. Surgery was performed by a young American doctor from the US military hospital at Frankfurt, and a week later Funk was back in his cell.

'I was treated like a private patient — a sort of mixture between Napoleon and Al Capone,' he said.

In August 1956, under the pseudonym of 'John Begonia', he was back in the same hospital, having gallstones removed.

When he was not feeling sorry for himself, Funk gossiped about the past at every opportunity. His favourite topic was Third Reich corruption. He claimed: 'Göring made a fortune by arranging shipment of military trainloads of women's stockings and undies from Italy for black-market sale in Germany.' Funk's policy had always been to know, if possible, everything about everyone of importance. 'Hermann had a little clique of friends who organized the racket for him.'

'Why didn't you tell Hitler?' Speer demanded.

'How could I? How was I to know who else was involved at the top and whether Hitler already knew and simply turned a blind eye to it all?'

It was through Funk that Hitler's last 'political testament' — the official transcript of his table-talk in February 1945, when he knew that the war was lost — had been conveyed out of the

Berlin bunker. Funk visited the bunker on 20 April 1945, ten days before Hitler's suicide, in order to seek the Führer's permission to convey the gold deposits of the Reichsbank from Berlin to Munich; and Martin Bormann took this opportunity of sending the records of table-talk out of Berlin. Funk deposited the document, sealed, in a Munich bank. Later, whilst imprisoned in Spandau, he feared that the document's discovery might incriminate him further, so he smuggled a secret authorization out of the gaol to a friend who promised to withdraw the transcript from the bank and burn it. In fact the friend opened it and, noting its historic value, compromised with Funk's instructions.

In accordance with his undertaking, the friend burnt the original document, but in the interest of history made a photocopy. It was this copy, signed and authenticated on every page by Martin Bormann, that was published subsequently throughout the world.

Promenading around the garden, Funk and Raeder kept each other well informed about their respective ailments. Funk was also a past master at *Herz und Schnauze* (heart and a fast, biting tongue).

'Herr Raeder,' he said (the prisoners always addressed each other as 'Herr'), 'you're a religious man, so do you know the difference between Catholics and Protestants?'

When Raeder remained silent, gazing at him blankly, Funk happily explained: 'Somewhat like the difference between Lenin and Tito.'

Funk never attempted to tell jokes to the humourless Dönitz, whom Raeder treated even in Spandau as an inferior officer. Hess and Speer were essentially loners. Nobody could get really close to Hess; he would not let them. The amiable Neurath consistently managed to remain dignified, but Funk and Schirach were forever quarrelling yet almost inseparable, gratefully sharing their mutual love of music and literature.

Each of the seven developed a behaviour pattern towards the prison's Directors and guards. Hess considered them all enemies and tried to act unruffled and contemptuous in their presence. Raeder and Neurath were polite but condescending. Schirach wanted to be friends with everybody. Dönitz continually switched between pulling rank, being remote, and seeking close contact; while Funk vacillated nervously, uncertain which attitude could be the most advantageous.

Debating the chances of some remission of their sentences, Schirach, who had told his gaolers that he had become an anti-Semite at the age of seventeen after reading a book called *Eternal Jew* by Henry Ford, said to Funk:

'Our whole misfortune came from racial politics.'

Anti-Semitism was a mistake, Funk replied. I wonder what would have happened if the churches in Germany had been more outspoken against religious persecution? It makes me think of the story of a Jew who was chased by the Gestapo and ran into a church to try to lose himself among the congregation. The priest spotted him pretending to pray, and also the very obvious Gestapo invading the church. Interrupting the service, the worried priest announced: "All Jews please leave the church!"

The Jew stayed in a pew, bent his head, and didn't move, so the sweating priest cried even louder: "I said all Jews must leave the church at once!"

Meanwhile, the Gestapo moved along the aisles methodically checking each one, but nobody moved. Finally the priest almost screamed: "For the last time, I insist that all Jews must leave the church!"

'Suddenly the crucifix over the altar stirred, and Christ descended from the cross, walked over to the Jew, and said: "Come, brother, we aren't wanted here."'

In his cell one night, Funk took his fountain pen and some paper, and wrote:

A ghost sonata in a Prison Cell
A Night in Spandau
By Walther Funk

My thoughts threaten to throttle me, and I have to pull them out of my soul.

What a human being has to suffer when the soul is crucified and sick nerves teased can only be judged by someone like me who has been in prison for years.

Yet I think somehow they all like me, and even feel genuinely sorry for me, but there are those rules and regulations for the treatment of prisoners to which warders and guards have to conform. Again and again, some have tried to ease my plight, but what remained was still enough to destroy more and more my strength for life.

The French doctors who treat me do their best to ease my pains with injections, but the nightly noise, and the 'Firework of Hell' — the lighting of the cells from outside and inside — robs me of sleep even though I pack cotton wool into my ears and use a dark cloth over my eyes.

I wake from the noises outside my cell, and when the light is put on, I can't fall asleep again. I feel like the blind of whom it is said, 'They feel the moonlight on their hands, and hear snowflakes falling.' When the heavy iron door at the entrance of the hall leading to the cells is banged — in one night I counted twenty-eight such bangs — I have a bad pain in my eyes as if a knife had been thrust into them.

It says in the regulations that every fifteen or thirty minutes at night a light must be shone into the cells, and that warders must patrol up and down checking whether we are still alive.

These marching steps we hear all night through the little barred window in the cell door, which must remain open. We also hear the conversation of the warders, and every sound multiplies in the cell corridor, for above us yawn the empty halls *of* that part of the prison which once accommodated hundreds of prisoners.

The healthier of my comrades don't suffer so much from the night disturbances. Only Dönitz and Von Shirach frequently complain of sleeplessness through light and noise. Like myself, Dönitz, who endures rheumatic pains, has a notice on the board of his cell stating, 'No Noise' and 'Switch on light only if necessary'. But the warders do not always strictly follow these medical orders.

Hess, who sometimes suffers from mental disturbances and acute hysterical pains, once had to spend a fortnight in the dark cell, the only furniture of which was a chair. But certain Directors have tried hard to ease rules and regulations, in particular the American Director.

It is now ten o'clock at night. The trumpeter blows the last call from across the barracks. Warningly, sadly, devotionally, sounds the bugle. All summer, the young bugler painfully but conscientiously practised. Now he can blow it like Young Siegfried.

The light at my cell door is switched off, only to be switched on again in fifteen minutes. Now the searchlights of the guards on the prison walls outside play against the window and through it on to the cell walls.

The orders of the changing guards bark through the night, but though it is night, with the light through the little window in the cell door one can still see everything in the cell's dim light.

Now the ghosts of the night will come, knocking, tapping, marching up and down, all part of Spandau's strange ghost sonata.

On that unforgettable night when I bled so terribly, I was in a semi-conscious condition and felt I had already left this world. I was a sleep-walker as a child, and accustomed to strange experiences, but my condition and experience on that night of illness was like a visit to the beyond in a state of complete happiness.

Nobody prays more devotedly than the sick prisoner in his cell, and I prayed that night.

It is twelve o'clock — midnight. Now starts the actual hour of the ghosts. But it is not easy for my ghosts, for my cell grows neither dark, nor is it quiet enough for them.

The control clock in the cell corridor buzzes its half-hourly signal, and midnight is the signal for the change of nations among the groups of warders. Russians hand over to Americans, Britons change with the French, or vice versa. All this happens with much talk, rattling of keys, closing of heavy iron doors, and either the retiring guard, or the new one, or sometimes both, shine the light into my cell, while the head guard, on his inspection, looks into my cell once more.

My hearing is as sharp as that of a dachshund. I know the various warders. There are about thirty of them. I know not only their voices, their coughs, whistling and humming, but also their steps, the way they sit down or play with the keys, or how they put or throw them on to the table.

I belong to those happy and yet unhappy beings born to love. I cannot hate. I cannot hate a single human being. Hate is nothing but an inferiority complex. I looked always only for the beautiful, the goodness in men, and that was my downfall. Doing favours can become a plague.

Visiting days are the great feast days of the year here. Before a visit, all our thoughts and feelings are keyed up for the great day. How much one has to tell and to ask, but most things remain unsaid because of the lack of time. The highly strung soul of a prisoner is overwhelmed during such visits. Conversation during a visit is carried on at a tremendous speed in order to be able to talk and ask as much as possible, but memories chase each other and become confused.

Sometimes memory stops and one tries in vain to remember a name one used to know quite well.

But the wire fence between the prisoner and visitor in the visiting room is depressing on such a day of celebration. A fence like this I remember having seen as a measure of protection in the aquarium against poisonous reptiles in the zoo.

After my operation in October 1949 an official of the French High Commission came to see me in the prison hospital room to inquire after my health. This official gave me permission for a special letter to be sent to my wife telling her about the successful operation. How grateful I must be for the outstanding operation of the great French surgeon. Yes, the French doctor and the professionally excellent, tender nurse were an oasis of human kindness and culture in this desert.

I am much better now thanks to the years of special treatment by deep injections into the central nerve points of the head and spine. The surgical treatment of my bladder every eight to ten days still has to continue, and I still require morphine, atropine, and other injections during the treatments. Generally, the improvement in my health continues.

I now receive two drugs of an interesting erotic(!) character. One drug is made from the testicles of bulls, and another is made from the afterbirth of mothers. What they really do here to keep me alive!

I dozed a while and have just had an unpleasant dream. I pulled out my hair — fistfuls of it — and yet, in reality, I am bald. And in another part of my dream I played cards with the Americans — with Attorney General Jackson and Judge Biddle. I think it was a game of poker. I lost heavily. Bad luck in dreams is supposed to bring luck in life. Yet I always said 'Twenty-two' when I should have called 'Twenty-one'. Why was I condemned to such a sentence?

Now the eerie sound of the owl is mixing with the nightly concert of the ghosts of Spandau. The owls, like the falcons, are nesting in the walls and towers of the prison. Together with the crows and rooks, they haunt this place. Once we unsettled one of the eerie fellows when we had to clean the corridors of this large prison building in readiness for an inspection by officers of the Occupying Powers.

It is now 6 a.m., and the bugler calls reveille. The full light is switched on. Keys are rattling in the cell door. Time to get up for washing. I need ten minutes to pull myself together. My head is buzzing, my eyes burn.

And so the day arrives — oh! that it would be over.

Funk was not permitted to send this essay to his wife. It contained too many subjects whose mention was forbidden in Spandau letters.

In November 1949, after five weeks in the convalescent room recovering from his major operation, he was passed as fit to return to his own cell, and special sanction was given for Dr Guinchard, his surgeon, personally to continue supervision of treatment. The day before he was due to return to his cell, and to the old prison routine, Funk, in a falsely jovial mood, told jokes, recited poetry — the unprintable kind — to nursing orderlies Boon and Prost, and talked about one of his favourite pastimes, which was whist. He was as fond of this card game as he was of telling a tall story to the eagerly gullible. Hitler's ex-financial adviser chuckled gleefully as he related how completely he had taken in Hess with a yarn involving himself and Richard Strauss, the composer.

'Do you know,' he asked Hess, 'that one night Strauss kept an audience of thousands waiting for him to appear as conductor of a symphony concert while he played whist with a friend and myself? There we were in evening dress, tucked into a little room behind the concert platform, and Strauss wouldn't leave for anybody until the hand was played out. What's more, we were back at the game as soon as the interval was reached.'

Hess, who was easy meat for this kind of fairy-tale, stared in amazement as he listened to Funk's romancing. 'You know,' said Funk later, shaking with laughter, 'he was completely taken in. Not a doubt of it. Hess was the living proof that the insane, the drunk and childish are always protected by God. When you thought of Hess and his impossible ways, it shows what irresponsible people once ruled Germany — and think of that drug addict Göring, fornicator Goebbels, drunkard Ley, and vain pompous Ribbentrop!'

Funk excluded himself from such criticism, of course, but added aptly: 'If everyone remembered the past, no one would forgive anybody.'

7: THE RICHEST MAN IN GAOL

> It is my guilt that I educated youth for a man who committed a millionfold murders; I carry the guilt for youth reared in an anti-Semitic State under anti-Semitic laws; and I assume responsibility for the kidnapping from Eastern occupied territories of from forty to fifty thousand children between the ages of ten and fourteen years of age and their transportation to Germany for service in the labour and armed forces.

This was the Nuremberg confession of Baldur von Schirach, Hitler Youth Leader, former Governor of Austria, and the creature responsible for perverting and poisoning the minds of the children of his generation.

'Youth', said Hitler, 'must be swift as greyhounds, tough as leather, and hard as Krupp steel.'

Schirach, his ardent disciple who prepared children for war and was for many years one of the Führer's closest associates, echoed devotedly: 'He who marches in the Hitler Youth is not one among millions but the soldier of an idea.' He also claimed that the object of Hitler Youth training was to ensure that 'a gun feels as natural in the hands of a German boy as a pen'.

It was Schirach who wrote many of the songs for the Stormtroop marchers of the 1930s, and songs like 'We Are the Soldiers of the Future' for boys and girls he led and taught blind obedience to the Führer. At the age of twenty-four, before he had completed his university studies, he became leader of the brown-shirted Hitler Youth and of the girls of the Bund Deutscher Mädel, in their uniform white blouses and blue skirts. By the time he was twenty-nine he was one of the most important of the Nazi hierarchy, reporting directly to Hitler.

Von Schirach working in the prison garden. A guard sits behind him. Once he announced his intention of replacing all Christian crosses with swastikas; later he had a crucifix in his cell.

As a young man, Schirach's plump eunuch's face surrounded by blond boys dominated all the propaganda photographs of the youth movement he led from 1933. He seemed like a man who might be dangerous to small boys, but was not as effeminate as he appeared. This big, soft, bisexual-looking, pampered upper-class boy with the *thé-dansant* eyes was an original Nazi. Hitler himself advised him to study in Munich and recruit students for the Party. Schirach saw himself as the Chief Scout of Nazism. Hitler loved his poems, and in praise of his leader Schirach wrote:

> That is the greatest thing about him,
> That he is not only our leader and great hero,
> But himself, upright, firm and simple,
> In him rests the root of our world,
> And his soul touches the stars
> And yet he remains a man like you and me.

Schirach converted one of Hitler's speeches into a poem, creating verses from his Führer's own words. Retrospectively, the words appear prophetic:

> Could be that the columns which halt here,
> That these endless brown rows of men,
> Are scattered in the wind, split up and dispersed
> And will desert me. Could be, could be...
>
> I shall remain faithful, even though deserted by all —
> I shall carry the flag, staggering and alone.
> My smiling lips may stammer mad words,
> But the flag will only fall when I fall
> And will be a shroud covering my corpse.

In fact the Nazis' swastika-emblazoned blood-red flag, about which Schirach wrote so poetically, affronted his artistic sensibilities. He thought it was vulgar.

Youngest of the Nazi leaders in the Nuremberg dock and an ardent disciple of the gospel of 'pure Aryanism', he insisted that he was a 'product of the Boy Scout movement'. Ten million German children looked to him as their guide and mentor. He repaid their hero-worship by warping their minds with Nazi hatred and, when they were old enough, sending them to their death fighting for the 'master race' myth.

From the age of six to eighteen, when conscription for the Labour Service and the army began, girls and boys were absorbed into the Hitler Youth. Parents found guilty of trying to keep children from joining the organization were liable to long-term imprisonment.

From six to ten, children were supplied with a performance book in which their ideological progress was recorded. At ten, after tests in athletics, camping, and Nazi-distorted history, they graduated into the Jungvolk (Young Folk) where the following oath had to be taken:

> In the presence of this blood banner, which represents our Führer, I swear to devote all my energies and my strength to the saviour of our country, Adolf Hitler. I am willing and ready to give up my life for him, so help me God.

The banner displayed across the entrance of the youth camps declared: 'We are born to die for Germany.'

At fourteen, children were admitted into the Hitler Youth proper, in which they stayed until eighteen. This paramilitary organization, which Schirach airily likened to the Boy Scouts, often indulged in 'camping expeditions' armed with rifles. Schirach taught girls soldiering, too; from ten to fourteen, girls were classified as Jungmädel (Young Maidens). From the age of fourteen, when the girls became members of the Bund Deutscher Mädel (League of German Maidens), emphasis was placed upon the great honour of bearing children for the Third Reich. At eighteen, thousands of girls did a year's service at farms, usually close to the Labour Service camps for young men.

By the close of 1938, Hitler Youth numbered 7,728,259. To suck in some four million more who managed to keep out of the youth organizations, Schirach instigated a law sanctioning conscription of all youth into his movement on the same basis as they were drafted into the armed forces. Parents were warned that their children would be taken from them and placed in orphanages or 'homes' unless they joined.

Schirach's poisoning of young minds was reinforced by three types of special schools: Adolf Hitler Schools, under his personal direction; National Political Institutes of Education; and Order Castles. The Adolf Hitler Schools took twelve-year-olds to give them six years' intensive training for leadership in the National Socialist Party or in public services. The Political Institutes cultivated 'the soldierly spirit'. These were supervised by the SS, which provided the headmasters and most of the teachers. Order Castles were for the most fanatical graduates of the Hitler Schools and Political Institutes, and these students specialized in 'racial sciences' and general Nazi ideology.

'It was through me that our young people believed in Hitler,' Schirach confessed in Spandau. 'I brought them up to believe in him. It was my task to dismantle this faith, which is why I wanted to be brought to trial and take the blame.

'That such shameful iniquities as the concentration camps could occur in a land with our noble cultural traditions — the home of Goethe, Kant and Humboldt — is almost incredible.'

On General Patton's orders, he wrote a message telling the youth of Germany that there should be no underground movement, no Hitler myth, no anti-Semitism.

He tried to discount part of his guilt for the corruption of a nation's children, but Justice was not deceived, and he was sent to Spandau for twenty years.

'I am surprised,' he said on arrival in the prison. 'I really did think they were going to hang me.'

Propped on the table of his ever neat and tidy Spandau cell were pictures of his daughter and three sons. But there was no photograph of the mother of his children. Like the millions of misguided youngsters she, too, became a casualty of his ideals, but got off much more lightly than they did. Henriette von Schirach divorced her husband in October, 1950.

His apparently poised manner and blatant vanity made him an uncomfortably repellent personality. Even in his Nuremberg cell he wore a smart dove-grey suit, as if dressed for a stroll along Berlin's Kurfürstendamm. But the carefully contrived surface bravado could not camouflage his inner fears. In time, his stance developed into one of smooth self-justification.

In Vienna, in 1940, he ruled as Governor and *Gauleiter* and lived lavishly with seventeen servants. There were endless stories about his famous white bedroom. His official titles were Reich Youth Leader, Lord Mayor of Vienna and Reich Defence Commissioner of Vienna. He dominated Austria until 1945.

On his birthday, in Germany and Austria, his home was always besieged by adoring members of the Nazi Girls' Association, who descended on him waving banners and bearing gifts. One girl brought a pair of gloves she had knitted for her beloved Baldur, with one hand embroidered 'Heil' and the other 'Hitler'.

When the so-called 'Thousand-Year Reich' collapsed, Schirach disappeared. Wearing a beard, he worked for a time as an interpreter at an American Army post, but when the hunt for him got too hot, he decided to surrender and gamble on the advantage of his strong American family background.

'I am giving myself up as a prisoner of the Americans to get the opportunity of putting my case before an international Court of Justice,' he scrawled in a note he delivered on 5 June 1945 to a United States Command Post in the Austrian Tyrol.

When his wife, Henriette, was first allowed to see him after his capture, she brought him some cake and a bottle of wine in a basket. As she walked into the room carrying the basket of food, he laughed: 'Ah, Red Riding Hood visiting the wolf. I am so sorry you married the wrong man.'

In 1948 the Austrian Government applied to the Allied military authorities in Germany for Schirach's extradition as a war criminal. They wanted to charge him, as former *Gauleiter* of Vienna, with responsibility for the destruction of the city and with racial and political persecution. Also in 1948, Schirach smuggled out a small slip of paper from Spandau gaol bearing a message to his wife. It read:

> We did not realize the luck that belonged to us. Now it is destroyed. That which is, is always threatened with danger. Only that which has been remains unchangeable. And though it never returns to us, the luck that was ours remains our luck.

It was always the same. Messages and letters, full of philosophic, poetic and idealistic talk, some of it contradictory, but never a word to his young wife on the upbringing and financial care of his children.

In August 1950 a letter was handed to Schirach in Spandau. As he sat in his cell reading it he might almost have heard his wife's voice:

> Have you ever once asked yourself how we manage to exist? Have you at any time, instead of sitting in your cell studying philosophy, Latin, French, writing poetry, and thinking how to straighten out your position in history, as you call it, actually faced reality and wondered where the next meal was coming from for your wife and children?
>
> You isolated yourself from everything and everyone, your head forever in the clouds as it almost always has been from the day of our marriage. As the years went by, I realized more than ever that your idealistic obsessions and dreams were taking you further and further from me and the children.
>
> Remember the day in 1943 when I came to Berchtesgaden after staying with some friends in Amsterdam, and the copy of a *Life* magazine I bought on my way back through Lisbon? I showed it to Hitler, who, as you know, hardly ever saw any foreign publication. I pointed out to him a feature in the magazine written about the war and its inhumanities.
>
> Do you remember what happened? You were in the room at the time. Hitler blew up and told me, 'You people must learn to hate, all of you. You are much too sentimental.'
>
> I could see that my presence irked the Führer, and as I made to leave, Martin Bormann walked over and put on a record to soothe Hitler's nerves. When I reached the staircase I heard the blare of Wagner's *Götterdämmerung* and, suddenly, the certainty came to me that those whose company I had just left, and you were among them, were doomed, finished absolutely.
>
> When you joined me later, I told you of my premonition and what I thought. You called me a fool who didn't understand that today's world was a world of men — hard men. I was always the fool. I never understood.

Then, when Hitler's Germany crashed in ruins around us, I fully expected you to ask me to take poison with you, as did Goebbels with his wife and children. Our best friend, Colin Ross, said, 'I played the wrong hand and now I must take the consequences.' Then Colin dug his own grave in the garden of our home in Urfeld, and shot himself in our sitting room.[4]

I buried him myself after wrapping him in the canvas of his favourite tent, and it was then that I was ready to face death with you. Your answer to me was, 'I cannot take my life. First I must make my place and my work clear in history.' As always, you would not face facts. Had I taken poison, it would have saved me untold suffering in my fight to live and keep my children alive. I have expressed my feelings so many times before to you, but you preferred to ignore them as being distasteful. Reality has always been distasteful to you.

That day of all days, however, Schirach had to face reality. Almost as a postscript, Henriette finished off her letter to him with: 'I intend to divorce you immediately.' He never replied to the letter, nor wrote to his wife again.

For days on end, at work in the prison or in the garden, he hardly spoke to anyone, until one morning a duty officer visited his cell on a routine check-up.

'Any complaints?' he was asked as usual.

'I am well, and yet I am not well,' said Schirach.

'What do you mean?'

'My nerves are upset, and I have terrible migraine headaches. I think my condition is due solely to a letter I received from my

---

[4] Colin Ross was an American-domiciled author who returned to Germany to work for the Nazis during the war. The Martin Dies Committee investigating un-American activities just before the outbreak of the war made accusations in December 1939 that Ross was a master intriguer whose activities 'appeared to come within the category of espionage'. The committee recommended that he should be prevented from ever setting foot again on American soil.

wife. She is divorcing me. Everything's gone now, everything is finished.'

The officer had already been told of Schirach's domestic misfortune by the prison censor. 'I'll see you get something for your headaches,' said the visitor.

'Thank you, but it's not pills I want,' urged Schirach in the flawless English that he spoke without a trace of accent. 'Some cyanide would be much more helpful. My family and friends will see you are paid well, and in advance, if you give me a hand to get hold of a phial.'

'Don't be a fool. My job is to keep you alive, not to kill you. Pills will do you more good. They'll give you time to get accustomed to the idea of losing your wife,' answered the officer as he walked out of the cell.

Schirach got his pills, but no cyanide. The idea remained with him for some time, however, and it got a further airing one day during a work period, when the prisoners were making paper bags and envelopes. Seated on stools around a wooden table in the inner cell block corridor, the seven shattered Nazi gods picked up sheets of cut paper for hour after hour, folded them, brushed glue on the edges, and put the finished bags and envelopes on an ever-mounting pile.

In turn, every prisoner was allowed to read to the others to break the monotony of their task, but whenever the guards became a little lax — they, too, knew the meaning of boredom — the prisoners would take advantage of the situation. When it came to Schirach's turn to read, he ignored the book and said to no one in particular, 'It has always puzzled me how Göring, who shared imprisonment with us and the others at Nuremberg, managed to secure and then hide the cyanide with which he took his life.'

Former Grand Admiral Dönitz offered the first theory:

'After his death, I remembered the days when I was escorted to the shower room with Göring, and noticed how enormous was his stomach with its folds of fat. When you consider this, it wouldn't have been at all difficult for him to have sewn a poison capsule in the skin under one of his enormous folds.'

Walther Funk also thought it likely that Göring had secreted the cyanide somewhere upon his body. It was easy to see, Funk said, how Göring always appeared to be fearful over the prospect of being removed from the prison and compelled to leave all his belongings behind.

This reference to Göring's belongings encouraged Dönitz to take a new line of speculation. 'Now I come to think of it,' he said, 'Göring's most prized possession, or so it appeared, was his long-stemmed pipe, which he would not allow out of his sight, not even when he bathed.'

'That's true,' broke in Schirach. 'One couldn't help but notice how watchful an eye he always kept on it. What appeared to worry him, and he mentioned it to me more than once, was that he had heard that those under sentence of death would know the hour of their end only when they were awakened one night, given a different suit for their execution, and ordered to surrender all personal belongings.'

Dönitz recalled that Göring had also pestered him with this problem, but it was Neurath who had the last word before the prisoners had to bring to an end their clandestine conversation.

'That favourite pipe of Hermann's may be the answer to it all,' he suggested. 'If you remember, when Göring's suicide was discovered, it lay on the floor, its stem broken in two.'

It was a thoughtful Schirach who returned to his cell at the end of the day's work. He filled his pipe with prison tobacco from a box that lay on the table and as he lit it he could hardly have been otherwise than preoccupied with the riddle of

Göring's end. He winced as he also recalled the end of his friend Colin Ross, who, though born in Vienna, was of Scottish descent. Staring at the walls of his cell, Schirach heard again Ross's warning words to Foreign Minister Ribbentrop: 'If we lose the war — and we *shall* lose it — they will put us on show in cages like wild beasts!' Unable to face trial when the Third Reich crashed in ruins around him, Ross took his own life.

Even in 1943 danger signals were already vivid. During a visit to Vienna that year by Göring and his wife Emmy, Schirach had steered them into a private room in a restaurant to discuss his concern with the only man he thought had real influence with the Führer.

'Things are going wrong,' Schirach said, 'and we shall lose the war if we carry on like this. We have to do something or we shall get the blame. We must make this a common cause. Speak to Hitler privately. Does he not realize something will have to be done?'

Looking at him sadly, Göring replied: 'Speak to Hitler alone — what an idea! I never see him alone these days. Bormann is with him all the time. If I could, by God, I would have gone to see Churchill a long time ago. Do you think I am enjoying this damned business?'

A few weeks after he got his wife's letter containing the devastating divorce news, Schirach received a tube of his favourite toothpaste, smuggled in by a co-operative guard. It could have contained a message, or even a phial of poison. But there was no more talk of cyanide after a visit to Spandau by his brother-in-law, Heinrich Hoffmann junior, son of Hitler's personal photographer, who came to discuss the divorce proceedings.

Young Hoffmann explained that his sister, in applying for the divorce, would probably obtain custody of the children. When he heard this, Schirach replied: 'I would like you somehow to obtain guardianship of them, Heinrich. I am told that I have no legal rights, but we must nevertheless declare that only because of this do we accept any court ruling in respect to parental rights. It should be possible in some way to safeguard our interests — which, for me, are the interests of my children.'

'Don't worry, Baldur,' said Hoffmann, 'there are other things in life that will compensate you.' The visit over, Schirach returned to the cell block and to his philosophical studies, poetry, and dreams.

At his brother-in-law's suggestion, he sent a letter to the court composed of three sentences only. They were: 'I have nothing against the divorce. I wish her the best. She must know what she has to do in this situation.'

This sparse statement was accepted by a Munich court as Schirach's affidavit. Although unwitnessed, it was in the circumstances (the Spandau prisoners being permitted no legal rights or representation) considered to be all that was required for the granting of a divorce of mutual agreement, the most frequent and easiest form of divorce in Germany.

In October 1950 the marriage between the little girl who grew up with Hitler and the Führer's favourite protégé was dissolved. Neither Henriette von Schirach nor Heinrich Hoffmann junior, nor in fact anyone connected with the family, was able to obtain the custody of the children. Owing to the lack of proper legally witnessed documents from the father, unobtainable due to Spandau regulations, the children became wards of the Kaufbeuren County Court in Bavaria.

The Soviet Director stopped Schirach being handed a notice of guardianship proceedings affecting his children, so the Western Directors advised his lawyer that his client could be notified, through a routine letter, of the general content of the legal document.

Fate, however, had not finished rubbing salt into the self-inflicted wounds of Schirach, who in his time had destroyed the lives of countless thousands. Exactly five years after his arrival in Spandau, in 1952, he was handed a letter that in unexciting legal phraseology informed him that he and his sister Rosalinde had become the sole heirs of a large family fortune, the bulk of which was vested in American gilt-edged securities.

It was tantamount to offering a corpse the comfort of champagne and caviar. Schirach, who was the son of an American mother and a Prussian aristocrat, must have realized from this left-handed stroke of fortune that there was no man poorer than he. For all his wealth he really owned nothing.

From Alfred Rosenberg, Schirach had parroted the reverberate mouthings that had proclaimed the racial purity of the Nazi supermen, although he was of considerably mixed stock himself. His mother, Emma Middleton Lynah-Tillou, was the daughter of a New York lawyer-industrialist descended from the Huguenots. She was burned to death when an aircraft crashed on her home in Wiesbaden. She died because she ran into the blazing building to try and save her Pekingese dog. His Prussian father, Carl von Schirach, was the son of a major in the American Army who stood guard beside George Washington's coffin and of Elizabeth Bolly Norris, who hailed from Philadelphia. Schirach's great-grandfather was a Chief Justice of New York; two American ancestors signed the

Declaration of Independence, and the legendary Sir Francis Drake was also said to occupy a branch of his family tree.

Carl von Schirach, who became a theatrical impresario, a director of the Weimar National Theatre, was by all accounts an improvident character who considered it tiresome to discuss money matters. Nevertheless, he knew how to squander his wife's money right up to the time of his death.

The fortune now inherited by Schirach and his sister came from the distaff side, via the Norris Locomotive Company of Philadelphia and other subsidiary firms. It was further enriched by additional shares and money from grandfather Tillou. The entire fortune was taken over by the Custodian of Enemy Property in the United States, but continued to grow with interest each year until the day Schirach left Spandau and could claim his share. He had been unaware that his father's will had been lying in the gaol's safe since September 1949. It had been sent to Spandau, but as a result of Soviet objection its contents were not disclosed to him.

When Henriette heard about her ex-husband's windfall she wrote to Spandau for the first time since she had informed her husband of her intention to get a divorce, asking for written authority to enable her to obtain a portion of the money to assist in the upbringing of their children. Schirach replied, through his brother-in-law, with a point-blank refusal. A little later, nineteen-year-old Angelica von Schirach made her second visit to Spandau, specially primed by her mother to ask her father to sign the necessary authority. The girl returned empty-handed.

Schirach confided to his brother-in-law: 'My refusals were prompted by the suspicion that Henriette might be trying to get her hands on the money for her own ends.'

'As always, he never even considered that I might be concerned solely with the children's welfare,' Henriette angrily replied to her brother when he reported the conversation. 'He knew that you and Rosalinde were helping me to meet the expense of the children's schooling and upbringing, but then I should have known better than to have asked. His answer was typical of his way of thinking.'

So the richest man in Spandau kept intact his new-found wealth; all of it. Perhaps his most valuable possession, however, was what he received on 1 December 1948, the day he and his guilty companions heard that the rule of silence had been abolished and that they could now talk to each other during working hours. More than anything else, even exceeding his passion for wearing uniforms, Schirach loved to talk, although the seven were not allowed anything like the same freedom when the Russians took control.

Tall and well built, still trying to disguise his innate femininity by assuming a military bearing, in the days of his freedom Schirach could never attend too many rallies or make too many speeches. 'Every boy who dies at the front is dying for Mozart,' had been one of his favourite effusions, and he would follow up with yet another choice sample of verbal whimsy. 'Vienna', he would declare, 'cannot be conquered with bayonets, only with music.'

Even on the day he had surrendered to the American forces in June 1945 he had wanted to talk, again to the youth of Germany and to the world, by broadcasting to them his brand-new ideas on what had been and what was to be. It was out of the question, but he still talked about anything and anyone — except his wife.

Of Hitler he said: 'I believed I was serving a Führer who would make our people and youth great and happy, but I was mad to ever meddle with politics. I was born for the arts.'

Of the future: 'I expect to be out of Spandau by about 1966, and a fit man in his sixties can still get plenty out of life.'

Of Speer: 'We do not get on well because he is a man who does not appreciate the artistic. He doesn't even appreciate good music.'

That was untrue; Speer was very fond of opera and serious music. There was, however, one thing Speer and Schirach had in common: their great interest in Hess. They both defended him whenever he was in trouble, as he continually was, and both liked to talk about him.

One evening Hess refused to take his supper from the food trolley, shouting, 'You are trying to poison me! I won't eat it!' Schirach could hardly restrain his impatience for the arrival on the scene of the Chief Warder, so that he might explain the tantrums of the Deputy Führer.

'Hess and his mania about being poisoned,' he asserted, 'were enough to drive anyone mad. I remember on one occasion at Nuremberg when he told me not to eat the biscuits with which we had been served, because he believed they had been impregnated with a drug. One day in the garden in Spandau when he was rolling with his usual "cramps", Hess said to me, "I am positive someone is trying to poison my food. Are you sure there are no Jews employed on the kitchen staff of the prison? There may be one of them on the staff who is acting for international Jewry and putting poison in my food on their instructions!" Although we all assured him there were no Jews in Spandau, the answer didn't satisfy him. "How can you be sure there are no Jews here when there are so many foreigners in the prison?" he asked.'

(In fact, an American guard in the gaol named Robert Dackerman was Jewish.)

Schirach recalled that Hess once inquired whether the vegetables the seven of them ate were artificially grown. He said the reason he asked was that for years he had followed a strict rule about not eating vegetables grown with artificial fertilizers. He even used to have a greengrocer deliver special vegetables cultivated only with natural manure. It was the only safe way to eat, Hess claimed.

A vegetarian as well as a teetotaller and non-smoker, he was as fussy over food when he went to Hitler's Chancellery or Berghof quarters — 'although Hitler had his own specialist diet chef and also preferred vegetarian meals', Schirach said. 'For a long time Hitler didn't notice that Hess made a habit of bringing his own vegetarian dishes in a container carried by his adjutant. He had the food heated up in the Führer's kitchens. I remember him once explaining to an irritated Hitler: "My food must contain certain biologically dynamic ingredients."'

To another Spandau officer Schirach offered his explanation of Hess's flight to Britain:

'Hess has always been a great dreamer. He worshipped Hitler, and the adoration was reciprocated. Indeed, you only had to find one to find the other. However, the pressure of military affairs during the war saw Hess move further and further down Hitler's table, with generals being given the favoured seats at the Führer's side. This used to depress him tremendously. His lord and master, he felt, no longer needed him. It was under this spur that Hess' mind began to swell flamboyantly on the possibility of achieving something tremendous for his Führer, something that would regain him the place he had formerly occupied at Adolf's side. And what was more likely to ensure a more glorious success than a flight to Britain as ambassador extraordinary dedicated to the task of persuading Britain that the war was lost, and that no hindrance should be placed on Germany's plan to liquidate Russia?'

Schirach had a final word to say about Hess, a rider as it were to a brief inquest.

'This man', he said, 'was never any different. It is really strange that he of all persons should have been deemed worthy to be Hitler's second-in-command. Then, of course, there was always Göring the drug addict — what a bloody fine pair they made! We had some prime types among the Party hierarchy.' Schirach apparently excluded himself from the category. 'Martin Bormann, the former estate bailiff who was known to us in the Führer's inner circle as "Hitler's Grey Eminence", was forever trying to sell the idea of creating a new National Socialist ritual because he was convinced that we needed to copy the Catholic Church. Bormann insisted that the only way to beat the Church was by patterning our political ceremonies like impressive Catholic celebrations.'

Recalling another corrupt ex-partner in crime — Julius Streicher, the sex-obsessed anti-Semitic *Gauleiter* of Nuremberg and one of Hitler's oldest friends — Schirach reminisced: 'Streicher loved showing off the talisman he always carried of a silver figure of a rabbi with a gold rope round his neck. Well, the rope they put around Streicher's neck at Nuremberg wasn't made of gold.'

As a brother-Nazi, Schirach possessed his own special brand of viciousness. He did not perhaps care to remember the incredible days when the children of Germany, under his tutelage, betrayed their parents to the Gestapo and believed that Hitler was the new Messiah, and Germany his kingdom.[5] He had children recite a prayer before their evening meal:

---

[5] In honour of the Führer, Schirach wrote poetry and songs for Hitler

> Führer, my Führer, given me by God,
> Protect and preserve my life for long.
> You rescued Germany from its deepest need,
> I thank you for my daily bread.

Hitler counted on the Hitler Youth Movement to educate Germany's children and teenagers for the purposes he had in mind. Schirach declared at a rally of young Nazis on 27 July 1936: 'An avowal of faith in the eternal Germany is the same as an avowal of faith in the eternal God. To Nazis there is no God but Germany.' He also emphasized: 'The lives of all German youths belong solely to Hitler. If a child asks its mother, "Am I yours?" she must answer: "No, you belong to the Führer."'

As for mothers worshipping God, he recited from the Nazi book *Thoughts for the People*: 'Only when the German woman is free from the Church can she develop her dignity and spiritual power.'

In Spandau, Schirach was no longer inspired by pagan beliefs. On the wall of his cell hung a crucifix bought for him by his brother-in-law at his request from a Munich shop. It was an Oberammergau crucifix made of light oak upon which was imposed the figure of Jesus carved in acorn wood. Wooden plugs were substituted for nails and, to meet further the requirements of the Spandau regulations, there was not even the customary metal inscription. The crucifix was three feet long; Schirach felt he needed a large one.

Youth song-books vilifying the Church and the Jews. When *Gauleiter* of Vienna, he set about exterminating and deporting the city's 185,000 Jews and announced his intention of replacing all Christian crosses with swastikas.

8: THE GARDEN OF EDEN

The garden had never looked lovelier. The lilac was a parasol of mauve beauty, the walnut trees stood heavy with fruit, and elsewhere in their own beds strawberries ripened into crimson lusciousness; tomatoes, celery, chicory, radishes, marrows, cucumbers, carrots, spinach, peas, onions, potatoes spread and multiplied. Everything was here in this garden of plenty, but there was one fruit that could never be plucked by the seven men who dug, hoed, and nursed the sandy soil and trimmed and pruned the trees in the garden of Spandau: freedom.

In August 1947, the month after they arrived at the gaol, the British Director offered to let anyone who wished work in the prison garden, which covered some five to six thousand metres. All accepted, glad of the distraction of being able to spend several hours daily in the open air — weather permitting — amid the old trees and lilac bushes.

In the early years at Spandau they were barred from talking to each other even in the garden, and the Russian Chief Warder submitted a complaint to the gaol Directors' meeting that prisoners Nos. 2 and 3 'habitually engaged in unauthorized conversations while working in the garden, on the pretext that they were discussing garden work'. The Directors decided that 'There will be no relaxation of the rules of silence because of work in the garden'; and the offending prisoners, Dönitz and Neurath, were officially reprimanded and warned that repetition of the offence could result in punishment.

Some of the prisoners stripped to the waist as they worked. In the tree-shaded solitude of the garden, three loaded machine-guns were trained down on them by teams of khaki-clad soldiers from high towers astride the surrounding walls. All that was grown at Spandau, except the strawberries and walnuts, went into the prison kitchen for everybody.

At 10.30 a.m. four blue-uniformed guards led the seven from their cells to a steel door at the far end of the inner cell block. The door was unlocked; and in single file, preceded and followed by their escort, the seven descended a narrow winding stone stairway to yet another steel door below. Beyond was the Garden of Eden, as the prisoners named it, after Britain's Foreign Secretary Anthony Eden.

The work and exercise in the garden were the only opportunity the seven had to be in the open, and they were under surveillance from the moment they arrived until they returned to their cells at midday. On a typical day, as the prisoners stepped into the spacious garden, they instinctively glanced at the sky for their friends the birds who made their home in Spandau's trees, winging and wheeling their way up and over the wall. Spades and rakes were quickly handed out, and the prisoners headed for the vegetable plots they worked individually.

Grand Admiral Karl Dönitz, watering-can in hand, joined Baron Konstantin von Neurath; Hitler Youth Leader Baldur von Schirach paired with seventy-seven-year-old Grand Admiral Erich Raeder. Walther Funk walked up and down a while, muttering and grumbling to himself, before moving over to Neurath and Dönitz, who often screened himself behind low-hanging tree branches whilst he cracked nuts he had gathered from a prison nut-tree. Albert Speer, always content with his own company, headed for his tomato bed. Rudolf Hess engaged in his favourite gardening pastime, the doubtful comfort of the nearest wheelbarrow on which to stretch out and sleep for an hour or so.

'It is below my dignity to carry a pail of water,' Hess insisted. 'What would people say if they saw me doing this? They might see me from some of the high buildings around the prison.'

But in letters home he constantly boasted to his wife and son of his gardening prowess, and how the work tired him. This was sheer deception, for he was the laziest man in Spandau, as his fellow prisoners and guards could have testified.

'I have had enough to do with vegetables to last me for the rest of my life,' said Hess once, when he managed to get up from the wheelbarrow. 'When I was at school in Godesberg we had to do some heavy gardening every week. Each pupil was given two square metres of ground of his own with which he could do what he liked. My efforts, however, did not travel beyond a liking for the gooseberries that were growing, and my teacher soon gave me up.'

In the beginning, 9,000 square metres of weeds had to be cleared before double-trenching could begin in the Spandau garden. Working unwillingly at this task, Hess commented: 'It is perhaps appropriate that I am weeding — as in my last profession — only now it is on a smaller scale.'

Raeder and Dönitz resented Hess's laziness, realizing that so many of his antics and dramatics were clearly designed to avoid doing his share of garden work. Raeder referred to him as 'His imprisoned lordship', and Dönitz mockingly called him 'The Baron'. The sight of Hess getting away with tantrums — and even, at times, securing preferential treatment because of them from the prison staff — infuriated the two naval disciplinarians, and they openly displayed contempt for their former Deputy Führer.

During one summer, Hess' malingering was so blatant that the four medical officers had a notice attached to his cell door instructing that he was required to work in the garden every day under supervision. Hess was warned that if he disobeyed, he would be severely punished and lose privileges. He complied unwillingly, moaning and groaning all the time, but was none the worse for it. His bluff had been called.

Walther Funk also had an intense dislike for manual labour and spent most of his time philosophizing or jeering and making fun of the other six. His usual trick was to pretend to be looking for something to do, and then stand beside one of the others with an unemployed hoe in hand.

In May 1954, Hess heard that the officer in charge of a unit of Guards assigned to the prison, was the heir of the Duke of Hamilton — the man Hess flew to Scotland to see in 1941.

Complaining of pains in the leg and hip, Raeder was given treatment and the use of a stick to help him in the garden on wet days. When the seven were informed: 'No garden today — it's raining,' they carried tables and chairs into the corridor. Piles of paper, brushes and glue were provided, and the men who had once threatened to dominate the world sat around tables making envelopes.

In 1952 the American Director advised that he intended to have them taught basket-making. They objected and Dönitz wrote to his lawyer, Otto Kranzbühler, asking whether refusal would justify punishment. Warning them not to provoke incidents, Kranzbühler said: 'It is essential for the Western Governments to regard you as gentlemen.'

The biggest achievement of architect Albert Speer was the rock garden he built by the skilful manipulation of old bricks. He worked as a mason, carpenter and glazier in the building of a greenhouse. He laboured most of the time in an old pair of white shorts that his wife had sent him, and was friendly with everybody but Schirach, whom he detested. 'His mind is warped by false ideals,' he said; to which Schirach retorted,

'Speer is only a so-called artist. He is devoid of any genuine artistic feeling.' These men, who once traded in hate, knew how to vilify each other. Dönitz and Raeder, who were bitter enemies before Spandau, remained so throughout their years of imprisonment.

Speer asked if he could sketch in the garden during break periods on working days and during walking periods on Saturdays and Sundays. The request was denied. The minutes of the Directors' meeting stated: 'The Soviet Director did not find it possible to authorize prisoner No. 5 to sketch during the time allotted to him for taking a walk in the fresh air.'

Neurath was advised by the doctors not to do work of any kind in the garden because any exertion could kill him. But for this tall, heavily built ex-farmer, the alternative relaxation of reading was severely restricted by the cataracts that affected his sight. The garden was his only interest within the prison.

On learning that the seven were also cultivating flowers, the Russian Director asserted that there was no provision in the rules for flower beds in the garden. He ordered: 'Remove them at once!' The Western Directors argued and compromised: 'No *new* flowers to be planted, but those already growing can remain.' The Soviet Director said he was against planting of flowers and tall plants 'for security reasons'.

When, in the summer of 1956, lofty sunflowers were officially declared to be a security hazard due to their height interfering with the clear view required by observation guards, Funk, Schirach, and Dönitz almost went berserk. They began hacking down flowers of all shapes and sizes. Dönitz, in a fit of temper, totally destroyed his much loved and carefully nurtured beds of beans. Frayed nerves were eventually calmed by some guards, who were professional warders brought from

American prisons. These guards were particularly adept at handling the psychological problems of long-term prisoners.

'Enjoying the splendours of nature was always my greatest pleasure,' said Neurath. 'What can be more beautiful than to experience a sunrise in the mountains, alone or with a dear like-minded companion beside you? That is now all over for me, and will never return, but the memory remains and can never be taken away.'

There was no Alpine mountain scenery at Spandau gaol. The only real solitude available was if, like Albert Speer, you were caught stealing cauliflowers for the third time and sentenced to a week's solitary confinement.

Moustached and distinguished-looking, Konstantin von Neurath, of the duel-scarred cheek, was a multi-linguist. Deliberate in speech and movements, he always contrived to appear amiable and polished, even in a gaol uniform. He was a resourceful diplomat, adept at masking true feelings and personal opinions; he hated fanatics and those he termed 'fantasists' who re-tailored historical facts to suit themselves. As a rule, he manoeuvred around problems, and it was perhaps this trait in his character, more than any other, that eventually led him into a Spandau cell. An aristocratic diplomat of the old school who had weakened, he disliked excessive involvement in social rounds and internal politics, but was forced to be deeply concerned with both. He became a convenient bridge for Hitler between the old and new Germany. Formerly German Ambassador in London and Rome, he was appointed Foreign Minister by the Führer, and then Protector of Bohemia and Moravia.

This soft-spoken, complacent, diffident man, who accepted every post the Führer offered him, contributed an air of respectability and acceptability to the Hitler gang. He claimed that brutality was abhorrent to him, but conveniently avoided potentially embarrassing curiosity about unpleasant aspects of Nazism. 'Decent' Germans like Neurath — conservatives of the old breed who thought they could keep reins on the Nazis and use them — worked to build up Hitler, and ended by being torn down themselves.

In a unique position as the favourite and senior Cabinet Minister of Germany's post-World War I President Hindenburg, if Neurath had resigned and openly opposed dictatorship it would undoubtedly have triggered a crisis that Hitler might not have survived. Recognizing his political strength at the time, Neurath reassured friends that he considered himself a rock in the middle of the Nazi brook, slowing down the course of water.

However, refusal to involve oneself in intrigues and personal 'decency' were not always virtues, as he discovered too late. All he finally got for compliance with the regime was the post of gardener-in-chief at Spandau gaol. So, with his practical knowledge of the land, he directed Spandau's crop planning. To everyone he was *Der Obergartenbaudirektor* — the overseer and general director in charge of garden development.

Always courteous, rarely complaining, and belonging to a different world and generation from those of his companions, Neurath commanded the respect of prisoners, guards, and administration staff by calm acceptance of his punishment. His sole grievance was the security check throughout the night, and on one occasion he suggested, 'Why not leave a dim light in the cell burning all night? A man can get used to that but not to the flashing lights.'

Allied medical officers frequently tried to amend the practice of cell security checks by declaring the flashing lights to be injurious to health. Rejecting their advice, the Soviet Director, formally putting on record his reason for disallowing any modification, stated: 'Medical prescription permitting turning off of lights is illegal and places the warders under the jurisdiction of the prisoners.'

Secret photograph of the octogenarian von Neurath in the Spandau garden. Leaning on a hoe at his left is Admiral Dönitz.

Neurath's condition became a daily anxiety, and in the garden a nursing orderly watched him constantly. As he worked there, Neurath often over-exerted himself, then suddenly stiffened and held out his arm for support. Slowly, aided by Dönitz and Speer, he would lower himself to the ground and sit there while the nurse broke one of the trinitrin capsules always available for such emergencies. Sniffing the capsule, he would rest until sufficiently recovered from the heart attack.

Repeatedly doctors warned him not to work in the garden or even to wash his own clothes, but Neurath always answered, 'One must work.' Whenever he felt in danger — the warning was a tightness in his chest — he had special permission to lie or sit regardless of where he was.

It was around this eighty-year-old prisoner's silver-haired, close-cropped head that Spandau's greatest political controversies raged. From time to time British, American, and French officials unsuccessfully tried to get him transferred to hospital, but the Russians refused to discuss a transfer. 'If the Allies want better medical treatment for Neurath, there are plenty of good Russian doctors available,' they said. Two comprehensive medical reports on his condition were ordered by the British Foreign Office.

At one stage, a notice signed by three American officials was attached to his cell door, stating: 'Complete bed rest from 9 p.m. to 6 a.m. All guards are requested to obey these medical regulations.'

Against those preaching a softer attitude towards a 'now harmless old man' were others quoting the evidence of Nuremberg:

> He cast the pearls of his diplomatic experience before Hitler; guided Nazi diplomacy; soothed the fears of nations who were prospective victims; was prepared to be the instrument of the Führer's policy so long as it added to the greatness of

the Reich; and brought the punishment of the world upon himself, which he must now serve — in full.

When Neurath talked in the garden of Spandau, the other six paid attention. They respected the opinion of this diplomat of the old school, and realized that his outlook extended far beyond the narrow viewpoint of the untravelled Nazi leaders. 'If we didn't have Neurath, we would all go crazy, he is so practical,' said Speer.

'His calmness and serenity sustained us all,' said Raeder.

To the six, Neurath advised: 'Think much, but say little. Feel much, but show little.' But his own diplomatic mask slipped sometimes, and in one letter home he admitted, 'I don't think I can stand it much longer.'

This man, whom butcher Heydrich replaced in Prague, was the last prominent figure of the pre-Nazi regime to hold office under Hitler. Neurath had really been out of office from the time he was evicted from the German Foreign Ministry in 1938 by Ribbentrop and given a nominal job as 'President of the German Secret Cabinet Council'. The following year the Nazis appointed him Protector of Bohemia and Moravia, since he claimed descent from a dynasty that once reigned in Hungary. But the Baron, who in earlier years had walked daily, umbrella on arm, regardless of the weather, to London's St James's Park to feed the ducks, proved in Bohemia to be too easy-going for Hitler. The Führer wanted the Czechs kept cowed and in terror, so Neurath was replaced.

Nevertheless he was one of the 'strong men' in the buildup of the Nazi regime. He played a sinister role in opposing world disarmament and helped to destroy the League of Nations.[6] He had this to say about the way events turned out:

---

[6] It was Neurath who advised Hitler to withdraw from the League of

'The war was the most gigantic piece of stupidity. My knowledge of the English people convinced me that Britain would keep her promise to Poland, and President Roosevelt's statements also made it clear that the Americans would ultimately enter the conflict. I foresaw that Germany could not win. With that good man and great friend of mine, Lord Halifax, I honestly worked hard for peace before the war, but we were wasting our time. Hitler had decided on war. Such is the way of things.'

Neurath's 'way of things' was choosing to ride storms by compromising integrity. Hitler's expansionist foreign policy ideas soon got beyond Neurath's control. *Lebensraum* ('living space') was the word constantly on Hitler's lips. He maintained that the 62.5 million people in Germany's 436,000 square kilometres needed a land empire in which to expand; as far as he was concerned, the simple answer was European conquest and even the annexation of territory from the great land empire of the Soviet Union. At the meeting in the Reichs Chancellery during the first week of November 1937, he told Neurath: 'Living space for the German people is the sole solution to Germany's problems. At the risk of war with Britain and France, I intend to conquer land in eastern Europe. Our situation can be solved only by means of force.'

Excusing participation in the disastrous consequences of Hitler's ambitions, Neurath ruefully explained to his Spandau garden colleagues: 'I frequently urged Hitler not to draw the bow too tight, but he didn't listen and told me lies. I was certain his aggressive, expansionist line would inevitably produce a European war. For years I held that we could only

---

Nations' Disarmament Conference. He also played a leading role in the conferences that led to Hitler's decision to reoccupy the Rhineland.

become a major power again by securing British co-operation, which is why I constantly sought gradual *rapprochement* through practical co-operation.

'I and others were totally opposed to actions that might precipitate military confrontation with Britain and France. Despite this counsel, Hitler was utterly convinced that Britain and France wouldn't lift a finger to oppose conquests in eastern Europe.'

For the first time, Neurath saw that Hitler was ready to launch a series of wars he was confident could be waged with impunity:

'What Hitler said at that meeting in November 1937 knocked the bottom out of the whole foreign policy I had consistently pursued, the policy of employing only peaceful means. I could only view my task as destroyed. Had Hitler not lost patience and replaced my previously peaceful policy with one of force, I'm convinced all remaining questions could have been solved.'

Following the fateful meeting, Neurath admitted to his daughter Winifred: 'I fear now there will be a war.' He was conscious of increasing isolation and powerlessness, and repeatedly informed his family that he was considering resigning. 'I would gladly hang my cloak on the nail,' he said, but he did not.

When, on 14 January 1938, Hitler revealed to two Polish leaders, Josef Beck and Josef Lipski, his determination to invade Austria and Czechoslovakia, Neurath warned him: 'I cannot be associated with an aggressive policy that must inevitably lead to a new world war.' When Hitler strode away without replying, Neurath offered to resign, but the following month — at the 2 February celebration of his sixty-fifth birthday and fortieth anniversary in the foreign service — Hitler attended a ceremony to honour him as a great patriot.

He presented Neurath at the reception with a large oil painting, of the Emperor Constantine's tomb!

Turning to Winifred von Mackensen, who was beside her father, Hitler confided: 'You know, this man's like a father to me. I can't let him go. I need him for foreign affairs.' A few weeks later, whilst still assuring Neurath that he wanted him at his side, Hitler advised him that he had appointed Joachim von Ribbentrop as Foreign Minister.

'What else could I have expected from a man like that?' Neurath later commented in Spandau.

Baroness von Neurath told friends at the time that her husband was through with public life, but within a week he was back in Berlin, at Hitler's request, to become President of a newly announced Secret Cabinet Council composed of five cabinet ministers and the three commanders-in-chief of the armed forces. The Council was Göring's idea to divert attention from the military crisis and save Neurath's prestige at home and abroad. The alleged aim of the Council was to tender 'guidance in the conduct of foreign policy'. The Goebbels propaganda machine made it sound an impressive super-cabinet and that Neurath's appointment to it was promotion. The Secret Cabinet Council never existed.

Although present in Munich in September 1938 when Britain's Prime Minister Neville Chamberlain secured Hitler's signature on the notorious 'peace in our time' declaration, Neurath's influence was waning until Hitler brought him out of cold storage to make him Protector of Bohemia and Moravia.

'I had terrible misgivings about taking the job,' Neurath confessed to his fellow Spandau inmates, 'and only did so because Hitler said my appointment to the post would reassure Britain and France that he didn't want to pursue a policy hostile to Czechoslovakia.

'The end of Czechoslovakia proved to be the beginning of the end of Hitler's Germany. And to think that the day Hacha [Czechoslovakia's President] handed his country to us on a plate, Hitler rushed into his office and embraced his secretaries, shouting: "This is the greatest day of my life! I shall go down in history as the greatest German!" He went berserk.'

In early 1942 Neurath returned to Germany from his Prague post. He was in Berlin later in the year following news from his son Constantin, who was diplomatic adviser specializing in Italian and African affairs to General Rommel in Africa. After discussing the deteriorating course of the war with his son, who had returned home on sick leave, Neurath was sure the war was lost. His warnings were ignored.

His counsel was later far more appreciated in Spandau gaol, for it was to him that the other six came with their problems. Dönitz, who hardly knew the Baron before his imprisonment, confided in him completely. One morning as they filed into the garden, Dönitz could hardly contain himself until the opportunity arose to talk privately with Neurath as they tended the huge plot of potatoes.

'I have heard some disgraceful news in a letter from my wife,' began the Grand Admiral. 'She tells me that all she is getting is the pension of a *Kapitän zur See*, which is really shocking considering my responsibilities. I became the highest commanding officer of the navy at the most critical time of the war. As a Reichs President, I had the thankless task of bringing the war to a finish, and now all the Government can give me is a captain's pension for my wife because they say I owe my promotion beyond that rank to Hitler.

'Without the existence of the Third Reich I would still have become an Admiral; and according to the old regulations from the Kaiser's days, Field-Marshals and Grand Admirals could not be pensioned at all. They were entitled to full pay until the end of their lives. The nation has the right to investigate every high soldier from the following viewpoints: was he actively responsible for the outbreak of the 1939 war and did he, once the war started, do everything as a soldier to win it?

'What is now happening is a deliberate insult. Nor do I intend to waive my salary as Reichs President for the month of May 1945. When I get out of this sanatorium I will attend to all this,' concluded Dönitz angrily.

Neurath calmed him, suggesting that he could ask his lawyer to investigate the pension arrangements with a view to receiving an increase.

The prisoners all usually avoided discussing matters concerning their families in order to retain some measure of privacy, but on rare occasions the barriers dropped, and one of them would raise a worrying family problem. Their past and possible future were frequent topics. The Russian Director tried to forbid them talking in the garden and insist on them walking singly, but the other Directors disagreed.

'We're in here largely because optimism is an incurable military disease,' commented Neurath. 'The mad military ambitions of Hitler and Göring have a lot to answer for.' He considered Göring, whom he usually called 'the fat one', a vicious bully and an upstart.

'He was a lazy, selfish coward and an irresponsible dope-addict,' said Speer.

Schirach laughed. 'Remember how furious he was with me over my Nuremberg confession that I brought up our youngsters to have faith in a man who murdered millions? Göring called me a fool, a traitor, a degenerate youth leader whom nobody would listen to in a few decades when all the democrats were done for. But with my statement I put an end to any flowering of a Hitler legend.'

To which Dönitz imperiously replied: 'I regard it as wrong that individual Germans should be constantly indulging, in the name of the whole German people, in public self-accusations and confessions of guilt. That sort of thing does not win for us the respect of other nations. The assumption that any one people is morally worse than other peoples is, in itself, a false premise.'

Speer, who was often accused by Dönitz and Schirach of disloyalty to the Führer, added: 'The nightmare of many a man that one day nations could be dominated by technical means was all but realized in Hitler's system. But the people of Germany will come to despise and condemn Hitler as the proven author of her misery.'

'One cannot condemn Hitler for holding out to the last,' Schirach interjected.

The discussion was brought back to earth by Funk: 'When people ask why we didn't get rid of Hitler ourselves, they overlook the fact that the Third Reich's early years brought us a significant economic upswing. Admittedly, this might have been because of our rearmament, but the abolition of the humiliating clauses of the Versailles Treaty increased our national unity and enthusiasm.'

Neurath commented: 'It never ceased to amaze me how the world let us get away with so much — dating right back to the 1934 June blood bath which, although viewed with international disgust, was regarded as our internal affair and not warranting intervention or influence from other countries. It was even more incredible that Britain and France did not act when we reintroduced conscription, despite the Versailles Treaty forbidding this unless it was internationally approved.'

Always the realist, Funk said: 'We're really all in here because we indulged in playing follow-my-leader games too much. We love impressive leaders, but there are three kinds of leaders — those interested in the flock; those interested in the fleece, and those who are only interested in themselves. Our Führer was the latter type and it suited us all to follow him, and his orders. The basic trouble is that most Germans believe in obeying orders, even bad ones. I remember when a fire almost destroyed an upper-floor Berlin restaurant. Flames made escape by the staircase impossible. When the fire brigade managed to lower all the diners and staff to the ground, a newspaper reporter asked one of the survivors:

"'What did you do when you saw the place was ablaze?"

"'We sounded the alarm.'"

"'But what did you do when the flames started to spread?'"

"'We all retreated to the corner of the restaurant furthest from the flames.'"

"'But what did you do then?'"

"'We awaited orders.'"

Early in 1953 Hess confided in Neurath: 'My wife needs an operation and I have advised her to go to a good nature healer. I can't remember his name just now, but I have told her that some of my men will remember him. He is just the fellow she should see for what is ailing her. I think I am wise to advise a nature healer; even the best pathological institutes can make mistakes. Perhaps you will just laugh at my beliefs, but nevertheless I know I am right.' Hess recalled that he had often been ragged about his faith in nature cures.

'No, I certainly don't find your suggestion amusing,' said Neurath; 'homoeopathic treatment has helped my high blood pressure and my heart condition, but, in any case, just believing something will help does one good.' Hess, having shared some of his worries, moved off to plant sunflowers all over the place, to the disgust of the others, who accused him of endangering their 'agricultural productivity'.

Neurath was not on such amenable terms with Hess during earlier years. Their paths had often crossed, for example in connection with German-speaking communities living abroad. As Hitler's deputy and Party secretary, Hess attempted to monopolize that aspect of foreign policy. The Baron had to compete with individuals such as Göring, Goebbels, and Hess, who constantly sought to meddle in foreign affairs, until he was driven to protest to Hitler: 'The uncontrolled activity abroad of irresponsible Party functionaries who are frequently totally inexperienced in the realm of foreign policy has already delivered many setbacks to our efforts among Germans abroad.'

Hess also interfered with Neurath's work when a Führer decree of 25 September 1935 made all appointments initially subject to Hess's approval. As a result of this, and of Nuremberg laws issued a few days previously that deprived Jews of citizenship, Neurath knew he could no longer retain Jewish officials in his Ministry. Two of his closest advisers on European affairs — Gerhard Kopke, Minister-Director of his West European desk, and Minister-Director Meyer, of the Russian and East European division — had to go. He could not easily replace them as they had been the principal designers of the policy to which he had adhered. Hitler accused him of 'protecting scoundrels and traitors'.

Throughout years when he was answerable to Hitler, and even to Hess, Neurath's career was confirmation that in politics good intentions, vague conceptions, and readiness to concede can be fatal. For years in Spandau, however, he failed to recognize the true basis of his own failure and guilt as a war criminal. Expounding the art of diplomacy to fellow prisoners, this diplomat, who had compromised too often and too much, asserted:

'A diplomat must know his own mind and accept the consequences of his own tactics. Foreign policies must be guided by principles which experience and history have demonstrated to be sound. Diplomacy has two key ingredients. First is the strategic plan and, second, the execution of it. Statesmen are responsible for formulating policy, whilst its execution is usually left to the diplomats. Diplomats really require every virtue but should at least possess confidence-inspiring integrity. They also need to be knowledgeable enough to have the ability to forecast possible consequences, and a sense of reality is crucial. Unrealistic policies can trigger appallingly destructive forces. In diplomacy as in every other enterprise, luck seems to run in cycles.'

Everyone stopped to listen in Spandau when Neurath recalled the old days, appreciating that he was known in many countries and once moved in exalted circles. He always represented the Nazis at events outside Germany and attended the funeral of King George V on their behalf.

Despite the ban on newspapers the seven managed to learn something about what was happening in the world outside. Neurath was greatly affected by the news of the death of Queen Mary. That day he had a severe heart attack. When he had recovered, and for many days afterwards, he could talk of nothing else but the royal lady with whom he and his wife had grown up.

'When I was a boy,' he recalled, 'I remember the Princess Elisabeth von Teck arriving with her daughter Mary at Ludwigsburg Castle [near Stuttgart]. I can still see the old Princess wearing what had just become the latest fashion, a tailor-made costume of black barathea, which buttoned right down the bodice with a hundred pearl buttons.

'The Princess was very large and buxom, and I remember the girls in the castle trying to guess the exact number of buttons on her bodice. She took a keen interest in the young ladies' dancing lessons in the great hall at Ludwigsburg, but Mary was unable to take part because of a bereavement she had not long suffered by the death of her fiancé, the Duke of Clarence. She was dressed entirely in black, and her appearance, together with the fact that she had lost a sweetheart at that early age, made her, in the eyes of many, a romantically tragic figure.

'My father was Lord Chamberlain to the King of Württemberg, and I was accordingly presented to Mary. But for my father and I, there might never have been a Queen Mary to rule England for so long. Late one evening, when I was seventeen, on arriving at Ludwigsburg Castle we were horrified to see the flicker of fire from one of the castle bedrooms. We rushed to the room and burst in to find the curtains ablaze from a petrol lamp and young Mary, asleep, unaware of her danger. We roused and escorted her to safety and then returned to put out the flames. Castle officials agreed that, but for the fortunate discovery of the fire, Mary might have been burned to death.'

Years later, the Baron, who married Marie Moser von Filseck of Württemberg, met Mary again in London. It was at a reception held by King George V and the Queen at Buckingham Palace early in 1930, soon after Neurath had presented his credentials as Reichs President Hindenburg's Ambassador.

'All the gentlemen at the reception were presented first,' said Neurath, telling the story to Speer, 'and when it came to my turn, Queen Mary exclaimed, "Surely it is not little Konstantin!"

'Later, it was the turn of the ladies of the diplomatic corps to be presented; and when my wife approached, Queen Mary cried, "Manny Moser! you are not an ambassador's wife!" delighted to discover a friend of the old Württemberg days. After that we saw a great deal of the King and Queen, paying regular but unofficial visits to the Palace.'

The best-liked anecdote Neurath told of royal days past was the story of Queen Mary and the apples:

'One day, when I was Ambassador in London, a large parcel arrived from the *Bürgermeister* of our home town in Ludwigsburg. The accompanying letter stated that the *Bürgermeister* had read in a local newspaper that Queen Mary was personally helping her grand-daughter Elizabeth with her German lessons. So he was pleased to offer a box of Württemberg apples to Queen Mary, the teacher from Württemberg, so that she might give one to her pupil whenever she did well with her lessons.

'After reading the note, we opened the box, an ordinary wooden crate, and my wife took out one or two of the apples to see what they were like. They looked much the worse for wear, having shrivelled considerably during their journey to England. The box was repacked, a note enclosed by us apologizing for their condition and my wife took them personally to Buckingham Palace by car.

'A Palace footman carried the box ahead of my wife into Queen Mary's suite, and, on being received, my wife explained the purpose of the gift. When the box was opened, Queen Mary read the *Bürgermeister*'s note, unpacked the apples, and holding one up said: "For my pupil, oh no! I'll eat these apples from the old homeland myself!"'

Albert Speer, looking ever towards the future, drew hungrily on Neurath's long experience as a diplomat. On opportune occasions he questioned him about his former life, and invariably the Baron had a story to tell that was worth hearing. There was, for instance, the weekend party at Chequers during Anglo-German political negotiations. The Neuraths, accompanied by German Chancellor Dr Bruening and his Foreign Minister, were the guests of Prime Minister Ramsay MacDonald and his daughter Sheila.

'We usually avoided English weekend parties because everyone was expected to play bridge, and we didn't play, preferring to spend our Sundays at home or in the Embassy garden,' Neurath told Speer.

'It was a pleasant weekend with plenty of invigorating conversation. George Bernard Shaw was one of the guests, but it remained unforgettable to my wife and me for an entirely different reason. Ramsay offered to show us round, and naturally we were interested to see what Chequers was really like. All went well until Ramsay suddenly pulled open the drawer of a chest in a room we were looking at and there staring up at us was the life-mask of Oliver Cromwell.

'My wife, as a diplomat's wife, knew how to control her feelings and merely said, "Very interesting", although she was nearly sick with horror.

'Perhaps if I had listened to Queen Mary, I wouldn't be in Spandau today,' said Neurath on one occasion. 'She had a premonition that my career was going awry when I was called back to Germany from London by Hindenburg. The day after I received these instructions, the Italian Ambassador arranged to chaperon my wife at a reception at Buckingham Palace. When their car drew up in the courtyard, a chamber-lain was waiting to tell my wife that he had orders to take her straight to the Queen.'

'Queen Mary at that moment was standing surrounded by a large group of people, and a new ambassador was just being introduced to her, but seeing my wife arrive the Queen surprised the ambassador by hurrying over to her. "Manny, your husband must not go back to Germany now; he would do so much better here as an ambassador," the Queen said.

'Manny explained that I was not willingly going because I, too, felt I should remain in London, but that I had given Hindenburg an undertaking to return at any time he needed me as Foreign Minister. Now the call had come.

'I returned to London a little later to put my affairs in order and my wife and I received an invitation to a farewell luncheon at Buckingham Palace. It took place in the Queen's private apartments and only the King and Queen and my wife and I were present. There was one servant only to bring in the food, and the Queen actually served the meal. So great were the portions she began to heap on our plates that my wife laughingly cried, "Too much! Too much!"

'Ignoring the protest, the Queen continued what she was doing and said, "You eat what I give you in my house." When the time came to say goodbye I left knowing that the Queen was convinced my career had taken a turn for the worse.'

And so it proved. Neurath, the man who settled once too often with his conscience, returned to Germany, Hindenburg, Hitler and Spandau.

One morning in September 1952, Funk was very much smitten with an idea that had occurred to him. He first approached Schirach, who was busy sowing cabbages; then he moved on to Raeder, visiting each of the six in turn to explain his scheme.

As a former journalist, Funk was fully alive to the power of the press and had conceived the idea of smuggling a petition out of Spandau to the Pope with a combined plea from all seven for help in securing a remission of their sentences. Funk had even drawn up the document; and he told the others that it was also his intention, after the Pope had seen it, to have a further copy made for America, where he wanted it placed with *Time* and *Life* magazines.

After the initial discussion in the garden, the document itself was secretly handed on from cell to cell for each of the prisoners to study before a decision could be reached in the garden the next day.

Immediately, when work began outside the following morning, Funk began to ask what the others thought of his scheme. Schirach, Raeder and Hess were ready to sign; Neurath held his hand because he had not yet heard the opinions of Dönitz and Speer. He found they did not approve and they told Neurath the reasons for their objections.

'We consider a petition to the Pope directly from us to be in bad taste and far more likely to react against us for openly defying Spandau regulations forbidding any political contact with the outside world,' said Speer. 'It is not that Dönitz and I fear any punishment for such defiance, but we are convinced it is bad diplomacy. It is far more effective that our wives, families and friends should make such appeals on our behalf.'

Said Dönitz: 'In this matter, Speer's answer is mine. I agree entirely with his views.'

Neurath, as 'chairman', told Funk to destroy the petition.

'Don't be disappointed,' Speer consoled Funk; 'it is far better to accept and resign ourselves to our punishment and captivity. The problems of captivity always remain the same from the human point of view. Many prisoners, in spite of spiritual depression, later recover their capacity to survive and live, and this comforts me to some extent.'

The seeds of another scheme were also sown in the garden of Spandau. Every day the cells and their contents were searched. For years nothing was found, until, one morning, a certain object was discovered under Schirach's bed. It was round in shape and tightly wrapped in paper.

The Russian warders conducting the search demanded to know what it was, but Schirach said he was mystified himself. One of the warders bent to pick it up.

'Don't touch it,' warned his companion, 'you never know what it might be.'

They agreed it would be wiser to call the Chief Warder, who in turn sent for a duty officer. Examining the object carefully in the glare of a spotlight, the officer decided to unwrap it. It could have been a booby-trap explosive, but there was only one way to find out. Slowly he untwisted the top of the paper to reveal a 'horse apple' — at least it looked like one and had the recognizable odour. But the officer knew that similar booby-trap tricks had been used by saboteurs during the war and thought chances should not be taken.

Still partly wrapped, the object was very gently transported to nearby cell No. 28, where it remained with a guard until given a preliminary inspection by all four Prison Directors, after which it was transported to the prison secretariat. After more detailed examination, it proved to be what it undoubtedly looked and smelt like: a 'horse apple'. How it got into Schirach's cell was a mystery that had to be solved, so a four-Power conference was called and the dung was the centre-piece of the table during the discussion.

It took several days to discover the truth, and it was found that the mystery began with Speer requesting and getting a load of horse manure for the garden from the nearby British barracks. A warder decided to present hypochondriac Funk with a 'nature cure' for some of his ailments. Smuggling the object into Funk's cell, the warder told him: 'It's a rare plant that's supposed to be a marvellous cure for bronchitis. Just rub it on your chest three times a day.' When the delighted Funk unwrapped the package to find the smelly 'horse apple' he fell about laughing. It was his style of joke.

'Put it in Schirach's cell,' Funk suggested. 'He's full of the stuff anyway with his high-and-mighty aristocratic airs, so he'd be absolutely right for it.'

Welcoming the idea of bringing Schirach down a peg, the warder obliged and transferred it.

Following thorough inquiries, the American Director confessed to the other Directors that one of his warders had been responsible for the incident. He apologized, and that was the official end to the 'Spandau bomb plot mystery', but the four-Power conference room and the garden were linked in yet another investigation in January 1953, which became known as the 'great chocolate inquiry'. The Baron was the culprit. One day as he was working in the garden, he slipped a hand into his jacket pocket, fumbled for a moment, put a hand to his mouth, then slipped something back into the pocket. A watchful warder, seeing the movements, rushed to Neurath, yelling:

'Spit out whatever is in your mouth!'

Neurath did so. It was a piece of chocolate, and from his pocket the warder extracted the remainder of a bar. The Chief Warder was summoned, the chocolate confiscated, and Neurath questioned as to its source. He would give no explanation.

Wrapped in a piece of paper, the chocolate was taken to the four-Power conference room and placed in the middle of the table to await the four Spandau Directors.

Secret snapshot of the drab "Four-Power conference room" in Spandau. It is here the four prison Directors meet.

The Directors arrived, and the chocolate inquiry began. Its terms of reference: chocolate was a luxury; luxuries were forbidden to the seven men of Spandau; therefore the chocolate must have been smuggled into the prison; which meant a breach of security.

For fourteen days the 'evidence' lay locked away in the conference room cupboard. At each meeting of the Directors to hear fresh information, the chocolate was brought from the cupboard and placed on the table while the officers deliberated. Every warder, every member of the prison staff, was questioned, but the mystery of the chocolate was never solved.

A fourteen-day inquiry into a piece of chocolate seems fantastic and farcical; but to the prison authorities the chocolate could have been a phial of poison or a gun. The Baron was warned that repetition of this offence would result in a drastic curtailment of privileges.

'I appreciate the seriousness of the matter from your point of view,' said Neurath to the officer reprimanding him; adding, 'If only chocolate had been the one weakness in my life!'

Neurath admitted that much of his past attitude found expression in a saying that became well known in Germany: 'God made a great mistake when he limited the intelligence of man but did nothing to limit his stupidity.'

9: A NAVAL ENCOUNTER

Throughout their years in gaol together the Grand Admirals of Spandau, Erich Raeder and Karl Dönitz, were at war with each other.

Erich Raeder, first Grand Admiral since Tirpitz,[7] was sacked by Hitler in January 1943 from his post of Commander-in-Chief of the German Navy. He was replaced by the newly promoted Grand Admiral Dönitz, his critic for many years and the rival chiefly responsible for undermining his authority. The demoting of Raeder was politely wrapped up in an announcement that he had been appointed Inspector-General and would remain Hitler's principal adviser on naval affairs.

In his order of the day, Raeder announced: 'I have been relieved of my office because of the state of my health.' The truth was that U-boat chief Dönitz had torpedoed Raeder's career, and everyone in the German High Command knew it.

Throughout the remaining convulsive death-throes of the war, Raeder and Dönitz sedulously avoided each other; they were never present together at the many naval conferences that took place in the presence of Hitler. Only at Nuremberg, where they faced charges of unrestricted naval warfare, did they find themselves in each other's company.

Raeder, for fifteen years in command of a German Navy he had helped to build, was, at the age of seventy, sentenced to life imprisonment. Dönitz, because his spectacular promotion was manoeuvred during and not prior to hostilities, was not accused with others of being a partner to the deliberate

---

[7] Tirpitz directed the submarine campaign against Allied shipping in World War I until his dismissal in 1915.

planning of an aggressive war. He received the lightest sentence of the seven men of Spandau: ten years. The two men who hated each other were transported together to a gaol where they could escape neither from their consciences nor from the presence of one another.

A picture from Raeder's photo album showing him as a young officer aboard the Kaiser's yacht.

Shortly after his arrival Raeder addressed a petition to the Allied Control Council. It asked for his life sentence to be changed to death by shooting:

> I prefer a soldierly death sentence to languishing in prison for the rest of my life. As I am seventy and my powers of bodily resistance are limited, life imprisonment could not last long for me. I should regard shooting as a lighter sentence, and, in the long run, it would be for my relatives a blessed release. This plea in no way means that I, in any way, confess my guilt.

Raeder pointed out that Article 29 of the Statute permitted the Control Council to lighten sentence, though not allowing any increase in severity. 'I would regard such a change in my sentence as an act of mercy,' he concluded.

He was not kept waiting long for an answer. The petition was rejected. To spend his last years in Spandau seemed all that was left for him. Erich Hans Albert Raeder, the naval counterpart of a traditional bullet-headed Prussian officer, whose destiny it had been to tend the dying embers of Kaiser Wilhelm's dream of a German Imperial Navy ruling the seas, became the custodian of the books in the prison library. He kept them in the disciplined order expected of a well-trained sailor.

The prison library was authorized to provide books 'according to the reasonable desire, character and aspirations of the prisoner'. It was a converted cell in the inner block. Singly, at specific times during the afternoon leisure period, the other six prisoners came there for something new to read. In the prisoners' early Spandau days, wives and relatives were allowed to send books, but the privilege was stopped because every volume required close examination for possible hidden messages, a security check involving too much time and labour for prison personnel.

It was decided to retain a certain number of books, including fifty volumes from Raeder's own library — among them several editions of the New Testament — but an additional arrangement was made. The men were asked to indicate what books they preferred to read, and the Spandau district's public library was instructed to stock the shelves accordingly. The choice was mainly highbrow: appreciations of painters and paintings, seventeenth-century German history, and translations of French and Spanish works. Magazines were *verboten* and the only newspaper allowed was a Protestant journal that dealt wholly with religious topics.

All seven prisoners helped to keep the library clean, but the books were Raeder's sole responsibility, and a book was as precious to him as a pet cat is to an old woman. In the navy he had been noted for the disconcerting habit of poking about in galleys and crew quarters to satisfy himself that everything under his command was shipshape. He was feared, too, in outlying bases under his discipline, for he would drop in unexpectedly, and could spot a slovenly uniform or an untidy flower-box in a barrack window a mile away. As a librarian Raeder was just as meticulous. His favourite saying was, 'A disorderly ship reflects incapability.' If a book was damaged, or a single page misused, he verbally disciplined the offender. If any warder disturbed his carefully organized and indexed shelves, the otherwise quietly spoken and respectful prisoner became a raging pint-sized martinet complaining bitterly of 'unwarranted interference'.

It was always possible to obtain a special book any of the prisoners wished to read. Works on philosophy were greatly in demand. Raeder, himself a doctor of philosophy, was also a keen amateur scientist. His *bête noire*, Dönitz, preferred historical biographies and loved adventure stories, a taste that Raeder sniffed at with contempt.

'I enjoy the books of Jack London, especially stories about dogs,' admitted Dönitz, who had always kept a wolfhound of his own. 'Dogs and little children are the best creatures in the world,' added the man who sank fifteen million tons of shipping during the last war. 'I read intensively for weeks on end until my head is full; then I stop for a fortnight and that gives me a chance to think things over before resuming once more.'

Dönitz read and re-read Forester's adventures of Captain Horatio Hornblower. 'These are books my little grandson Peter should read so that he doesn't become a landlubber,' Dönitz told Speer, advising him to try the stories.

Speer lost himself as much as possible in books, seeking in historical reading parallels with current times. 'During my first three years here I read over five hundred books, from Greek drama to the famous plays and novels of contemporary literature,' he said. 'At least a hundred of them were on the history of art and culture, and seventy of them dealt with the Renaissance — there's a subject worth studying.' Pausing, he then said reflectively, 'It took me three weeks to get through Tolstoy's *War and Peace*, which is terribly long, but I must admit I liked some of it quite well. I have to confess, however, that most of what I read I forget very quickly. I've no intention of becoming a mental acrobat, but anyhow I do get something out of it, whether I remember or not.'

In his reading, Speer found an answer for Raeder's frequently repeated defence that whatever he did for the Third Reich was done under the Führer's orders. Raeder insisted: 'A soldier's first duty is to obey the orders of his military superior, otherwise he could suffer severe punishment, even be shot, for refusing to carry out orders.'

To which Speer countered: 'I read in an English history book something that blows that contention to pieces. The commander of the guards at the trial and execution of King Charles I was tried for treason and murder. The commander's defence was that all he did "was as a soldier, by the command of his superior officer whom he must obey or die". The court dismissed this with the declaration: "When the command is traitorous, then the obedience to that command is also traitorous." And that was said more than three centuries ago.

Subordinates obeying an order are liable to punishment as an accomplice if they knew the order involved an act that constituted a crime.'

Schirach's reading tastes matched his ideals. He cared most for books on the ancient Greeks, music, and literary criticism. Once, as a diversion, he read a book on the love-life of snails. 'Having now read about the habits of these vineyard snails that taste so well,' he said, 'I feel ashamed at having eaten so many of these amorous beings without considering their feelings.'

Ex-Reichsbank Minister Funk particularly liked works dealing with the intricacies of finance and economy, but also read widely on such subjects as world history, psychology and philosophy, although his favourite possession was a book on chess sent to him by his wife in 1949. He tried out master-moves over and over again.

With his failing eyesight Neurath restricted his reading to the Bible and historical works, but librarian Raeder had a difficult task trying to satisfy Hess's ever-changing tastes. These switched from astronomy to history and from medicine to travel. Returning a copy of a book called *Nearest to the Pole*, Hess commented: 'You know, Grand Admiral' — he still called them all by their old titles — 'this book contains very interesting information on the Eskimos. Young marriageable pairs change partners several times until they find they are suited. Such marriages then usually last for ever. Very reasonable! This kind of arrangement corresponds to our Bavarian probationary marriages.' Saying which, Hess departed with the first volume of *War and Peace* so that he could study his ideal, Napoleon, leaving Raeder fussing over his library shelves.

Raeder had once been a swashbuckling figure in a heavily padded, wide-lapelled uniform, set off by a gold dagger of ornate design. In gaol he became a mild-mannered bibliographer; and it was hard to realize that this blue-eyed man of just five feet six, once so corrupted by power that he became a law unto himself, could have been anything but a schoolmaster — which was, indeed, his father's profession. If Raeder felt he had to explain himself he did so in terms that many Germans readily understood and endorsed: the means always justified the ends. On the wooden table in his cell was a picture of Christ, which was given to him by the French chaplain; close at hand were copies of two of his favourite quotations. One of them, 'Quickly march through life; act and don't think too long; don't rely on others; don't ever expect gratitude', stood on his desk at the German Admiralty from 1926 to 1943. The other, 'Our fate is in God's hands; to know this is our greatest strength', he had kept in the privacy of his home, also suitably framed.

Although ostensibly religious, Raeder joined with Dönitz and Schirach in objecting to sermons delivered by the French chaplain, Casalis. They did not like their consciences being disturbed.

The French chaplain was often in trouble with the Soviet Directors who were suspicious or contemptuous of religious worship. At one meeting of the Prison's Directors the Soviet representative complained: 'During last Sunday's religious service, the French Pastor Casalis spoke with the prisoners about the atomic bomb, by which he offended anew against the Allied Prison Regulations.' At another meeting the Soviet Director questioned post-church conversations of the chaplain with prisoners, so the chaplain formally requested permission to talk to inmates individually after services. The Russian's answer was: 'The Pastor was given the responsibility of conducting religious services in the prison and he should conduct services at the appointed times. I further consider that in view of the standard of education of prisoners Number 1 and 5 [Schirach and Speer] it is unnecessary to give lectures on religious subjects. I am of the opinion that any religious instruction should be given during the time allowed for church services.'

Morning and evening Raeder read daily Bible quotations from the calendar that hung from the wall above his cell bed. This thin-lipped and devout Protestant was always a man with two religions — the other was the German Navy.

He liked to recall his days as a young officer in the Imperial Navy and how, while he was navigator of the Kaiser's yacht *Hohenzollern*, he came to meet Franz Hipper, 'the agent of my destiny'. Hipper, who was to play a significant role at the great Battle of Jutland, and later commanded the fleet, apparently took a liking to Raeder, who became his favourite junior officer. 'When I become an admiral, I'll make you my chief of staff,' Hipper boomed. He kept his word. Six years later, in 1916, when the German High Seas Fleet headed into one of the greatest encounters in naval history at Jutland, Vice-Admiral von Hipper's chief of staff on board the flagship *Lutzow* was Captain Erich Raeder. The *Lutzow* commanded the scouting force ordered to make contact with the British units, and during the ensuing devastating forty-eight hours was so severely mauled that she had to be abandoned. It was Raeder who was responsible for getting his chief transferred to another battle cruiser. He never forgot the power of the Royal Navy's guns, and continued to declare, 'Britain's strength at sea should never be underestimated.'

It was a bitter blow to him when the remnants of Germany's sea power, seventy-four ships in number, were scuttled at Scapa Flow on 21 June 1919. From that moment he became imbued with a single burning idea: Germany's navy must be rebuilt, and Germany must become once more a great sea power.

On his appointment as Chief of Naval Construction in 1928 Raeder became adept in piloting Germany's rearmament programme through the gaps in the Versailles Treaty. One of the answers to the treaty limitations on naval strength was the 'pocket battleship', which Raeder had built to his own specifications. By having ship plates welded or riveted, he tossed overboard a substantial part of the weight and the idea that the construction of battleships was impervious to change.

In other directions, too, he was as tricky as a fox. In arming new ships he was shrewd enough to realize that the treaty restricted the calibre, but not the length of the guns. Germany had turned over to Nazism by the time Raeder had added the *Deutschland* (later renamed *Lutzow*) to his pocket battleships, and he had two more on the stocks as well: the *Graf Spee* and the *Scheer*. Hitler was soon clamouring for more big ships and long guns, and in time the *Bismarck*, *Scharnhorst*, *Gneisenau*, and *Tirpitz* were added to the fleet.

In Spandau, Raeder the sailor and Neurath the diplomat of the old school often discussed past decisions and tactical errors. Neurath was three years the elder.

'At the beginning, when Hitler and I first met, he told me that he had no intention of challenging Britain's predominant position at sea,' Raeder reminisced. 'Hitler was anxious, he said, to put this on record by negotiating a special agreement between the two countries concerning the respective strengths of their fleets. In this way he hoped to show Britain clearly that a clash between the two fleets would never enter his mind. He was thinking of a ratio of perhaps three ships to one. I agreed with the idea. The idea of a future clash of arms with the United States appeared equally out of the question.'

It was Raeder's job to keep an eye on the development of the navy as a whole, including political and financial factors, ship-building, armaments, harbours, and docks. The Commander-in-Chief of his submarine arm, Captain Dönitz, favoured a highly mobile, powerful medium-size submarine, which could be built in large numbers within the tonnage limits accepted in the Anglo-German Naval Agreement. Such subs would be able to attack convoys in groups, or 'wolf packs', as recommended by Dönitz from 1936 onwards. The 'packs' proved to be a significant advance on the submarine tactics of World War I and became largely responsible for the great successes of Hitler's submarines.

Whatever Nuremberg did to Raeder it certainly did not strip him of his old beliefs or his contempt for the rules of warfare. As ruthless as the next Nazi, he considered that unrestricted attacks of submarines on neutral and unarmed merchant ships needed no explanation other than that provided by the so-called exigencies of war. Humanity did not enter into it at any time.

Throughout his career he had always disliked consultations and the routine of the round-table conference. Whenever he could, he gave orders without reference to anyone, and this was the situation in the early days of his association with Hitler. In the beginning Hitler thought highly of him. He was answerable only to the Führer.

'The trouble with you, Erich, was that you were never accessible,' Neurath, his closest friend in Spandau, told him one day in the garden. 'Holding yourself aloof from Hitler as you did lost you a great opportunity of convincing him that you knew what you were doing and that your strategy was correct. Another mistake you made was your failure to come to terms with Göring. Surely you must have realized how important he was to you in securing the air support you needed?'

Raeder was never happy in his relationship with anyone other than those subordinate to him, a fact well known to other high-ranking Nazis. 'How could one get sense or cooperation out of Göring?' he demanded angrily. 'He was completely unmanageable, vain, selfish, and an arrant liar. It was his fault entirely that we failed to invade Britain in 1940. His infantile delight in pompous ceremonial and the luxury with which he surrounded himself set a very bad example to his subordinates.'

Raeder's association with Göring — personally and officially — was bad. The Reichsmarschall's failure to acknowledge the necessity for a naval air arm was one of the sorest issues between them. Raeder explained to Neurath: 'I told Hitler that I could not guarantee the success of landing operations unless we had full air cover and that it was necessary for at least part of the Luftwaffe to be placed under my command. Göring wouldn't hear of it. He couldn't bear that anyone should have even temporary authority over a single squadron of his air force, and the pity of it was that Hitler backed him up. Hitler let this wonderful opportunity slip through his fingers, and by late September all hope of an invasion had gone. When it was too late the Führer realized that he had allowed Göring to persuade him against his better judgement. Göring's influence was enormous and disastrous, and Hitler never succeeded in restraining him.'

The first shadow over Raeder's professional career had come with the defeat of the *Graf Spee* in what was to become known as the Battle of the River Plate. The opportunist Dönitz did not hesitate to knock a few nails in the waiting coffin of his rival whenever he had the chance. On one occasion in talking to the crews of submarines lately returned from duty in the Atlantic he had plenty to say about the wasteful policy of his Commander-in-Chief, and suggested that if the manpower employed in a surface fleet that was suffering from paralysis could be transferred, together with dock facilities, to submarine construction, Germany's strength in underwater craft could be tripled.

As the war went on and the prospect of victory receded, Hitler, no longer buoyant and cocky, could hardly have been less than grateful for a scapegoat as a diversion from mounting reverses and strategic withdrawals that could not be hidden from the Germans. On 30 January 1943, the tenth anniversary of Nazi rule in Germany, the following official proclamation was released to the public:

> The Führer received the Commander-in-Chief of the Navy, Grand Admiral Raeder, at his headquarters today. In recognition and appreciation of his history-making accomplishments in building the new German Navy, and in view of his accomplishments as Commander-in-Chief of the Navy during the Greater German War for Freedom, the Führer has appointed Grand Admiral Raeder Inspector-General of the Navy of the Greater German Reich.

Bluntly, Raeder had been sacked. Nevertheless, for his part in the preparations for, and the ruthless conduct of, aggressive war, the man who had never failed to express his hatred of the British (yet kept a signed photograph of Britain's Admiral Jellicoe on his desk) was sentenced at Nuremberg to imprisonment for life. From his cell, he sent his family an inscription:

> Weep not but thank often,
> Though things do not work out as hoped,
> Much is left to be grateful for.
> God's love is large and rich and
> Though you do not realize it at once — It has no barriers.
> Doubt not if you would keep your sanity.
> Get into line to strengthen the front.
> Though you may not be distinguished from the formation,
> Unity is solidarity, and you are part of it.

An unbending disciplinarian, Raeder ensured that his cell was always tidy and used a number of dusters that he kept in various places. He quickly lost his temper if these were disturbed during the daily searches, yet never complained of the crippling arthritis from which he suffered. His dentures were his biggest annoyance. He had a set of false teeth made in America with intricate springs and bridgework; 'an engineering masterpiece', he believed. Although his jaws, which were contracted with age, spoiled their balance and fit, Raeder was reluctant to have the dentures replaced.

Despite an operation for hernia in 1949, he found it necessary to wear a truss and was awakened earlier than the other prisoners to give him time to adjust it. He liked to spend a few minutes on deep-breathing exercises, watched his weight carefully, and enjoyed working in the garden. 'Visitors are always amazed by my appearance,' he boasted. 'They can't believe my age. Looking after about twenty strawberry beds, among other things, gives me plenty to do and keeps me fit.'

Until his wife came to Spandau for the first time on 15 March 1950, after she had been freed from Russian imprisonment, Raeder's visitors were Anita, the daughter of his first marriage, and Hans, the son of the second marriage. Hans became the great disappointment and tragedy of his life. 'He could not join the navy because of poor eyesight,' Raeder regretfully explained, 'but he fought with the army in Russia.'

When Hans returned from the war he took up farming, but not being over-strong had to turn to book-keeping and worked for a firm in Lippstadt, where he lived with his mother. In January 1953 Raeder learned that his son was in hospital and dangerously ill with a rare blood disease. His lawyer, Dr Otto Kranzbühler, who had defended him at Nuremberg, informed the German Government of the circumstances. An immediate approach was made to the four-Powers requesting permission, on compassionate grounds, for Raeder to leave Spandau for a couple of days to visit his son.

It was refused. Kranzbühler tried telephoning one of the Directors at Spandau. 'Nothing can be done,' was the reply. The next move was an appeal to US Government officials, and West German Chancellor Konrad Adenauer intervened on Raeder's behalf. Nothing came of this either. On the afternoon of 17 January the prison chaplain entered Raeder's cell as he was finishing a letter to his son.

'Your son...' the visitor began, but it was not necessary to complete the sentence. Raeder knew. He sat on the bed staring at the photograph on the table of his wife and Hans. Life had dealt him his greatest defeat since imprisonment in Spandau.

The German Government suggested that Raeder should be allowed to attend the funeral on 21 January, his wife's birthday. Following refusal of this further request, Kranzbühler called on US High Commissioner Conant.

'It would be impossible to get all four-Powers to agree about this, and we can't start a war over Spandau,' were Conant's final words on the subject. Frau Raeder went to the funeral of her son, and Erich Raeder remained in his cell.

His books, library, and the garden where he could discuss the blunders of the past were all that was left for him. 'If only Hitler had listened, things might have been very different,' he said. 'It was because of our activities in Holland and connections with the Spanish and Finnish navies that we were able to create a basis for building a submarine force despite the Versailles Treaty. In this way it was possible for the first launchings to take place in 1935, immediately Hitler had agreed to the signing of the Anglo-German Naval Treaty in London.

'Submarine crews were at first trained abroad, and later in an anti-submarine division that served as a camouflage for our real purpose.

'In the summer of 1939 the Führer didn't think England would enter the war if we attacked Poland, and a programme of naval expansion was sanctioned by which the construction of a really powerful fleet could be completed by 1944 or 1945. However, as events turned out, the navy was compelled to go into action against the greatest sea power in the world and at a time when we were just beginning to expand.'

Early in 1941 Raeder expressed strong doubts about the value of continued American neutrality to Germany, and advised Hitler that American entry into the war could even prove 'advantageous for the German war effort if Japan thereby became a belligerent on the side of the Axis'. Hitler did not go along with this line and warned Raeder to avoid risking incidents with American ships. The Battle of the Atlantic was at its height, the Allies were not winning it, but American Lend-Lease supplies were still managing to pour into Britain. Raeder told Hitler: 'Our naval commanders cannot be held responsible for a mistake if American ships are hit.'

Raeder pinpointed a day in December 1942 as fateful to Germany's fading prospects. He was given an account of a meeting at which Hitler fulminated against the uselessness of big ships and the lack of ability and daring on the part of older naval officers. The Führer even went so far as to accuse the navy of attacking merchant ships only when it was apparent that there could be no answering fire.

'What I heard', Raeder said, 'convinced me of the futility of reasoning with Hitler. Shortly afterwards I was informed officially that the Führer regarded my ships as nothing but breeding grounds for revolution, idly lying about and lacking any will to go into action. It was made plain to me that it was his irrevocable decision to do away with the High Seas Fleet and put the personnel, weapons, and armour-plating to better use.

'On 6 January 1943 I saw Hitler and warned him that if Germany's large ships were put out of commission the repercussions would be disastrous, not only to our own situation but with respect to all naval strategy everywhere. It would be a victory for our enemies without any effort on their part, and would be viewed as a sign of weakness and lack of comprehension of the supreme importance of naval warfare.

'The removal of our threat from the Atlantic would enable our enemies to concentrate either on settling the Mediterranean situation or massing their forces for a decisive blow against the Japanese fleet. Nothing I said was of any use. By direction of the Führer, as Supreme Commander of the Armed Forces, the German High Seas Fleet ceased to exist.'

Addressing himself to Dönitz in the Spandau garden, Raeder explained:

'Hitler lectured me for about an hour that day and, apart from your submarine arm, couldn't find a good word to say about the German Navy throughout its whole history. His arguments revealed Göring's influence in the background. Our heavy ships, which had always particularly interested him and of which he had once been particularly proud, were now condemned as useless as they needed constant protection both by the Luftwaffe and smaller ships.

'He was obviously trying to offend me personally. When he had finished I asked for permission to speak to him privately. He agreed, and during the discussion that followed I asked him to relieve me of my post as Supreme Commander of the Navy on the grounds that he had just expressed himself as dissatisfied with the effectiveness of the navy under my leadership. As always when he found himself resolutely opposed, he climbed down and stressed that he had not wished to criticize the navy as a whole, but only the capital ships.

'I replied that I was ready to agree that my retirement should take place so that it would cause no disagreeable talk in the navy. He could give me some title that would indicate I was still connected with the navy. Realizing that I was determined to resign, Hitler finally agreed to it and, at his request, I suggested two officers whom I considered suitable to succeed me: Carls [Admiral Carls of Group Command North], and you [Dönitz].

'You were at your Paris headquarters at the time. I telephoned and told you I had tendered my resignation and proposed Carls or you as my successor. You and I were in complete agreement that in the long run the only way to achieve real success against the enemy was with our submarines, though with regard to the importance of surface craft we occasionally disagreed.'

Dönitz said: 'It's possible that Hitler chose me as your successor because, as Flag Officer, Submarines, he expected to find me an ally on the question of getting rid of the capital ships; whereas I persuaded him not to scrap the very big ships, because their withdrawal from service wouldn't have resulted in any appreciable increase in either manpower or material. Hitler was astonished and indignant, but finally accepted it, although reluctantly and with bad grace.'

Oddly enough, if Raeder had had his way he might have escaped his fall and eventual imprisonment. In the spring of 1939, then aged sixty-three, he had occupied his high post for eleven years and he asked Hitler to let him hand over his command to a younger man. The Führer declined, as he did on three further occasions — twice in 1941, and again the following year, when Raeder was advised by his doctor to seek retirement.

He little guessed that one day he would retire to a gaol to spend most of his remaining days.

10: HITLER'S SUCCESSOR

Grand Admiral Dönitz's sentence of ten years made him the shortest-term prisoner in Spandau. To hear him talk of his plans when the gaol opened its gates for him one would have gained the impression that the martial fires within him had long since been damped for ever. Tall, lean, and thin-lipped, the man said to have been chosen by Hitler, at his last gasp, to be President of the Third Reich and Supreme Commander of the Armed Forces confided to anyone who cared to listen the simple programme he allegedly had in mind to end his days in peace and goodwill once he was free. 'I am going to try not to be a nagging old man,' he said. 'Despite my age, my heart is young and certainly young enough to understand youth.'

The Grand Admiral's heart-warming sentiments did not end in mere day-dreaming. 'I want to care for children, orphans, and those in need,' was his plaintive cry. 'I think I shall start a kindergarten, a mixed one for puppies as well as children.'

This belated paternalism was not perhaps as coy as first appeared, when one recalled how he had laboured ruthlessly to add to the world's orphans. In his underground headquarters on the French coast, built to ensure immunity from any stray bomb, wattle-necked Dönitz of the unsmiling mouth, windmill-like ears, and ice-blue eyes directed the most murderous campaign in maritime history. 'Kill and keep on killing,' he exhorted submarine commanders. 'Remember: no survivors. Humanity is a weakness.' Nevertheless he insisted that the Nuremberg verdicts made a mockery of justice; the judging nations, he said, would not have behaved differently from the Germans. 'The British didn't really want to prosecute me, because the Admiralty acknowledged that our navy largely fought a clean war.'

Dönitz in Spandau. A photograph secretly taken outside the entrance from the prison garden.

Radar, and the courage of the men who guarded Britain's lifelines on the sea and from the air, tipped the scales in the momentous battle with the U-boat wolf packs. But in those critical days when Dönitz had stood in the wings and watched the drama being played out under his direction, he was a man with murder in his heart. Neither prison nor the condemnation of the civilized world wrung any radical change in him. Fellow criminals such as Speer, Schirach, and even Funk confessed to the enormity of their offences, but for all his chatter about children and puppies Dönitz remained unrepentant and a dangerous character. He was dangerous because he remained a Nazi by every unnatural instinct; dangerous because prison neither blunted his ambitions nor destroyed his belief that he was ordained to lead the German people back to glory as the master race.

Dönitz's enmity towards Britain, and his refusal to acknowledge Germany's defeat as a salutary lesson from an outraged world, endeared him to what became known as the 'Dönitz Brigade', a powerful and influential organization dedicated to hoisting him into the saddle as the new Führer-cum-saviour. Among its members were no fewer than thirty-six of the Grand Admiral's former U-boat commanders, who contributed their share to a fund expected to be more than useful later on, but which in the meantime helped to pay the expenses of the Dönitz family for every visit to Spandau. The fund was managed by Ahlmann & Company, a bank trading in the old naval city of Kiel; and it was no mere chance that one of its directors happened to be Eberhard Godt, one-time Rear-Admiral and Dönitz's chief of staff and operations.

The Dönitz 'legend' stayed alive in Hamburg, Kiel, Dusseldorf, Munich, and West Berlin. He was *Der Löwe* (The Lion), and true-blue Nazis asked, 'How soon will he be out to lead us the way we want to go?' It was not a question that could be answered with any certainty. There were in fact three possible dates on which Dönitz's sentence could be deemed by the authorities to end: either May or autumn of 1955, or October 1956. It depended on whether Dönitz's sentence was regarded as having begun from the moment of his arrest at Flensburg on 23 May 1945, or in the autumn of the same year when he was transferred to Nuremberg for trial, or in July 1947 when he was taken to Spandau.

A precedent could be said to have been established in the case of a number of German generals who were released early in 1953 from the British zonal prison at Werl on the basis that their sentences began from the time of their arrest rather than from the time of their conviction at Nuremberg. It did not follow that this rule would be applied to the criminals at Spandau, however, and Dr Otto Kranzbühler, lawyer for Dönitz and Raeder, kept trying to clarify the situation regarding Dönitz.

When the largest part of his sentence lay behind him, Dönitz watched the calendar; he knew that, when his time was up, many would be awaiting his return to society as Hitler's successor, ready to back him in a bid for power. Despite the rigid security measures at Spandau — no prison had ever seen their like — it was impossible to achieve complete isolation. The traffic of smuggled letters into the prison enabled Dönitz to interest himself in the activities of the Sozialistiche Reichspartei, a neo-Fascist organization that was banned in January 1953. He could also receive messages from Werner Naumann, the most important Fascist uncovered in Germany since the war, who was anxious to know if Dönitz was prepared to become Head of State in the event of former Nazis securing control of the country. Naumann, State

Secretary in Goebbels's Ministry, was arrested by the British, who hoped to nail him for plotting against the State. Subsequently handed over to the Germans, he was later released on the order of the West German Supreme Court without ever being brought to trial.

According to his admirers Dönitz had no political ambitions and was interested simply in the welfare of Germany. In Spandau, though, in devious ways, he got to know about everything written about him anywhere in the world, for he was jealous of his prestige.[8]

The man who never failed to allude to the free world that defeated him as 'the enemy' managed to look immaculate even in prison garb. The bane of his life was the rheumatism he suffered, and his customary reply to the daily duty doctor's inquiry if he had any complaints to make was, 'Ach! I get no relief from these bloody cramps.' A non-smoker when he came to Spandau, he drew his weekly ration of tobacco and divided it among the others until the day he decided to try a pipe himself and found he liked it. He became a confirmed smoker, but a great pipe breaker; his wife had constantly to send him new ones.

Keeping fit was an obsession, and Dönitz was irked by his inability to take regular exercise. Even in his tiny cell he paced up and down. 'I have to keep healthy to get out of this hole,' he said. Early to bed was another rule he observed and he retired long before any of the others. He explained: 'If I go to

---

[8] Ever a man with a passion for personal investigation, on one occasion in 1937 Dönitz, dissatisfied with official Admiralty reports on currents and tides around Britain's naval base at Portland, decided to find out for himself — aboard the submarine U-37. The British destroyer *Wolfhound* located the sub and depth-charged it to the surface. Dönitz remained below while the U-boat's captain went on deck to make profuse apologies.

bed a couple of hours earlier than is usual here, I sleep away little more than a month of my sentence each year. It means that of the ten years I have to serve, over a year of it can be spent in sleep.'

Karl Dönitz was born near Berlin in 1891. Although he had no particular love for the sea he joined the navy when he was nineteen. The outbreak of World War I found him serving as an ensign on the *Breslau* when that vessel, in company with the battleship *Goeben*, fled to Constantinople to escape Britain's Mediterranean fleet. The episode appeared to convince the future Grand Admiral that his talents lay elsewhere; he became a pilot, but without ever developing enthusiasm for seaplanes, although he flew them skilfully. He returned to the sea by joining the submarine service and was a fully-fledged commander when he ordered his U-boat to attack a British convoy off Malta one day in October 1918. The convoy's escort took command of the situation, however, and forced the raider to the surface with depth charges. Dönitz nevertheless succeeded in scuttling his submarine before being taken prisoner. He had nothing to learn about guile and cunning even in those days; simulating madness, he was sent to an asylum in Manchester. 'That enabled me to be among the first prisoners of war to be repatriated when hostilities ceased,' he boasted.

The emergence of the Nazis as the new masters of Germany could not have been more timely to his ambitions. It had become clear that the Treaty of Versailles, for various reasons, was no longer a shield against German rearmament. Dönitz did not need to be persuaded to make his genuflection to the swastika; having the captaincy of corvettes and frigates behind him, he was quickly put in full control of U-boats. He developed over the years the mannerisms and approach of one who considers himself a leader. Young officers, his 'boys' as he called them, could be as wild as they cared. He would excuse their escapades and protect them as long as they did not fail him at sea and endorsed his conception that they and all U-boat officers belonged to 'one vast family of sons'.

To the lesser ranks among submarine crews he was equally vehement in his demand for unconditional obedience, high courage, and devotion to the last breath. He never met them in a formal way, but would stand among them whipping up the gospel of German supremacy and what was expected of them. The hard glow of his fanaticism made the Grand Admiral a figure to be remembered. He later believed he would not lack men willing to follow him blindly on the day of his release from Spandau.

In days when he devoted considerable energy to building up the submarine fleet and evolving new methods of attack, he gained powerful support from within the Nazi inner circle. With Göring's help, he perfected a tie-up between his underwater raiders and the Luftwaffe, and in the course of their work together the two men became close friends. Startlingly different in appearance, they had at least one thing in common; both had been inmates of mental asylums, although for different reasons.

Prone to violent seasickness at the slightest swell, fat, blubbery Göring was hardly a heroic character aboard ship. Among the Nazis, however, he was immensely powerful, and Dönitz was willing to cultivate anyone who could give him an influential lift along the road he was travelling.

On the outbreak of war he had not progressed as quickly as he had hoped but nevertheless had become chief of the German U-boat force. He boldly asserted that it would make no difference to his submarines whether enemy ships sailed alone or in convoy. He had quickly to revise this opinion and later withdrew a large proportion of his fleet to the Baltic.[9] When it emerged again its commanders had new orders. They were to hunt in packs — the day of the lone U-boat prowling the sea routes was over.

Dönitz had his eye on the post of Commander-in-Chief, but at that time Raeder's position was still strong and secure, mainly because of the success of the campaign in Norway. However, when he judged the time opportune, the wily U-boat specialist began to ask: 'What's the use of a German fleet bottled up in the Norwegian fjords?' The poison could only work slowly, but Dönitz had nothing to learn about the art of intrigue. Gradually Raeder's authority was undermined and in the end he had to make way for his rival. The escape from the French Channel ports of the *Scharnhorst*, the *Gneisenau*, and the *Prinz Eugen* in 1942 drew the venomous comment from Dönitz: 'It was a remarkable feat; there's no doubt about that. But it was not a naval battle. It was the retreat of a frightened navy and shed no glory on Greater Germany.'

In Spandau, Dönitz only rarely got to grips with Raeder, arguing over blunders that helped fracture the German war machine. The older man invariably reserved one repeatedly used torpedo in readiness for his final assault. Whether or not there was an audience, Raeder sooner or later fixed his glance on the rival he loathed, nodded his head significantly, and dismissed him with a final objurgation, 'Just a bloody scribbling admiral.'

---

[9] Some of Dönitz's other boasts were: 'I will demonstrate that the U-boat can win the war alone. For us nothing is impossible'; 'The enemy ships will go down — and keep going down. Germany's fate depends on this'; 'Aeroplanes can no more kill U-boats than a crow can kill a mole.' He lived to reflect on the bitter emptiness of that final assertion.

Admiral Karl Dönitz, commander of Hitler's submarine fleet, giving a pep talk to crews of the First U-Boat Flotilla at Brest in July, 1942. 'We will catch the enemy wherever we meet them.'

It was in the presence of Speer, responsible for the production of prefabricated U-boats when Germany's day was almost done, that Dönitz preferred to hold a postmortem on defeat. His country's overthrow was forever a humiliation to him, and the memory of it galled him.

'You know, Albert,' he once said to Speer, 'the war was really lost before it had begun because we had no answer to Britain's great naval strength. The only effective counter to it would have been for Germany to have entered the war with a thousand U-boats, and if the situation had been better understood we should have had them. War with Britain was never envisaged by the Government, and our armed forces were equipped, in fact, for war in Europe. That was the intended theatre of operations and it was based on calculations that Britain would either remain neutral or become our ally.'

Who was to blame for this miscalculation? Dönitz realized that there was no simple explanation but he knew that, once committed to war against Britain, Germany's naval resources had to be directed against the enemy's shipping and communications; failure to turn the seas into a vast cemetery of dead men and dead ships had assuredly encompassed Germany's defeat.

'It was Hitler's complete misconception of the British mentality, which in no circumstances was prepared to tolerate a further increase in Germany's power, that led to the war,' Dönitz claimed to Raeder. 'More than anyone, it was Ribbentrop who was responsible for the war due to his total misjudgement of possible British reactions. As a result of having lost World War I, and thanks to the unwise provisions of the Versailles Treaty, we got into ever-increasing political and economic difficulties. We were then set on the road to dictatorship. Most Germans regarded Hitler as a saviour. The demoniacal side of his nature I perceived only when it was too late.'

Before he at last recognized Hitler as an evil demon, Dönitz had rendered lip-worship service to the Führer. In a 1943 speech overflowing with adulation he declared: 'We are all worms compared with Hitler.' He also referred to 'the heaven-sent leadership of the Führer'. But in the chilly reality of Spandau gaol, he spoke differently:

'We had no fleet air arm, thanks to Göring, and there were other factors that sapped our strength. To begin with we had to contend with formidable anti-submarine devices, poor intelligence, particularly in the vital period towards the end, the failure of our air reconnaissance, and the Allies' massive bombing offensive.

'At one of Hitler's tea-parties, I took Göring to task for disastrous Luftwaffe failures. He hit back at me, but the way I took his lashing infuriated him so much that he decided instead to vent some of his anger on Ribbentrop for his foreign policy failures and even threatened to strike him with his Reichsmarschall's baton. When Göring called Ribbentrop a dirty little champagne salesman and told him to shut his damned mouth, Ribbentrop shouted: "I am still Foreign Minister, and my name is *von* Ribbentrop!"'

(Ribbentrop had been a champagne salesman and married the daughter of Germany's foremost wine producer.)

In the midst of these reflections, Dönitz paused suddenly as if memories of lost battles were too lacerating to recall. At last he continued: 'In November 1943 I wrote in my diary that the enemy held every trump card, covering all areas with long-range air patrols and using location methods against which we still had no warning. I told Hitler this, and that the enemy knew all our secrets although we knew none of his, but he dismissed it all as nonsense.

'It might have been different, Albert, for both of us, and the war itself, if only you had been in charge of production before 1943. Those U-boats of mine, the new type, would have been ready in time and they might have pulled the trick. Instead, from the winter of 1944 until the end of the war more submarines were being destroyed by bombing than were lost at sea. The strength of the service was about thirty-eight thousand men and of these all but eight thousand fell.

'The real mischief started with the radar used by both ships and aircraft. Our losses, which previously had been thirteen per cent of all ships at sea, rapidly increased to between thirty and fifty per cent. It was terrible. In one month alone, May 1943, we lost forty-three U-boats in convoy attacks and elsewhere, and nowhere in the Atlantic were our submarines safe.'

A sore point with Dönitz was that he claimed to have pressed for the development of radio-location in Germany before the war, but nobody took any notice as he was only an unimportant *Kapitän zur See*. He conveniently forgot that when Britain armed her anti-submarine forces with radar he really did not know what had hit him. At a naval conference he had declared: 'Everything possible is being done to discover the nature of this new anti-submarine device.' As a thwarted radar pioneer he appeared to have been singularly uninformed.

Dönitz quickly pointed out that neither superior strategy nor tactics influenced the battle against his U-boats. 'The scientists who perfected radio-location were hailed as the saviours of their country, and this indeed was the truth,' he said. 'Superiority in this technical achievement helped to win the day. Germany on her part blundered badly by allowing her scientists to be called up for service with the armed forces, and not until later were many of them released or exempted.'

The war, as Dönitz saw it, took a turn for the worse through Germany's failure to occupy the Eastern Mediterranean, through which lay the route to the Far East and to vital oil supplies. The situation was brought about, he asserted, by the unwarlike qualities of the Italians and the land supply problems of Rommel's army. The combined German-Italian naval forces were not strong enough to achieve even temporary command of the Mediterranean, and it was this weakness that prevented Germany circumventing the invasion of North Africa.

By 1944 Germany was ready to give up the ghost, and the smell of defeat was high in every Nazi nostril. In a situation pregnant with disaster the attempt on Hitler's life by the German generals could not have surprised Dönitz in the least. However, he understood well enough what was expected of him and in an order of the day said: 'A small clique of mad generals sharing nothing in common with the brave armies that are defending the Fatherland has attempted to murder our beloved Führer. This cowardly and treacherous act against our Leader and the German people will receive the punishment it deserves. The German Navy — under orders from its own Commander-in-Chief — will deal as ruthlessly with any traitor discovered in its midst.'

Dönitz was present at the Führer's headquarters shortly after Hitler's escape, at a reception for Mussolini. Hitler was moody and his rage suddenly burst into flame. 'I am beginning to wonder whether the German people are worthy of my great ideals,' he roared. 'If they are not they deserve to be destroyed.'

Before the curtain dropped on the last act of the Wagnerian drama in the Berlin bunker, Hitler appears to have made four copies of a will in which he named Karl Dönitz as his successor. The documents were to be delivered to the persons Hitler was anxious to acquaint of his testamentary wishes, but the emissaries who were to take them failed to arrive at their destinations. The corpses of the two messengers were discovered later and the rest is speculation, except that no copy of the will was ever found. Therefore, for what it was worth, Dönitz's promotion rested on a signal sent to him from the bunker by Martin Bormann, informing him of his appointment. The 1 May 1945 signal from the Chancellery in Berlin was addressed: 'Grand Admiral Dönitz (Personal and Secret). To be handled only by an officer.' It stated:

> Führer died yesterday at 1530 hours. In his will dated April 29 he appoints you Reichs President, Minister Goebbels Chancellor, Reichsleiter Bormann Party Minister, Minister Seyss-Inquart Foreign Minister. The will, by order of the Führer, is being sent to you and to Field Marshal Schörner and out of Berlin for safe custody for the people. Reichsleiter Bormann will try to reach you today to explain the situation. The form and timing of announcement to the Armed Forces and to the public are left to your discretion. Acknowledge — Goebbels, Bormann.

The will's instructions were at variance with Dönitz's ideas on the choice of advisers and ministers whom, he felt, he needed around to help him end the war on the best obtainable terms. So he ordered that if Goebbels or Bormann appeared they were to be arrested. He began recruiting Ministers for a new provisional central Government. To direct the Ministries of Industry and Production he chose Albert Speer. He found an ally in Speer, who was ready to assist in trying to re-establish communications and get some kind of order from the indescribable chaos, although there was little that could be achieved. Dönitz was at the helm of a sinking ship from which all effective authority had been swept overboard.

Dönitz recalled the momentous telegram from the Berlin bunker:

'Himmler's attitude on the day upon which the telegram announcing my nomination arrived had shown me that he expected to be named as Head of State. Now that the responsibility for the appointment of ministers was mine, there could be no question of collaboration between him and me. I had to have a swift and final showdown with him. I told my ADC to telephone him and ask him to come and see me. He refused until I myself spoke to him.

'He arrived accompanied by six armed SS officers. I offered Himmler a chair and myself sat down behind my writing desk, upon which lay, hidden by some papers, a pistol with the safety catch off. I handed him the telegram containing my appointment. As he read, an expression of astonishment spread over his face. He went very pale. Finally he stood up and bowed and asked to become the second man in the State. I replied that there was no way I could make use of his services, and he left. I was, of course, by no means sure that he would not take some action to oppose my orders, but so far we had avoided the open conflict which I had feared, and which would have had such disastrous effects on internal order.'

Dönitz did not have to be called upon twice to become Führer. In a broadcast to the country as Reichs President and Supreme Commander of the Armed Forces he explained that Hitler had died fighting at the head of his troops. The need to sustain what little was left of public morale convinced Dönitz that it was unwise to reveal that the Führer had died by his own hand. Ending a brief peroration that made his own position clear to everybody, he declared: 'The fight goes on.

My mission is to save the German people from destruction by the Bolshevists.'

On Speer's final visit to the Berlin bunker, Hitler sought his opinion of the leadership qualities of Dönitz. Speer guessed that the Führer was preparing to choose his successor and diplomatically praised the Admiral without laying on the compliments too heavily. Experience had taught him that the erratic Hitler often listened to advice, then jumped in the opposite direction.

'So you got me into all my trouble,' Dönitz said ruefully to Speer in Spandau's garden.

Disputing the constitutional legality of Dönitz's succession to Hitler, Speer said: 'You can't really claim it was truly legal because the constitution of the Reich would have required an election.'

'I disagree!' Dönitz snapped back.

'Moreover, Hitler seeking to impose on you Cabinet Ministers of *his* choice was a preposterous idea,' said Speer. 'If you were compelled to respect all the terms of the will, then the imposition of ministers meant that you couldn't sack any of them even if they proved unfit for office. If this was to be so, then Hitler would have denied you, as President, the most important power you were supposed to possess.'

Dönitz did not reply for a moment, then, terminating the argument, concluded: 'Resignation, then the voluntary renunciation of the position that the Allies had recognized was legally mine, would have been the one great mistake I could have made after the capitulation. I am still, and will remain, the legal Chief of State until I die.'

Then, ignoring Speer as if he had just been dismissed, but continuing the discussion with Neurath about their final days of freedom, Dönitz said: 'I needed you then — searched everywhere — but couldn't find you. I felt it to be a matter of great urgency that, to help me deal with the external political problems that would arise, I should have at my side an experienced adviser, a man who was untarnished by any contact with German foreign policy of recent years. I hoped that you, whom I had known personally since 1915, would assume the post of Foreign Minister and Prime Minister in the Government I proposed to form.'

When Dönitz ordered his aide-de-camp to locate Neurath, the aide telephoned Ribbentrop, hoping he could help. Ribbentrop hurried to Dönitz to suggest that not only was he legally entitled to be appointed Foreign Minister but he was also the best man for the job. He said that the British had always been pleased to deal with him. Dönitz refused the offer and toiled long and hard to select Ministers for a 'new Germany', but the 'cabinet' never met. Three weeks later, with other Nazi war leaders, he was made prisoner. At his trial at Nuremberg it was said that he was no mere army or divisional commander but in charge of the U-boats, the most formidable arm of the German fleet. Nor was it forgotten that as Head of State he had ordered the war in the East to be continued.

Perhaps only in Germany, with its fantastic history of political pillage and murder, could the question of a war criminal's right to succeed Hitler as Head of State be discussed as a serious proposition. Elsewhere it would have been regarded as a joke in deplorable taste or an admission of congenital idiocy. Dönitz was not without influential supporters, those prepared to press what they were pleased to call his constitutional rights. Others — probably the more dangerous elements — claimed that *Der Löwe* was above politics.

Dönitz was credited with helping two and a half million Germans to escape to the West by playing for time in the armistice negotiations with General Montgomery. This, plus his hatred of Britain, put him on speaking terms with more than just a few Germans.

Though he was appointed Führer only on Hitler's death, captured official German naval documents for the first four months of 1945 reveal that Dönitz became *de facto* Führer several months before. The German conduct of the war in its final stages had almost entirely passed into his hands. Apart from maintaining U-boat attacks as a first priority to the bitter end, he increasingly involved himself in the direction of land operations, into which naval personnel were heavily drawn, and in economic warfare. He even had himself appointed 'coal director', or Coal Czar, to use his own expression.

During the last months, war records now in the British Admiralty's possession record Dönitz almost daily closeted with Hitler and dominating discussions in the Supreme War Council. He held forth with a stream of detailed proposals, businesslike, completely unshaken, and invariably following his statements with the remark: 'The Führer agrees', or 'The Führer decides accordingly.' He did most of the talking and decision-making; little was done by the exhausted, broken man Hitler had become.

Displaying an imperturbability bordering on schizophrenic insanity, Dönitz stubbornly continued tactical warfare routines without real strategic sense. Even during the first week of May 1945, while negotiations for unconditional surrender were in progress, he kept U-boats 'of an improved type' at sea and sank three Allied ships at the cost of twenty-five German submarines. Throughout the long period of collapse, problems of defeat were never once discussed by Germany's Supreme

War Council, largely due to Dönitz's blindly efficient irresponsibility and dismissal of reality.

For the day Spandau's prison gates were to open for him, he arranged to be taken to the nearest airport and flown to the West. He was certain Communists would organize a demonstration outside to mark their bitter disapproval of his freedom, but was assured by the lads of the Dönitz Brigade that his supporters would also be outside in force, ready to deal with any awkward situation that might arise.

It seemed as if history's pages were being turned back.

11: THE WOMEN OF SPANDAU

Perched three thousand feet up on the flank of an Alpine mountain in Upper Bavaria is a cluster of half a dozen wooden houses that bear the postal address of Gailenberg. Tourists would tell you that Gailenberg was worth seeing for its modern art gallery — half restaurant and part music club — and because it was the place where Frau Ilse Hess chose to live.

The presence of Frau Hess in this little community, as isolated as a monastery in the heart of a forest, was the reason for my visit. I took the road to Gailenberg beyond the picture-postcard village of Hindelang (not to be found on any road map) and began the curling, testing journey by car along the last stretch of a mud track from which the mountain-side dropped away dizzily. This was only the first stage of an investigation that was to add up to thousands of miles before it was done and I had met and talked to the women of Spandau. These women, it is no exaggeration to say, shared the sentences of Nuremberg with their men. They belonged to an exclusive 'club', which had a simple set of rules:

> To exchange all information on what was taking place in Spandau.
> To work politically to improve conditions within the prison.
> To secure the release of the seven men there as quickly as possible.

In July 1947 the wives of Hess, Funk, Schirach, and Göring were held with the wives of other prominent Nazi officials in a Bavarian prison camp. After their release, and almost from the day their husbands entered Spandau Prison, the wives decided to work jointly and individually for alteration of the Nuremberg sentences. Four of the Spandau wives approached the Pope. Baron von Neurath's daughter, Winifred von Mackensen, was the first of them to see His Holiness personally to ask for help. She had a private audience with him at his Castel Gandolfo summer palace. So did Inge Dönitz. As the Spandau prisoners were all Protestants, it was questionable as to what motivated the Vatican authorities to grant Papal audiences to women pleading the cases of husbands condemned by an international tribunal for inhuman crimes against the world.

Inge Dönitz not only appealed to the Vatican but also asked the Archbishop of Canterbury to intercede on behalf of the men. Erika Raeder hoped that her acquaintance with the Pope, whom she had known when he was Cardinal Pacelli and a Papal Legate resident in Berlin, would be remembered. Always meticulous in pleading the cause of the seven, rather than that of her husband alone, Luise Funk spent an hour and a quarter with Cologne's famous Cardinal Frings, and during the audience offered to become a convert to Catholicism. Immediately afterwards a personal interview was arranged with West Germany's Chancellor, Dr Konrad Adenauer.

Winifred von Mackensen was the undisputed leader of the 'Spandau club', which included all the wives, and even Henriette, Baldur von Schirach's ex-spouse. The solitary male associate member was Heinrich Hoffmann junior, Schirach's brother-in-law.

At the start of my tour of all the Spandau families, at the first house I passed in the little village of Gailenberg in Bavaria, two women and a man peered suspiciously from different windows, but otherwise ignored my presence. I knocked again and again until, at last, the front door was unlocked and unbolted — it was still broad daylight — and a taciturn individual directed me to the home of Frau Hess. The route was by way of a slippery grass slope to a sprawling wooden house that had for a close companion a great barn. It was difficult to find anyone, but a woman finally appeared; in answer to my question she pointed to the door of the barn and said, 'That is where Frau Hess lives.'

In the darkness of the barn I could make out cattle stalls filled with logs, and there was a flight of steps whose door led to a landing and a couple of other entrances. I came across the woman whose directions I had tried to follow and it appeared that this part of the barn belonged to her. 'The other door,' she said. In the end I got out of the maze to reach a door opened by Frau Hess, a tall, heavily built woman who smiled a greeting. If you did not know you would have sworn she was Rudolf Hess's twin sister. She had the same deeply set eyes, penetratingly blue, the identical facial bone structure and strongly cast jaws. She was the other half of the incredible Hess story; the woman left behind by a letter dropped from the cockpit of an aeroplane; the only woman in Hess's thoughts; the wife he was afraid to meet again; the invited and the rejected.

Frau Hess took charge of my overcoat, and I followed her into a room that served as both kitchen and bedroom. On one side stood a big Bavarian cooking stove, heated by logs. Above it were a few shelves for the pots and pans Frau Hess used. In a corner was a single box divan, covered by a chintz spread and cushions. On the wall above the divan hung a striking painting of a handsome boy, and alongside it a crude pencil drawing of a man descending by parachute watched by a solitary farmer gazing up at him from the fields below.

Frau Hess

I stared at the drawing for an instant. Frau Hess said, 'My husband drew that when he was a prisoner in England. He sent it to my son. He thought it would amuse him.'

'Come this way,' she said a moment later, and we walked into another room that, despite being part of the barn, the top corner of it in fact, was surprisingly cosy.

I settled down in a comfortable old armchair immediately behind a couple of small windows that overlooked the snowcapped Alps. Facing me, across a circular table, Frau Hess sat, at her side a smaller table on which was the portable typewriter that she used. The room was full of pictures, photographs, and piles of letters, many of them heaped up on a roll-top desk that could not have taken much more. Amidst the collected photographs of Hess junior, taken with his mother and his friends in the years of his growing up, was one of his father, beetle-browed, eyes lowered and brooding. Rudolf Hess was on the wall too, the subject of a striking head in watercolour done by Professor Hom, Hitler's favourite painter.

Rudolf Hess had owed his former exalted position to his unquestioning loyalty and to the circumstances of being Hitler's companion from the earliest days. Hitler was partial to surrounding himself with mainly stupid, inferior men, but in the days of peace Hess was intelligent enough to make stock speeches around the country and strut on to platforms at Party gatherings. War required something more. When he found himself relegated to the background to permit real organizational and strategic minds to take over alongside Hitler, he did not like it. So, to prop up his waning prestige he attempted to bring true his dream of a separate Anglo-German peace, and flew away from his wife and son.

I looked at the bookshelves laden with works on philosophy, science, astrology, and the writing of Goethe, and saw that Frau Hess was watching me. She has always been described as the typical German *hausfrau*. She was a *hausfrau*, of course, but there was nothing typical about her. There was much more to her than that, even if the mousy blonde hair, straight cut and caught up at one side by a single clip, and the freckled and rosy complexion of a peasant that she made no attempt to hide with make-up, tended to discount this impression. She admitted having put on considerable weight during the last few years, but looked far younger than her true age. The collar of a striped blouse peeped over a high-necked sweater; a plain black skirt, nylons and low-heeled walking shoes with silver buckles completed her outfit. In her disciplined appearance there was only one concession to femininity: the chunky silver bangles she wore on each wrist.

Wives with a reputation for knowing how to cook (Hitler liked her dishes) and how to stay at home can be assured of an appropriate label, but to suggest that Frau Hess was just another German wife and mother would have been an underestimate of her extraordinary character. She was wedded to a loose-leaf letter file that she kept on a table beside her, for that was all she possessed of a husband, or would ever possess, unless the Nuremberg sentences were modified. Her account of her parting with her husband, cryptic as it may appear, was understandable in the circumstances. Hess was Hitler's deputy, and the ferment of war drew him constantly away. Frau Hess understood this readily enough.

She began to talk and said: 'In the conversation I had with my husband outside the nursery at our home in Munich on 10 May 1941 I asked him, "When will you be back?" He said he didn't quite know and that it might be on the following day, but certainly not later than Monday evening. I replied, "I don't believe it. You won't come back so quickly."'

He did not. It was 28 years, 6 months, and 25 days before Ilse Hess and her son, Wolf Rüdiger, who by then had become an engineer and airport designer, saw Rudolf Hess again. He had flown to Britain in May 1941, remained a prisoner there until taken to Nuremberg for his trial, and not until Christmas 1969 did he summon up enough courage to see his wife and son.

Telltale sentences in various letters to his wife hinted at the thinking behind his refusal to see her. In one letter he wrote:

> I no longer wish to see beauty and allow my spirit to be moved by it. The protective skin around my soul grows thicker and starts to develop the rings of years. Only those who have lost freedom know what freedom means.

And in another:

> My *real* thoughts are shared with nobody nowadays. They pursue their way inside ... I had to learn to stretch the thread of hope that reached out towards the day of liberty — to stretch it more and more!

One wonders whether, when he wrote those phrases in his cell, he gave even a passing thought to the millions in concentration camps to whom he denied not only the precious freedom for which he now yearned so much, but also the very right to exist.

'We were not apart,' his wife assured me. 'Telepathy, astrology, and his letters kept us together.'

Her gaze was drawn to a glass cabinet in the room and I turned to it and saw that it contained a lion's claw, a few Egyptian archaeological souvenirs, astrological charts bearing the signs of the zodiac, and a tin model of a soldier, about four inches high, of a type that was popular in Germany in the early 1930s. It was a little Nazi soldier with painted brown shirt and breeches and a black tie. It had the face of Hess.

Frau Hess went on: 'My husband and I remained in constant telepathic contact. People frequently turned up here whom I had not seen for years, and inevitably in Rudolf's next letter there were questions about these very visitors. My husband and I received and sent to each other in this way.' I wanted an explanation of Hess's illnesses, and Frau Hess was by no means unwilling to discuss her husband's condition. 'We frequently quarrelled because I felt there was nothing wrong with him, and this was proved by the many examinations he had. It was only his imagination and nerves, but nothing would convince him. During the first year and a half when he was a prisoner in England he was always writing to me about his aches and pains. Then one day the complaints suddenly ceased and I knew that at last he had accepted the fact that he was a prisoner and could do nothing about it. Only then did the anger and pain in his stomach and chest vanish.'

Both Hitler and Hess were forever taking pills for almost everything and going on 'health diets', but most of their ailments were psychosomatic, often hysterical symptoms. Nor was hypochondria Hess's solitary weakness. He disliked or was incapable of dealing with practical matters in his domestic life, as Ilse Hess freely admitted. The impracticalities of his character spilled over into his Party work to such an extent that exasperated regional leaders, pouring problems concerning Party politics or procedure into Hess's sorting-house of an office, described his attitude as: 'Come unto me all ye that are weary and heavy laden, and I will do nothing.' This was confirmed by Walther Funk who, discussing Hess's ability as Party deputy, delightedly informed Neurath in Spandau gaol that Hitler had once remarked to him:

'I only hope Hess never has to take over from me. I wouldn't know who to be more sorry for, Hess or the Party.'

Illustrating further his woolly-mindedness, Ilse Hess said, 'Rudolf and I used to come to Hindelang a great deal in the old days and we agreed it would be a good idea to buy a place here. We decided that the Modersohn house [the art gallery/restaurant] in Gailenberg would be just right for us. But Rudolf forgot about it until it was too late and it was sold to someone else. It could have been mine to run as a guesthouse.'

Snow fell heavily on the first night of my visit, and the following morning Frau Hess telephoned my hotel to say she would be coming down to join me. She came, on a toboggan, down the snow-covered mountain track, suitably dressed for the journey in brown corduroy trousers. She was less cautious and suspicious and at this meeting talked to me about her son Wolf.

'The school our boy goes to at Berchtesgaden is coeducational and sometimes this worries me a little. Two of my son's closest friends say it is very nice, but they wouldn't like their own sister to go there.

'I was very much taken by my son's former teacher. He was a brilliant man and I asked him to discuss my husband's letters with the boy, which he did. He seemed to me to be a good influence and I was shocked when he was arrested on a charge of perverting some of his pupils and sent to prison. It was a tragedy. He was such a happily married man and the school no longer seemed the same without him. Wolferl's progress appeared to slow up and I seriously thought about taking him away.'

Although none of the boys at school ever ragged Wolf about his father, he kept a collection of photographs of him tucked in a leather case. 'Why should I have the pictures by my bed and let the other boys stare at them all the time?' he said.

Most of Hess's letters to his son, the advice they contained, and the subjects he wrote about were far too involved and greatly above the boy's understanding. I remarked on this to Frau Hess. 'It is true his letters were difficult to comprehend,' she admitted. 'That is why I needed the teacher to explain and simplify them for the boy.'

In her mountain home, Frau Hess read letters from her husband over and over again, smiling to herself as she relished the flavour once more of a familiar passage, and editing the Nazi philosophies he deliberately injected into them for posterity or future publication. They were intended to be the basis for the new *Mein Kampf* from the man who had helped Adolf Hitler to write the original.

When Rudolf Hess assisted Hitler with the writing of *Mein Kampf*, Ilse Hess helped check the proofs. Hitler two-finger-typed the original version on an ancient typewriter, and Ilse Hess claimed to have revised the first typed manuscript, although changes in the text were made only as a result of her husband discussing them with Hitler. She says that both she and Hess wrestled with Hitler over proposed amendments because, as she puts it: 'Hitler was slow to admit we were right.'

While her husband languished in gaol, Ilse Hess wrote a book, *England-Nuremberg-Spandau*, which still defended Nazi ideas; then another, *Between London and Moscow*, which included an account of her and her husband's friends commemorating Hitler's birthday since his death. She maintained the Hess home as a kind of National Socialist shrine for visiting Nazis from all over the world.

As she studied afresh writings from Spandau Prison, she must have thought of the night she had sat in a restaurant with Adolf Hitler and her boyfriend Rudolf. She had just lost her job with a bookseller, and was undecided whether to begin studying at Munich University or to find work elsewhere.

Hitler said: 'My dear girl, has it never occurred to you to make a job of marrying this man here?' pointing to Rudolf. A few weeks later they were married.

Without any apparent financial support from her husband since early 1941, she had contrived to live and send her son to a good-class Berchtesgaden boarding school.

'People say that you have at least a million pounds tucked away abroad, Frau Hess,' I fired at her during my visit to her home.

I hardly expected an answer. She responded simply with a slow smile, 'I have managed to pay off all debts'; then she added, 'When my husband went off without notice, I had a large house on my hands with fifteen servants. I had only two thousand marks in ready cash.' Her husband's 'men', as he frequently referred to his Nazi comrades in his letters from Spandau, looked after her interests until her son was old enough to do so.

I said goodbye to Ilse Hess at her lonely mountain home. Whatever else other people had been led to believe, it seemed to me that her influence on her husband's life and affairs must always have been powerful and directional. She was that kind of woman. As I left I noticed an open book on the table before her. The title was *How Green Was my Valley*.

My next meeting with another member of the 'Spandau club' took place in Munich where Henriette von Schirach lived and worked. At weekends she returned to the village of Urfeld, where she owned a bungalow spacious enough to contain three large reception rooms and several small bedrooms, bought with the money she earned as an assistant in her father's photographic laboratories.

Eva Braun, before her friendship with Hitler, had also been an assistant in the laboratories — which made Henriette's father, Heinrich Hoffmann, a millionaire as a result of the monopoly he was able to establish under the Nazi regime.[10] The daughter of a Munich teacher, Eva Braun used to enjoy distracting customers with her low-cut dresses when she served in the Hoffmann photographic shop. It was in that shop that she first met Hitler.

---

[10] Heinrich Hoffmann senior is said to have started in business in 1933 with a capital of 900 marks. When Germany surrendered he had amassed a reputed fortune of £1,450,000. Hoffmann became a millionaire because he had the sole right to photograph Hitler and other Nazi leaders. In June 1950 a sentence of five years' hard labour was confirmed by a Munich de-Nazification court on Hoffmann, which also banned him from taking pictures for ten years.

During the second year of the imprisonment of the seven in Spandau, the following handwritten letter arrived in London:

To Excellency Winston Churchill

Dear Sir,
Please, excuse my request. My husband is one of the seven prisoners sentenced by the Nurnberg Tribunal 1946 — now in the Allied Prison Spandau Berlin (British Sector) former youth leader Baldur von Schirach.

It is forbidden to send food or tobacco to the prison.

Dear brother enemy could you allow that we can send our prisoners a Christmas parcel, they are your prisoners too.

With all good wishes for yourself

Henriette von Schirach

Kochel am See
US Zone, Bavaria
5 November 1948

Churchill declined to answer personally. The Foreign Office replied instead saying that, as Spandau regulations were governed by the four nations, it was not open to the British to waive these regulations in order to permit her to send a parcel containing food and tobacco. Nor were Churchill or the Foreign Secretary prepared to ask the prison Governorate to consider making an exception in her favour.

Slim and attractive, Henriette von Schirach, with only the grey tinge in her boyishly close-cropped hair as a telltale sign of the passing years, was the outcast of the 'Spandau club'. She remained a member, but since her divorce from Baldur von Schirach most of the other wives preferred to exchange information on prison affairs with Henriette's brother Heinrich, who looked after his brother-in-law's affairs.

'It may be hard for others to understand, but I did not desert my husband because he was in trouble,' Henriette asserted. 'I was a "widow" of the Nazi regime years before Spandau because Baldur was married to the Nazis and his Hitler Youth.'

Although she put her case cautiously and measured her words, from the moment she began to talk she evidently felt she needed to defend herself. While she spoke she became more excited as she recalled the relationship between herself and her husband and her disappointments. She found it impossible to remain calm and suddenly let herself go.

'Baldur lived the life of a Tibetan monk and that is how he now thinks of himself. He isolated himself from the world. This began soon after his imprisonment in Nuremberg in 1945, and it precipitated the divorce. It was not a new experience for me because in our married life together he was always remote from everything and everyone, including myself and his children, but then it was less unbearable. He thought only of his ideals.

Not once during my visits to him in Nuremberg Prison, and certainly not in any of the letters I received from him until I divorced him, did he ever ask, "How do you and the children live?" To find the money in order to smuggle a bottle of schnapps into his cell at Nuremberg I had to sell something. When my boys needed boots, my treasured collection of baby clothes went to the farmers who bought them. I sold bottles of Coca-Cola in the streets to earn a little or worked as an usherette in a cinema. My husband could acknowledge my struggle only by sending me idealistic out-of-this-world poems, and I couldn't feed my children with his poems.

'Baldur would never face facts. We argued constantly about this. His sister Rosalinde was brought up in Britain and America and was a complete Anglophile. Baldur himself also naturally liked the Anglo-Saxons because he was himself of

American extraction, yet he burned his boats frequently and in most extraordinary ways.

'On one occasion in 1943 I was listening to a BBC broadcast to Germany and heard that he had made a particularly silly speech at a Vienna rally, full of hatred against the British. I telephoned him from Munich at once and said, "What the devil do you think you are doing and saying with the war at such a dangerous stage?" He became furious and, cursing me, said warningly, "Keep your mouth shut, even for Frau von Schirach there is a concentration camp."'

In 1940, in Vienna, Henriette was accused of buying a pair of stockings from a Jewish shop, and in 1943 she defiantly criticized to Hitler's face the deportation of Jewish women she had witnessed during a visit to Amsterdam. Hitler advised her not to be sentimental. Following this incident, the Schirachs were cold-shouldered by the Nazi leaders, yet Baldur was still authorized to receive regular secret reports on Reinhard Heydrich's mass execution of Jews and other opponents of National Socialism in occupied Eastern Europe.

The family link with the United States, Henriette revealed, gave her husband the idea that he expertly understood the character of the people there. More American by blood than German, he was described as looking in the Nuremberg dock 'like a contrite college boy who has been kicked out of school for some folly'. With Colin Ross, his US-resident writer friend, he had discussed the necessity of trying to placate the United States by timely diplomatic gestures and at all costs keeping her out of the war. Schirach hoped that President Roosevelt could be persuaded to support Germany's territorial claims in Europe, and found Hitler and Göring more than mildly interested in his theory. Ribbentrop, however, did not think much of it, which was sufficient to kill its appeal to the Führer.

'That was another of my husband's dreams blown away,' said Henriette.

'I know that my husband was the victim of his upbringing,' she said in extenuation, 'and that at the time of his arrest and trial he really wanted to make amends. He had always said that German youth could not be blamed for Auschwitz and the barbarities of other concentration camps. But because my husband was an idealistic ostrich who could never face the truth about himself or others he could not escape his share of the guilt.'

Henriette von Schirach's storm of reproach halted a moment; the estranged wife began dutifully to defend the father of her children: 'I believe that when Baldur went into captivity, making statements against Hitler and thus accusing himself, he realized his mistakes. Unfortunately he woke up too late. He admitted his wrongs and declared that he, who after Auschwitz still pursued a policy of racial hate, had to share the guilt of Auschwitz.'

Then bitterness crept into her voice again. In May 1947 Henriette, together with the wives of other convicted major war criminals, was arrested on the instructions of the Bavarian Minister Loritz, and taken to an internment and one-time labour camp near Augsburg in which Russian slave workers of the Messerschmitt works were accommodated during the war. Walther Funk's wife, Luise, was there; and so was Göring's wife, Emmy. Two American officers handed Henriette a batch of photographs taken when Allied troops marched into Dachau, Buchenwald and Belsen concentration camps. She was ordered to look at each picture for five minutes. It was while she was in this internment camp that she heard that her Baldur and the six others sentenced at Nuremberg to imprisonment, had been sent to Spandau. After a de-

Nazification trial — held, appropriately, in one of her husband's former Hitler Youth Centres — Henriette von Schirach was given the benefit of her past protests against Hitler policies and was freed.

Working under an assumed name, she then earned a livelihood from various sources. She became a saleswoman for French and other subtitled foreign films distributed in Germany. In addition she was assistant editress of a television magazine and helped produce television films for Germany and America. Although her children, Angelica, Klaus, Robert, and Richard, were made wards of court, she looked after them with the help of her brother.

Angelica, who studied art at Wiesbaden and designed advertising posters, also felt the weight of being a Schirach and avoided using the family name. She adopted the name of one of her American ancestors. Her Christian name was the uncommon one that belonged to Hitler's niece, Angelica Rabaul, who committed suicide at seventeen. The circumstances of the death were never disclosed, and according to several of his biographers, Hitler never recovered from the shock. When Baldur von Schirach chose the name of Angelica for his first-born, Hitler was delighted.

Throughout our conversation Henriette von Schirach made no attempt to defend her own association with the march of Nazism. 'I am not entitled to any sympathy,' she said. 'I was responsible for my own mistakes and in the end I finished in the gutter crawling for a living, while Baldur, in Spandau, kept his head in the clouds at a safe distance from reality.'

'Luise Funk, the wife of Walther Funk, on trial at Nuremberg as a war criminal, is reported to have made an attempt on her life. She is expected to recover.' This message sped round the world on 5 December 1945. Frau Funk stayed alive, to become one of the most active workers in the ceaseless political manoeuvring to free the seven men in Spandau or at least lighten their sentences.

The wife of the former wealthy Reichsbank Minister became a paying boarder at a *Gasthaus* in the little hamlet of Hechenberg, a few miles from the Bavarian health resort of Bad Tolz. In the heyday of Nazism, fashionable Bad Tolz was a favourite country retreat of Hitler's high-ranking lieutenants, their wives, and their women.

Gasthaus Zoehr is a large, rambling Bavarian farmhouse whose two upper floors have been converted to accommodate paying guests. The smell of the cattle stall was strong as one entered the farmhouse, and this was not surprising when one recollected that in Bavaria it is the custom of the farmer and his family to share their home with their cattle. Gasthaus Zoehr was no exception to this rule. The proprietor, Herr Zoehr, was an ambling six-foot-three-inch peasant with enormous hands and a greasy handshake. Frau Funk's landlord had once been general handyman and farmer on the Funks' own estate.

The day I visited the *Gasthaus* I was shown into a room on the first floor. Frau Funk rose to meet me in a smart rose-coloured costume that her lipstick and nail varnish matched. Her auburn hair was brushed smoothly back into a snood. She wept as she spoke of her husband.

'Walther was framed if ever a man was,' she said, using an unexpected Americanism and nervously twisting a handkerchief. 'He was framed on the evidence of SS Obergruppen-führer Pohl,[11] who was tortured by men working

---

[11] SS General Oswald Pohl, former chief of the concentration camp administration, and a senior director of the Reichsbank, signed an

for the US Attorney in Nuremberg. Pohl said he arranged for the transfer of gold teeth taken from Jews murdered in the concentration camps to the vaults of the Reichsbank, which my husband controlled. I say my husband didn't know of the existence of these teeth.

'Pohl was tortured and beaten so that he would testify in this way against my husband. Hot salve was smeared on his face and then shaved off with rusty knives until he bled. Salt was then rubbed into his wounds. In agony, he was made to sign this damning confession, which was then rushed into court a few minutes later by the American Attorney and presented as evidence against my husband.'

'What proof have you that Pohl was tortured in this way or in any other way?' I asked.

'I just know it, I just know it,' she replied emphatically. She had to admit that she was unable to offer any evidence to support her allegations.

From 1942 the SS deposited large quantities of gold teeth, platinum and gold rings, diamonds, watches, earrings, and silver knives, forks, and spoons in the Reichsbank. Twelve kilos of pearls arrived in one consignment. Under a secret agreement with Himmler, Funk deposited melted-down gold from teeth and other valuables grabbed from condemned concentration camp inmates in an SS account given the cover name of 'Max Hediger'. Apart from valuables stolen from

---

affidavit at Nuremberg respecting the contents of the SS safe deposit account kept in the strong-room of the Reichsbank Frankfurt offices. When raided by the Allies, the deposit contained huge bags filled with rings, bracelets, cuff-links, jewellery of all kinds, money, and thousands of false and gold-capped teeth. Pohl, who was also Himmler's departmental executive for the entire extermination policy, stated that the subject of these valuables in the Reichsbank vaults had been twice fully discussed with Funk.

camp inmates who were promised 'resettlement', there were mounds of banknotes. Within the initial year of this policy, Reichsbank vaults were so filled to overflowing with jewellery, silverware and cash that Funk commenced converting valuables into cash by disposing of them through municipal pawnshops. By 1944 the Berlin pawnshop was so overwhelmed by the flow of these stolen goods that it notified the Reichsbank it could accept no more. Admitting that shipments came regularly from the Lublin and Auschwitz camps, the manager of the Reichsbank's precious metals department confessed:

'It was in the tenth delivery in November 1943 that dental gold appeared. The quantity of dental gold became unusually great.'

These gruesome Reichsbank deposits were used as security for loans to the SS to finance schemes for concentration camp labour. Even in Spandau gaol Funk persisted in denying knowledge of the contents of the deposits, despite the fact that soon after his arrest, racked with fear and guilt, he confessed that he had been personally responsible for having Jewish prisoners killed so that gold could be extracted from their teeth. He had gold teeth knocked out of their mouths even while they were alive, but removing gold fillings was easier when they were dead. He also admitted that he had issued orders in all slave labour camps for gold to be collected, and even spectacles, so that they could be distributed to Germans. He retracted this confession in the Nuremberg witness box, in spite of evidence from an SS witness who claimed to have visited vaults with Funk and discussed the contents.

Towards the end of 1949 a letter was received by the Spandau Prison authorities from the Land Commissioner of Bavaria requesting permission to interrogate Funk in connection with foreign exchange funds that had disappeared from the Reichsbank. It was alleged that at the beginning of 1945 Funk, then President of the Reichsbank and Reich Minister, had obtained Hitler's consent to move gold and foreign exchange. One hundred tons were hidden in potash works in Thuringia, but in April 1945 this was discovered by American troops. Later that month the balance of the Reichsbank gold reserve — 728 ingots of 25 kilos each, plus one milliard of Reichsmark banknotes, and 25 hundredweight of other currencies and jewellery — was sent to Bavaria and buried by the Walchensee.

The letter to the Spandau gaol from Bavarian Land Commissioner Dr Albert Roll stated that it was possible Funk had intended to escape to Switzerland. He was said to have had among his personal possessions three sacks stuffed with foreign currencies and two 25-kilo gold ingots. Dr Roll enclosed a questionnaire to be submitted to Funk.

'An emissary from Eisenhower came to see me at the beginning of the occupation and asked me to tell him where Reichsbank gold had been buried,' Luise Funk continued. 'I didn't bury any, so I couldn't tell him. My husband was the most incorruptible man in Germany,' she went on tearfully. 'All our years together we were never interested in politics. How can my husband be held responsible for something he didn't know about? If a murderer places a corpse in a trunk and leaves it at a bank for safe keeping, is it to be assumed the police on discovering the body are justified in accusing the bank director of murder?'

This was a familiar argument with Frau Funk and it fitted the pattern of every move she made to disturb the verdict of Nuremberg. She did not easily retain her composure, but shrewdness never deserted her. She wrote to the US High Commissioner for Germany:

> The execution of punishment in Spandau is diametrically opposed to the conception of the civilized world of conditions prevailing in penitentiaries and prisons. The conditions may be compared only to the dungeons of the Middle Ages you read about in thrillers. Prisoners undergo the cruel torment of flashing lights in their eyes in conjunction with modern mental cruelty and cleverly thought out rules of control, ruining the prisoners mentally and physically. It is worse than a death sentence, for the men are buried alive — physically and mentally.

She never stopped writing in the same vein, no matter how much gaol conditions improved; and she continually 'leaked' stories to newspapers, politicians, and eminent Church personalities regarding 'inhuman gaol conditions', including lurid versions of Hess's 'harsh treatment'.

The room that was her home and battle headquarters could have been in any musty boarding-house in any third-rate English seaside resort. It was filled with undistinguished period pieces, together with a heavy wardrobe and mahogany chest. There was the inevitable ancient marble-topped washstand and china water-jug and basin.

'Look at that primitive bed!' she exclaimed, pacing the room with almost the same degree of tension that her husband exhibited in Spandau. 'I could sleep on one of the fine beds from my old home, but it is on this bed that I have suffered most and spent so many sleepless nights thinking about my Walther. No, I shall not use another bed until he is free.'

She drew my attention to the oil painting of her husband and other pictures of him that hung from the walls; here and there I came across the bric-à-brac that spoke of more lavish and comfortable days. Tea was served on an exquisitely embossed, solid silver occasional table of oriental design, the top of which was a separate tray supported by three curling silver arms. Lower down, these merged into a thick stem and then emerged again as legs. The table must have weighed about a hundredweight. Frau Funk showed me some of her husband's possessions, among them a large watch in white gold that she explained had run for thirty years and was supposed not to have lost more than two minutes during that time. I opened it and saw the inscription: 'Der Reichs-Handwerkermeister Schramm von der dankbaren Reichs-Handwerkskammer', (literally: 'To the Reichs Artisan Master Schramm from the grateful Chamber of Reich Artisans'). I remarked that I was surprised the watch contained nothing to show it belonged to Walther Funk.

My admiration for the timepiece prompted Frau Funk to rummage in a bedside drawer, from which she drew out a glittering golden dollar piece. She touched a hidden spring at the edge of the coin and it opened to reveal an enchanting little watch that had been set within. 'I don't think there is another like it in the world, and it is one of my dearest treasures,' she said. 'My husband always carried it with him whenever he wore evening dress.'

Jewellery appeared to be a family passion with the Funks. Frau Funk, I noticed, wore a single-strand pearl necklace, pearl earrings, a gold ring mounted with two large pearls, and in her hair a pearl comb. She shared with Frau Hess a belief in telepathy and was convinced that she was constantly in touch with her husband.

'When Walther is very ill I know it before he writes and tells me. I, too, become affected with heart trouble, jaundice, abdominal disorders, and my eyes suffer. Recently, when his condition became serious again, I woke up one night and clearly felt his hand gripping my shoulder.'

Frau Funk allowed a graphologist in Munich to examine her husband's letters. 'He is a very experienced man, and able to reveal to me much more of my husband's innermost feelings than I know already. My graphologist repeatedly pointed out the extraordinary superior aloofness of my husband.'

Funk kept his wife informed of the books he intended to read so that she could follow suit. They felt that by this arrangement they were brought closer together even if Funk's forays into psychology and philosophy puzzled his wife. She also told me of her interest in astrology, and although she was not willing to reveal what the stars foretold she admitted that on one occasion a great spiritual change had been indicated. Shortly afterwards she had sought the advice of a Church cardinal regarding her husband and was so impressed with the advice and counsel given to her that she decided to change her religion.

'I am handicapped by my inability to memorize the instruction I am given, but I am sure I shall be able to overcome the difficulty in time,' she said. 'Perhaps my husband will be released one day and then he can help me with my studies; because he, too, has also decided to become a convert to Catholicism after reading my letters.'

In Spandau, Funk would just smile indulgently over his wife's certainty that he would change his religion. 'I have plenty of time to make up my mind,' he would point out with logic.

Frau Funk regularly attended Mass and arranged for prayers to be said for all the Spandau prisoners. As she continued to speak of her husband, her eyes (they were affected by cancer) became swollen and bloodshot from continuous weeping, and she reached for a pair of dark glasses. She often wore them at Spandau to hide this misfortune from her husband.

She beckoned me to the window of her room and pointed across the fields to a gleaming white mansion on a nearby hill. The place was The Berghof, the fabulous twenty-two-room Funk family home that had been confiscated. General George Patton, who lived in it for a time, described it as the finest house he had seen in Germany. It commanded a large farming estate with vast fields and extensive woods.

As I left Luise Funk, she sat, as she did so often, gazing through a pair of powerful binoculars at the luxury home she had lost. The binoculars helped to create the illusion that she was closer to her old possessions.

Frau Winifred von Mackensen, daughter of an ambassador and the wife of one, was the diplomatic brains of the 'Spandau club'. She did more than anyone to change conditions within the formidable prison. There was not a diplomatic trick that she did not know. Since the death of her husband in 1949, her only interests were her father, Baron von Neurath, her mother the Baroness, and the remains of the family estate in Württemberg, where Queen Mary spent her girlhood years.

The families of the men of Spandau lived modestly, but they were not impoverished and managed to get to the prison on visiting days however considerable the expense. Once they had enjoyed luxury, and nothing had troubled them. Their 'age of loot' ended only with Germany's defeat. After the war the Allies located historic treasures that overflowed secret storehouses and returned them to their rightful places in the art galleries, museums and cathedrals of countries that had been under occupation. That was just part of the story, however, for millions of pounds in hard cash, jewellery and valuables —

easily negotiable loot — still remained unaccounted for. Not all this wealth left Germany. A great deal was salted away as private fortunes in the banks of neutral countries, held in cover accounts for top-ranking Nazis. Only the unwillingness of the banks prevented an investigation that could have exposed the full truth.

State allowances, pensions, and other sources of income, not always possible to specify, kept the families of the men of Spandau on a comfortable keel. However, most hoped their early restricted postwar mode of living would be temporary; they believed they had a strong case in negotiations and manoeuvres for the return of confiscated property and funds that would make them rich again.

The Neurath estate, with its houses and farm buildings, nestled beside a trout stream at the foot of a vineyard hill. Its small acreage, dominated by the family mansion, cream-painted and with green-shuttered windows, was confiscated shortly after the end of the war. The Baroness had inherited wealth of her own. Her grandfather was Edward Cooper, who married Mary Westerveldt of Long Island, US, and both came of distinguished American families.

The Neuraths had other American links. Sumner Welles was related to them, and one of the Baron's ancestors was the famous Danniel D. Tompkins, Governor of New York from 1807 to 1817, who played a great part in the War of Independence and gave his entire fortune to the cause. *The Public Papers of Danniel D. Tompkins,* published in 1898, is part of American history.

When I visited the Neurath mansion, I met the Baroness walking in the grounds. Time had not laid an unkindly hand on her and, despite her crown of white hair, wavy and silken, her skin was smooth and firm. In a billowing blue-and-white dress, and wearing a straw hat that shaded her face from the sun, she looked no less graceful than when, as she often had done, she had attended the Royal garden parties at Buckingham Palace.

I took tea with the Baroness and her daughter Winifred in the Neuraths' private drawing room, a room that belonged to more leisurely days and the long-forgotten past. Everywhere, on the papered walls, on the old oak writing desk, on occasional tables, were photographs, miniatures, and paintings of branches of the Neurath family tree. Largest of all, facing the Baroness's favourite chintz-covered settee, hung the first oil portrait ever painted of her husband, when he was a young diplomat in Turkey.

'I always told my husband he was much too serious-looking and that I preferred to see him smiling,' the Baroness said as we stood beside it. We sat down before a large table, carved and old, to an English tea complete with slab cake, buns, pastries and biscuits, and the best tea I had tasted anywhere in Germany. Few Germans understand the simple art of teamaking. The only intruder in this room of silver and china bric-à-brac was an electric kettle that stood beside the table.

The Baroness served, and I could not but think how strikingly she resembled her girlhood friend, the late Queen Mary. Her conversation, in perfect English only occasionally halted by a difficult phrase that found easier voice in German, was tea-table conversation of bygone days in England; of parties and the activities of the various diplomatic corps in London; of the Neurath estate, but not a word of Spandau.

Her husband was in the gaol because among other misjudgements he had mistakenly believed that the professionals — diplomats and civil servants — would eventually help curb dangerous excesses and smooth rough edges, she said. He did nothing to help the Nazis attain power, but nor did he try to stop them. Yet another of his errors was thinking that it was sufficient to take private moral refuge whilst still continuing a public career. He failed, consequently, to salvage both his integrity and his country, and wrote from Spandau gaol: 'Destiny was stronger than I.'

Neurath viewed National Socialism in the light of lessons he had learned in Mussolini's Italy, where things had been very wild at first but had settled down. He believed that the Nazis could be used to win advantages, and that in time Nazism's more radical aspects would mellow. He considered it his duty to make the best of Hitler and his cronies. Optimistically flattering himself that he would gradually help tame them, he told Britain's Ambassador in Berlin: 'The Hitler experiment has to be tried some time or other.'

Convinced that the Third Reich was a 'national resurrection', he asserted: 'It was nothing more than the logical continuation of the century-old search for German unity — an inevitable historical development, not a Nazi innovation.' But he never believed that Hitler would use restored German power to launch an aggressive war.

When, on 4 May 1945 in Austria, French troops arrested him and his son-in-law, Hans-George Mackensen, who had served as Ambassador in Rome, he told his wife: 'Don't worry. Nothing will happen to me. I have a good conscience, and most assuredly I will return to you.'

Only when we had finished tea and the Baroness, seated for a moment at her desk, picked up her husband's last letter from prison and began to read it deliberately and firmly, did emotion intrude. Then suddenly, as if remembering she was the wife of a diplomat, she recovered herself and finished what she was reading, carefully folded the letter into its original creases, and slipped it back into its envelope.

'It would be nice if he could die here with me,' she said quietly. She got up, and I took my leave. As the door closed behind us, Frau von Mackensen said, 'We diplomats always learn to control our emotions.'

As we started to descend the staircase, the old world of Baron von Neurath, Protector of Bohemia and Moravia, butted in with the pointed horns of a stag mounted on wood, inscribed, 'Shot, November 1940, in Moravia' — Moravia, where thousands of men and women were also shot or died in concentration camps.

At the foot of the staircase was the room from which we had previously come, a large reception hall. This, too, was crowded with full-size paintings of Neurath and Mackensen forebears. In one corner on a pedestal stood a white marble bust of Frau von Mackensen. 'My husband wanted it done. It's not very good,' she said. I disagreed with her.

We turned into an adjoining room, Frau von Mackensen's study, where this daughter-in-law of Field-Marshal von Mackensen — leader of the Kaiser's 'Skull and Crossbones' Hussars — planned operations to free her father. She told me:

'It would have been better for my father to have been hanged at Nuremberg than to live in Spandau. I am his daughter. I love him and I can say that knowing it to be true.

'I make no defence for him. He made a mistake and has been tried and found guilty, and one doesn't argue about it. But he is so old and sick that, even had he once been dangerous, he can no longer do any harm. If he were allowed to return here, to his home, he could be placed under some form of restraint. His only wish is to be able to die in his home and to be near the wife to whom he has been married for so long. My father was never a member of any Party and that is officially admitted. He is a German.'

Almost as soon as the Spandau gaol doors closed on her husband, Baroness von Neurath began appealing for help to everyone of influence she knew — from Queen Mary of England, with whom she had grown up, to the Pope. With her daughter's shrewd collaboration, she employed her years of experience as wife of an ambassador and Foreign Minister to explore every diplomatic avenue that might possibly secure remission of her husband's sentence. Initially she concentrated on Britain, where her husband had been Germany's ambassador to the Court of St James, and on the Vatican. Then she selected other friendship targets for her letters. One of the earliest was Lady Astor:

To Viscountess Astor, MP
London, SW1
4 St James' Square

Leiufelverhof
Post Euzweihuigen Württemberg
Germany, American Zone
November 14th 1947

Private

Dear Lady Astor,

I hear you are in Germany and want to help the German women, therefore I address this letter to you, whom I know personally from former times, as kind-hearted and strongminded, hoping you can help me to reach a more humane treatment of my husband, whom you knew well as German ambassador in London 1930-32. He is imprisoned since 2½ years and now in Spandau. He is one of the chief political prisoners condemned to 15 years' imprisonment and now in Spandau delivered to the Allied Control Commission. Since then, their already very hard treatment in Nürnberg under American care has augmented and is that of common, not of political prisoners, against all Völkwrecht. Our bishop of Würm of Württemberg, well known to the English bishops of Chichester and Canterbury, tried lately to come in contact with my husband, who as Minister of Foreign Affairs freed him from imprisonment from the Nazis, but has totally failed and writes to me desperately. No visits whatever allowed until now, not even from doctor or clergyman, 3 months without church service, a French Pastor is allowed to preach to them once a week now but may not speak to them or know them personally. Not even his children may write to him. One short and very strictly controlled letter between him and myself is allowed, but often sent back and retained mostly for 4 weeks. Later, when a visit will be allowed for *15 minutes* for one person, it will be under most degrading circumstances, so that my husband will not allow me or my daughter, who has just lost her husband, a former Ambassador, to undertake this terrible long journey even when it is allowed.

My husband is now 75 years. I am 72. We are married 47 years. He is, although very courageous and believing in the world's and God's justice for him, now beginning to lose his former strength in health. As he always had a heart disease, he feels especially that he is not allowed to sleep one night through, because every 5-10 minutes they are wakened by an electric 'Bleur' light. This against an old gentleman, who once upon a time has done good service between our two countries. A pity Sir Nevile Henderson is dead. He was a good friend of ours and could tell a lot about my husband's work for your country as Foreign Minister in Berlin, 1932-37.

Please excuse my long letter with my great anxiety and my remembering you as a friend in our London time. Perhaps you can help spreading the real facts, which I am sure are not known in England and to Parliament especially.

Thanking you in anticipation, I am, dear Lady Astor,
Yours sincerely,

Baroness Marie von Neurath

PS In answering this letter you will better address it to Mother-Superior Mary San Maurice, Villa Beasa, Fribourg,

Suisse (Switzerland). She will send it to me. Quicker and surer as the Post.

In the same envelope, an additional letter was enclosed, dated the same day:

Dear Lady Astor,

I reopen this letter, because today's post brings me the account of a lady friend, who has at last been allowed to see my husband in Spandau for 15 minutes. Her account upsets me greatly. She writes that he was so dreadfully neglected and dirty and quite apathetic, spoke scarcely to be heard through double glass windows and could not hear himself as his deafness and sight has greatly diminished, and a crowd of 12 men were around listening and writing up every word. His hands full of dirt, his hair and beard shaven, lost 20 pounds. Could you not help at least that my daughter could take the international train from Frankfurt to Berlin used only by English and Americans? She is born in London and has her birth but from there. The best time for a visit would be 20 December and could she stay for at least ½ hour? Can you help me that my husband from his bad state of health and weakness could be brought in an English or German surveyed hospital, where he would be cared for, so at least not to take another bad cold, which he has had several already? Of course if I were allowed to accompany my daughter and see him together, this would be such a beautiful Christmas present.

Do not think badly of me, that I have so many wishes, but I am in such anxiety, because nobody will help him. Even the Pope and Queen Mary, whom I knew so well and to whom I have written several times, have not answered, probably they dare not do anything. You, who have seen now what thousands of German women suffer, often like we unjustly, will perhaps have the courage to try and help. I have such confidence in your help. Please do not leave this letter unanswered without a little gleam of hope to your ever so thankful,

Marie von Neurath

X We both have never been members of the Party and are treated as free.

Lady Astor sent a copy of the letter to Lord Pakenham, who at the time held the Foreign Office post of Chancellor of the Duchy of Lancaster. An accompanying note simply said: 'Dear High and Mighty, Do, please, read this letter. Can anything be done?' Within two weeks Lord Pakenham sent Viscountess Astor two replies. The first reported:

> Visits by a chaplain would not count against the allowance of one visitor in each period of two calendar months.
>
> Officials asserted that the Spandau regulations compared favourable with those of British prisons and it was therefore doubtful if any relaxations were warranted.
>
> A further point was that the two fundamental conditions, that prisoners should be given organized work and that work, exercise and religious services should be communal, were secured by the British.

Pakenham's second note advised:

> The regulations are the subject of quadripartite agreements and there is little hope of our obtaining the agreement of our allies to any amendment. In fact, two of them hold the view that the existing conditions are quite lenient and it was a long struggle before we obtained agreement to communal work and religious worship.
>
> I don't like the idea any more than you do, but I expect that the difficulties I have mentioned are insuperable for the moment. However, we must see whether anything can be done later on.

Lord Pakenham wrote to Britain's Commander-in-Chief in Germany, Lt General Sir Brian Robertson, enclosing copies of his correspondence with Lady Astor. Commenting on Neurath, he said:

> I am not asking for any concessions in the treatment of von Neurath, but I would be most grateful if you could take an early opportunity, possibly when the British are in charge, of seeing that such comforts to which von Neurath is entitled by the regulations are in fact accorded to him.

The following month, in a third letter to Lady Astor, he explained:

> My dear Nancy,
> I wrote to you on 10th February about Baron von Neurath and the difficulties in the way of any relaxation in the prison regulations which are governed by quadripartite agreement.
> I have made further enquiries into von Neurath's welfare and learn that he is being accorded all the comforts to which he is entitled by the prison regulations. In addition, he is fully aware of the fact that he may apply for the services of a Chaplain whenever he wishes to do so, but has stated that he has no particular desire to take advantage of this privilege.
> Baroness von Neurath need have no fears for her husband's health, which I understand is extremely good considering his advanced age. The prison medical officer has in fact stated that in his opinion von Neurath is 'very fit'.
> Yours ever affectionately,
>
> Pakenham

The Baroness then looked to another old friend: Britain's former Secretary of State for Foreign Affairs, Lord Halifax. Diplomatically recalling the past, she wrote:

Dear Lord Halifax,

Perhaps you remember me from the time of your visit to Berlin, when you came for an informal family lunch to our house, before leaving for Munich-Berchtesgaden with my husband, for a visit to Hitler?

You were very earnest then, but I so well remember your sympathetic smile, that lit up your face, when my daughter entered the room with one of our beloved 'Dachshunds' in her arms, which you caressed so dearly. My daughter, now a widow, as her husband Herr von Mackensen died from a terrible illness a year and a half ago, lives with me here near our old home in the house of my husband's brother, full of dogs, who all miss their imprisoned master, as we do now already since nearly 4 long years.

He undergoes in Spandau a most severe treatment under the care of the Controllrath, never in accord, whenever the smallest relief for the prisoners is suggested. He now will be 76 years old and we cannot even undertake to pay the allowed visit to him every 2 months for 15 minutes, which my daughter undertook in a very difficult long journey from here over Hanover and passing the Russian zone 3 times last year, which now is quite impossible. As also our usual letters, allowed every month between my husband and myself, are lately not always delivered and Baron Ludinghausen his Nürnberg advocate living in Berlin has died a few days ago, the relations between us are practically broken, and you can imagine, that we feel most uneasy about this, knowing that his forces diminish permanently from the bad food in Spandau and in consequence of a very serious great operation, which nearly cost his life in imprisonment and has augmented the permanent bad state of his health. We cannot even help him with parcels of food that are strictly forbidden.

Now there would be a chance to get him in an American prison in Stuttgart, for preparation of a process in Stuttgart for which we have succeeded to engage a new *Rechtsanwalt* who, as he does not know my husband, is unable to get permission to fly to Spandau Prison as he has found a law, which permits him claim transport for my husband to a Stuttgart prison. If you could help me interest Lord Robertson, whom I do not know, for the matter, I think I could do so with M. François-Poncet, an old friend of ours, who now is in Baden-Baden with General Koenig, and I also think that the Americans would not object to the plan.

The aim of the new process is to take away our old family farm (except our own whole fortune), so that you can imagine how important this judgement will be for us. Being only women we, my daughter and I, left alone, do not look into matters at all. Moreover we hope to propose of a lot of new attests from diplomatic colleagues in Germany, who were not obtainable in Nürnberg (also my daughter and I were then unobtainable in Austria, which was absolutely cut off from Germany, and friends from all our posts in the world), that my husband has never wanted war and he warned Hitler most earnestly to make Ribbentrop his ambassador to England, a post that he himself was very sorry to leave on Hindenburg's request and his Fatherland's great need of him, whose good relations with England were known. I am so sorry that Sir Nevile Henderson, who was a great personal friend of ours, does not live any more, he could attest how often they tried together to convince Hitler to a peaceful arrangement in world matters and to maintain the good understanding with England.

For both of them it was tragic that they failed in their mission and only a diplomat like you can understand the great risks such exposed high positions have to overtake. As wife of a diplomat I hope you will understand I come to you for help and as the wife of a country gentleman of old style I think you will best understand me.

Thank you in anticipation,
I am yours sincerely,

Baroness Marie von Neurath

The letter hit the right note, because Lord Halifax immediately started working in British Foreign Office, Washington State Department, and Paris diplomatic circles to see if he could assist his former fellow diplomat and friend. In a 17 January 1949 letter to a Foreign Office colleague he said:

> I have always thought that old man had rather a rough deal, for I cannot believe he was more than a pretty unwilling passenger, though in this capacity no doubt he did reprehensible things, and he was surely demoted from Czechoslovakia for not being rough enough with them.
>
> That, however, has I suppose all been taken into account by the Court, and it now looks as if it is a question of somewhat more humane administration of the court sentence.
>
> Would it be in order for me to send the letter direct to Brian Robertson, or would it be proper for one of your people to forward it for such action as might be possible and for me to tell her that this has been done?
>
> Yours ever,
>
> Halifax

The pending legal proceedings against the Neurath family referred to in the letter the Baroness sent to Lord Halifax involved what was known as the 'Liberation Ministry' of the new state of Baden-Württemberg. On 1 October 1948 formal charges were opened against Neurath in a de-Nazification trial; the object was to confiscate his property, estimated to be in excess of 400,000 marks. A Stuttgart lawyer, Dr Helmut Fischinger, retained by the Baroness, saw the proceedings as an opportunity to reopen Nuremberg allegations and requested that Neurath be brought from Spandau to defend himself at the hearings. The Soviet Union refused permission.

In February 1950 Baden-Württemberg's public prosecutor decided that, in view of the case's importance and the danger of Neurath dying, a public accusation should be made and Neurath tried *in absentia*. When the first public hearings began on 4 October 1950 the court agreed that his presence was necessary, but as the Allies would not let him leave prison the case was postponed. Eventually, through successful legal actions, Winifred von Mackensen saved the family's Austrian hunting lodge and their Baden-Württemberg estate.

The Baroness and her daughter never eased an instant with their campaign to alter gaol conditions and free the Baron until they achieved the results they wanted.

Strangely, the Neuraths were yet another Spandau family who believed in telepathy. Whenever the Baroness told her daughter that she knew the Baron had suffered a heart attack during the night, it was always confirmed in his next letter from the gaol. Walking in her garden, Winifred von Mackensen sometimes felt her father strangely near. 'A few days later,' she said, 'he would write and mention a particular tree I was looking at that day.'

Frau von Mackensen was born in Forest Hill, London, when her father was a young vice-consul. In appearance she could have been taken for the wife of an English squire, with her straight-cut, silver-streaked hair, neat blouse, and tailored suit. She spoke good English, though not as fluently as her German-born mother, for she still betrayed a slight accent. She had the poise and assurance of a born aristocrat, and only when she talked of her father did one sense how deeply she felt his exile to Spandau.

Excusing his actions, he had told his wife, his daughter, and others: 'I believed that, in a war in which the existence of the German people was at stake, I could not, as a German — which I am with full devotion — refuse my service and my knowledge. After all, it was not a question of Hitler or the Nazi regime, but rather of my people and their existence.'

When indicted as a war criminal he was convinced the accusations were a mistake, and he largely conducted his own defence. Added to this stress was the knowledge that his son was interned in Switzerland and liable to arrest if he returned to Germany; his son-in-law was in prison (where he would soon die); his wife and daughter were far away in Austria, and his estates had been confiscated.

Accused of having sold his honour and reputation because of his continuous co-operation and association with Hitler's Government, in his defence Neurath told Britain's deputy chief prosecutor, Sir David Maxwell Fyfe, that he had never heard of a Cabinet Minister resigning if he disagreed with one particular thing. To which Maxwell Fyfe devastatingly replied: 'Every Cabinet Minister for whom I have any respect left a cabinet if it did something of which he morally disapproved.'

After his imprisonment, the Baron confessed to his wife and daughter that his post in Czechoslovakia — the job that more than anything else consigned him to Spandau — was nothing more than a travesty; and his daughter asked:

'Then why did you agree to serve?'

'Because I was such a blockhead and still believed Hitler,' he replied.

On a bedroom wall in a tumbledown house standing high above the ruins of Heidelberg Castle and the old university town itself, I saw a strange pencil drawing within a simple wooden frame. The drawing, little more than a miniature, depicted a lonely woman in a black shawl seated beneath two massive broken Grecian pillars, the ruins of lost dreams. Towering in the background was a range of mountains.

In the right-hand corner of the drawing were the initials 'A. S.' — those of Albert Speer, Hitler's favourite architect and Minister of Production. The drawing was finished by Speer on 24 April 1948, and released to his family by the prison authorities as a special privilege; it brought a personal message of deep significance.

The woman in the drawing was Speer's mother, 'widowed' and in mourning for her lost son, surrounded by the ruins of his ambitions, hopes, and all that he built and yet destroyed. The mountains that he had once loved to climb symbolized Speer's lost freedom.

I stood in the cramped little bedroom gazing at the drawing with Speer's wife, Margarete. In May 1953 the Speer family — Frau Speer and her six children — moved into a brand-new apartment house in the town of Heidelberg itself. Until then they lived for years in an overcrowded outhouse in the grounds of her father-in-law's estate. There was a wonderful view of the old town far below and of the lovely Neckar valley, one of Germany's natural show-places.

On the brickwork of one of the two entrances to the Speer estate I could still see in black lettering the name 'A. Speer'. A steep, winding path led to a car park just below the ground level of the strikingly spacious white Speer house, with its sun-trap windows and broad, neatly kept lawn. But the Speers were dispossessed of this home, and in their place lived American Army Brigadier-General John B. Murphy and family. To reach the post-war Speer home you climbed an even steeper hill to arrive breathless at the little wood-and-brick outhouse, surrounded and almost swallowed up by unkempt bushes and flowers.

Swinging on a rope strung from a bent and tired old tree beside the house was a straight-haired, bespectacled girl in her teens. She ran into the house to inform her mother of my arrival, and reappeared with a slim, attractive woman who had the harassed look of a hen with too many chicks to handle. Despite her family handful, Margarete Speer managed to look smart and presentable in a simple white pleated blouse, long-sleeved beige cardigan and plain grey skirt, and had the figure to fill them. Her hair was cut short into a neat back roll, the kind of trouble-free style that a woman of many domestic dilemmas and no domestic help would choose. Although her hair was short, she kept brushing it back nervously, and the children evidently worried her even though they were playing in that part of the Speer estate still remaining to them.

There were four boys and two girls. Cello-playing Albert junior, the eldest son, wanted to be — and later became — an architect like his father and grandfather. He was apprenticed to a carpenter, studying for a carpentry master's certificate, and also attended evening classes to prepare himself for a technical university. His father directed the course of young Albert's career by correspondence from Spandau:

> I agree, Albert, to your taking carpentry lessons as part of your training as an architect on condition that later you work for a time as a bricklayer. This is necessary because you cannot ever give orders on a site without command of the trades, otherwise you feel stupid, and a decent fellow would even feel a bit of a fraud.

When Albert junior later entered an international town planning competition, he dutifully sent his proposed plan to the gaol before submitting it. He came second and won a substantial cash prize.

Fritz was the scientist of the family. Natural science, chemistry, physics and geometry were his speciality. 'As for you, Fritz,' his father wrote from Spandau,

> it is difficult to write a real fatherly letter; you know, one of those with lots of fatherly warnings. When I was as young as you are now, I too was a little irresponsible, and disinclined to work at school. Sometimes I was bad-tempered, which I now know was due to the natural growing pains of a boy. I know all about those complexes that often plague a boy, but they disappear as you grow older. And, because I know all this, I would dearly like to help you now. I took to rowing and thereby got rid of all harmful tendencies. I suggest you do the same.

Fritz, the family's photographer, took most of the pictures of his mother, brothers and sisters to send to his father in Spandau.

'Then there is the shy one, Margaret, whom you saw when you arrived,' said Frau Speer, counting her brood to me. 'Margaret and Arnold — he is a year younger — come next. As far as school is concerned, he is the black sheep of the family. Ernest is the youngest, and then there's my elder daughter Hilde, but I would like to tell you more about her later. She is away from home at present. I always try and find somewhere for one of them to stay because I haven't got enough room.'

Looking around the crowded house, I could see why. Frau Speer shared a bedroom with Ernest, and the other five had two small bedrooms between them when they were all at home. Double-tiered wooden bunks for the boys in one of the rooms helped out.

The house was full of odd bits of nondescript furniture and had an air of planned disorderliness. The kitchen, out of all proportion to the family it had to serve, was the main room.

Next to it was a narrow lounge with two occasional tables and a floral-patterned settee. Some early nineteenth-century Italian landscape drawings that decorated the lounge walls were the only pictures salvaged from the ruins of the Speers' former home in Berlin.

Frau Speer and I strolled through the grounds to a garden table away from the children's inquisitive ears.

'My husband lived only for his children but for years we never allowed any of them to visit him in Spandau. I was against it. They would get a wrong impression of a father of whom they knew very little before because he was away so much during the war. The youngest, for instance, was only eighteen months when my husband was arrested in 1945.

'I don't want to argue the rights and wrongs of my husband's case. He was tried at Nuremberg because he used foreign slave labour, although I do say he was not the one who actually employed them. But don't you think he has already paid a big enough price?

'His most terrifying recurring nightmare in the prison was visualizing going to the governor to point out that his twenty years were up, only to be told by the governor that he didn't know anything about it so Albert would have to stay.'

Then Margarete Speer abruptly dropped the subject. She knew her husband was one of the few Nazi war criminals who admitted the mistakes and wrongs committed against humanity.

'It's strange what a career can do to a marriage,' she said. 'Albert had to meet so many demands that we became almost strangers. Yet it wasn't always like that. The early years of our marriage were great fun. As soon as the sun appeared, in March or April, off we would go with skis and rucksacks, travelling through the Alps from one Alpine Union hut to another, keeping wherever possible to the heights and not going down into the valleys. We climbed the easier peaks, and even today I remember how cross Albert was when, despite his physique, he could not make the last few metres of a lofty peak. Albert liked getting what he wanted.

'In the summer we undertook much longer tours with a tent and folding canoe on the Danube, Moselle, or Mecklenburg lakes. But driving was my husband's greatest joy. We always had a two-seater sports car and I was the spare driver. Albert never lost this enthusiasm and when he became Minister of Production he even learned to drive a tank.

'Rowing, flying a plane and Rugby were his other favourite pastimes, but our beautiful carefree days were gone after a few years, sacrificed for his career. And that's how it was. Albert looked forward impatiently when we might travel and find enjoyment in our old excitements, but there was always something to keep him back, and then came Spandau.'

Margarete Speer changed the subject once more. It was about her daughter, Hilde, she wanted to talk; the daughter whom Albert Speer hoped would set an example to the rest of his children — a democratic example.

In the summer of 1952 Speer was upset by the news that his daughter Hilde was not to be allowed to benefit from her success from earning an award under a youth exchange scheme that entitled her to spend a year in the United States. Objection had been made to her because her father was a war criminal.

John McCloy, the US High Commissioner for Germany, who had organized the scheme, said it should not be American policy to let the sins of the father be visited upon the children. McCloy appealed to Secretary of State Dean Acheson, who himself happened to be the son of a pastor.

Acheson overruled Hilde Speer's disbarment from the United States for an academic year. The following summer she changed her home in Heidelberg for another in Hastings-on-Hudson, New York State, chosen by the American Board of Re-education of the US Information Services in Germany as one of a number of pupils to spend twelve months at an American school learning the democratic way of life. She was even elected president by classmates of the Hastings school she attended. The identity of her father remained an official secret, and she lived with Dr Richard Day, a children's doctor and psychologist, at Circle Drive, Hastings-on-Hudson.

Hilde shared the Day family's home life, attended the local school with Dr Day's three daughters, aged eleven, thirteen and fifteen, and was a regular speaker at international youth discussion groups. The only people in the locality aware of her background were Dr Day and his wife.

Invited to tea at John McCloy's mother's home in Hastings, Hilde discussed her father with McCloy; he told her that the US State Department was prepared to review his case, but that the Soviets flatly refused.

'Hilde was a pretty child, very musical, and very popular,' said Frau Speer proudly. 'In her letters home and to her father, which I passed on to Spandau, her German became Americanized. Her father told her that on her return she could take over from me and try what she knows of child psychology. My husband felt that what Hilde learned in America would be good for the rest of the family.'

There are stranger things ... as Shakespeare said.

For twenty-four desperate days during the month of May 1945 a silver-haired, sharp-featured woman was the First Lady of what was left of Hitler's Reich. Frau Inge Dönitz, wife of

Grand Admiral Karl Dönitz, never forgot the experience. She lived and waited for the time when her husband — the man with the shortest sentence and biggest hopes in Spandau — would assume, as she said, 'his rightful place at the head of the State'.

Frau Dönitz

To see Frau Dönitz I drove for about thirty minutes from the port of Hamburg Centre to No. 1 Dora Sprechstraße, Aumühle. This was just a mile from the estate of the father of modern politics and militarism in Germany, Bismarck, the 'Iron Chancellor' and power behind the throne of the first Kaiser.

Frau Dönitz had a three-room ground-floor apartment comprising bedroom, living room, kitchen, and bathroom. The spacious rooms were furnished in a severe style. Dominating the few pictures in the living room was a naval artist's impression, drawn in 1941, of her husband's massive U-boat pens under construction at Laurient. High on top of a cabinet stood a life-size bronze head of Peter, the eldest Dönitz son, who was killed when serving as an officer of the watch aboard one of his father's U-boats.

On the Saturday we met, Frau Dönitz was off duty from her work as a nursing sister at the Hamburg Rautenberg Hospital, the very hospital declared at one time by the German Government to be a centre of neo-Fascist activity. Frau Dönitz had exchanged her hospital uniform for a plain but elegant woollen dress. She was tall and thin and her hair was disposed of in a bun. Disciplined from head to toe, she had the command over herself expected from the daughter of a family of four generations of professional soldiers — and from the wife of an ambitious man who became a Grand Admiral and Reichs President.

Both her sons were killed in action: Peter, early in the war, and Klaus, drowned in an E-boat action. Only her daughter Ursula, married to former U-boat commander Guenter Hessler, survived. During the war Hessler had received the Knight's Cross from his father-in-law and then took a desk job on his personal staff.

'When my husband comes out we will both need rest and peace,' was Frau Dönitz's careful opinion. 'It will be the first time I shall really be alone with him. As long as I can remember, his profession has always come first. I realize, of course, that sooner or later I shall have to "look into the bucket", which is a naval wife's way of saying she knows that she will lose out once more.'

A heavy smoker, as she talked of her husband she reached for another cigarette, her favourite Egyptian brand, jabbed it into a small holder, and a moment later was exhaling the smoke through her nostrils.

'At the Nuremberg Tribunal my husband learned about many terrible things of which he was not aware before. He knew nothing of concentration camps; nor did I, though admittedly I had heard of Dachau and other such places and that it wasn't very comfortable to be in any of them.'

She seemed to repeat the statement, then, continuing the defence, went on: 'When I occasionally mentioned the question of concentration camps to my husband he would reply, "A lady in your position should not associate herself with rumours."'

'Didn't your husband ever question Himmler about the camps?' I asked.

'Oh no, he wouldn't do that because he always maintained that one department was not justified in questioning the affairs of another merely on the strength of rumours. My husband would have thrown anybody out of his office had they come to him in such circumstances.'

The horrifying 'rumours' of mass persecution and torture did not prevent him from telling naval officers in the autumn of 1944 that they had to be anti-Marxist and anti-Semitic, and he repeated these statements to interrogators at Nuremberg. So Grand Admiral Dönitz's 'surprise' in learning at his trial of the revolting history of the concentration camps was somewhat difficult to explain away. My recollection, which I confirmed later from captured records, was that Dönitz seemed much more informed on the subject than his wife was apparently aware of. Not only had he made mention of the use of concentration camp labour at Hitler's naval conferences, but on one occasion he had made a personal request to the Führer for the release of a prisoner whose specialized technical skill was required.

Frau Dönitz's conversation switched suddenly from the uncomfortable past to more pleasant thoughts of the future.

'We might move in with my daughter-in-law,' she volunteered, and then added with a slight smile, probably remembering her brief period of glory, 'but the day may come when demands will be made on my husband. If the present head of the German State were to die, influential people might decide to ask my husband to take over. Knowing his sense of duty, which is not prompted by vanity as some appear to think, he would accept.'

Frau Dönitz paused and the only sign of tension was the way she gripped the cigarette holder in her hand. Her face, free of make-up, gave nothing away.

'My husband has the right to hold the first position in the land for two reasons. Firstly, because he was responsible for saving two and a half million Germans who were able to escape from the Russians during the time he was *Staatsoberhaupt* [Head of State], and played for their safety by delaying the armistice. Secondly, because he was nominated in Hitler's will as his successor.'

Dönitz had devotedly followed his Führer. On 15 February 1944, more than a year after Germany's terrible Stalingrad defeat, he told his senior officers that he was in complete agreement with Hitler's strategy. Everyone, he said, should follow Hitler without question. The following month, in a message to the German people, he declared:

> German men and women! What would have become of our country today if the Führer had not united us under National Socialism? Split parties, beset with the spreading poison of Jewry, and vulnerable to it because we lacked the defence of

our present uncompromising ideology, we would long since have succumbed under the burden of this war and delivered ourselves up to the enemy who would have mercilessly destroyed us.

Even a month before capitulation, this political admiral, who at his trial and afterwards in Spandau gaol maintained that he had merely been doing his duty as a serving naval officer, insisted: 'Europe will realize that Adolf Hitler is the only statesman of stature in Europe ... Europe's blindness will one day come to a sudden end.' On 1 May 1945 he broadcast:

> The Führer has nominated me as his successor. In full consciousness of my responsibilities I therefore assume the leadership of the German people at this fateful hour. My first task is to save German men and women from destruction by the advancing Bolshevist enemy. It is to serve this purpose alone that the military struggle continues. For as long as the British and the Americans continue to impede the accomplishment of this task, we must also continue to fight and defend ourselves against them.
>
> The British and the Americans in that case will not be fighting in the interests of their own people, but solely for the expansion of Bolshevism in Europe.

I asked Frau Dönitz: 'Are you suggesting in all seriousness that your husband is entitled to inherit a right from a regime that had no power to confer it, is no longer in office, and is wholly discredited?'

She had never before discussed the future with anyone outside her husband's circle. I reminded her that Hitler's leadership hardly established a dynasty and that his Nazi laws died with him. She rapped back coldly and precisely:

'Hitler was made Chancellor when Hindenburg was president. The Reichstag then voted him absolute power for four years, during which time Hindenburg died, and Hitler, using his rightful authority, combined the positions of President and Reichs Chancellor into that of *Staatsoberhaupt* or Führer.

'Hitler threw out the old constitution, and in its place established his own — by which, among other things, he gave himself the right to appoint his successor. This right is now a German law.'

I replied that a law established by such a regime and in such a way could be disposed of without any difficulty: 'It's really quite simple. If Hitler made his own laws by conveniently throwing out the old constitution, the present German Government is equally justified in annulling the Führer's so-called constitution and with it the right of succession.'

About to say something, cigarette holder poised in mid-air, Frau Dönitz paused, realizing that she had said all she wanted to say. The hand was lowered, and she replied quietly: 'I must say, my husband will not try to insist on this right, but would always be ready to take the wheel if the people desired it.'

She then produced a letter received from the Archbishop of Canterbury. 'You can see that the Archbishop says that he has every sympathy with me in the matter, which shows that he agrees that my husband and the other Spandau prisoners were the victims of injustice, and the Allied prison with its medieval conditions would not exist at all but for the terror of the Russians.'

The Archbishop's reply to her plea for help was unquestionably written with human consideration. She, however, was using it to rally support for the sympathy campaign concentrated on a stage-by-stage easing of gaol conditions, with the ultimate object of easing the inmates out of prison altogether.

As for her 'medieval conditions', the only truly medieval aspects of the gaol were the cells with iron hooks upon which inmates had been strung up to die of strangulation. But the hooks were used in the years when the seven were the masters.

Before I left, Frau Dönitz agreed to let me take away a large batch of her husband's prison letters to enable me to translate or photocopy a selection. I subsequently found among them one mailed in the Charlottenburg district of Berlin, to a Fräulein in Hamburg. It was not an official prison letter, but the small sheets of paper were covered with familiar-looking, closely cramped pencilled handwriting. Although satisfied that the writing matched Dönitz's authorized correspondence, I nevertheless photographed it for subsequent examination by a graphologist. It proved to be an important message for former colleagues, which he had arranged to have smuggled out of the gaol then mailed in an ordinary envelope to an accommodation place to avoid bearing the conspicuous Dönitz name and home address. Frau Dönitz had clearly forgotten having put the illegal document amongst her file of official gaol correspondence. The letter's secret contents did not match Karl Dönitz's open utterances, nor his wife's claims, as to his future intentions.

All that his wife later said of his release was: 'For ten years he had no relationship with the outside world. For him, coming out of Spandau was like being born again — into a new world.'

It was in Berlin, where she had gone to visit her husband, that I first met the eighth and last member of the 'Spandau club': Erika Raeder, second wife of the Grand Admiral who had built Hitler's navy and was condemned for life. At first Frau Raeder did not want to see me. Then, changing her mind, she said she was prepared to make a statement, but was not willing to enter into any discussion. I said I wanted her to discuss everything with me frankly, or nothing. Finally she agreed.

This was my first insight into the character of the woman I was to meet, but it was not in Berlin that I really got to know Erika Raeder. I wanted to talk to her in her own surroundings; so a few days later I met her at Hanover airport, and we drove off to her home in Lippstadt, Westphalia, a three hours' journey along the autobahn. On the way I realized how much hatred she bore: hatred of Russia, hatred of Britain, America, France, and everyone remotely connected with her husband's imprisonment; and hatred of defeat.

With every word this tall, pallid-faced woman in her mid-sixties, still wearing mourning for her thirty-year-old son Hans, poured out unqualified bitterness. It was anathema to her when Hitler replaced her husband as C.-in-C. of Germany's navy with the 'new boy' Dönitz. Her country's defeat was yet another blow, and in 1946 she vanished from Berlin; with her husband she was flown to Moscow.

The Russians returned her husband to Germany to stand trial at Nuremberg, but for four years she herself remained a prisoner behind the Iron Curtain, her whereabouts a Soviet secret. In Minsk, and in the Bimau, Buchenwald and Sachsenhausen concentration camps in Eastern Germany, she savoured the dregs of misery and the heaped-up indignities.

When Grand Admiral Raeder was convicted as a war criminal the Russians were requested by the Nuremberg Tribunal to allow his wife a special visit to her husband; but she never appeared.

'They fed me on caviar in Moscow but let me go hungry in Minsk. In Sachsenhausen I had to peel seven hundred potatoes a day, was interrogated all the time, and finally released without explanation,' she complained.

She left Sachsenhausen, a former Nazi death prison, exactly four years to the day after she and her husband were captured by Russian troops when their home near Berlin was overrun.

'On my release, my orders were to stay in the Soviet zone, not to speak to others about the Russians, and to live in the Potsdam district.' But at the first opportunity, wearing a pair of men's shoes and carrying a small rucksack, she took a train into the American sector of Berlin.

'I never belonged to the Nazi Party and yet I was punished.' Everything Erika Raeder said to me during the journey to Lippstadt was coloured with venom. 'The International Court of Nuremberg had no legal right of existence and no legal powers. The accused never had a chance to produce any evidence or witnesses for their defence who might have helped them.'

It was no use arguing with her, however wild her accusations. Frau Raeder had begun a long tirade, and nothing was going to stop her.

'What about the bombing of German towns as an example of Allied inhumanity?' She did not mention the Luftwaffe blitzes and flying-bomb attacks on British cities and towns. 'British inhumanity in the conduct of the war was shown in many ways, including the use of U-boat traps,' she declared. Apparently Germany's submarines should have been left to destroy shipping unmolested.

Until we reached Lippstadt and her modern apartment house, Frau Raeder fulminated against Britain and the Allies, and extolled the humanity of the German forces.

In a comfortable lounge scattered with photographs and inscriptions she spoke acidly of the conditions at Spandau and said she thought relatives should be granted free air travel to the prison. Then, amid the Goebbels-style outpourings of this embittered woman, came: 'In Churchill's book, *The Gathering Storm*, he admitted that his intention to invade Norway was forestalled only by Germany. Yet the invasion of neutral Norway was a charge on which my husband was convicted at Nuremberg.'

This was the first point in all my long conversations with Frau Raeder that really made me pause. Then her voice cut in again:

'The treatment that we Germans have suffered is far worse than anything that happened to the Jews.'

I left unsaid the picture in my mind of concentration camp incinerators, of mass graves. No words could temper this torrent of hate, yet she and her husband claimed that he had protected Jews in the navy from persecution; that he had intervened on behalf of a number of Jews of his acquaintance and even secured the release of Jews from concentration camps. Denying knowledge of what went on in the camps, Erich Raeder maintained:

> I did not learn the full scope of these terrible happenings until the days of the Nuremberg trials and then, like all other decent Germans, I was deeply ashamed. Up to that time I would not have believed it possible that Germans could have sunk so low, could have behaved in such a bestial fashion towards a defenceless minority. No excuses are possible for such behaviour.
>
> It is to my religion, and the Christian background that my parents gave me, that I owe the inner serenity that supported me during the difficult days of the Nuremberg trials and throughout the years in Spandau.

Frau Raeder returned to discussing the British Navy:

'The reason why the British detest us, and my husband in particular, is because his brave little ships *Scharnhorst* and *Gneisenau* and the tiny German Navy made the British look silly and proved themselves better fighters. There is no doubt that the little German Navy was much better than the great British Navy.'

She accused Britain — not Hitler — of bearing responsibility for World War II. Her husband told her: 'Britain went to war in 1939 because Greater Germany, growing in strength and united with Austria, was becoming a menace to British imperial and economic interests. The destruction of this political and economic power of Germany was Britain's war aim, an aim in which she was supported by the United States with a zeal that was even greater than her own.

'The only aim that the Anglo-German nations declared was, of course, the purely moral aim of a "crusade" against National Socialism and Hitler. That it was not this crusade, but war on the German people and their industrial power that was their principal war aim, we well realized in the years immediately following 1945, after Hitler was dead and National Socialism had been eradicated — at a time, that is, when both had lost their significance for the German people. Such an aim was less a justification for the measures taken by the Allies than was the knowledge, which we Germans gained only after the war, of the crimes which the Hitler regime had committed.'

Consumed with bitterness and hatred, as far as both Erich and Erika Raeder were concerned they had no cause for self-reproach or guilt. Of all the wives of the 'Spandau club' she was the most talkative and its worst propagandist.

12: EMERGENCY

The khaki-clad batman roused the sleeping figure by quietly nudging his shoulder and then bent over and said, 'An emergency call from Spandau, sir.' It was 2 a.m. The man on the bed, the duty doctor, yawned and asked, 'Who is it this time?'

'Hess, I'm afraid, sir.'

'Oh, lord! It would be.'

The doctor slipped out of bed and began to dress. He was one of four representing each nation, whose job it was to keep the prisoners in good health, as far as possible, and to ensure that nobody could ever accuse the authorities of neglect or indifference. The task conferred on the doctor the right to exercise his authority to an extraordinary degree, even to brushing aside almost any of the Spandau regulations.

Leaving the officers' quarters near the prison, the doctor approached the main entrance. He stamped his feet as he walked, as did everybody entering the prison after dark, so that the guards would not be tempted to shoot first and ask afterwards.

At the Directors' office the doctor waited while a secretary telephoned news of his arrival to the Chief Warder in the inner cell block; and then he walked down the corridor to an iron door at the end. He whistled through a small hole in the door, saw an eye fixed on him through the peep-hole, and heard the sound of a key being turned. Keys of the inner cell block were retained by warders inside. Accompanied by the Chief Warder, the doctor entered the cell of prisoner No. 7. Chief Warders acted as interpreters, and with the exception of Chisholm, the

British Chief Warder, who was not fluent in Russian, they all spoke Spandau's four languages. Not one ever remained alone with a prisoner.

Rudolf Hess was lying on the floor, hands clutching his stomach and moaning: 'Help me! Help me! Why can't you help me?'

An examination, the doctor knew, would serve no useful purpose. The symptoms, for which a physical reason could not be discovered, never varied. At one time Hess was even allowed a hot-water bottle to relieve cramps.

'All right, Number Seven, this will help,' the doctor said, extracting a hypodermic syringe from his bag. Hess stopped moaning immediately and looked at the doctor.

'What are you giving me?' he asked as the syringe was filled with a colourless liquid from a small container.

'Morphia. Your arm, please.'

The injection completed, the doctor said, 'Now you will sleep and we'll talk about it again later.'

Hess slept without further trouble. The colourless liquid pumped into his arm was sterile water.

When the doctor had caught up on his disturbed rest some hours later, it was time for Spandau's daily medical checkup. Occasionally the duty doctor visited prisoners in their cells, or perhaps in the garden; but more often, as on this morning, the men were brought in singly to the surgery outside the main cell block.

Baldur von Schirach came into the surgery rubbing his hands in anticipation of the privileges he hoped would be granted. He came to attention, clicked his heels, and stood close to the doctor's table until told to take a seat.

Smiling, Schirach glanced at the record book in front of the medical officer and said:

'Now then, may I have some fruit for my constipation?'

The doctor knew that the other six would also make similar requests. Their only chance of obtaining extras was to request them for health reasons, although Schirach believed in the efficacy of coffee and fruit as a laxative. His first wish was granted.

'And black coffee and black bread?' he suggested, trying to increase his initial gain.

'Let's wait and see how the fruit helps,' answered the doctor.

Schirach moved across to the scales where a medical orderly checked and registered his weight on a card.

'What is it this week?' the prisoner asked. On hearing that he had dropped a little he protested, 'The right weight is most important to my well-being, Doctor, and in the circumstances I think you should consider my application for extra bread and coffee.'

He was ignored.

Maintenance of the prisoners' weight was considered important. When the Russians took over, some of the prisoners, due to the change of diet and nervous strain, lost from two to four pounds each during the month.

'You had trouble with Hess again during the night, Doctor,' said Schirach, switching the conversation. The former Deputy Führer was the talkative Schirach's favourite subject, and he babbled on: 'Perhaps there is really something physically wrong with him. He is certainly not normal. Some of his actions are undoubtedly prompted by the inferiority complex from which he suffers. I am sure it was this that induced him to fly to England and to attempt, in one stroke, to become the most important man in the world.

'When Hitler informed Göring that, in the event of anything happening to the Air Marshal, Hess would be next in succession, Göring became so furious that he began to shout at the Führer; he said it was an insult that a man of Hess's inferior intelligence should be thought fit to take his place.

'I advise you, Doctor —' But Schirach got no further.

'Shut up, Number One! You're talking too much again,' he was admonished by the doctor. Schirach became silent; he knew just how far he could go.

'Here are your new glasses, Number One, though you don't really need them.' The doctor handed them to him in a case.

'If others are permitted to see an eye specialist and are issued with spectacles, I don't see why I should be excluded,' Schirach answered in his usual clipped manner. 'Please may I know the prescription of the glasses?'

The doctor asked the reason for his curiosity.

'It's nice to know these things,' was the reply, but he had to leave without his request being satisfied.

Karl Dönitz was the next to be shown in. He, too, clicked his heels, looking round the barely furnished surgery with its examination couch and medicine cabinet. After asking for fruit, black coffee, and black bread 'for constipation', the Grand Admiral explained that he was still troubled by his 'bloody cramps'. To illustrate the truth of his assertion he cocked his right leg up in the air, and as he tried to straighten it yelled, 'J-e-s-u-s C-h-r-i-s-t!'

Dönitz believed that he had thrombosis in the legs. 'The operation that the King of England had, that's the operation I need,' he said. 'The King had cramps, did he not?'

An electro-cardiograph had shown Dönitz's heart to be free of any disease. His general condition was good, and the doctor assured him, in ordering massage, that he was not a thrombosis case. Dönitz undressed, and for fifteen minutes Proost, the medical orderly, massaged his legs and body to encourage better circulation.

'I think part of the trouble is that I am no longer able to take long walks,' explained Dönitz. 'The cell is too small for the exercise I need. Would it be possible, Doctor, to allow me, when my cramps are really bad, to walk up and down the cell block a few times?'

'Yes, I think so,' replied the doctor.

Albert Speer came limping in for his medical check-up.

'Oh, no, not you as well,' said the medico in mock despair.

'Come now,' said Speer, suddenly straightening up and walking quite normally, 'you can't blame me for trying.'

Speer wasn't at all remiss in asking for more fruit, black bread, and coffee.

'Is there anything else you'd care for?' inquired the doctor.

'Yes, I would like to ski,' answered Speer with a grin.

Speer, too, was a self-appointed guardian of Rudolf Hess, and began to talk about the emergency call during the night.

'Hess must be a great trial to you. The problem as I see it is at which point does hypochondria and deliberate faking end and a form of insanity begin?' he said. 'One day at Nuremberg, Hess asked me to try some sugar from a packet he had been using and to tell him whether I thought it caused diarrhoea. The following day I deceived him by telling him that I was becoming constipated and he replied, "No doubt in certain quantities it can have the opposite effect." Now what can you make of such a man?'

Hitler's old Minister of War Production wanted a Vitamin B injection because he used to be given a number of them to relieve strain during the war and had found they did him a lot of good. The British and American duty doctors always declined, however, and as usual Speer responded: 'I will wait until I see the French doctor.'

He was usually in excellent physical condition, except one December when, suddenly weak and feverish, he had started to spit blood and complain of severe chest pain. Portable X-ray equipment brought from the American hospital had confirmed pulmonary infection, and he was transferred to the prison infirmary, where his wife visited him on Christmas Eve.

The tall figure of Baron von Neurath entered the surgery.

'How are you?' asked the doctor.

'No better than a man of my age can expect to be, I suppose,' came the reply. 'My angina causes great pain, but the digitalis I have had to tone up the heart has helped a little. I must say, however, the homoeopathic treatment I receive from the French doctor seems to do me the most good, though I am afraid that it will not be approved by the rest of the medical staff.'

He was right. For several months the four doctors — who had jointly to agree on all special treatment and surgery — argued about the effectiveness of homoeopathic treatment. Finally, when Baroness von Neurath and her daughter Winifred visited the prison in May 1953, they were informed that this treatment was to be continued indefinitely.

'Your husband realizes that his angina can only be relieved,' the visitors were told.

Before leaving the surgery Neurath turned to the doctor to ask the question he put to every officer in Spandau:

'Tell me, will I ever be free again?'

The answer was always, 'Yes, some day.'

But the Baron knew his heart condition was grave and would cause his death. He required regular sedation to control his blood pressure.

'My sentence was a terrible blow to my pride,' he admitted.

Bow-legged, arthritic Grand Admiral Erich Raeder was weighed and examined. 'I limp only for a moment or two after I get up from a chair, doctor,' he said; 'otherwise I walk normally, though my knee undoubtedly needs constant attention.'

When he underwent an operation for a hernia in Spandau, Raeder received blood transfusions for four days from an American source. He received massage regularly for his arthritis, and on this particular morning the doctor said he could have impregnated wool for the knee. Raeder bowed, gave his usual '*Schönen dank*', and left.

Fat little Walther Funk shuffled in. 'Herr Doctor,' he said, cringing as he usually did when about to complain or ask for something, 'can't you help me? These bloody Russky warders still ignore the authorized notice on my cell saying that I must not be disturbed after treatment. They kept me awake again all last night.'

The doctor made a note to raise the matter once more, knowing that as always the answer of the Soviet Director would be: 'In the name of the Union of Soviet Socialist Republics I wish to point out that the flashing of lights in the cells throughout the night is a security measure that takes precedence over everything according to the regulations.'

The Russians forever quoted from the book, and among the Spandau personnel were many who agreed with their strict interpretation. When the other Directors insisted that the nightly inspection should be cut down, the Soviet Director answered curtly: 'I will refer it to a higher authority.' So the East-West tug-of-war began, but at the next weekly meeting of the Directors the reply of the higher authority was 'Net', and that was the end of it.

Funk, stripped naked, stood on the surgery scale. 'Why am I losing so much weight, Herr Doctor?' he whined.

'Losing a bit of fat won't do you any harm,' the doctor answered. 'You're paying now for the over-indulgence of the past. You were always greedy for too much of everything.'

At the mention of the old days, Funk's lips parted in a semblance of a smile and he recited:

> How I like to remember the times
> When all my members were limber —
> All but one.
> Oh, the wonderful times are gone;
> Stiff are all my members —
> All but one.

He stretched out on the surgery couch, and the medical orderly began to massage his right leg. Because of muscular inflammation in this limb he had walked with a stick for some time. Apart from diabetes, he was prone to hypertension, pulmonary and urine problems, and a whole string of ailments. Doctors who checked him again and again found his heart still in reasonably good shape and considered he would simply have to put up with his other conditions, as he had done for years — long before he was imprisoned. In August 1956 he underwent an operation for the removal of gallstones in the British Military Hospital in Berlin.

'Apart from the bloody Russkies disturbing me at night, Herr Doctor, I have quietened down considerably after the last treatment for nervous disorder,' Funk volunteered. 'The dreadful condition of over-excitement has gone, and now perhaps the heart disease will disappear, especially as I feel that the medicine I am receiving is doing me a lot of good. All my suffering originates in the soul.'

The massage finished, Funk began to dress. As he was about to leave he said, 'Herr Doctor, I have one more request to make. May I have some pills for my migraine headache?'

'Do you know, Number Six, that it costs between 240 and 280 marks a month to supply drugs and medicine for you?' the doctor said.

'Let me out of Spandau, Herr Doctor,' Funk replied, 'and I will gladly pay twice that much myself.'

Funk once admitted to Neurath: 'I manage to deceive the doctors so much about my health because I believe my own lies.'

Funk's migraine, which was genuine enough, was prescribed for, and a few moments later prisoner No. 7 took his place in the surgery. When Hess undressed to mount the scales, the small scar on his chest, relic of an attempted suicide during his imprisonment in Britain, was visible. It happened at Maindiff Court Hospital, Abergavenny, Wales, when Hess snatched a bread-knife, tried to stab himself through the heart, and succeeded in inflicting only a slight wound. It was his second try; prior to his removal to Maindiff, where he spent the last three and a half years of his detention, Hess — in full air force uniform and flying boots — flung himself over the banister of a long flight of stairs. A guard, hearing the crash, drew his revolver, and Hess was saved from being shot only when an officer realizing his peril called out in the nick of time, 'Don't fire!' Hess was found at the foot of the staircase crying for morphia. He had broken a leg.

Hess explained the suicide attempts to his companions in Spandau by saying, 'I felt I was going mad, and I was also depressed because the future looked so hopeless for Germany. One of my mother's brothers committed suicide, and my father's sister was taken to a mental hospital and died very young. I believe the reason for her condition was that my grandfather was drunk at the time she was conceived. I am certain that, when I was in England, Secret Service agents intended to kill me either by driving me to suicide, murdering me in a way that would look like suicide, or by putting small doses of poison into my food so that it would appear I had succumbed to a lengthy illness.'

Personnel who guarded Hess in Britain knew all about these suspicions of his. They reported that even when food was served from a common dish he would never take the piece of meat nearest to him because he believed it was intended that he should do so.

'Number Seven,' said the Spandau doctor, 'we have decided to give you some further psychiatric and physical examinations, including an X-ray.'

Hess's stained false teeth showed in a slight smile of satisfaction. 'That is good, Herr Doctor, but there is one thing I would like to ask you about. I have heard that X-rays can make a person sexually sterile. This concerns me greatly because a woman astrologer, who guided me for many years, once told me the stars showed that I could not expect to have more than two additional children, although at the time nobody knew I would have to spend so many years of my life in prison.'

Hess was not apparently taking into account the fact that he was due to spend the rest of his life in gaol. He was quite satisfied when the doctor assured him that he had nothing to fear from the X-rays.

A few days later a large truck drove up to the main entrance of Spandau Prison with mobile X-ray equipment from a nearby American Army hospital. Hess, who received more medical attention than any of the prisoners, was due for further treatment. He was brought into the surgery and ordered to strip. 'I would like some protection against the X-rays, Herr Doctor,' he said, cautious as ever. (The people of Munich used to say: 'If ever the Führer passes this way on the rampage you'll see Göring shooting wildly while our Rudi runs home to make sure that his licence to carry a revolver has not expired.')

The doctor emphasized once more that there was no danger. Hess was nevertheless X-rayed with his hands spread over his middle as a precaution. The X-ray showed clear lung fields except for a small calcified area in the upper right zone; a blood test was negative; no evidence was found of organic disease. There was no physical reason for the chest and stomach pains of which he complained almost every day.

'I am going to give you charcoal biscuits to aid your digestion,' said the doctor, 'and some medicine to tone you up.' The medicine was produced from the dispensing cupboard, and Hess, who had a formidable knowledge of drugs, asked what were its exact contents.

'Iron and strychnine,' was the reply.

'In that case, Herr Doctor, you would have no objection to taking some of it.' The doctor laughed. Knowing Hess's phobia with regard to being poisoned, he obliged him by swallowing a spoonful of the tonic.

When over-exhausted, Hess was convinced he had heart disease. 'I am tired all the time. Why is this?' he asked. His obsession that this was a symptom of a serious condition was probably not unrelated to certain long-standing fears referred to by Göring when questioned about Hess. The basis of them dated back to self-gratification during adolescence.

Cancer was another of Hess's great and abiding fears. 'I feel that nature doctors are more likely to find the answer to cancer,' he said. 'I have more regard for them in this respect than for the practitioners of modern medicine. I do not say that every homoeopath is an artist, but the genius of the homoeopath doesn't simply lie in exact thinking. A Hamburg homoeopath told me that the recipe for his drugs came to him when he was dozing at night.

'It cannot be explained why, in our time, so-called quacks are often successful. With understandable horror, doctors discovered that farmers were putting fresh cow manure on wounds. However, this therapy proved surprisingly successful especially with gangrenous wounds. Some time before the war it was found that cow dung contained extraordinary antiseptic properties. Homoeopaths will never outrun the scientists in the medical profession — it is the other way round — which is why I have always sympathized with homoeopaths.'

Hess's interest in nature-healing went back a number of years. In the early days, when the Spandau prisoners were still permitted to obtain books from their families, he was convinced that modern medicine was not helping him very much; he secured a collection of books filled with folklore on the treatment and care of all known diseases dating from 500 B.C. to the present.

Hess's hypochondria was further illustrated by the precautions he took when he parachuted into Britain. His pockets were filled with 'emergency' pills and potions, mostly homoeopathic. He was armed not only with vitamin tonics, glucose, and sleeping tablets, but with a so-called elixir said to have been brought by a Swedish explorer from a Tibetan monastery. Hess believed it to be a miracle cure for any gallbladder trouble.

In a comment on this aspect of his flight, Britain's Medical Research Council had stated:

It seems quite clear from the remarkable collection of drugs that he was intent on protecting himself against an assault of the devil so far as his flesh was concerned, and, if he knew the action of all the drugs he carried, he has obviously missed his vocation and ought to have made a very handy general practitioner.

He seems to have protected himself (1) against the pains of injury by opium alkaloids; (2) against the discomfort of headaches by aspirin; (3) against the pains of colic by atropine; (4) against flying fatigue by pervitin; (5) against the sleeplessness following pervitin by barbiturates; (6) against constipation by a saline mixture, and against every other ailment to which flesh is heir by mixtures of unknown products made up along homoeopathic lines — i.e. so dilute that it is impossible to say what they are. This reliance upon allopathy for bodily ailments, and his further belief in homoeopathy for other discomforts, seems to represent a curious outlook on medical science.

There was ample guidance available to Spandau's doctors in his dossier. Records showed entries and notes such as the following:

> Prone to long moody periods during which he took to his bed and lay with his fingers in his ears, he would smile to himself, or stare straight ahead for hours.
>
> Whenever aware of being under observation, his most frequent reaction was one of suspicion and complete unwillingness to talk about his past life. He always attempted to prevent thorough examination of his mental state, declaring, 'I cannot remember.'
>
> Out of touch with reality except for immediate requirements, problems or complaints.
>
> Obvious that much of his amnesia was assumed.
>
> A psychopathic personality of the schizophrenic type with marked depressive tendencies and delusions of persecution.

Unjustifiable suspicions give simple incidents a sinister judgement; subject to hallucinations of grandeur.

A hypochondriac who rolls on the floor, arms folded round his stomach and groaning with apparent pain. When asked the extent of the pain, instantly stops to discuss the symptoms, but, having finished his detailed description, begins again.

Hess had unquestionably a Jekyll-and-Hyde personality: the ruthless Nazi capable of anything and the individual professing interest in the happiness and welfare of children. But the conclusion of physicians and psychiatrists from the four-Powers was unanimous and unequivocal: 'Hess is not insane in the sense of being incapable of distinguishing right from wrong, or fully realizing the consequences of his acts.'

It was the Spandau Directors' difficult task to prevent unnecessary mollycoddling and to ensure that only measures absolutely essential to maintain or improve the prisoners' health were introduced as prescribed in the agreed four-Power rules. Only hard experience compelled changes in the original regulations, and these were substantially introduced at the insistence of the gaol's doctors, who were in many respects all-powerful. But they had no say whatsoever in the disposal of the bodies of any inmates who might die in the prison. This was, above all, a political problem, and one of the most delicate that had to be faced.

The gaol's regulations provided that a prisoner's next of kin be informed, if necessary by telegram, of serious illness; and a prisoner could, if he so desired, request other persons to be notified. The question of special visits in the event of serious illness was not explicitly covered by the regulations, but extra private visits in connection with urgent family affairs could be sanctioned by the prison Governorate.

It had long been uneasily felt that the previously agreed measures to be taken on the death of a Spandau inmate were unsatisfactory. Cremation involved the disregard of certain provisions of German law, which required the production of a certificate from relatives of the deceased that cremation had been carried out in accordance with their wishes. Neurath's health, in particular, precipitated reconsideration of the problem at a meeting of the Allied High Commissioners held in June 1951. The most recent medical report on the Baron, supplied by the Officer Commanding the British Military Hospital in Berlin, stated:

> This prisoner is in general well preserved and in good condition but he has arterial and heart disease with a high blood pressure. He has occasional heart attacks of an anginal nature which have not hitherto been really severe. His expectation of life is not good, the chances being that sooner or later he will die after such an attack, but it is not possible to put any period to such a forecast; it may be several years.
>
> There is not anything in his life in prison which specifically hastens the progress of the disease. He does not exhibit any psychiatric abnormality.
>
> He also has senile cataracts in both eyes which, as always in this disease, causes progressive failure of vision. At present he can see, with glasses, to read. A time will come when his vision will be limited to the perception of light. However the progression of the cataract is slow and at present it appears unlikely that this stage would be reached in less than three years. An operation is not indicated at the present and it is considered unlikely that by the time the cataract is mature, which is the time for the operation, he would be a good case for it. Again, this condition is not affected by his prison life. For neither condition is there any special treatment which is unobtainable by reason of his being a prisoner.

In June 1951 Chancellor Dr Konrad Adenauer tried yet again to influence Neurath's release from Spandau by personally presenting to US High Commissioner McCloy a German Government request for the Baron, then seventy-eight, to be transferred to a hospital. The move was clearly intended as the initial step in engineering Neurath's complete release. Shortly after discussing the problem with Dr Adenauer, McCloy, answering as current Chairman of the Council of the Allied High Commission, informed the Chancellor that the Commission could not support the request. The reply pointed out that Neurath was visited by doctors every two or three days; then, following the line of the most recent medical report, it added that his physical condition was 'the result of age and not of imprisonment.'

At that June's meeting of the Allied High Commissioners, McCloy suggested that the matter of disposal of the body of a Spandau prisoner be raised with the Soviets. André François-Poncet of France asked for time to refer to his Government. McCloy proposed that the question of a new 'less barbaric procedure for disposal of remains should be taken up with the Russians by the three Governments in Berlin, each acting separately'. He thought that, even if the approach proved unsuccessful, the gesture would have some ethical significance.

At the following month's High Commissioners' discussion, François-Poncet reported that he had consulted his Government and that they were not in favour of pushing the issue with Moscow. They thought the matter could be dealt with when a case actually arose, but McCloy reported that there would not then be time for prolonged discussions, with a body lying around awaiting disposal. François-Poncet referred to the demonstration that had taken place after the execution of seven Landsberg prisoners whose bodies had been handed over to the next of kin. McCloy said that the funerals of the Landsberg prisoners in the US zone had been dignified, and that, although there had been a demonstration in the British zone shortly after the executions, he understood that the families of the executed men had nothing to do with it. When McCloy pressed the point further, François-Poncet agreed to consult again with Paris.

Sir Ivone Kirkpatrick, for Britain, said that if the Soviets were unwilling to accept any modification of the procedure previously agreed on by the Kommandatura, no more action could, or should, be taken. However, the Western authorities would then be in a stronger position to defend themselves should a prisoner die and the existing procedure, which would certainly cause widespread indignation in Germany, have to be applied.

Three days after this meeting, Major-General Bourne, the General Officer Commanding the British sector, wrote to the Principal Legal Adviser of the British Army in Germany:

Action on the death of a Prisoner in Spandau

I agree that the present procedure for disposing of the body of a prisoner is not suitable. I consider that a new procedure, on the following lines, should be introduced:

On the death of a prisoner, an autopsy should be performed in the presence of doctors of each of the four nations, and a death certificate signed by these doctors in accordance with the result of this autopsy. One copy of the certificate should be retained by each nation. The body, together with a copy of the death certificate, should then be handed over to the relatives for burial.

No announcement should be made of the funeral, and it should be attended by relatives only and by representatives of the four nations.

> I do not think that anything can be achieved by raising this question at the meeting of the prison directors. I would suggest that it be considered by the High Commission.

A few days after Major-General Bourne's suggested revision of burial arrangements, London authorized Sir Ivone Kirkpatrick to agree to John McCloy's proposal for an approach to the Soviet authorities in Berlin about the remains of Spandau prisoners who died. The Foreign Office concurred with McCloy's view that, even if unsuccessful, the approach would at any rate place on record that the Western Allies had done their best to get the regulations on a decent footing.

Kirkpatrick was advised to point out to the Russians that there was no reason why the burial of Spandau prisoners should give rise to extremist demonstrations if the authorities took precautionary measures. Furthermore, if the Soviet authorities renewed the argument that acceptance of the revised procedure would contravene requirements established at the International Military Tribunal, they should be told this contention had no legal basis. The only procedure laid down by the Tribunal regarding sentences stated: 'In case of guilt, sentence shall be carried out in accordance with the orders of the Control Council for Germany.' The Russians were clearly referring to procedure adopted in the case of major war criminals who were condemned to death by the Tribunal and whose ashes were scattered after execution. The quadripartite committee responsible for carrying out those executions decided on the disposal of the remains. It could be further argued that the case of those condemned to death was not analogous with that of those imprisoned. Accordingly, rules affecting the disposal of remains had the same legality as other Spandau regulations; they were passed by the Allied Kommandatura, so revision — now that the Kommandatura had ceased to exist — could be effected only at intergovernmental level. It was such intergovernmental assent that was being sought.

It was agreed that the three Western Commandants should make a verbal approach to Soviet Commissioner Dengin about the disposal of remains. It was like talking to a brick wall. He repeated that the proposed amendments were contrary to the intentions of the Nuremberg Tribunal, and arguments contradicting that got nowhere. As usual, Soviet intransigence blocked reasonable changes.

During 1952 Neurath had a severe angina pectoris attack. The heart pain almost killed him. The Soviet doctor who was supposed to be on duty was summoned but could not be found, so the British medical officer was called. Neurath had been nursed through a similar attack the previous month, but at times his deteriorating heart condition made it difficult for him even to speak. An adjustable hospital bed had to be installed in his cell, and warders were instructed not to use the night inspection light — only a diffused light.

When his daughter, Winifred von Mackensen, heard that he might not recover, she was anxious to know if the family would be allowed to take possession of the body should the worst happen. The Directors again discussed procedures in the event of his death. It was decided that the body should be taken to the Wilmersdorf crematorium for a brief service, and the ashes returned to the gaol. The Directors felt that the journey to the crematorium should be made at night. Police would be notified and road-blocks established to stop demonstrations in front of the prison if news of the death leaked out. The prison chaplain, Military Governors, Directors, warders, and twenty military guards would accompany the body, which would be transported in an army truck to avoid attracting attention. A decoy cortège might also be necessary. The ashes would remain in the prison safe. All the Western Directors were agreeable for the ashes to be given to the Neurath family. The Soviet Director undertook to seek authority to permit him also to comply with this.

Flowers that might be sent to the gaol would be placed in the chapel for a time, after being checked for possible hidden explosives. Inscriptions on accompanying *in memoriam* cards would, if necessary, be censored.

An all-night Directors' meeting covered every possible aspect of the funeral, including the choice of music, which it was decided should be determined by the chaplain.

To Winifred von Mackensen's inquiry regarding burial regulations on the death of a prisoner, the Directors officially replied:

> Custody of a prisoner's body is vested in the Four-Powers even after death. Permission for private family burial cannot be granted. Nor can any information regarding official burial procedure be disclosed.

When the families of the men of Spandau learned that under no circumstances would the body of a prisoner be handed over they agitated for relaxation of this rule. Finally the three Western High Commissioners yielded to pressure from the German Government and proposed a modification of the procedure. On the ground that it violated the four-Power agreement governing custody of the prisoners, the Soviets refused to grant families the right to arrange a private burial, saying that it would pander to Nazi fanatics throughout the country.

While their relatives continued to press their case, the seven men speculated on the grisly problem.

'I hear the American Government has forced reconsideration of the question of our corpses,' gossiped Schirach in the summer of 1953. 'Anyone who dies here will no longer be incinerated, but will be given a grave here in the prison cemetery, and relatives will be allowed to visit it once a year.'

On the night of 2 September 1954, hearing sounds of choking and gasping coming from Neurath's cell, a night guard checking through the spy-grille saw him fighting for breath and rushed an oxygen cylinder and respirator to the cell. The British and French doctors stayed with him throughout the night. An oxygen tent was fixed over his bed, and a British nurse brought in to keep watch. Asked by the British Director whether he wanted his family advised by telegram and whether he wished to see the chaplain, Neurath just about managed to whisper, 'Yes.' A telegram was sent to the Baroness and her daughter suggesting that they come immediately. He was so ill that the chaplain was notified that the last rites could be administered.

By the time the Baroness and her daughter Winifred arrived, he was in the gaol's infirmary. The two visitors were allowed to sit on chairs at the foot of his bed for thirty minutes. For two days he stayed in the oxygen tent with doctors alternating in constant attendance. This time the four Directors decided against cremation. Neurath, it was agreed, would be buried in the prison garden he had tended lovingly for years, dressed in his own civilian clothes. Funeral arrangements were finalized and everything was ready — except the Baron: he recovered.

13: SPANDAU LETTERS

There was a ring at the door and, to the woman who opened it, the postman handed a blue-green envelope with a Berlin postmark. Printed in bold black letters in the left-hand corner of the envelope were the words:

> SPANDAU ALLIED PRISON
> (1) BERLIN-SPANDAU
> Wilhelmstraße 23

Albert Speer had written his weekly letter to his mother.

> My dear Mother,
> Though you assure me that you are quite well, I read somewhat differently between the lines. Please write and tell me the truth. After all I am strong enough and can take it. I don't want to shirk bad news, and certainly not when it concerns yourself.
> Don't get bitter, and don't make your life more difficult because of my imprisonment. Neither aggravating yourself, arguing, nor despairing can help either of us. I therefore consider it right that you should all try to get over it as best as possible, and if, for once, you could really be merry, it would please me immensely.
> That we should understand each other is my greatest wish. I am fully aware that trouble and aggravation can only worsen the condition of your heart and lower your power of resistance, so please be sensible about everything.
> I am weaving through time so that I can come out unbroken and full of enthusiasm for my profession, in order that I can make money straight away for Gretel and the children.

I hope very much, Mother, that you are better. Both of us must never stop hoping for *auf Wiedersehen*. Always remember this when you are fed up with life. Never lose the will to live. It is so important to me. How sad it would be if I should learn in here that you no longer exist, and have gone before my return.

Your Albert

Every Sunday afternoon in Spandau, seven men sat down in their cells to write a letter home. This was their only official contact with the world outside the prison walls. When they first came to Spandau they were informed of the letter-writing regulations:

> All letters to be in Latin handwriting [Germans write in two styles, German and Latin]. Letters, to be written clearly, are, for the time being, unrestricted in length, and strictly limited to personal affairs. Politics and discussion of international affairs are barred. Unrestricted reference to internal Spandau matters is also not allowed. Nor are wives and relatives permitted to send prisoners national or international news.

At first the seven were permitted to write and receive two letters once in every six-week period, but a little later this was altered to once every four weeks with letters restricted in length to 1,200 words. In April 1948 the rules were again revised:

> Letters 1,300 not 1,200 words as stated previously. Nothing may be underlined. Abbreviations are not permissible, and that applies to initials; signs not allowed without an explanation for them. Anything contrary to these regulations will result in letters not being sent.

During Easter 1950 Speer in his small neat handwriting wrote his children a Spandau nature story. He had a florid style, although the details and descriptions in his letter were not exaggerated:

My dear Children,

How is the cat getting on with the dachshund? We too here have many animals, but only birds. They may come and go without permission.

Before I rise in the morning, and again in the evening, a blackbird gives me a concerto. Just a few moments ago she started the evening concert, and then we listened to two wood pigeons, who, inseparable, sit on a branch in front of my cell window, busily kissing.

Recently, a falcon attacked them. The pigeons let themselves drop from the branch very quickly, and so got away. As a punishment, the falcon lost its way in our prison, and he didn't seem to like it at all, which I could understand only too well. Actually, falcons only go where it is so lonely that 'foxes' can openly say 'good night' to each other. And that is why the falcons are here.

I can also see from my window a pair of magpies which built their nest last year, a large nest right in the top of the tree, but so well built that all the winds can't do a thing about it. I think that's why the falcon likes it, for recently he stepped into it and the magpies had to sit next to the nest, and, of course, took umbrage.

When the magpies saw that the falcon wanted the nest, they started a large meeting of all the magpies of Spandau. There were eighteen in the tree. I don't know what was decided, but, since then, some more magpies have arrived for the protection of the nest, and the falcon has not the courage to continue his poaching.

We also possess an owl, and she'll start hooting any minute now. At present she is peeping out of her hole in the roof, maybe she is a little surprised by us, and sometimes she may even laugh about us.

Four weeks ago, a company of crows flew off after having spent the winter here. They are probably somewhat north now. The crows kept together well. Twice buzzards were nearby. The crows started a hue and cry, assembled high in the air — there might have been three hundred of them — and attacked the buzzards, who immediately fled when they saw so many birds.

Since the buzzards left it is much quieter, and more and more of the smaller birds arrive, starlings, robins, finches.

I have told you all this so that you, too, may study the life of birds when you are in the woods. Life changes so much all the time, like all of you. Please send me — all of you — your latest measurements. I have those from last year, and can compare them and see how much you have grown.

Your Papa

Speer's letters to his mother bore unmistakable indications of a guilty conscience:

My dear Mother,

Another six months are gone. It is unbelievable how quickly time passes here. I can only say 'Thank God.' I only hope I live to see all of you again, therefore please remain well and mentally alert. Be sensible and don't get excited so that you can enjoy life once I am back with you. I wrote this letter in a larger handwriting than usual, thinking of your eyes. Is it better like this?

I sunbathed in the garden, and when that bored me, occupied myself a little in my small rock garden, which I planned on a bank. I started it with marguerites, camomile, poppies, strawberries and other wild plants which thrive in this sandy desert here. I am as happy over it as I was about the first rock garden which I built twenty years ago. What a pity however that it can't be in our own garden.

It is always dreadful for me to have to send you birthday greetings while still a prisoner. It reminds me too much that you have had to spend another year of your life parted from me.

Your Albert

Always keen on exercise and physical fitness, once a useful Rugby player, he wrote:

My dear Children,

I have now started my winter sports. Every morning and evening I start peculiar twisting of arms and legs and call it gymnastics. It might be quite healthy. I am keeping in good training for my work in the garden. Nevertheless you will leave me standing when we all ski together again.

There is an English book here telling of gymnastics of the eyes so that one can do without glasses. I have had a pair for reading and writing for the past year, and needed a stronger pair. So four weeks ago I started the eye exercises as per book. The experiment is indeed a success. I never would have thought it. I read now without glasses and this letter is written without them. I am writing all this so that you, Margaret [his daughter, who wears glasses], will understand that with patience and perseverance your eyes can improve, and, should you be at all interested, I will tell you the name of the book.

I have given you a lot of advice, Margaret, but like all fathers, I make the mistake of thinking you will really take any notice of it.

As for you, Fritz, if you don't like music right now, it doesn't really matter because you might get to like it in a few years. I don't care very much for operas, but I do like concerts.

Thanks for your last letter, Albert. I am thrilled and looking forward to seeing the new types of cars when I am free. Much must have changed.

Your Papa

And, to his wife:

My dear Gretel,

All day long you have to contend with the children and their troubles while I sit here reading, drawing and playing around in the garden a little. I really have a bad conscience about it all.

When I come home one day, I must get used again to climbing. For years I have not scaled a single height, not even a staircase, but with a little effort I might again become a mountaineer.

I don't agree that it would help to send Fritz to a boarding school. I am no friend of boarding schools. I have just read two books on child psychology. One of them, the most interesting, was in English and, unfortunately, I could not understand it so well. Find out whether there is a child psychologist in Heidelberg, and if so get him to take Fritz in hand.

Please send me fifty labels with 'S' marked on them for my laundry.

Your Albert

Proposals drafted by the Law Committee of the Allied High Commission, discussed and approved by the High Commissioners on 15 March 1951, were recommended to mitigate somewhat the severity of letter-writing regulations at Spandau. An improvement of visiting arrangements was also sanctioned at the same meeting.

To overcome Soviet obstruction, the Council of the Allied High Commission decided that any attempt to reach complete quadripartite agreement to the amendments should remain strictly unofficial. Rather than a negotiation, it should take the form of personal action on the part of each of the three prison

Governors supported by his other two colleagues. The note from the Allied General Secretariat advised:

> It is desirable that the discussion on problems to be solved should be initiated by one of the three Western Governors in the course of his duty month as Chairman. It is no less desirable that the contemplated discussion should be conducted in such a manner as not to reopen the question of improvements already achieved.

Changes to make postal regulations more liberal included: authorizing prisoners to receive and to write a letter every two weeks instead of every four weeks; granting greater freedom to send and receive additional letters in 'exceptional cases', for example at Easter, at Christmas, and on the birthday either of the prisoner or of his usual correspondent. It was also intended to reduce appreciably the time required by the Governors to examine correspondence addressed to prisoners in order that letters could be delivered within twenty-four hours after they reached the prison.

The Governors also wanted to make it possible for a prisoner to rewrite a letter if the one originally submitted for checking before mailing required partial or total censoring. Authorized correspondents were also to be specially warned to avoid deviations from correspondence regulations, which would cause deletion of passages. It was further recommended that there should be greater freedom to send or receive, in addition to private correspondence, strictly business letters.

A few months after the new policy was pushed forward, the three Allied Prison Directors unanimously opposed the attitude of the Soviet Director in seeking to deny Speer's request to be allowed an extra letter to be sent to his ailing father-in-law. The Russian stated that Speer had not exhausted his regular letter rights. The British Director called attention to the Soviet Director's own remarks at a meeting a few months earlier when he had classified an emergency, within the sense of the Prison Regulations, as 'family problems and grave sickness'. At that same meeting the Russian would not agree to a special visit to Raeder by his wife on the occasion of his seventy-fifth birthday, because this did not constitute an 'emergency' within the meaning of the regulations. After conceding family problems and grave sickness as justifiable circumstances for additional privileges, the Soviet Director told his Allied associates: 'A birthday is not an exceptional case. There are all types of anniversary holidays. A big war criminal [Raeder] should be satisfied with receiving wishes and congratulations for his birthday in a normal letter. The crimes committed by the war criminals should not be forgotten. It is much too early to forget them.'

A few days before Speer's eldest daughter, Hilde, left in August 1952 on a Government-sponsored visit to America to learn the democratic way of life that her father had scorned, the following *bon voyage* letter arrived at the Speer family's Heidelberg home:

My dear Hilde,

You cannot possibly imagine how delightful it is for me to travel with you in thought. It is so beautiful that you should have this great experience. I nearly envy you. If you have inherited anything from me it is my delight to travel, so I can well imagine how happy you are.

I have every trust in you that in spite of success you will remain modest. That attitude will take you the furthest. It is a pity you can't write everything to me. Have you considered starting a diary so that later we can share your experiences together?

Wishing you happiness and joy,

Your Papa

Within a few hours of writing this letter, Speer learned of the death of his mother. His next letter was to his wife:

> My dear Gretel,
> Please don't feel that the severe loss I have just sustained in my lonely life presents a difficulty that I shall not be able to overcome. Admittedly, in prison I feel much more of what a family can mean to one than ever before, and how irreplaceable it is to lose my mother. But Nature ensures that, above a certain and bearable measure, pain does not increase, and besides that, one somehow becomes blunt towards sorrow and need. You know that, too, from the difficult times of the past years.
> On the outside, I am as before, my feelings are my own.
> Your Albert

Denial of the privilege to write or receive letters was the punishment most feared by the Spandau prisoners. On occasions Rudolf Hess was not allowed to send or receive letters for a month because of repeated insubordination.

Hess's correspondence was clearly undertaken with a deliberate eye to publication of a book. For the benefit of those faithful Nazi followers who still clung to the Hess 'Führer-of-tomorrow' myth, letters were carefully injected with phrases of patriotism and guidance; for example:

> My dear Ones,
> If I should catch him later, this devil who has cost me eleven and a half years — and who knows how many more years of real life with all their heavy sacrifices — I would kill him, in spite of all the good which he might finally produce.
> I have reached an age in which to youth I have become a hindrance. I hope that the young people concerned will draw the right conclusions. What I could do to bring them to that point I have done, very difficult as it was.

Even through silence one can talk. Give youth my greetings with all my heart.

Yours

Hess signed most of his letters *der Deine*, copying the ancient Roman style of ending a letter with simply 'Yours', or *der Euer*, 'Your One'. He never used his own Christian name. When, in October 1952, the prisoners were told they could now write a letter every week, Hess wrote informing his wife of the new regulations:

My dear Ones,

Well, now you are astonished! Hardly did I write the letter of the 19th instant and here is another one today. In short, sensation in Spandau!

From now on, every week, one letter in exchange with the whole family. Up to one thousand three hundred words, if possible typewritten to help the censor, but don't imagine that I can really sweat out a weekly letter of one thousand three hundred words. For that purpose I am lacking material and the spirit. Don't forget that eleven and a half years do not pass without leaving their trace.

My next letter probably follows in a fortnight to friends in all circles.

Your One

But he changed his mind and wrote every week, most of it culled from books. One letter was mainly concerned with his favourite subject: Napoleon. In many ways Hess attempted to pattern himself on the Emperor, as the letter indicated:

My dear Ones,

The will of Napoleon was concentrated on glory at any price, even the cost of millions of dead, and so his desire to do good for the French people and the world became meaningless.

Even as a human being, too, he was lacking the tiny spark of kindness which history demands from the great ones. You see it is all-important to what purpose will-power is put. For will-power Napoleon certainly had to a tremendous extent, probably unequalled by anyone else. The control of his body and mind was so potent that he could sleep wherever he was sitting, yes, even on a trotting horse when he wanted to or even before the beginning of a decisive battle.

He revealed the secret of this extraordinary aptitude. When he had to ponder about a problem he opened a particular drawer of his mind, and when he wanted to sleep he closed all his mental drawers. And then he rested.

A good exercise for will-power and self-control is to force one's self to go easy on food. For instance, not to eat meat on a given day, though one has quite an appetite for it, or to get along with an apple and just a few pieces of dry bread while hiking.

Yours

Writing about the planes continually flying over Spandau, former pilot Hess said:

My dear Ones,

What utter nonsense to convey a few dozen people at a speed of 400 kilometres an hour through the air when none of them is really in such a hurry that they might not just as well go by train.

Every time, thousands are disturbed in a very impertinent way. Even bird song is interrupted; the peace of nature disturbed all along the route of their flight. Shameless. Headline — 'Cultural Progress'.

I would be happy to know whether Wolferl [his son] prefers anything special in his reading, or if he merely reads anything that comes his way. At his age I was particularly interested in nature study and especially astronomy.

I am just reading an interesting book by Camille Flammarion, *The Puzzle of the Life of the Soul*. The author was once Director of the Paris Observatory. When I was young I read so many books on astronomy that I neglected my book-keeping course, and failed my exams.

I hated everything connected with business, which, however, does not mean that I consider business unimportant, far from it. Men in a big way of business have their parts to play in society, as I know from my experiences in Egypt. Fate however had other plans for me, among them to put me here.

Now back to the book by Flammarion. The author discussed unexplained supernatural phenomena in France, such as the vibrations in the brains of dying people, which can be heard thousands of kilometres away. Schopenhauer and Goethe have also commented on like phenomena, and Shakespeare says, 'There are more things in heaven and earth…'

Oh that I could be a ghost among you at Gailenberg, and with my men of days gone by.

Yours

And 'silent' Hess, self-conscious about his garrulous correspondence, wrote to his wife:

Mutti,

My 'writeritis' must not mislead you. I am still the old Hess, as tight-lipped as ever.

I wonder whether Wolferl has inherited my thrift in money affairs? I can be thrifty to the point of miserliness and yet am not above throwing money about to the point of extravagance. On occasions I have often walked to save a twenty-pfennig fare and then without rhyme or reason squandered my cash on a flight in a sports aeroplane.

As for you, my son, whenever you play chess, watch your pawns. I have always looked out for them and thereby once enjoyed a notable success. In 1916, in an army hospital, a chess world champion, Cohen by name, played a number of simultaneous games. The only one which he lost was the one played with me, due to 'extraordinary anchoring' as he angrily expressed it.

According to what you write about your new teacher, he must have known, not long before the war, one of our cousins, probably your grand-uncle, Hans Hess, Professor of Geometry at one of the higher schools in Nuremberg. He had a passionate liking for studying glaciers, and yet another hobby, Marxism.

He was, until 1933, a town councillor in Nuremberg and a Social Democrat. It is said that every time my name was mentioned his hair stood on end. We considered each other as the black sheep of the family, and at least I was amused.

Your One

News of the Coronation of Queen Elizabeth prompted Hess to write as follows in June 1953:

My dear Ones,

In a little book on the Germanic races, I have just read that the Lower Saxons distinguished themselves by possessing a mixture of common sense and blockheadedness. Obviously I don't regard you, my dears, as belonging to this famous and notorious community, not when it comes to blockheadedness.

That the Anglo-Saxons took along with them something of this characteristic when they crossed to the island no one will argue. Not so much the common sense but their blockheadedness, a will of their own, is shown by the way they hold on to measurements, weights, and things like 'Fahrenheit', which undoubtedly are famous only because they are so impractical. This nation prefers the time-robbing and complicated ways of counting and measuring rather than falling in step with the rest of the world. I marvel that they made the mistake of accepting the same system of time as do the rest of the people of our globe. They must have overlooked the fact that they could have reckoned time by the rising of the moon, which is a very complicated way of counting, as every day it differs by thirty minutes from the sun. It would have been a nice old-fashioned way of measuring time, at least the forefathers of the ancient Greeks found it so.

As an alternative the offspring of the Saxons could have adopted accounting time from the movements of the stars. Adjusting the star-time to the sun again would be just as complicated as trying to transfer English coinage and measures into those based on the decimal system.

For example, an Englishman travelling to the Continent would have to work out how many days have passed since the 21st March, multiply the figure by three minutes and fifty-six seconds, and add the result to his British time, after deducting twelve hours from it. Then he would have 'the time of the day of the damned foreigners'!

To be serious, however, I wish our nation possessed more of this characteristic of the old Saxons, without showing it in the strange usage of old-fashioned measurements and time.

Your One

A birthday letter to his son read:

Philio Mio,

Maybe you will become a brilliant engineer, something I wanted to go in for when I was young, but could not achieve because grandfather's firm was waiting for me.

When things didn't turn out well, I turned back to my old love, only on a bigger scale. I wanted to engineer the world, and indeed did so a little until Fate said 'Enough' and seated me into Spandau, where I am still sitting.

My wish for your birthday, my boy, is that this puzzling power which we call Fate may have cooled off on me a little and may direct your life in a calmer, steadier, straighter path and not take you for a scenic railway ride.

Life can also be compared to an escalator which may carry you rather well, but becomes rather embarrassing if it goes down and gets stuck in the cellar.

Your One

Almost all Walther Funk's correspondence concerned the great variety of his illnesses, describing with much self-pity and in detail symptoms of the treatment he had to undergo. His letter of 16 December 1951 was one of the exceptions:

My dearest beloved little doe. My dear, good, brave little wife,

You will remember the day many years ago when I gave you a little silver heart on a silver chain, which you wore for such a long time. It was a good talisman and it protected you through many dangers until with other possessions it was stolen from you by people whom you trusted. [Frau Funk buried her jewels in her garden but they were filched.]

I have made many mistakes in my life and have been disappointed on many occasions, but never so keenly as in discovering how vile and treacherous some people can prove to be. And yet there is no one in the whole world who can say that you or I have intentionally or consciously committed an injury or an injustice against anyone.

But you are right in what you say, true love gives lovers always the feeling of shelter, the feeling of being protected in the breast of the one person one loves.

Please bring me a new pipe. The last two which I received are not in smoking order any longer. The pipes here have to suffer more than usual as the proper nursing and cleaning of them can't be undertaken with the appropriate instruments. Also I have to suck and pull harder to keep them going because of the scarcity of matches. [The guards lit up for them.]

I am smoking my most satisfying pipe now as I always do when I write to you. I think I must have smoked some seven hundred bowls of this masterpiece of a pipe since you gave it to me on our thirtieth wedding anniversary. It is as if I had smoked seven hundred Havanas [cigars were his favourite in the old days], but this pipe too is very sensitive. I have only the other one left, also very tasty and English.

Your Pumpelmann

When he was really ill, Funk's letters conveyed the fact in a peculiar way to his wife; he untidily scrawled lines diagonally. When well and normal, his handwriting was neater and more readable.

My dearest beloved little doe. My dear, good, brave little wife,

On the 29th of April just gone it was exactly seven years since the black day that I had to part from you. That was a Sunday and the first swallows had arrived. It is the same this year. I saw the first swallow in the prison garden.

The cuckoo, too, is calling for the first time. For the past fortnight I have spent several hours every day in the garden enjoying the beautiful spring.

When I was so very ill with inflammation of the nerves, a high temperature of 101 degrees, and the cramps in the bladder, I cried for you as I have never done before in my life. That is gone now and I am improved. Above all I sleep better, though still with tablets.

By the way, because of my illness, I completely lost my hearing and sense of taste for a time. Now I can taste again a little, but can't smell a thing. I received Vitamin B_1. My diabetes has disappeared and left only slight traces, I haven't needed insulin injections for three weeks.

Recently I dreamt of lice. In the old times that meant money to me.

Your Pumpelmann

In a post-Christmas letter, Funk told his wife:

The Christmas days in the cell, which you made into feast days through your beautiful presents and visit, are now over. I had bathed and groomed myself with more than usual care so that everything around me should be proper for the feast, and in readiness for your visit in my quiet retreat, and you came indeed, though only in my dream.

Holy evening between four and five in the afternoon I was lying on my couch and thinking with longing of the loving care bestowed by you in putting the final touches to the Christmas tree in that little refuge of yours when quite clearly I saw you surrounded by the flickering Christmas candles.

That was the most ennobling moment of my life, and I was as happy as never before on any of the Christmases I have so far spent in prison. It was as if an angel had entered my cell, and when I opened my eyes the half-moon, visible through the window of the cell, seemed eager to give me a greeting from you.

On Christmas Day during our ceremony the large wax candles you brought were burning so bright and were flickering so friendly towards me that I was reminded of the light in your loving eyes. During a walk afterwards I wore the new scarf, gloves and one of the nice new shirts.

Your Pumpelmann

Just before a visit from his wife was due Funk wrote once more:

My dearest beloved little doe. My dear, good, brave little wife,

My thoughts are wholly concerned over your impending visit. During the last few days I am certain you must have thought of me often and very longingly, especially throughout the nights of the full moon when I have been aware of your devotion.

When I hear this light sweet singing in my inner hearing, then I have the sensation as if all my being were filled with a melody of love which you too comprehend with your soul, and enter into the harmony. About the extraordinary experience of the soul reaching its climax I will reveal my thoughts more fully one day.

This afternoon we shall again have a gramophone concert. We are going to hear Beethoven's sixth and his last sonata, played by Wilhelm Kempf. I am looking forward greatly to it.

On Friday I again had surgical treatment for the bladder and diseased nerves. It is always very painful in spite of morphia and cocaine injections and for twenty-four hours after I feel very ill indeed. I find myself in a most irritable condition and become oversensitive to all noise and light. Sleep is impossible, though I take double the quantity of sleeping pills. Oh my dear, how I suffer then.

In my religious diary [diaries containing a thought for every day were given to each of them by the padre] I find for today the following consoling theme:

'God knows what you do, where you live. He will never leave you, and will not forget you.'

Believing in this, please receive my kiss for you.

Your Pumpelmann

Because of censorship, there were delays of several days, sometimes as many as ten, before letters were handed to prisoners or posted to their families. The men were instructed to use only one side of the paper, and to leave a border around their writing to enable photostat copies to be made more easily. Every letter written and received was photographed and filed in the Spandau records. Censorship was strict, and offending lines were simply scissor-snipped right out of a letter. Originally letters were censored by only one official; then two 'approved' initials appeared on the censor's stamp on each page.

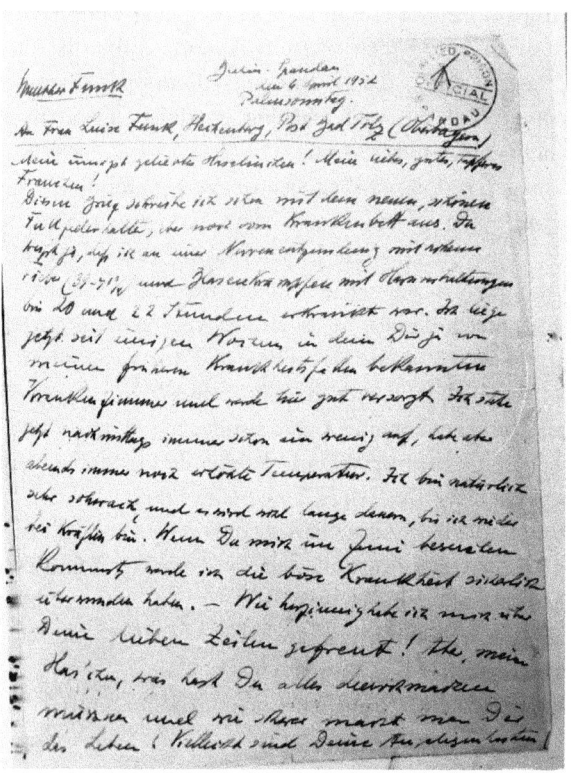

Actual letter from Funk to his wife. The official censor's stamp can be seen.

Frau Dönitz said there was little complaint about the censorship, but on one occasion when a letter to her husband was returned to her, she felt its contents to be so innocuous that she sent it on to Richard Stokes, MP, who at that time was particularly concerned with German affairs. Frau Dönitz asked

Stokes to read the letter and judge for himself whether it contained anything indiscreet, and if not, to see whether the censor's action could be reversed. The letter was forwarded to the Foreign Office, and apparently considered harmless, for it was then passed through the Spandau censorship.

Baldur von Schirach wrote a warning to his brother-in-law, Heinrich Hoffmann junior, concerning censorship:

> My dear Heine,
> The children's letters caused objections because they contained drawings and letter text on the reverse side. Please remind them from time to time to leave the reverse side blank as the censorship regulations demand. It has, furthermore, to be observed that no photographs of buildings (school buildings or homes) are allowed here.
> At present I have the pictures of the boys and you and Annemutz before me and I offer up a smoke-offering to you all with my new Pipe.
> I would like to dissuade Klaus from studying journalism. For this calling study is of little value, while on the other hand legal studies are a very good basis for nearly all vocations. And, if he still wants to be a journalist, he has more prospects as a Doctor of Law than if he presents himself with just a journalistic degree, which is nowhere taken really seriously.
> With regard to letters sent here. These are to be typewritten if possible, although it is very painful to me to renounce the sight of your handwriting. All handwriting is a picture of the writer.
> I would like to ask you to comply with this regulation if possible as it facilitates the censorship of the letters and the distribution is speeded up. With regard to the children, they will, of course, continue to write.
> Nothing has changed here. The following passed through my mind this morning:

No human being is as good as he thinks he is, and nobody is as bad as he appears to others. There is a certain comfort in this reasoning, though it is expressed in a pessimistic sense.

Greetings from the heart.

Your old Baldur

Idealist and dreamer, Schirach filled most of his letters with thoughts on music, his own brand of philosophy, and 'spiritual' advice to his children. To his son he wrote:

My dear Klaus,

How nice that you have encountered the 'Fifth'. Big parts of this symphony I cherish in my mind and I often delight in them. The violin concerto, too, is in my mind with its themes and its variations. With regard to chamber music, this is another world and a very big one which is still strange to you. You can only penetrate it if you take one step after the other and with reverence. One does not know Beethoven if one does not know his sonatas. The chamber music of Haydn and Brahms is one of the most glorious manifestations of the human spirit.

In the ancient world the Greeks brought to a fine art epic works — poetry, drama, philosophy, architecture and sculpture. A similar accomplishment has been achieved only once in modern times through the birth of Occidental music. One must realize this in order to understand what was accomplished in Europe. In my opinion, it is even greater than ancient achievements.

In the language of music, not only can human beings understand one another, but the world itself and also the other world. Or, as Beethoven says, 'Music is a higher revelation than all wisdom and philosophy.' Technical science has made us alike poor and rich — this is a very good theme for an essay!

'What use would it be to man if he should gain the world and lose his soul?' The problem of modern man is the danger of losing his soul. This is not only the fault of technical science. Man is the servant instead of being served.

Greetings and love from your true friend Pap.

Although he was a man who had turned away from the principles of human duty, Schirach appeared to be untroubled in a further letter to his son in which he discussed the ethics of a career:

Dear Klaus,

You always return to the subject of newspaper writing. I had hoped you would express an opinion on the proposals which I made to you in my last letters. I think such possibilities as a school for journalism or an apprenticeship with a 'revolver paper' should not even be taken seriously by yourself.

It sounds almost frivolous when you write of editors who feel themselves superior to what they write. Does this not mean that they act solely because of their greed for money? Such people have the lowest possible moral standards, although they are supposed to fill young people with ideals. With regard to such people I am of the same opinion as the great composer Max Reger who once wrote to a critic, 'I sit here in the smallest room of my house and have before me your critique. Soon I will have it behind me!'

The true test is whether in accomplishing his professional duties a man can feel that he has not sacrificed his ethics. I fear because you have a certain talent for writing you have let yourself be persuaded that writing is a profession for life, yet there are numerous other professions in which such talent is needed daily. In journalism only the top performances represent essential work. Nowhere is there worse writing than is to be found in newspapers written by people who have nothing to say.

> Though I do not know anything of world affairs, I advise you to postpone travelling to foreign countries until after your examinations.
>
> You write, Klaus, that you are enthusiastic about dancing, but I never hear anything from you about sport. At your age one has to take up athletics intensively.
>
> Greetings and love from your true friend Pap.

When it was the turn of the Schirach children to write to their father, each contributed a separate section of the 1,300 words, and the letter was then rounded off by the prisoner's brother-in-law. This arrangement sometimes caused delay and, if a letter arrived at Spandau too late for the regular weekly delivery to prisoners, it had to wait until the following week. Schirach wrote to his brother-in-law's wife about this:

> Dear Annemutz,
>
> Your letter has arrived too late, and so I must write to you without knowing what you have to say to me. The next day for letter writing is the 19th of October. Please try to arrange that your letter reaches here about ten days earlier. Of course I realize how tricky is your task in gathering in good time the letters of four children living at different places. This is certainly not easy and will need many reminders.
>
> When I think how lazy I was in writing when I was a boy and unfortunately, also later (please do not mention this to my young men), I think it very remarkable how punctually my three boys write. Angelica does not come into these observations because she is now grown up, and can be relied upon to do what is expected of her. I do not want to imply by this that all girls are like this. But, generally speaking, one observes that when a girl becomes a young woman she has the knowledge of what is right.
>
> After this excursion I come back to my first point, which is to send off the post without regard as to whether it is

complete or not. The main thing is that I should get news and punctually.

There has been no summer at all and certainly not more than eight consecutive sunny days. You can imagine how this, with my dependence on weather, has caused migraine very frequently. Plants and trees are withering earlier, which is not a good sign. I, like many other 'merry' natures, have a more tragic conception of this world. To regard it cheerfully one has to be convinced of the senselessness of existence.

Humorists are often outspoken pessimists. Other dear fools among our fellow men, the optimists, excel in a so-called earnestness for life. This sounds like a paradox, but exactly corresponds with my experience. The optimist has a sense of comedy, and he expresses this in a joke which is essentially superficial. Humour has depth, smiles are very close to tears.

Despite the world as I know it, I now think of it neither as the best nor the worst of all possible worlds, but it certainly contains more misery than joy.

You cannot alter things if you are misunderstood, for that is human Fate. More and more I have learned to see that so-called influences can be temporarily very strong, but cannot change a man's inner self. The gardener must leave the main work to God.

Greetings from the heart,

Your old Baldur

And to his brother-in-law, Schirach wrote:

My dear Heine,

If one 'celebrates' at forty-six one's ninth birthday as a prisoner, one can hardly be expected to exhibit a festive mood.

The Western man is on the way to becoming a termite.

I am reading my beloved Molière, also a novel by Maupassant ... and a work of Shakespeare. I only mention this so that you can see that I am not quite down in the mouth.

I admire nothing more than a firm character which courageously asserts itself under difficult conditions and rises above circumstances. Of course I know only little of the details of the struggle for life since 1945, but I have not become such a stranger to events that I cannot imagine what you have been through and what still lies ahead.

Baldur

14: TOUCHING IS NOT ALLOWED

After a thorough scrub down and grooming, the old farm-cart was ready for duty. A strip of Persian carpet, worn and discoloured, partly covered the weathered floorboards, and on it stood a comfortably upholstered chair, roped firmly to one side and awaiting the solitary passenger for whose benefit everything had been arranged. As the horse and cart drew up outside the Bavarian farmhouse, the driver climbed down from his seat to vanish for a moment into the house. Then he reappeared with a pair of wooden steps, which he propped against the tail of the cart.

A moment later he was joined by a woman dressed in a rose-coloured costume, over which was draped loosely about her shoulders a beige woollen coat. She wore a small brown felt hat. The driver helped her up the steps and into the cart, and as she began to settle herself a plump *hausfrau* emerged from the farmhouse carrying a couple of medium-sized travelling cases. It was time for *auf Wiedersehen*.

Slowly the cart moved off along the rough, narrow road that linked one village with another. Frau Luise Funk was on her way to Berlin to visit her husband at Spandau. The little cart took its time covering the few bumpy kilometres to the tiny hamlet of Hechenberg, where the passenger exchanged the chintz-covered chair for a seat in the local single-deck bus travelling the fifty kilometres to Munich.

From Munich another bus took Frau Funk to the airport, where she was met by Hans Rechenberg, a trusted friend and former public relations spokesman for Walther Funk's Economics Ministry. Rechenberg always accompanied Luise

Funk on her journeys to Berlin. Sometimes they flew from Munich and on other occasions from Dusseldorf. 'I didn't want the Russians to be certain of the route each time,' she explained. 'They don't like the Funks and might take it into their heads to attack my plane.'

A little over one hour and a quarter after leaving Munich, the plane touched down at Tempelhof aerodrome, Berlin, where a waiting car took Frau Funk and Rechenberg to the Hotel West-Pension, Kurfürstendamm, in the British sector. This hotel, favourite Berlin home of Unity Mitford in the days when she was smitten by Hitler,[12] was also popular with Spandau wives whenever they visited their husbands.

As she opened the door of her bedroom, Luise Funk looked for the large bunch of flowers she knew would be displayed in a vase on the dressing table. Every time she arrived on a visit, there was always a bouquet of pink carnations awaiting her, on the express orders of her husband and provided by Herr Rechenberg as part of the services he still rendered his former chief.

After removing her coat Frau Funk immediately crossed to the telephone beside her bed and requested a number — the secret number of Spandau Prison. Within a few seconds there was a click at the other end of the line, and Frau Funk announced herself, adding, 'I am now in Berlin.'

'Ring again later,' came the answer.

In another three hours' time she made the second call and was told, 'At eleven o'clock tomorrow morning.' It was in this

---

[12] Unity Mitford, one-time friend and admirer of Hitler, died in hospital at Oban, Scotland, in May 1948. The thirty-three-year-old daughter of Lord and Lady Redesdale and sister-in-law of Sir Oswald Mosley, she returned from Germany in January 1940, with a mysterious bullet wound in her head. It was said to have resulted from a suicide attempt.

way that a visit to the prison was finally fixed. The routine was always the same. A wife or close relative wishing to visit Spandau first fixed a convenient date and then left it for the prisoner to make formal application to the Directors. When this was granted it was the visitor's turn to apply for permission, and not until the request was granted were arrangements made to undertake the trip.

It was the practice not to allow more than two of the prisoners to receive visits on the same day. On the eve of a visiting day the excitement and mood of expectancy and tension communicated themselves to other prisoners as well. When the medical officer saw them for their daily examination he could 'diagnose' a pending visit without difficulty. Schirach developed a migraine headache and desired a strong sedative; old Neurath just asked for 'something that will make me sleep a little better tonight', and the same went for Speer and, naturally, Funk. Only Dönitz and Raeder, steeped in service discipline, were almost invariably able to dispense with sedatives. Hess never saw visitors — for years.

Always before a visit the men busily laundered and pressed their clothes and all wore bright-coloured shirts given to them by their families, and specially reserved for visiting days. Speer's favourite was a 'hillbilly' model with dazzling red squares, but Dönitz outdid him with even gaudier cowboy shirts. For 'dress occasions' Funk wore a brown cashmere scarf, and Schirach a red scarf that, when it arrived at Spandau, had a rose pinned to it. The flower was removed, but the scarf still contained a hidden gift. It had been drenched in eau-de-Cologne to enable its wearer to enjoy a perfumed luxury from the world outside.

On visiting morning everyone carried a hairbrush and perfumed soap to the washroom. Dönitz usually had a large tablet, lavender scented, Neurath a French soap with a carnation perfume. In the early days neither soap nor towels were issued. When this came to the knowledge of General Lucius D. Clay, Military Governor of the US Zone of Occupation in Germany, he demanded to know why the prisoners were so treated and was told that it was because a political prisoner in another gaol had used his towel to hang himself. General Clay compromised with security by allowing the seven to use towels under guard, after which the towels were taken away.

At 10.30 on the morning of her visit, Luise Funk and Rechenberg left their hotel in a hired car, which twenty-five minutes later drew up in Wilhelmstraße, Spandau. Frau Funk got out and walked alone along a stone pathway to the main entrance of the prison and past the wooden signs, 'No Entrance' and 'Warning — Danger — Do not approach this fence. Guards have orders to shoot. By Order.' She reached the massive iron-studded gate and knocked. Immediately a guard peered through a small window and asked:

'Are you Frau Funk?'

She replied that she was, then a small door opened in the gate and she stepped through. Waiting for her on the inside was round-faced paunchy Monsieur Darbois, the French Director of the prison, who escorted her to the guardroom, where she began to fill in the necessary details in the visitors' book:

> Surname: Funk. Christian name: Luise. Full name: Luise Funk. Date of birth: 7 June 1888. Nationality: German. Religion: Protestant. Residence: Gasthaus Zoehr, Hechenberg bei Bad Tolz. Time: [here a guard standing beside her showed her his watch. It was 10.57].

While Frau Funk was thus engaged, the contents of her large black handbag were emptied on to a desk for examination. The bag itself also came under observation and so, too, did the coat that the visitor had brought with her. When the guards were satisfied, her possessions were placed in a cupboard until the visit was over.

These formalities completed, in the company of Monsieur Darbois and an armed guard Luise Funk stepped out of the room and made her way up a flight of stairs to the conference room; after a brief delay there, she was taken into the visitors' room next door. The strange light-and-shade contrasts of the medium-sized room, the walls of which had been given a new coat of primrose paint, took some little getting accustomed to. Overshadowing everything and splitting the room into two was the high partition of single close-wire mesh. The mesh used to be double until it was decided to modify the barrier to improve the view on each side and give prisoner and visitor a better look at each other. The room was equipped with a Plexiglas screen, but this was also later removed.

Frau Funk sat down on a wooden stool in front of a long table facing the wire partition. The stool had been placed where it was so that a powerful spotlight could be directed on the face of the visitor to enable officials to watch every expression and signal. The only natural lighting came from the solitary window behind the wire mesh.

Close to her left sat Monsieur Darbois, while on her right was the Russian Director. There were two stenographers, one each side of the wire, ready to take down a full note of the conversation. Leaning against the wall behind her were the British and American Directors. On one occasion only has every Director been absent and the room been occupied by just a solitary guard. That was on 28 February 1953, when Frau

Erika Raeder came to see her husband after the death of their son, and it was tactfully decided to restrict the number of persons present.

As Frau Funk waited, the Russian stenographer smiled suddenly and said in easy German, 'Noch nicht fertig mit Sonntagskleider' ('He's not yet ready with his Sunday clothes').

A few moments later the room's second door on the other side of the wire opened, and Walther Funk shuffled in ahead of the guard to seat himself on a stool opposite his wife. Both of them placed their hands on the table before them, as required by the regulations, and the visit began.

The prisoner opened the conversation as he always did: 'Now I am happy again because I can see you'; then he inquired if his wife had had a good trip. As a former journalist Funk was once able to turn a good phrase, but he found it extremely difficult to talk easily in the visiting room. Politics, prison routine and world events were forbidden subjects, so he chattered mainly about his illnesses and his wife's clothes. He knew every dress and costume of her ample wardrobe. On this occasion he saw that she was wearing a new outfit.

'Stand up so that I can see your new suit,' he said. She did so and then he commanded, 'Turn round and let me see how it looks from the back.' Frau Funk obliged, feeling awkward before the others who were present.

'Did you buy it at the fashion salon where you used to shop?'

He was pleased when his wife nodded, knowing it to be a very expensive place. Luise Funk, never at a loss for conversation, talked about their friends, the farm tenants, and anything and everything she could think of. Then, driven by some impulse, she suddenly said, 'I wish I could touch you.'

As if moved by the same thought both tried to push their little fingers through the mesh. At once the Russian Director sprang from his stool and began to shout and storm at this breach of the regulations. Man and wife shrank back in terror at this outburst, but the other Directors intervened on their behalf, and the conversation began again. Funk started to talk about his operation, nervously twisting a handkerchief throughout the interview, as always.

'Don't put that on record,' the Russian Director ordered the stenographers.

'Are they still shining lights in your eyes?' Frau Funk asked.

As the prisoner nodded and said, 'I have to cover my eyes with three handkerchiefs,' the Russian Director again interrupted angrily.

'Such talk is forbidden here! Not here! Not here!'

The reprimand galvanized Funk, usually as timid as a rabbit, into an outburst of uncontrollable fury. Yelling and cursing, he jumped up from his seat. 'Is it a crime to speak? Is it a crime?' he shouted at the top of his voice, raging and cursing at everyone.

His wife, terrified at the possible consequence of such behaviour, suddenly sagged as if about to collapse, and the British and American Directors, aware of her weak heart, hurried forward to prevent her from falling. She was carried out of the room, propped up on a sofa in the adjoining room, and given a drink of water. Not until she had rested and was judged to have recovered from the slight heart attack was she allowed to return and assured that the time lost by the incident would not be counted.

Walther Funk was led in once more. Contrite, wringing his hands, he apologized to his wife and explained, 'It is because my nerves are frayed by the amount of drugs I have to take.'

The talk went on until the French Director glanced at his watch, rapped on the table, and called out, 'Noch drei Minuten'

— there were just three minutes left. When the time signal was at last given, man and wife stood up, threw each other a kiss, and then Luise Funk walked out of the room. The half-hour visit was over. Prior to November 1952 visits were allowed only every two months and restricted to fifteen minutes. The rules were amended to permit visits once a month, but because air fares were expensive most of the Spandau wives fixed the date of their trip to Berlin towards the end of the month so that they could pay their husbands a second visit a few days later.

Permitted to walk slowly along the corridor, Frau Funk caught a last glimpse of her husband as he was ushered towards the great iron door leading to his cell. He quickly turned his head to meet the eyes of his wife and then moved out of sight. Accompanied by the French and Russian Directors, who walked silently at her side, Frau Funk returned to the guardroom to retrieve her belongings and sign the visitors' book again so that there was a record of the exact time of her departure. Not until she reached the main gate and walked from the prison and away from her husband did the two Directors leave her.

At the next meeting of the directors, the Soviet representative placed on record that prisoner No. 6, Funk, and his wife 'violated prison regulations by touching fingers through the screen'.

Secret snapshot shows the austerity of Von Neurath's cell.

Frau Winifred von Mackensen was the first relative ever to visit Spandau. She did so in December 1947, when travel was a nightmare in Germany. Trains were unreliable and air travel impossible, so the Baron's daughter thumbed a lift on a lorry bound for Berlin. For four days and nights she lay at the back of the vehicle on a bed of merchandise and froze in the wintry weather. When she reached Berlin she was in an appalling state, her face and hands black from the lorry's diesel fumes.

At Spandau she was met by steel-helmeted guards carrying machine-guns, and she signed her name in the visitors' book, the first to be written in it, with a gun pointing at her back. Another guard searched her pockets and even felt in her hair.

Baron von Neurath was the only prisoner permitted two adult visitors at the same time, his wife and daughter. This privilege was allowed because of the age and health of the Baroness. Like her husband, she had a weak heart and it was necessary for a companion to be with her. A similar concession was also made in the case of young visitors accompanied by a guardian.

On 30 January 1953, when the prison had a new British Director, Frau von Mackensen asked whether she might be allowed to touch her father's hand. Permission was refused. 'It is just as well,' said her mother. 'I do not think it would be advisable. It could break his armour.'

Neurath had walked into the room upright and unaided despite his eighty years. Only when his heart condition was particularly troublesome did he use a walking-stick, and then his face revealed the unmistakable flush of cardiac strain. The Baron peered at everyone in the room. Cataracts in both eyes affected his sight; doctors considered an operation inadvisable owing to his condition.

On this occasion the Soviet Director so crowded the two visitors by his presence that the British Director asked him to move over a little.

'I always sit here,' was the reply.

'I insist that you move over at once.'

The Russian gave way and the visit began. Neurath opened an exercise book he had brought with him, and his wife, who wore a flower from the garden of their home, placed a sheet of paper on the table in front of her. Because of their failing memories both had to prepare for a talk from previously prepared notes. At the beginning, the Baron's tongue nervously explored his dentures. They were the second set with which he had been fitted since his teeth were extracted by a Spandau doctor, but he still experienced difficulty with them. One by one he ticked off the items on his conversation list: work to be done on the estate, news about his relatives, friends, and neighbours. His wife told him that she had brought him soap, underwear, shirts, socks, handkerchiefs, and pipes. Then came the signal that time was nearly up, and shortly afterwards the Baroness and her daughter rose to leave.

In May 1953 Spandau received one of its youngest visitors, ten-year-old Richard von Schirach. His father, who had not seen him since he was a baby in arms, had asked that the youngster should be allowed to visit him, and the boy was accompanied to the prison by Frau Hoffmann, wife of Heinrich Hoffmann junior. He had known for some time about his father's imprisonment and explained to schoolboy friends that his father was being restrained just as were certain noblemen in olden times. 'Like Richard the Lion Heart,' said young Schirach. But Baldur von Schirach wore no armour, shining or otherwise, when his son saw him within the fortress.

On seeing his father, the boy said:

'I couldn't remember what you looked like.'

'I don't know myself,' Schirach said. 'I have no mirror.'

'Papi, do you know who Lollobrigida is? Do you know what bebop is? Do you know what uranium is?'

Prisoner No. 1 was ignorant of them all.

'Do you ever see any animals?' Richard then asked.

'No. Where should I see animals? Occasionally a robin comes to my barred window, but only for an instant. Who would go into a cage of his own accord?'

A few weeks later, the prison authorities received a letter asking them to permit a terrier named Nylon to join prisoner No. 1 in gaol. The writer assured them that the dog was 'clean, healthy and happy'. The letter was signed 'Richard'.

When the older Schirach children visited their father they were given special leave from school and travelled alone from Munich airport. Until their eighteenth birthday they were always accompanied; and in Berlin family friends with whom they stayed made the telephone calls to the prison. For Angelica, golden-haired, blue-eyed, and a little dumpling of a girl, a visit to Spandau always posed a great problem. Which of her two costumes should she wear: the pepper and salt or the stewardess blue? On one visit it was the latter. She arrived at Spandau with a large bunch of red roses and asked that her father be allowed to see and smell his favourite blooms. The flowers were examined but she was told that she could not leave them as a gift. Angelica took the roses into the visiting room and had a smile for every guard she saw — being, on her own proud admission, 'a successful little flirt'. But, as she said afterwards, 'I tried my rather poor English on one of the guards but nothing happened. Not even the good-looking Russians looked my way!'

In the visiting room the girl kept her hat on at first so that her father could see the latest fashion. She also stood up to show off her costume and drew his attention to the new skirt length. 'I don't want you to become a Rip Van Winkle of a father,' she said.

Like Neurath, Schirach also made a note about the subjects he wished to discuss, such books he thought the children should read, and questions about their school reports. Robert was the only Schirach child to have seen his father in a cell, although not at Spandau. When he was five, the boy was smuggled into the cell at Nuremberg under the cloak of a padre, just before the Tribunal passed sentence. The youngster glanced round the dreary cell and said, 'You seem to be very comfortable here, Father.' This anecdote was never forgotten by the relatives of Schirach.

Before Schirach's sons left the visiting room they always climbed on to a stool so that he could see how much they had grown. So, too, did the three other children who went to

Spandau, the grandchildren of Grand Admiral Dönitz: Peter, Ute and Klaus Hessler. The latter little boy, the image of Dönitz as a child, bowed to his grandfather when he came into the room for the first time and did the same on leaving. Throughout the half-hour he called Dönitz 'Opus' — the children's favourite nickname for him — and spent most of the time explaining how he needed a transformer for his electric railway, and other things. He got them.

Turning to his daughter for a moment, Dönitz, who once ordered U-boat commanders to kill and to keep on killing, said, 'I am happy to have this leggy, straight-as-a-rod boy for my grandchild. His merry and lively eyes, ever ready to smile at the silly things I tell him, give me great pleasure and I long even more for all my tomorrows.'

As Frau Dönitz was signing the visitors' book in the guardroom on her very first visit she was startled by several loud reports, and then one of the guards came limping into the room with a bullet in his leg. Through the door she could see three other soldiers being carried away, injured when a machine-gun had been fired by accident. Frau Dönitz explained that she was a nurse, but her offer of help was refused. In those early days everybody in Spandau was racked with anxiety, and the tension came to a climax very easily at the end of a visit. That is why the guards were more than usually considerate to the prisoners, realizing how greatly they must have been racked by despair and regret.

At the first opportunity the six who received visitors talked excitedly together, but at night came reaction, often fearful. Then they needed opiates more than ever — something powerful enough to dull frayed nerves and erase the memory of a lost world that once knew their ambitions, and their cruelty.

Funk recalled the indictments and verdicts of Nuremberg in his own special way; for, whenever his wife left the main gate of Spandau after a visit, she was presented by her waiting travelling companion Rechenberg with a second bunch of carnations from her husband. They were dark red — in memory of a future destroyed by the past.

15: THE PUNCHING BAG

The Cold War began almost the instant World War II ended, and Spandau Prison stood like an isolated fortress, smack in the middle of the battle zone. Exercising its free choice, the Western two-thirds of Germany became integrated into the Western bloc led by the United States, whilst the rest of Germany remained in the Soviet orbit.

Of paramount importance to both East and West, the city of Berlin was an unhealed wound in the very heart of divided Germany. Despite the comradeship and shared fighting purpose of the war years, relations between the Western democracies and the Soviet Union were never those of true friends. Moscow began the first moves in its game of brinkmanship with the Western Allies as soon as war in Europe ceased, and Berlin was used as a counter in the dangerous game. Using Berlin as a weapon of political blackmail, the Soviets exploited every angle as a tactical expedient, applying pressure in accordance with their strategy.

The policy was short-sighted. Through her magnificently courageous war efforts the USSR's credit had been raised emotionally to great heights. Britain and the United States would have done almost anything to help her recovery. Instead, Stalin reverted to his old antagonistic ways. Soviet leaders swiftly returned to those attitudes of suspicion and hostility towards the West that they had expressed consistently and openly before entering into the wartime alliance against Hitler. The Russians and the three Western powers repeatedly found themselves drawn into tests of will; and in consequence,

Spandau Prison was plagued by conflicting or uncomfortable co-existence.

Although during each country's month of office at the gaol its senior representative automatically became chairman of the Prison Directors for that month, every important decision was required to be agreed by all four-Powers. Opportunities for bureaucratic obstruction and the use of the veto were therefore limitless. The monthly meetings to discuss the prisoners invariably became social occasions and tension-easing opportunities as well. The Power in charge of the gaol for the month vied with its predecessor in laying on food and drink for the Directors in an ante-room; and the cooks always gave the luncheons an appropriate national flavour, ranging from Russian bortsch to French consommé, from American corned-beef hash to British steak-and-kidney pudding. The luncheons often helped soothe strained tempers, but the Soviets always made it clear that they had come to regard the prison almost as a piece of diplomatic territory.

The Russians politically manipulated the prison, just as they did everything else outside, constantly seeking to throw the other three controlling Powers off balance and keeping them on the defensive. Similarly, as with all their international dealings, they made agreements only when it served or conformed with their point of view. They admitted that their primary weapon was economic power, and the constant political-economic contest with the Communist bloc was also at the heart of Spandau prison four-Power tactics.

The vulnerability of East and West was heightened by the struggles of both sides to overcome their fears.

The Soviets officially informed the Allied Powers:

> How is it that the present situation in Berlin arouses such fears? The first and most important reason is that the

Governments of the United States of America, Great Britain and France, exploiting the privileges granted to them by the Allied agreements on Germany, have separated the Western part of Berlin by making it into a kind of state within a state.

About two hundred miles east of the Iron Curtain, Berlin was uncomfortably isolated, and West Berlin had become an anomaly. Its inhabitants' affinity was with West Germany, although West Berlin was not recognized as part of West Germany and not governed by it. Four-Power agreement was supposed to guarantee free communications between West Berlin and West Germany and undertook that West Berlin's ties with West Germany would be respected.

The city, which the four-Powers took over in 1945, comprised a population of some 3,300,000. The Soviet sector, the largest, was in the east. The small French sector, taken from the two thirds originally allocated to the United States and Britain, lay to the north. British forces occupied the western sector, while the south-western area was taken over by the United States. The city, as a whole, was under the control of four commandants acting in unison as the Kommandatura; occupation personnel and German citizens were permitted freedom of movement in all sectors.

The western sectors of Berlin, separated from the British zone by 115 miles across Russian-controlled boroughs, were linked to the West by surface routes, including an autobahn, a single-track railway from the border opposite the city of Hanover, and water traffic routes. There were also subsidiary rail connections from Hamburg and Frankfurt. Three air corridors, each twenty miles wide, were allocated for Western traffic.

The people of Berlin had greater opportunities than other Germans to compare democracy with dictatorship, and regardless of their criticisms of the Western Powers the overwhelming majority chose democracy and freedom. The Soviets did not like this, because the Kremlin regards Germany as the key to power in Europe. The USSR decided that if Germany could not be totally united under Communism, then it should be kept divided with Berlin as the key. Spandau Prison and its inmates — in the city's British-controlled sector — became a valuable extra pawn. This was the sole place in West Berlin in which Soviet Russia still retained an absolute legal right to be.

One of the major Communist aims was to destroy confidence in West German currency, but the value of the Western Deutschmark in relation to the Eastern mark persisted in mounting steadily, despite ceaseless manoeuvres to undermine it. Furious with their inability to shatter the West's currency, the Soviets switched tactics, and the spark that flared into the blockade of Berlin was ignited at a four-Power Allied Control Council meeting in Berlin on 20 January 1948.

Marshal Sokolovsky, then Soviet Military Governor for Germany, alleged that the agreement between the Americans and British — to administer their two zones of occupation jointly in the interest of increased economic efficiency — constituted the establishment of a separatist German government and was therefore a gross violation of inter-Allied agreements. The French delegation reserved its position and stayed out of the argument. The dispute between the Russians, Americans and British over Germany's future, kept under the surface for three years, was about to explode.

Renewed representations from several influential quarters for revision of conditions in Spandau gaol were instantly dismissed by the Russians, and a note from the Control Commission in Berlin to London concluded:

> Any proposal for a relaxation of the present regulations would be objected to by the Soviet and French authorities, and would be opposed at the Co-ordinating Committee if not at the Control Council level. This is the view of the Legal Division, who have stated that the French and Russians consider the present regulations too mild.
>
> It is also for consideration how any such proposal would be regarded by the Occupied countries, e.g. the Belgians, Dutch, Norwegians and Danes.

Increasing East-West tension influenced a crisis spin-off within Spandau gaol when, early in 1948, the four-Powers called in the American psychiatrist Dr Maurice Walsh for yet another examination of Hess's mental condition. The Russians insisted that the examination be conducted in the presence of a battery of medical representatives and interpreters, and the Prison directors from all four countries. Dr Walsh, unhappy at having to examine someone in such public circumstances, had no option.

When he asked Hess whether he believed in a 'master race', Hess replied: 'This expression was employed by German propaganda for foreign consumption. It was not used in Germany. Anyway, I do not believe in this concept.'

The two-hour interview did not permit a very extensive survey, especially in front of so many witnesses. Yet solely on the basis of this comparatively brief examination, which the psychiatrist himself admitted was unsatisfactory, the conclusions he reached were considered so dangerously sensitive, in view of the Cold War, that he said he was asked to omit references to mental disease from his report. Dr Walsh was advised that the Russians would be unhappy with a report attributing medical reasons for Hess's behaviour, as they considered that he and other leaders of the Third Reich should be held fully responsible for crimes committed while they were in power.

In an assessment that was suppressed at the time, Dr Walsh wrote:

> The impression was gained that Hess is an individual of superior intelligence with schizoid personality traits, and that he has no psychosis at the present time; but there would appear to be adequate evidence that he has experienced at least two episodes of hysterical amnesia and depression with suicidal attempts. Both apparently occurred at a time when he was exposed to strong emotional stress.
>
> The former second highest officer of a modern State was found to have a chronic and extremely severe psychiatric disorder which should have incapacitated him from any post of responsibility for the lives and health of human beings. How was this possible in a contemporary State? This was indeed made possible by the fact that the leader of the State, Adolf Hitler himself, as clearly shown in his numerous published writings and pronouncements, also was schizophrenic and had experienced psychotic episodes; with a last lapse into frank psychosis at the time of the collapse of his brutally homicidal plans for the domination of Europe and ultimately the world.
>
> But how then was it possible that persons with such severe psychiatric illnesses should have gained control of this modern nation which had one of the highest literacy rates in Europe?
>
> Indeed the seductiveness of the schizophrenic has not been commonly realized. It is unquestionably true that in all periods of history individuals with this type of psychiatric disorder have succeeded in capturing the allegiances as well as the imagination of large numbers of people. This represents a serious danger to the stability of government and the safeguarding of human life and therefore must be taken into

account, together with economic, sociological, political, and anthropological factors, in the maintenance of world peace and the prevention of war.

It is of course precisely this seductive attraction which gained an audience for narcissistic leaders such as Hitler, or for some of the disturbed leaders of fanatic movements and less scrupulous politicians who have attracted masses of followers. Since many of these people are either psychotic, or nearly so, and are unable to have relationships with others except as narcissistic objects, the danger for the peace of the world if such individuals are allowed to come into a position of power is evident.

For almost a year, relations between the Soviet Union and the Western Allies had been steadily getting worse. In March 1948 General Lucius D. Clay, Military Governor and Commander-in-Chief of the United States in Germany, sent a special report to General Omar Bradley, Chief of Staff of the US Army, to notify his concern at a change he had sensed in Soviet policy. Soviet representatives in Germany were behaving with a new arrogance and disregard for the processes of Allied consultation, according to General Clay, who felt that this portended new Russian tactics. On 20 March the last meeting of the Control Council had been broken up by a concerted walk-out of the Soviet delegation. Hitherto, General Clay had insisted that war was impossible. Now he warned the Pentagon that it could no longer be excluded.

By the end of that month the initial steps were taken to blockade Berlin. The Cold War, which had begun in the city in 1946, started to range over the whole of Europe. The Russians and East Germans decided to harass Western garrisons in Berlin with the aim of forcing all three out of the city, thus leaving Moscow free to liquidate what it termed 'the centre of reaction' east of the Iron Curtain. The Communists repeatedly tested Allied resolve with provocative incidents such as the stopping and searching of a British train from Berlin, despite agreements precluding such actions. The reason for this particular incident was that the British had persuaded a German scientist to work for them. Russians stopped the train to kidnap the man to research for them. Fortunately the British had got the scientist out of the city the previous day.

The Soviet Union embarked upon the conquest of the country and the Western Allies joined with West Germans in resisting her. Soviet forces threatened to isolate Berlin completely. The United States, United Kingdom and France warned Moscow:

'Berlin is not a part of the Soviet zone, but is an international zone of occupation. Free access thereto as a matter of established right derives from the defeat and surrender of Germany confirmed by formal agreements among the principal Allies.'

The Western Allies declared that they would not be induced by threats, pressure, or other actions to abandon these rights. They hoped that the Soviet Government entertained no doubts whatsoever on this point.

The news blazed through the city like a forest fire and reached Spandau's prisoners via warders. Officially the seven were cut off from the world and barred from reading newspapers or magazines. Guards were strictly forbidden to tell them anything of current political developments, but there was always either someone who could not resist talking, or Walther Funk's secret news-bulletins smuggled in to him from friends outside.

They debated possible consequences of the East-West crisis.

'If there is a permanent break in relations, we will each probably be returned to the nation that captured us,' Dönitz ventured.

Raeder, who had been caught by the Russians, was not happy with the prospect.

Day after day tension mounted inside and outside the gaol. Ex-newspaperman Funk, adept at obtaining information from beyond the prison's walls, frequently supplied the others with news.

'Incidents are repeatedly occurring at border check-points when Soviet inspectors try to board Western military passenger trains, demanding the right to check travellers' identities,' Funk reported. 'Trains have been delayed through Western authorities refusing to allow Soviet officials to board. If the Western Powers were compelled to evacuate Berlin, their prestige throughout the world would suffer a shattering blow.' Then, almost prophetically, he added: 'By the simple act of cutting communications between Berlin and Western Germany, the Western Powers could be forced to abandon their plans for a West German Government.'

'If the Allies withdraw from Berlin, the effects will be catastrophic for the people of the city … and for us,' Neurath warned.

The fear of being abandoned by the Western Powers persisted in the minds of almost everyone in the city. It was plainly recognized that, in a military sense, the Soviets had Berlin at their mercy and could just walk in.

At a Moscow meeting of Allied Foreign Ministers, Russia's Vyacheslav Molotov had demanded 10,000 million dollars' worth of reparations from current German production, and the establishment of a strong central government for the country. The United States and Britain wanted German federation, economic rehabilitation, and their respective countries' occupation costs to be met. When the conference failed, the Soviet Union tightened its grip on all the territories it was occupying, and post-war Europe began to divide into two camps. By the time a new currency was launched in the Western zones of Germany in June 1948, Berlin was already virtually blockaded. The currency reform was the occasion, though not the reason, for the final East-West break, although the Soviets initially claimed that it was the root of the crisis. But they had been threatening for months.

'The Communist press is almost daily headlining alleged murders, robberies, black market, spying, and sabotage activities by so-called criminals from the Western zones,' announced Funk, reporting afresh from his smuggled news sources. 'The Russians are building up to something really big.'

On 16 June 1948 the Russians walked out of the Berlin Kommandatura. A week later the new West German Deutschmark was introduced to Berlin, and the following day warders reporting for duty at Spandau brought the seven the worst news they had received since hearing their sentences at Nuremberg; complete blockade of the city had started. The Russians had stopped all mail and passenger traffic from West Germany to Berlin by both road and rail. Pedestrians and motorists were forbidden to cross the frontier of the Soviet zone from Western Germany. Russian sentries posted on the autobahn were refusing to allow cars to continue their journeys eastwards. The city was isolated. Simultaneously there were electric power cuts, which the Russians attributed to 'coal shortage'. The suspension of rail traffic was due, they said, to 'technical faults'.

By stopping rail traffic and cutting power supplies, the Soviets, using their two most effective weapons, began the full-scale economic siege of the Western sectors of Berlin.

'See how far we stand from each other — at opposite poles,' Spandau's Russian Director bitterly warned his American, British, and French counterparts.

The Russians ended the Kommandatura, and the breakup of the Allied Control Council meant that all vestiges of four-Power control in Germany disappeared — except within Spandau gaol, upon which the Russians vented their fury and frustrations. The prison and its prisoners suddenly represented the only fixed punching bag in the gymnasium that the Russians could continue to flail with their fists in defiance of America, Britain and France. The Prison Directors' conference table was the only place where East and West continued to talk every week, and the arguments frequently dragged on all day and even far into the night.

Berlin was strategically useless to the West, but politically it was crucial. At stake was not half a city but all Western Europe. If the three Powers abandoned Berlin because of Soviet coercion, from the Elbe to the Atlantic it would be looked upon as the beginning of a long retreat before the onward march of Communism. If the Allies caved in, two hundred million Europeans could lose their freedom, and many of them perhaps their lives.

Early in July drastic cuts in electricity and gas supplies affected every facet of the city's life. Domestic power was limited to four hours a day. The current was totally switched off for two daily periods. The city's main power station and central control point happened to be in the Soviet sector. Other stations were used mainly to boost supply at peak hours.

There was also the problem of supplying food for the three Western sectors. Their populations of some 2,300,000 had to be fed with food imported from the West. There was enough in hand for five weeks, and enough coal for about six; 13,500 tons of coal was needed every day.

Funk, who seemed to come alive only when cracking jokes, commented: 'God knows, even the best blockade is no bargain. But if there must be a blockade, then it's better to be blockaded by the Soviets and fed by the Allies. Just imagine if it were the other way around.

'Even though we're in here, we can at least be thankful we're in the West and not the East, with the way things are there. I heard about two old men sitting on a park bench in East Berlin. One of them kept spitting on the ground until the other said: "Please, no political conversation, or I shall call the police."'

Through the smoke-screen of crisis around the city, Western Germany, the United States, Britain and France were subjected to a combination of military menace and political intimidation. Fear hung over the city. Everyone felt trapped. If the Russians marched into West Berlin, where would its citizens be able to go?

General Clay, the US Military Governor, favoured an armoured breakthrough from the Western occupied zones to Berlin, but this was dismissed as impractical by the Chief of Operations of the US Army, General Albert C. Wedemayer, who forecast that a conventional land attack on the Soviet forces would result in the annihilation of the Western Allies' armies.

The blockade was more psychological than economic. From the Soviet sector the Russians offered blandishments — more food, more coal, more consumer goods, sweets for the children, if the people of the Western sectors would sign themselves over to Russian domination. The Soviet action was seen as a plan for gaining control of as great a portion of Europe as possible, and for keeping the remainder so weak that it would not be able to withstand Communist subversion from within and would eventually fall into the Soviet orbit.

The blockade mentality intruded into the August monthly meeting of Spandau's Prison Directors. The Soviet Director, at his obstructive worst, blocked every proposal. In answer to the question whether prisoners could lie down and sleep after completion of the evening meal, he insisted stubbornly: 'The prisoners should not be allowed to lie down or sleep in their cells after they have been locked up for the night, prior to the time the lights are turned out at ten o'clock.'

The gaol's Russian warders and military personnel, confident at first that the West would cave in, irritably began to admit that Berliners were not reacting as expected. Then, one morning, the gaol, the skies above, and the entire city vibrated with the ceaseless roar of massive air fleets; the blockade-breaking Berlin airlift had begun. All day and all night, aircraft droning overhead became part of the pattern of life. People became so accustomed to the rhythm of the aircraft that they woke up when, during bad flying weather, they missed the regular beat of planes landing and taking off every minute and a half. Every morning the first thing Spandau's prisoners and the rest of Berlin did was listen for aircraft engine noise. The sound of engines was like beautiful music to them.

In spite of official assurances, Berlin's situation was militarily hopeless. The United States had 3,000 troops in the city, the British 2,000, and the French 1,500, while the Soviets had 18,000 soldiers in East Berlin and another 300,000 in the East Zone. They could at any time overrun the city. The dominant question was: would the Western democracies risk a world war in the interest of a few million Berliners?

Cold War flared into hot war within Spandau gaol when directors and medical officers disagreed violently yet again over the prisoners' food and conditions. The Soviet Director informed his Allied colleagues that he had been instructed to press for the reimposition of severer measures. The development was considered sufficiently serious for General Sir Brian H. Robertson to raise the matter directly with Britain's Foreign Secretary, Ernest Bevin. In a letter dated 26 October 1948, written from his Control Commission headquarters in Berlin, Robertson informed Bevin:

> Sir,
> Regarding the question of amending the regulations of Spandau Prison.
> Instructions were given on 18th June that an amendment to the existing regulations should be raised, but on the following day the meetings of the Allied Kommandatura were brought to an end.
> Since that time the quadripartite Governorate has continued to meet. Although the western representatives have pressed to improve conditions in a number of directions, nothing has been achieved. Indeed the Soviet representative wishes to make the conditions still more harsh and has put forward proposals to reimpose solitary confinement, to limit the hours of sleep and rest, and to impose further restrictions in regard to library books, family visits and incoming letters.
> I propose to ask my US and French colleagues to agree that our representatives in the Governorate shall put forward agreed proposals for ameliorating the conditions. If the Soviet representative refuses to co-operate, as I fear he will, I am sure that nothing is to be gained by attempting to raise the

matter either with the Soviet commandant or Commander-in-Chief so long as the quadripartite machinery remains in suspense. I believe that the only chance then of getting any alleviation is to expose by full publicity the state of affairs and the failure of our attempts to rectify them. This could probably best be started in Parliament.

Military Governor General Clay despatched the following message to Washington:

> Top Secret
> 5 November, 1948
>
> From Clay for Department of the Army.
> Yesterday I attended a conference with [Gen. Pierre] Koenig and [Gen. Sir Brian] Robertson which had been called by Koenig to discuss the general situation. At this conference, we all agreed that the treatment of Nuremberg prisoners at Spandau jail under quadripartite government was inhumane. We further agreed to advise our Governments that we propose to inform Soviet Military Administration that since the Allied Control Council was not functioning due to Soviet action, we considered that quadripartite control of Spandau under the Allied Control Council could not be sustained until the Allied Control Council started functioning again. Thus tripartitely, we would arrange for better prison management.

Washington authorized General Clay to take steps to place the gaol under tripartite control and formally notify the Soviet authorities regarding the repeated and unsuccessful attempts to get their agreement to the modification of prison regulations in accordance with civilized and humanitarian standards. It was suggested that the three-Power note should contain a warning to the Soviets that on a certain date the Allies would take over control on a tripartite basis, but that Soviet representatives would be allowed to come and inspect the prisoners. General

Clay wanted the note, and its reply, fully publicized. He requested General Robertson, of Britain, and General Koenig, of France, to refer the matter to their Governments and meanwhile authorize advisers to confer to evolve a more precise plan and study possible consequences pending the outcome of the note to the Russians. Clay wanted to tell the Russians that since their Cold War had brought quadripartite machinery to an end, they need take no further interest in Spandau Prison.

Britain's senior Foreign Office authority for Germany, Sir Ivone Kirkpatrick, preferred removing the seven from Spandau to the Western zones and justifying this to Moscow by saying that it was policy not to support any unnecessary mouths in Berlin when the Allies were being compelled to carry food there by air owing to the blockade. In these circumstances it would be better for the prisoners to be moved to where neither they nor their guards would have to be fed at the expense of the airlift.

All three Powers realized that the Russians were likely to resent unilateral action in this matter strongly, because of their suspicions of the motives. It was intolerable, however, that because of the Soviet refusal to maintain good standards, the Allies should appear to share responsibility for the cruelty and uncivilized methods of the Russians — which would certainly not be approved by the United Nations Commission on Human Rights. But, loath to take action that would increase the division of Berlin by ending what was virtually the only quadripartite machinery still operating, it was recommended that alternative tactics be tried before any attempt at instigating tripartite control. A Foreign Office memorandum declared on 23 November 1948:

We entirely agree that these people should be properly treated, but there are other considerations.

In other words, these people are in Spandau because they caused the last war, and we have no intention of doing anything rash which might make them the cause (indirectly) of another.

In view of the very delicate quadripartite situation in Berlin we do not feel at the present time that we are in a position to use the fortuitous accident that these 7 criminals are in the British Sector to substitute the kind of treatment that we in the United Kingdom feel is good prison practice for quadripartite views. As soon, however, as an opportunity occurs, rest assured that everything possible will be done towards putting things right.

The four Directors argued bitterly. The Russians would not budge; so the American, British, and French Directors sent urgent complaints to their respective Governments. The immediate American response was a directive to their Spandau Director:

It has come to our attention that we, as representatives of the US, are guilty in permitting inhumane treatment of war criminals now interned in Spandau Prison. It appears, due to Russian obstruction, Russian vetoing and Russian interference at the prison, that we have been unable, even during the months of American chairmanship, to carry out the prison agreements in the humane manner and in the spirit in which the agreements were originally made. Therefore you will immediately put into effect the following measures:

1. You will liberally and in a humane manner, interpret these agreements which have been signed by us and by the other three Powers concerned in the care of these prisoners.

2. Those changes in diet which were authorized, whereby those prisoners suffering from diabetes were to be given

substitute food ... [and] those prisoners suffering from anaemia were to be given small quantities of additional food, are to be immediately put into effect during our chairmanship.

3. You will obtain and ensure distribution to these prisoners ... [of] small quantities of butter, jam, meat and powdered milk. Under no circumstances will this additional food exceed 1,000 calories, and will be approx. 500 calories a day.

The purpose of this additional food will be to arrest the deterioration of the physical condition of the prisoners who are continuing to lose weight under the present harsh conditions and who are approaching a point beyond that of expected malnutrition.

You will permit prisoners when in their cells to sit or lie in their beds as they see fit, at any hour of the day or night.

You will permit the prisoners to speak to each other within reasonable limits when they are together. For security reasons conversations should be checked to ensure that they are not of a political or security-threatening nature. You will permit prisoners to have one visitor for 15 minutes every two months. The visitors will be permitted to bring food packages: each package not to exceed two kilos in weight and no prisoner to receive more than two packages per month.

You will provide a minimum amount of recreational facilities as determined by the US medical adviser. This recreation will be consistent with normal prison practice.

The exclusion of the Russians from the customary four-Power procedure had its dangers. They could retaliate by imposing punitive counter-measures when their turn came to administer the gaol for a month. Major Miller insisted that, unless he received orders to the contrary, the revised policy would be continued during the remainder of the American chairmanship of the gaol. To forestall any attempted Soviet obstruction of revised menus, two soldiers with fixed bayonets guarded the prison's kitchen door.

In all respects the Russian months were infinitely harsher. As soon as the Soviet medical officer came on duty, he cut out nearly all special allowances of food granted for health reasons; he rarely visited the prisoners, and generally took less interest in them than the other medical officers. Seeking to restrict the freedom of the seven as far as possible, the Russians took every opportunity to confine them to their cells.

The noise of the airlift never halted. At any time there were at least three heavily laden aircraft approaching the three Berlin airfields. The small Western garrisons could have been swiftly overcome, yet not a shot was fired between the forces occupying the city. The Kremlin was unsure how far it dared push the confrontation to the brink of World War III.

'West Berlin is a lighthouse of freedom in a threatening stormy totalitarian sea,' commented Neurath to Dönitz. 'For two thousand years Christians and others have been discussing the Last Day and speculating on the time and manner of its advent, yet it never occurred to anyone that we should come so close to organizing the Last Day ourselves by inventing nuclear weapons. All I pray is that the Berlin confrontation doesn't precipitate nuclear counter-attack.' (In those days the United States had exclusive possession of atomic weapons.)

'The blockade is a substitute for war,' Neurath added. 'It is a deliberate assault on the whole democratic position in Germany, and on America's commitment to Europe.'

One man did his utmost to sabotage or defy any Spandau gaol reforms: Soviet Chief Warder Baldin. Baldin, five-feet-two with close-cropped ginger hair and a domed head out of all proportion to his nine-stone body, was detested even by his own staff, who were aware of his attempts to get the personnel of the other Powers to report to him any Russians who read, slept, or spoke to a prisoner while on duty in the cell block.

Baldin was suspected of being the secret political officer of Spandau's Russian staff, for he was greatly feared, and at mealtimes it was difficult to carry on normal conversation in his presence. During the tension of the Berlin airlift Baldin was instructed by Marshal Sokolovsky — Commander of the Soviet Occupation Forces in Germany and Soviet Military Governor — that, in the event of blockaded Berlin escaping the Soviet stranglehold, he would personally be held responsible by his Government for ensuring that the seven men of Spandau were not removed by the Allies. Troops would be at his disposal if necessary.

To Baldin, then, the power and influence of the Spandau doctors were a challenge that he tried to meet in every way so that it might be destroyed. The Spandau rule that the prisoners could be addressed in German only was one of the biggest cards in his hands. Doctors unable to speak German were directed to employ a Chief Warder as interpreter; but as most of the prisoners spoke English, the American and British doctors ignored the rules and addressed the prisoners in English. Whenever Baldin heard a prisoner spoken to in English he laid an official complaint, and the officer was charged and punished for the offence.

One night a British doctor, whose turn of duty it was, answered an urgent call when Neurath was taken ill with a heart attack. Making his way to the prisoner's cell, he was stopped by Baldin, who curtly demanded:

'Sign the register.' The register contained the daily record of every visit to the cell block.

'I've already signed it once a short time ago, so there's no need to do so again,' the doctor replied.

'Sign the register!' the Russian warder repeated.

'I shall do nothing of the kind. I have an urgent call to answer, and seconds may be important,' said the doctor, furious at the delay.

Baldin stood against the cell block wall, refusing to open Neurath's door. 'You cannot go in until you sign.'

'Right,' said the doctor. 'I have two witnesses here, both British guards, who can testify that you refused to allow me to enter. If the prisoner dies, it is your responsibility.'

Baldin hesitated a moment, then unlocked the door. The following morning the doctor was summoned before the Directors to face a charge of breach of regulations and insubordination to a high-ranking officer. Baldin was, of course, the instigator and was determined to have the last word; but on this occasion he lost.

'As I have never previously been introduced to Chief Warder Baldin, and he wears no rank insignia on his uniform, I was not to know that he was a senior officer,' was the doctor's answer to the case. His defence was convincing because Baldin preferred wearing the ordinary type of Spandau uniform without any insignia to denote his rank. The charge was therefore dismissed.

Throughout the years he served at Spandau, Baldin attempted to smash the power of the prison doctors. One day, however, a photograph taken inside the prison was smuggled out and published in Germany. This was alleged to have happened during a period when he was in control of the inner block. One morning Chief Warder Baldin failed to appear on duty. He was not seen or heard of again, nor was any explanation ever offered by the Soviet authorities for his disappearance.

It was inside the gaol that the first significant glimmer of light in the blockade darkness appeared. Contrary to expectations, when the Russians took over in March 1949 for their month's tour of duty they continued the revised regime instituted by the Western Powers. The diet deteriorated as usual, but new privileges were not withdrawn. The Soviet Director even authorized an extension of the duration of visiting time, although the concession was as yet academic since the blockade had prevented visits. Nevertheless the softening of the customary hard line appeared to be an indication that the Kremlin was on the verge of accepting that the blockade had been a psychological and tactical error. East Germans had also suffered because of the blockade resulting in trade and economic restrictions that gradually crippled East Germany.

In the early months of 1949 West Berlin was shaping as an independent and self-contained city. Although it depended entirely on outside help, it was developing its own efficient administration and economic systems. Moscow saw Western support for West Berlin as evidence of the faith of the entire Alliance, as well as of the belief of West Germans that one day Berlin would again become the capital of the entire country.

On 9 May — almost to the day the fourth anniversary of Germany's capitulation — Moscow ordered the lifting of traffic restrictions with effect from one minute past midnight on 12 May. The Spandau seven and their warders also celebrated. Everyone in the gaol, including the Russians, was relieved that the blackmail was over. The blockade's final day was happily the same day upon which the constitution for the new West German Government was approved. General Clay said: 'The firm stand by our Government and the Governments of France and Great Britain nullified this last desperate risk of the Soviet Government.'

From the start of the airlift Allied aircraft had flown in more than 1,500,000 tons of supplies in almost 200,000 flights. No one had starved or died of cold in the city, although thirty-one American and thirty British airmen were killed in airlift crashes.

Soon after the blockade ended, the Spandau prisoners heard that the Western zones of occupation were to become an independent State called the Federal Republic, and that the Russians and East Germans, after dividing Berlin politically and administratively, had proclaimed the East Zone the Democratic Republic.

Meanwhile Berlin's sky was peaceful again. The non-stop roar of blockade-busting aircraft had stopped, and as the Spandau seven tended the prison garden they discussed the future of the nation they had brought to ruin.

'So four years after the downfall of the Reich, Germans are governing themselves again,' said Neurath.

'America, Britain, and France occupied Berlin as conquerors, but within three years they were its allies and the defenders of more than two million of our people,' Funk commented.

Neurath added with relief: 'Berlin and Germany have just been reborn.'

The end of the Berlin blockade was accepted by the West with caution. More proof was needed than this single gesture of a Soviet change of heart from the cynical aggressiveness which the blockade had typified.

The caution was justified. After backing away from further confrontation by allowing three-Power amelioration of Spandau's prison conditions to continue, it did not take long for the Russians to resume their old obstructive behaviour and seek to reimpose a harsher regime. As a result, the whole question of the gaol's continuance as a war crimes prison was revived. Berlin's city administration fired the first shot when West Berlin's Mayor, Dr Ernst Reuter, complained that the seven top Nazi war criminals had fifty-two servants and were costing his Council £40,000 a year. Reuter wrote to the three Allied Commandants requesting a meeting to discuss 'this intolerable burden in view of Berlin's financial crisis'.

His data was incomplete because it failed to take into account the numbers of persons engaged on maintenance at the prison; in addition to which there were the United States, British, French and Russian Directors, warders, guards, and servants attending Allied officers in charge. Part of the prison's upkeep was being borne by the city's administration, the Magistral of Greater Berlin.

In October 1949 the city authorities reported to the Allied Commandants that in their budget estimates for the 1949 fiscal year the amount of 450,000 Deutschmarks had been fixed for maintenance of the Allied Prison, Spandau. Estimates listed the following expenditure:

> For wages, amounting to about DM 300,000.
> For business needs, amounting to nearly DM 150,000.

The cost of wages covered twenty-one civil employees and fifty-one wage-earners (workers). There were employed:

> 1 head of the administration, gross monthly earnings: DM 701.19
> 1 delegate, gross monthly earnings: DM 546.27
> 1 storekeeper, gross monthly earnings: DM 436.46
> 8 cooks, gross monthly earnings: DM 350.90 (each)
> 2 waiters, gross monthly earnings: DM 350.90 (each)
> 3 house stewards, gross monthly earnings: DM 350.90 (each)
> 1 man of all work, gross monthly earnings: DM 293.63
> 1 messenger, gross monthly earnings: DM 293.63

1 assistant cook, gross monthly earnings: DM 180
1 female clerk, gross monthly earnings: DM 278.78
1 technical employee for buildings, gross monthly earnings: DM 510

Also employed:

2 ambulanciers
1 electrician
10 craftsmen (among them 5 stokers)
1 watchman
1 waiter
6 waitresses
14 kitchen helpers
2 cooking women
12 charwomen
2 laundresses

The Berlin city authorities further complained that prison employees were over-paid, their pay exceeding those of other municipal wage-earners by nearly 33 per cent. In addition, official flats attached to the prison had been given to eighteen workers free of charge. The city requested complete reconsideration of the number of staff used at the gaol, pointing out that in comparison the penal administration of seven ordinary prisoners cost approximately only 8,000 Deutschmarks a year.

After the Council's representations, the three Berlin commandants produced a survey for the Allied Council. Steps were immediately taken to effect substantial reductions in staff and costs. The municipal protest also sparked off reassessment of the gaol and the imprisonment of the seven.

On 6 December 1949 the Control Commission for Germany raised with the Foreign Office the question of terminating the current arrangements at Spandau, and it was recommended that the problem should be taken up with the United States and France. François-Poncet, France's High Commissioner, proposed that the commandants should be authorized to negotiate with the Russians regarding the transfer of the seven to another prison. Britain replied that if this were done and a negative response was received, the three Powers would have suffered a rebuff unless they were prepared to go further and act themselves. It was suggested that authority should be obtained from the respective Governments that, in the event of unsatisfactory Russian reaction, the prisoners should be divided up, with each country taking charge of those whom its own forces had captured.

The British envisaged Dönitz, Hess, and Funk being housed in Werl Prison where other war criminals in British hands were held and where there was a British Governor and British supervisory staff. Any additional security measures considered necessary for prisoners of this importance would not have presented great difficulties. It was expected that the Americans would house Speer and Schirach in Landsberg Fortress, where war criminals sentenced in subsequent Nuremberg trials were held. Neurath would go to the French, and Raeder to the Russians. The alternative was to transfer them to another Berlin prison.

A disadvantage was that the United States and Britain might lay themselves open to criticism for allowing Raeder and Neurath to pass into Russian and French hands. The Russians were notorious for their severity; and at the time that the Spandau regulations were drawn up, even the French wanted to enforce a tough regime, including unrelieved solitary confinement and no employment. The French differed considerably from the United States and British authorities in their views on penal conditions.

Suddenly, arguments over the custody and disposition of the seven developed into a battle between France, on the one side, and the United States and Britain on the other. The French accepted that the charter of the Allied High Commission for Germany made the control of the care and treatment of persons sentenced by tribunals of the Occupation Authorities an individual responsibility of the High Commissioners, but the difference in the wording was significant. The International Military Tribunal was set up by the Occupying Powers, but not by the Occupation Authorities. This meant that if Spandau inmates were removed to the Western zones they would have to stay in the custody of the Allied High Commission, rather than of the individual High Commissioners. All that would be required to achieve this would be an order from the Allied High Commission to each of the Directors of the gaol, directing him to hold specific prisoners. The Control Commission had the power to order the release of any of the men if it considered detention to be irregular.

The United States and Britain were prepared to make a test case of the issue before a court. The French were absolutely against this, as they were convinced the Russians would never let the Spandau seven out of their hands without a fight — inside and outside the gaol. Unwilling to shatter three-Power co-operation, Washington and London reluctantly shelved closure measures for the prison. But the battles over the seven continued, although their emphasis shifted, largely at the instigation of the one woman who never stopped stirring up Spandau controversy by using every manoeuvre in the political book.

London-born Winifred von Mackensen, Neurath's daughter, ceaselessly manipulated pressure from every angle — involving the Pope, Church of England and Protestant German bishops, French cardinals, and high-ranking statesmen. Understandably striving for the early release of her father, she bombarded dignitaries incessantly with letters containing details of prison conditions; she sought and obtained interviews to raise issues personally, and even secured a Vatican audience with the Pope specifically to discuss Spandau.

Through her father's Nuremberg lawyer she engineered an appeal from General Sir Brian Robertson to Sir Ivone Kirkpatrick, who was Permanent Under Secretary of State for the German Section of the Foreign Office at the time, and a few months later was appointed Britain's High Commissioner for West Germany. Until then Sir Brian Robertson had been shouldering the multi-responsibilities of Commander-in-Chief of all armed forces in Germany, Military Governor and High Commissioner.

On 24 May 1950 Sir Ivone Kirkpatrick advised General Sir Brian Robertson:

> I am at last in a position to let you have approval to the suggestion made in your letter of 18th March that you should propose formally to your colleagues that the Soviet authorities should be approached on the question of removing von Neurath to a hospital in the Western Zone where he would be held under custody.
>
> I am sorry that it should have taken us so long to let you have a reply. As you know, however, we feel bound to look very carefully at any question relating to Spandau. We have, too, been reluctant to sanction any proposal which might appear as a first step towards the break-up of the existing quadripartite arrangements, and it seemed to us not unlikely that the Russians might interpret a proposal to remove von

Neurath from Spandau as such a step unless he were clearly an exceptional case whose removal would not be followed by other similar proposals based on medical grounds. We therefore felt it necessary, in the first place, to obtain further information about von Neurath's health and that of the other prisoners, but as the medical reports which the office of the Legal Adviser has forwarded to us show beyond doubt that von Neurath's case is an exceptional one we think that his case can be raised with the Russians without any undue risk of repercussions. We hope that you will act as proposed and do your best to secure Neurath's speedy transfer to hospital.

The particular case of Neurath has some connexion with the question of the general standard of conditions at Spandau which has recently evoked renewed representations from the Minister of Works and the Bishop of Chichester. This is, of course, a question which is always liable to be raised here and although the present regulations as originally approved have been relaxed by the three Western Governors I do not think that it can be denied that conditions remain in some ways harsh. We should therefore be glad if you would raise also with your colleagues the possibility either of approaching the Soviet authorities with proposals for improving the conditions generally or of introducing improvements, as was previously done, without first consulting the Russians.

The points put to us which we feel call for consideration are as follows:

(a) that there is no provision for the prisoners to be visited by a German chaplain;
(b) that medical attention is inadequate;
(c) that no provision is made for notifying relatives in case of illness;
(d) that no previous notification is given of the date and time for visiting prisoners;
(e) that the standard of food during the Russian months of control is bad;

(f) that the prison cells are lighted periodically throughout the night.

Some of these are not of great moment in themselves but cumulatively we feel they go to show that Spandau still falls below the standards of civilized prison administration and that there is still a case for doing what we can to effect improvements.

I. A. KIRKPATRICK

Prior to Kirkpatrick writing this letter, the Foreign Office had requested an up-to-date medical report on all of Spandau's inmates. As a result, the following document arrived on Sir Ivone's desk:

Secret

Medical report on prisoners at Allied Prison Spandau

1. *SCHIRACH* aged 43 sentence 20 years imprisonment.

   Fit man. Muscular athletic build now deteriorating due to age and confinement. Mental adjustment to present condition good.

2. *DÖNITZ* aged 59 sentence 10 years.

   General health good. Osteoarthritis (rheumatism) of right hip contracted after prolonged exposure to cold in 1945. He has occasional severe attacks of this trouble and also of rheumatic pains in the hands and knees. These improve rapidly with infrared light and exercises. Mental outlook optimistic. He exercises vigorously.

3. *VON NEURATH* aged 77 sentence 15 years.

   History

   Up till 10 years ago patient led a vigorous life which included skiing and mountaineering. About 1940 he first became troubled by attacks of precordial discomfort and pain following exertion and relieved by rest. This was diagnosed as 'nervous heart' and palliative treatment given. During the past 2 years these attacks have been more frequent and more easily induced. At present they are brought on by hurrying upstairs or by gardening.

Patient suffers from breathlessness on exertion, gradually increasing in severity over past 2 or 3 years. It is now induced by the same activities as the precordial pain.

Patient has had one attack of dyspnoea at rest. This was accompanied by some discomfort in the chest and was relieved by rest and sedatives. This occurred 2 months ago and about that time he was treated for attacks of giddiness and flushing with sedatives and diuretics.

Patient has had recurring coughs and colds during the past 2 years and these attacks make his breathlessness and precordial pain more severe.

Recently he has had frontal headache and blood-stained nasal discharge.

He has never had oedema of the ankles. Appetite is good and there is no loss of weight.

Examination

Patient is elderly man, tall and erect with plethoric complexion. His mentality is very good and emotional outlook optimistic.

Cardiovascular system Pulse rate 72/min. Regular. Arteries show marked hardening. Blood pressure 225/120. Apex beat not palpable. Heart enlarged to left on percussion. Sounds are regular, faint and of poor tone. No murmurs heard. No evidence of congestive cardiac failure at time of examination.

Lungs Chest expansion is poor. No dullness to percussion. Breath sounds are of poor intensity, vesicular in all areas and equal on both sides. Loud inspiration and expiration rhonchi present at both bases posteriorly.

Abdomen Sound healed sub-umbilical mid-line scar (prostatectomy 1945). Otherwise nil abnormal.

Other systems Nasal discharge and pain on pressure over frontal sinuses. Otherwise nil abnormal.

Diagnosis

Hypertension and arteriosclerosis. Angina of effort. Chronic bronchitis and emphysema. Frontal sinusitis.

Opinion

This man's expectation of life may be measured in months. The recurring attacks of acute bronchitis to which he is subject under present conditions are likely to produce heart failure. The possibility of sudden heart failure due to coronary thrombosis is ever present. He may be regarded as an exceptional case among the prisoners at Spandau.

4. *RAEDER* aged 74 sentence Life Imprisonment.

An elderly man whose general health is good for one of his years. The hernia operation which he had is satisfactory. He complains of occasional pain in the chest following exercise or strenuous work and in my opinion care must be taken to ensure that he is not forced to overtax his heart. Mental attitude usually depressed.

5. *SPEER* aged 45 sentence 20 years.

Fit man. Still retains sound physical constitution. Mentally he is well adjusted to present condition.

6. *FUNK* aged 60 sentence Life Imprisonment.

History

For 30 years patient has suffered from a urethral stricture which required dilation by bougies at intervals of 4 to 6 weeks. During recent years he developed in addition benign enlargement of prostate and his urinary troubles became so great that bougies or catheters had to be passed at least once a week. In October 1949 prostatectomy was performed. Thereafter bougies were passed every 2nd day. This interval has gradually lengthened till at present he requires dilation every 8th day. This procedure is attended by considerable pain and exhaustion for the following 24 hours.

He also has attacks of right-sided lower abdominal pain.

Examination
Small plump pale man. Excitable and depressed by turns.

Cardiovascular system Pulse 64/min. Regular. Blood pressure 155/100. Arteriosclerosis. Otherwise nil abnormal.

Lungs Nil abnormal.

Abdomen Mid-line scar in lower abdomen, soundly healed. Tender in lower abdomen and area of more acute tenderness over appendix.

Eyes Vision in left eye only in upper outer quadrant. About 85% loss of vision.

Other systems Nil abnormal.
Diagnosis
Urethral stricture. Arteriosclerosis. Primary optic atrophy.
Opinion
This man in addition to his urinary trouble is prematurely senile.

7. *HESS* aged 56 sentence Life Imprisonment.
Physical examination reveals no abnormality other than flatulence. He complains constantly of abdominal pain and is capricious in his response to the same palliative medicine. He affects difficulty in recalling to mind any information which the examiner wishes to know. His attitude is usually one of extreme dejection.
Opinion
Physically in good health. Mentally sane within the meaning of the Lunacy Acts of Great Britain.

Within only three years of the imprisonment of the seven in Spandau, the campaign for easing their conditions, remission of sentences, and early release was massively intensified. Dr Konrad Adenauer, the Federal Republic of Germany's first Chancellor, was among those whom the prisoners' wives repeatedly pressed for support. Adenauer had been elected Mayor of Cologne at the age of forty-one; he was then summarily dismissed soon after Hitler came to power, on account of his open opposition to the National Socialists. For eleven years he led the precarious life of a fugitive, and for a time was harboured in a Benedictine monastery. He was arrested in 1934, then released. In May 1945 the Americans reappointed him Mayor of Cologne, but within a few months the British dismissed him. He was then seventy years old, and he decided to found his own political party: the Christian Democratic Union. In August 1949 he was elected Chancellor of the new Bundestag — the German Parliament — and less than a year after he had assumed office, the Spandau wives managed to enlist his help.

Adenauer sent his complaint to André François-Poncet, Chairman of the Allied High Commission, who had been the French Ambassador in Berlin before the war, and was the French Government's High Commissioner in Berlin afterwards. Adenauer also discussed the problem with General Sir Brian Robertson, who was a close friend.

The next diplomatic onslaught on Spandau came from England. The Lord Bishop of Chichester launched a series of letter allegations addressed to various Government Ministers. Sir Ivone Kirkpatrick and Foreign Office colleagues instituted further investigations into the fresh crop of accusations, then placed on official record the following comments:

They advised against pressing for relaxation of the prohibition of food parcels, pointing out that even English prison rules did not permit the receipt of food parcels; furthermore, the possibility of allowing parcels had been debated earlier by the Western Prison Governors and rejected as unnecessary and, on the grounds of security, unacceptable.

Nor was any relaxation recommended in respect of letters, since the Spandau regulation under which prisoners could write and receive one letter every four weeks compared favourably with English prison rules, under which prisoners may write and receive one letter at intervals of not more than two months.

Although English prison rules go no further than to lay down that the Prison Governor should, wherever practicable, inform relatives when a prisoner is dangerously ill, reconsideration was nevertheless recommended regarding the question of notifying relatives in the event of any of the Spandau seven falling seriously ill.

Dealing with complaints about prison work made in a letter from the Bishop of Chichester, it was felt that an element of compulsory labour was not improper. The British view was that organized communal labour is a principle of civilized prison conditions, which is why Britain insisted on provision being made for it in the Spandau regulations. Regarding the Bishop's allegation of insufficient food during the Russian months, the information was that the food during Russian control was now good in quality and reasonable in quantity.

On visiting rules it was noted that English prison regulations permitted visits by up to three persons but at intervals of not less than two months, whereas relaxed Spandau conditions brought into operation by the three Powers the previous December, although allowing a visit by only one person, did allow visiting every month. As for the periodic lighting of cells throughout the night, this was the original system, but the practice was discontinued when the relaxations came into effect. Cells were illuminated until lights out at 22.00 hours by a single electric bulb shining through a nine-inches-by-six door-grille. At 22.00 hours, lights were extinguished and the bulb moved to a position at the side of the door. The light was switched on every fifteen minutes for the warder to inspect the prisoners. It was not a direct light.

Like other church dignitaries, the Bishop of Chichester was a repeated target for 'Free the Spandau Prisoners' campaign propaganda. It reached him from Neurath's friends in France, and from Bishop Würm, head of the Protestant Church in Germany, who knew the Neurath family personally.

Was it coincidence or an orchestrated campaign that ensured that, within a brief period, the Bishop of Chichester received pressing communications from Bishop Würm, Baroness von Neurath, and Hans Raeder, Grand Admiral Raeder's son?

Refuting a substantial part of the allegations, Kirkpatrick asserted that there was no foundation for the charge that the British, United States and French authorities were complacent towards the Russians. Furthermore, he added in his July 1950 reply to the Bishop:

> Indeed, and I must ask you to respect the confidential nature of this information at present, the Council of the High Commission have instructed the three Western Commandants to raise with the Soviet authorities the whole question of conditions in the prison. The reaction of the Soviet authorities to this approach is not yet known, and indeed the approach has to be conducted with some caution lest its outcome should merely be exactly the opposite of that which we wish to achieve — that is to say lest the Soviet authorities insist on a more strict interpretation of the existing regulations than at present.
>
> We naturally hope that they may be persuaded to co-operate, but even if they should not do so, the Western Commandants are under instruction to consider what can be done to ameliorate conditions at least during the three Western months of control of the prison.

I am also doing what I can to help Neurath. But I was disconcerted today to be told by the American High Commissioner that the American prison doctor had recently reported that Neurath's state of health did not warrant any special treatment. I asked Mr McCloy to look into the matter again and he undertook to do so.

A month later, in answer to a further report from the Bishop of Chichester about Spandau conditions, Kirkpatrick wrote to him again:

Confidential

4th August 1950

Thank you for your letter of the 22nd July about conditions in Spandau Prison.

My colleagues in the High Commission have also shown interest in this matter, and have helped me to pursue it. We have agreed to take certain steps amongst ourselves to improve conditions during the three Western months of control, without approaching the Russian authorities, while on the other hand discussions have already been instituted with the Russian prison Governor on certain other aspects. My colleagues and I agreed, after due consideration, that it would be in the best interests of the prisoners themselves, as offering more hope of success, to work for a more liberal interpretation of the existing regulations by all four prison governors rather than for the adoption of new regulations. (The governors are competent to alter their interpretation of regulations without formal reference to higher authority.)

We have already ensured more satisfactory conditions on three points. The prison warders of the three Western powers have been instructed to reduce to an absolute minimum, compatible with security requirements, the use of lights in the cells, and searches of the cells. Censorship of correspondence and books has been speeded up to a point which has eliminated cause of complaint at present. These measures will affect three out of every four months.

Meanwhile negotiations with the Soviet Prison Governor have been opened on the following points. It has been proposed to him that longer visits should be permitted; that the number of letters permitted to be despatched and received should be increased, and that longer incoming letters be allowed. In the hope of improving the lighting of the cells during all four months of control, agreement was obtained from the Russians that an expert, provided under British auspices, should visit the prison to advise on the installation of a more satisfactory and less oppressive lighting system, and then report to the prison Governors; and finally the question of permission to receive visits from legal counsel has also been raised. I am afraid that I cannot yet report any positive results from these approaches to the Russians, but I draw some comfort from the circumstances that the Russians have agreed to discuss the matter.

As regards religious ministration, the prisoners themselves profess to consider the situation satisfactory and the Berlin Commandants therefore feel that it might be desirable to leave this point for the present.

The food supplied to the prisoners certainly appears to be adequate, though admittedly monotonous. Even during the Soviet month of control they receive practically the same rations as the Soviet guards.

I mentioned in the last paragraph of my letter of the 11th July the case of Neurath, about whose health I am concerned. I am glad to say that my approach to the Soviet Commander-in-Chief has in this case had a positive result, since he has now agreed to make an investigation into Neurath's condition. I cannot at present say what the result of the investigations will be, but it is at least something to have obtained Russian agreement.

In general, after my recent careful personal investigation into the conditions in Spandau during my last visit to Berlin, I feel that many adverse reports of conditions there are exaggerated. The Deputy Director of Military Government in Berlin recently visited the prison and heard no complaints from any of the prisoners except von Schirach, who only had a frivolous complaint to make. Gauneval, the French Commandant, also visited the prisoners recently and received no complaints. Taylor, the American, assured me that during the three Western months conditions were not worse than in the American prison at Landsberg. The prisoners are allowed to work in the garden, to rest in the cells whenever they desire, and to indulge in intellectual pursuits. Speer, for example, devotes himself to making architectural designs. While I was in Berlin I paid a formal call on M. Semichastnov, the Soviet Deputy Political Adviser, and took the opportunity of raising the general question of Spandau Prison with him. He then gave me an undertaking to look into the question of the health of the prisoners, and this promise has since been confirmed, in the case of Neurath.

I shall raise the matter again at the next meeting of the Allied High Commission in order to follow up what has already been done.

I. A. Kirkpatrick

In December 1950 renewed efforts were being made to find an alternative to Spandau gaol and then present the proposition to the Soviets. Officials were ordered to find a smaller prison in the British zone where the war criminals could be confined apart from common criminals.

Towards the close of 1950 two more political pressure moves occurred. As a result of representations made to the Pope by Neurath's daughter, Winifred von Mackensen, the Papal Nuncio strongly pressed Britain's Foreign Secretary 'to prove during the Holy Year that justice could still be tempered by mercy, and not overlook the fact that Western Germany is strongly Catholic'. The second political action, which was taken on behalf of all the war criminals including the Spandau seven, was a letter sent in December from Martin Niemöller, as spokesman for the Council of the Evangelical Church in Germany. It was addressed to 10 Downing Street and to Prime Minister Clement Attlee:

> Far be it for us, in drawing the attention of the governments to these cases, to assist actual criminals to fly from justice. In view of the fact, however, that many condemned persons have already served many years of their sentence and that many of them have already experienced the expiating force of punishment; in view of the circumstances that the desire for peaceful understanding among the peoples is growing stronger, we believe that the time has come to submit the following petitions to the governments of the victorious nations:
> 1. We beg for an amnesty
>   a. for condemned persons who were of a youthful age at the time of committing the deed laid to their charge;
>   b. for prisoners who on account of advanced age or illness suffer particularly in serving their sentences.
> 2. We beg for commutation or the repeal by an act of pardon of the punishment
>   a. of condemned persons whose punishment would seem too severe because at the time the sentence was passed a stricter standard was applied than was later the case in pronouncing sentences on the same or similar constituent facts;
>   b. of condemned persons who were sentenced according to principles of law to which members of other nations under similar

       circumstances, were not subject, especially in cases where sentence of death has been passed;
   c. of condemned persons in whose cases principles of law were applied, the validity of which has been questioned by leading lawyers of those countries which were at war.
3. We beg that Committees of Mercy be established to whose activities no time-limit shall be set, and whose members have previously had nothing to do with the condemnations. We beg also that a system of reprieves may be introduced on condition of good behaviour or of probation, and that German advisers be given a hearing in the matter.
4. We beg that proceedings which have not yet been concluded, may be discontinued to as large an extent as possible.

This extraordinary attempt seeking the complete overturn of the Nuremberg judgements, the abandonment of the hunt for and prosecution of other war criminals, and the placing of all those already sentenced and imprisoned into the hands of 'committees of mercy' totally unconnected with those who previously condemned the guilty, was utterly rejected by Britain, the United States, France and, of course, the Soviet Union.

On reading this letter from the distinguished Martin Niemöller, Prime Minister Attlee commented: 'Christian charity is one thing, but as George Bernard Shaw said long ago: "The secret of forgiving everything is to understand nothing."'

16: FORBIDDEN WORDS

No prison is as invulnerable as it looks from the outside. If they were, this book could never have been written. I smuggled questions in to Spandau's prisoners and obtained replies and details of many of their conversations with each other, by the same routes. The authorities knew that, through cracks and crevices in Berlin's ringed fortress, a sly traffic filtered that all the watchful and preventive measures introduced could not stop.

Initially denied newspapers or magazines and guarded by men who were forbidden to discuss outside political events with them, the seven kept abreast of external news by the simple expedient of reading the cut-up newspapers provided as toilet paper, until the introduction of paper toilet rolls ended the lavatory news service. But the toilet rolls offered another opportunity; they became a paper source for illegal correspondence. The prisoners, or friends outside, 'softened up' gaol personnel, persuading the gullible, or those who found it difficult to accept the depths of infamy for which their gaol charges had been convicted.

Denied authority for writing a book, Speer started collecting toilet paper sheets by strapping them with rubber bands in the bend of his knee so that they could not be seen. Every page of official notepaper issued to the seven, stamped with the Spandau seal, was checked off in the office when it passed through again as a letter. In his customary minuscule handwriting Speer wrote the main basis of his *Inside the Third Reich* book and, subsequently, diary thoughts on Spandau. By the time he was released, two thousand pages in his own handwriting, including letters to his wife and children and vast quantities of smuggled notes, were awaiting him at his home — most of it written on odd scraps of paper, toilet paper and cardboard. He later admitted that his key smuggler was a Dutch gaol orderly who passed the material to Speer's wife.

Schirach was also at it and secretly undertook to write his memoirs for 500,000 Deutschmarks for a German magazine. Maintaining that it was his 'duty to write for the sake of history', superficially affable Schirach knew how to turn on the charm and persuade naïve young guards that he 'really wasn't such a bad chap'; he got them to smuggle for him at considerable risk. It did not take all seven long to begin attempting to soften up the guards, some of whom had been children of the war and were therefore unfamiliar with the enormity of the inmates' crimes. The seven, and friends and relatives outside, always found conspirators among the Allied warders and displaced persons who worked in the gaol.

One warder smuggled in bottles of wine, passing them from cell to cell until everyone except Hess became merry. Schirach was persuaded to stop singing at the top of his voice only when scared warders and fellow prisoners finally made him understand that his singing could result in serious punishment for them all if Russian warders due on duty found them drunk. The Soviet Director even banned Communion wine because it could be intoxicating.

The seven were officially permitted to learn a little more of the world outside when, from May 1954, each of the four nations administering the gaol agreed to provide a different German-language daily newspaper for the inmates. 'Unsuitable stories or features' were censored from the newspapers, with the Prison Directors being responsible for this censorship. Former newspaperman Walther Funk, who knew more devious tricks than any of the other prisoners and was always the best informed, operated his own message shuttling service throughout the years he was inside. In May 1957 this service brought him a copy of a letter from West German Foreign Minister Heinrich von Bretano, confirming Bonn moves on Funk and Speer's behalf. The West German authorities had long been manoeuvring to obtain an amnesty for them. That month did in fact bring Funk's freedom, and even when he finally got outside, he still used his secret Spandau communications service to notify Schirach during October 1957 that the four-Powers were scheduled to meet in Berlin to discuss closing the gaol by the end of the year. The information was accurate, but the closure talks came to nothing.

Concern for security was behind a decision that on the surface seemed rather mean, which ended the privilege prisoners enjoyed of receiving books sent by their families. It was, nevertheless, a necessary precaution. Incoming books, together with the letters prisoners were allowed to write, could be used, it was realized, to establish a code to outwit prison security, and it was Grand Admiral Karl Dönitz who inadvertently first drew attention to the loophole.

The censors noticed that in letters to his family Dönitz frequently referred to the books he was reading, mentioning the author, publisher and edition, and invariably adding, 'Guenter will be interested to know of this.' Guenter was the Admiral's son-in-law, who had become one of his most trusted officers during the war. This connection, and Dönitz's pointed references, suggested the possibility of a code to the censors. They knew enough about what happened at the German Admiralty in wartime to give colour to their suspicions. For instance, before any U-boat commander was assigned to operational duty for the first time he was interviewed alone, by either Dönitz or Eberhard Godt, Chief of Operational Staff. Under an oath of secrecy the commander would be given a simple letter code, based on the word 'Ireland', so that in the event of his capture he could in the first few letters written to his family as a prisoner-of-war disclose how his submarine had come to be sunk, information crucial to Dönitz and his officers. To distinguish a coded letter from the usual letter home the date had to be underlined, and it was then the duty of the commander's wife or family to forward it at once to naval headquarters.

The formula is very much the same in using books for coded messages. Spandau's censors realized that if Dönitz was operating one of his wartime codes he would require to change the key book frequently, as prisoners were not permitted to keep a particular book beyond a certain period. And so the right to gifts of books was stopped. In the following letter to his wife he had something to say about the rules of censorship:

> Your letters were censored for the following reasons: references to subjects of a political character; unclear writing; and, thirdly, the use of abbreviations.
>
> You must not write about politics. The interpretation of the word is very broad. It includes all public matters, and most probably utterances of yours, which you may have made in connection with my birthday, concerning the loyalty of certain old comrades.

The following month, Inge Dönitz's letter from her husband advised:

> Meine Ingeliebste,
> It is not true that the prison is dirty and don't worry about me, my little Inge. I am unchanged. I am taking matters calmly and quietly. Everything takes its time.

I spent six hours today in the garden and am dog-tired, but it was very pleasant to be there. In Nuremberg, in the yard, there was a little green, and eleven kinds of singing birds. To watch the young ones growing and to see their first attempts at flight was delightful. Just the same, one can enjoy the growing of plants.

Does Guenter walk with little Peter? There is nothing that sticks in a child's memory more than walking with its father and asking him so many questions he wonders what is coming next.

Six of the photographs you sent me are on my little table. In the middle are the pictures of Klaus and Peter, our greatly beloved sons, the unforgettably brave and good boys who are always with us, my Ingefrau. In the evening I read mostly history, astronomy, biology, and also some novels, but I go to bed early, therefore don't worry about me. You know my calmness is unchanged, and really it is unnecessary to write more. Wait a moment, I received the soft warm underpants you made for me and they came at the right time.

My inner feelings and thoughts are the same as they were at Nuremberg. My old life was never one of comfort and relaxation, but the daily fulfilment of duties, in other words a life of deeds and actions. Now it is the other way round. That is why I now love to read what men of ripe experience, wisdom and philosophical calmness have written.

I have read the biography of Washington with great interest and prefer such books to novels, even historical novels, which are always somehow too coloured. Truth is what I want. I want to read how things really were, as far as can be at all ascertained objectively. Patience.

Dein Junge [Your boy]

Like Hess, Dönitz wrote many of his letters with an eye to his proposed autobiography, which, in fact, he had already arranged to publish soon after his release from Spandau. A considerable amount of preparatory work had already been done on it for him by friends. Dönitz referred to this in another letter:

> Meine Ingefrau,
>
> On the question of an autobiography, I want to point out once more that its weakness lies in the fact that nobody can see himself objectively. Everyone, though maybe unwittingly, presents himself as he wants to be seen.
>
> The most likely reason for a work of this character is self-apology, or self-aggrandizement. It is my belief that man's highest ideal is a wish for selfless duty.
>
> Materialism as a fulfilment of life, such as the accumulation of wealth or the pursuit of a comfortable and carefree existence, cannot tempt me.
>
> Your boy

The Dönitz home was said to have been looted after his arrest, and in his next letter the subject of material possessions was mentioned again:

> Meine Ingeliebste,
>
> That our things were stolen in Graberkate I am still sometimes furious about. They were collected with so much love. But don't let us cry about material losses.
>
> Mice have increased astonishingly in the garden and run across our feet, realizing how harmless we are. The owlet that lives here is getting its full share of them at night. There is also a pair of falcons here. I have been feeding the mice with lupin seeds, which I put outside their holes and watch them come out and take them.
>
> I am now growing an American kind of tomato which is larger than our own, but yellow instead of the usual colour.
>
> It is remarkable how, in the absence of normal distractions, one remembers all that has gone before. Things that really

meant something to one become clearer, among them the many songs one learned as a child. When I am with you again we shall have to buy a dog. What I will do when I come out I do not know. My liveliness and vitality have considerably decreased; only my character remains the same. I now find it difficult to recall names. Tell that to Eberhard [Dönitz's former U-boat Operations Chief of Staff]. He will be happy, for my excellent memory always frightened him.

Your boy

On another occasion Dönitz wrote about his dead sons:

Mein Ingefrau,

On the 20th of March, my dear Ingefrau, our thoughts will be united, thinking of our dear brave Peter. It was a bitter time in Bitterstraße [their Berlin home]; Peter missing at sea; and the sudden and considerable losses in the service; everything was so serious, heavy responsibility and nothing to lighten our affairs.

But it was like that during the long years of peace when one had daily to fight for opinions one held and to strive for recognition. It would have been better had my views been accepted in time and not when it was too late. That is where the tragedy in my affairs lies.

My dear, among the few personal possessions of Klaus is his wrist-watch, which he wore when he died, and which, despite being so long in the water, was still ticking. Maybe you can use it to replace the one you lost.

One day here is like the other. I am well except for a painful thumb and rheumatism.

I have a number of wishes for later on. I would like to hear the song of a nightingale. I don't remember ever hearing one in my life. It would be a pleasure, too, to see the snowdrops and violets growing in a beech wood in early spring. Sometimes I hear a dog barking on the other side of the wall and I think of Wolf. How nice it is to possess a dog.

Yesterday I watched the nearly full moon. These are my links with the outside world.

I'm deeply grateful to those who are good and kind to you. But to those who should be nice to you because of what we have done for them in the past and are not, I can only show my behind.

Your boy

Thinking of freedom, Dönitz, the first man due out of Spandau, wrote in another letter:

Meine Ingeliebste,

Please send me a star chart which I can adjust according to the month. The wind is blowing the clouds about, ideal weather for sailing. I am trying to learn by heart whole passages from the books read in order to exercise my mind. The days here roll on, one after the other, like waves in the Atlantic, only out there it is more beautiful and wider, freer and grander.

We shall soon meet again, and the past years will seem as short as a watch at sea to me. May is our month of Fate, in which we were married and also lost our two sons.

I would like to be at sea just once more, though not as a guest and stranger on the deck of a passenger liner, but down below, closely linked with the world of water, or fighting my own way at the rudder of a yacht. If only I could do that again; but I guess my rheumatism will say 'No.' When I do a thing like this I must put my life at stake. I cannot live as a normal citizen.

I am tired now and go to my bunk.

Your boy

Ilse Hess could not resist trying to challenge censorship by including political comments in a letter to her husband. It was confiscated and he was informed that he would not be permitted to have the letter — not even with censorship deletions — as a punishment for his wife's deliberate flouting of the restrictions. Warning against a repetition of such futile defiance, Hess wrote to her: 'Swallow it down, even if it wants to rise in your throat — like I do by the cartload!'

Also writing to his wife about censorship, Neurath told her that a page of her last letter to him had been removed because she had exceeded the limit of 1,300 words. Every word written by the prisoners, and sent by their relatives, was counted. The *Herrn Zensoren*, he added, were aware that she was unable to type (typewritten letters were insisted upon), which made it important that she should write clearly.

After his wife's visit to Spandau the Baron's next letter to her contained a little slip of paper from the censors warning her once more that political remarks were forbidden. In another letter he wrote:

> Dearest Manny,
> I don't need to tell you how your visit here, though short, has made me happy and refreshed me. The winter was bad and I did not think I would live through it.
> It is splendid that some friends are visiting you on our wedding anniversary. That I can't be with you is particularly painful, but circumstances forbid me to tell you of my feelings. I can only thank you for all the love which you have given me in good and bad times during the fifty years.
> On the 30th, my thoughts will be with you more than ever, that you know. I wonder whether it will be as hot on that day as it was fifty years ago?
> My very best greetings,
>
> C

Many of Neurath's letters contained advice to his daughter, Winifred von Mackensen, on the management of the family estate. An experienced farmer, he could write with authority on horticulture, drainage and sowing. On 3 June 1951, however, he was concerned with the legal battle over his confiscated estates:

> My dearest Manny,
>
> Today I am thinking of Father's death. Were it not for you I could not but wish that soon I should be with him in our little graveyard at Glattbach. But as it is, I am trying hard to hold on.
>
> I have intended for quite some time to make a new will in place of the one that was stolen [this occurred when the Neurath home was robbed] but have not had the chance to do so yet. During all these years of seclusion I feel that I can hardly draw up such a document without knowing how I stand legally.
>
> Have something drawn up by Fischinger [their lawyer]. The document that he sent to me is not likely to be handed over. It is advisable that anything prepared by Fischinger should be split up into several letters. I confirm again that a great part of the estate was bought in my name with your money.
>
> I have smiled a little over your description of the mosquito plague. More than that I cannot do here.
>
> I am suffering from angina pectoris and sometimes the pains are awful. I have a heavy burden to carry under the circumstances, but to complain is not to my liking.
>
> My very best greetings,
>
> C

One letter simply said:

> My dearest Manny,
>
> I find it difficult to write a sensible letter today, for what I would like to write I can't. It is better I don't write.
>
> C

Sending a birthday letter Neurath said:

My dearest Manny,

I thought of you all on February 2nd. How often we celebrated this day [his birthday]. I wonder whether I shall ever see Leinfelderhof [his Württemberg home] again? I remember our departure from there on Palm Sunday seven years ago. How right I was to feel heavy and depressed when we left.

It is now just twenty years ago since Hindenburg demanded that I take over the Berlin post and we said goodbye to London. Remembering all our years together, I realize what they meant to us and, too, what you meant to me. My only regret is that after everything we shared together I now have to bring you sorrow. But I could neither foresee nor prevent it.

It seems an eternity since you were here. Time flies and yet crawls here. Unfortunately my eyes are growing weak, as you can see from my writing. Naturally my letters from here are pretty empty. I am feeling much better thanks to the homoeopathic treatment I am receiving from the French doctor.

My trouble can't be overcome; after all, my days are numbered, and I can't be sorry about it in my present situation, though I would have loved to have come home just once more. I suffer great annoyance and worry and it is difficult to carry on, but carry on I must.

My hearty greetings,

Your C

When Christmas 1952 was over, he wrote:

My dearest Manny,

We are entering 1953, and with it, into my eightieth year of life, and though I have really lived long enough, I want to die at home and not in prison.

For the New Year I am sending you and Wini all the best wishes, above all, that your health may remain good. I, on my part, will try my utmost to remain well and hold on, difficult though it is.

The Christmas days, always so hard for the soul to bear, are over. How difficult they must have been for you, I know also. I have been thinking of the Christmases that we had with our parents. Those days are gone, but I must be grateful for them.

Your C

One Palm Sunday the censors passed through a Neurath letter with comments on his Nuremberg sentence — a forbidden subject in all correspondence:

Dear Manny.

I received your letter punctually. Handwritten letters make one feel closer to home than do typed ones. Palm Sunday 1945, I believe it was the 27th March when we left to go to the children and it will always remain in my memory. The farewell to our home, and all the things which I had built and planted there in more than forty years, was particularly hard, maybe because of a premonition of a long parting. But I had a clean conscience and never thought that I would be held responsible for the deeds of others — deeds of which I knew nothing and which I would never have approved.

The truth about this, though too late, will yet have its day. Anyhow, I would not act differently today if again faced with the same situation.

I wish you the best of health and tenderly embrace you.

Your C

This was the only occasion in all his letters from Spandau in which Neurath attempted to defend himself.

The letters of Grand Admiral Erich Raeder always opened with a quotation, either Biblical or from Goethe, and these words of wisdom invariably called for a close scrutiny from the censors, on the alert for a possible code message. Awaiting his wife Erika's visit to Spandau after her release from Russian imprisonment, he wrote on 12 February 1950:

> Dearest Etachen,
> Let me know the day of your arrival in April. Write down all questions to be discussed and in the order of their importance. I am doing the same. They take down everything one says here. Tell them when you arrive of your intention to give nothing to the newspapers, especially interviews, so that they will realize here that it is not your fault should anything go wrong.
> My valuables here are: wedding ring; cuff-links with initials 'A.V.'; gold chain for my monocle, which was a present from you; dental plate in platinum gold; fountain pen; brown leather purse with some gold teeth in it; a cheap wristlet watch without value but in working order; about forty books and a picture of Christ.
> Erich

And after the first visit:

> Dear Etachen,
> Thank God for fulfilling a part of my prayer, which was a wish to see you again. The only trouble was that the many business things we had to discuss left us so little time. Let us hope we get more time on your next visit. It is certainly a great excitement for the soul to meet again after such a long parting.
> In the morning and evening I read the quotations that appear on the calendar in my cell. It comes from the Herrnhut Brethren.

In the garden we observe the life of crows, magpies and two falcons, all meeting here and fighting large air battles daily. It is remarkable that the falcons hold their own against so many crows, who try to outmanoeuvre them.

Thank you for the two silk shirts, the dark red and the dark blue, which are greatly admired here, and thank you very much for the nice soap you sent. You know I don't like strong perfume.

Erich

In fact Raeder detested perfume, bobbed hair, short skirts, lacquered fingernails, and smoking. It had been his custom to badger young naval officers into passing the information on to their wives so that they would know his views regarding feminine habits and dress. Abstemious himself, he imposed his will on the German Navy by forbidding any drinking immediately before duty hours and he saw to it that this was observed. An alcoholic breath never went unpunished. Smoking on an empty stomach was also considered injurious, and Raeder discouraged this practice.

The son on whose future he had set so much store died. Raeder, whose ruthless U-boat warfare had sent so many fine young men to unknown graves, was deeply moved by this loss, writing, on 18 January 1953:

Dearest Etachen,

Hardly had I finished a letter to Hans when the chaplain informed me that our dear son, the hope of our old age, had passed away.

What was it that made him die so quickly? He looked so well during his last visit, and I was surprised when you wrote and told me about his illness. Since then I have asked God daily to allow him to become well again. I pray for you and your health twice a day. But the ways of God are unknown and in spite of our sufferings we must not doubt Him.

You know how I loved Hans and how I always worried about him. But great as is my sorrow for him, I know he is better off now than we are. I am troubled above all by the thought that you, my dearest, had to part from the son who gave you, despite your suffering, such pleasure to cherish.

Don't worry about me, my dear. I am glad that I can, in my love, be something to you still, hand in hand.

Tell me how Hans died and everything the doctors said.

Remember that it is up to you to keep yourself well for our ever-to-be-hoped-for reunion. God bless and take care of you.

Erich

Whatever hopes for the future Karl Dönitz expressed to fellow inmates, and openly in correspondence with his wife, he secretly had other ideas. But these were reserved for letters smuggled from the gaol.

Through a smuggled message received from his son-in-law, he learned that his prestige was holding up well, according to a survey conducted by the Allensbacher Institut, the country's foremost public affairs research organization. An opinion poll conducted during the summer of 1952 logged him as scoring a top 46 per cent rating among formerly prominent personalities whom the German public still held in good esteem. Former Minister of Finance Schacht scored 42 per cent; Göring, 37; Speer, 30; Hitler, 24; Schirach and Hess, 22 per cent.

Although filled inwardly with overwhelming hate for the peoples who defeated and imprisoned him, in letters subject to prison censors' scrutiny Dönitz declared innocuously: 'When I am freed, my task will be to remain silent and feel my way back to life'; 'I shall be emerging from a cage, so it would be foolish of me to express opinions as they still have to be formed.'

An illicit pencil-written letter dated 14 March 1953, however, exposed the other Dönitz — the true Dönitz. It revealed that his current courier was about to be transferred from the gaol, which meant illegal correspondence would halt for an unforeseeable period until a replacement smuggler could be arranged.

The incriminating 14 March letter contained a number of names, including code names. References to two apparently different people — 'Carolus' and 'Tante Lotte' (Aunt Lotte) — were both Dönitz's code names for himself. 'Guenter' was his son-in-law; 'Frank', his former Navy propaganda chief; 'Uncle Erich', Grand Admiral Erich Raeder; 'Otto', Dr Otto Kranzbühler, his lawyer; 'Elisabethe' referred to Elisabethe Heinemann, the person whose home was used as the accommodation address for the letter; 'Ursel' was his daughter; the 'Rudolf-People' were the Russians, and 'Eberhard' was Eberhard Godt, his wartime Naval Chief of Operational Staff.

The revealing letter confirmed indisputably, in Dönitz's own handwriting, concern for his prestige and political future. He still divided the world into 'the German nation', and 'the enemy'. The letter read:

> March 14, 53. My dearest, thank you for your letter the beginning of February, which had no date. Now the most important thing: end of May this chance of traffic ceases. Until then it is my intention still to write several times because I request answers for several questions before the curtain comes down between us. It is therefore important now my dearest that you should answer my questions or have them settled by Guenter as soon as possible because there are delays here through collecting and handing out. There is therefore very little time left before the end of May and we have to work quickly and accurately. Therefore, dearest, please be my good chief of staff and write without me asking

for it if you should have anything to report of interest and meaning. Also tell Guenter that he himself should write using this way. It is only such a short time that I request this burden from you. Here now come some of my questions. Those you can answer straight away please answer soonest, otherwise it is advisable to copy them before you give this letter away, or tear it up, especially of those questions concerning Guenter, so that you can hand over everything properly. In case you don't think Guenter's postal address a safe one, bring the copy personally to him when you visit at Easter. So be clever. Questions:

Firstly. There is supposed to be a Prien film in the making about Scapa Flow. Who of us has his hands in it? In the interest of historical truth? Eberhard is the one who knows all which led to the operation at Scapa Flow. Frank, too, is of importance in this matter, he wrote a book on Prien and was a friend of his. Besides that there is a book of Prien's by himself which gives important details about the Scapa Flow matter. So please, dearest, clear the matter and write to me. In any case inform Frank about the film and intentions.

Secondly. There is supposed to be a series in an illustrated paper on Uncle Erich. It seems similar to the one on Carolus in the *Post*. Please organize it that someone reads the Uncle Erich reports and tells me what silly things are alleged in it about Carolus.

Thirdly. I have no judgement about the *Post* articles on Carolus which are running now. It is said that Otto managed them. Is he satisfied with the printing? Is it correct that in one of the instalments it reads that Schwerin-Krossig is supposed to have said that he didn't think much of Carolus and that he was only a Hitler boy? What do you think of the overall effect on the articles on (a) the German nation; (b) the enemy? And do the advantages outweigh the disadvantages or the other way round? Do they serve Carolus in his prestige? So please, dearest, write me your opinion and answer the questions. Please tell Guenter that after the *Post* articles are finished he is to send me *his* answers to my questions and I would also like it if Otto could report his opinion to me.

4. Has a clause mentioning the possible deflation of money been considered in the contract which was drawn up with the Athenaeum publishing house for Carolus, so that he does not have to work one day for half the value of the mark? Has that been considered? In no case would Carolus turn as much as one finger if the full value of the present mark is not paid when day of writing comes.

5. Please ask Guenter when you visit him at Easter whether he thinks his address Hoffrnannstraße safe enough so that Tante Lotte might use it for sending him a letter there before end of May? If not would he please mention an address of the Elisabethe kind.

6. Some young, unwise and politically immature people are alleged to have been sworn in by oath on Carolus. They were then arrested. Does this comic bagatelle have any disadvantages for Carolus? Always the viewpoint has to be considered that he can as soon as possible change the air.

7. You must definitely consider that the Rudolf-People will insist on Carolus being released at the latest date possible, and will see to it that a counter-demonstration is started outside here by people inspired by Communists. It is the wish of Carolus that on his day of release he will be driven directly from the Sanatorium to the airport and fly to the West. That has to be prepared accordingly. Carolus points out all this already, because he does not know whether he will have the chance to do so at a later time.

8. Long experience with rheumatism has taught Tante Lotte that woollen blankets are the best bed cover. Looking ahead Tante Lotte asks that such blankets be purchased. They must be of real wool, though, not made from the beech or oak wood ersatz.

9. Ursel, while visiting here, mentioned the name of the man where you always stay here. Guenter also mentioned the name in his last letter. I don't think this is very advisable.

10. Tante Lotte has had for quite some time a blood circulation trouble in her right leg, which gets worse … veins on the leg, violet coloured, and cramps and pains. What does one do against it, how does one treat it, how does one behave in a case such as this?

11. My dearest, you best of all, you wrote to me about Frau H. on the lines that you could not forget and blamed her that she behind your back had intercourse with me. It is right that it was *me* who had intercourse with her behind your back. You must blame *me*. But things should be forgotten and that's why I will not contradict. What you did write hurt me, but as I did not wish to hurt you I told Ursel when she was here to tell Frau H. not to come. I had however with this refusal the feeling that I was not doing the right thing, for the woman, whose visit was offered in kind spirit, would also be hurt. Now, dearest, you are writing in your letter 1st March so kindly about the whole affair, that I am touched and happy. I will write to Guenter tomorrow that Frau H. could come. Then all of us are doing the right thing. Anyway, my dearest, I am grateful. You are my little crown.

12. How was the evening with Otto? Did he mention anything special? Is there anything else of interest to me? Hearty regards for Elisabethe. I hope she is well again. You, my dear, are, after all, the only one. Was there anything else unfavourable or silly in the *Post* about Carolus?

Dearest, is it now sure that Ali will come in April? Can I announce him? Are you coming end of May beginning of June? I am looking forward to you, you best one, you beloved. When will Eberhard come? I would like very much to see him.

I handed a copy of this letter to Secretary of State for Foreign Affairs Selwyn Lloyd when he interrogated me about the prison. As I said in Chapter 1 of this book, I am certain that, more than any other factor, this smuggled document saved me from being prosecuted and possibly imprisoned for breaking through Spandau gaol's official secret security barriers.

On another occasion, however, illicit correspondence routes were used for a far more laudable purpose than a would-be future Führer issuing instructions to followers eagerly awaiting his release. When, in 1953, sixteen-year-old Hilde Speer experienced for the first time in her young years American thinking and living, she suddenly had a desperate need of honest answers to questions tormenting her mind. There was no escaping the fact that her father had been tried and convicted as a major war criminal. During Hitler's final days in the besieged Berlin bunker, there were only seven men with the right to be directly connected to the Führer by phone: the Commander-in-Chief of the Luftwaffe, Reichsmarschall Hermann Göring; Minister of Propaganda Joseph Goebbels; the Gestapo's Heinrich Himmler; Supreme Commander of Armed Forces, Field Marshal Wilhelm Keitel; the Führer's so-called 'Secretary', who, in reality, was in control of all domestic policies at the time; and Hilde's father — Albert Speer.

Hilde, only nine when her father was arrested, knew that he had made the most straightforward impression of all on the prosecutors and judges at his trial by not attempting to shirk responsibility. But did he speak honestly? Did he regret complicity in the terrible crimes, or merely that it all went wrong? Was he shrewdly confessing shame when confronted with inescapable guilt, or because he wanted to try to rescue his neck from the hangman?

Hilde needed to know. Spandau visiting restrictions, however, absolutely forbade discussions of politics; nor was such discussion permitted in authorized correspondence. She had to obtain answers to questions, somehow, and wanted her father to consider long and hard before replying. The issues were far too important to her for quick, off-the-cuff replies.

Appreciating the depths of Hilde's dilemma, Margarete Speer told her daughter to raise the questions in a letter that she promised to have smuggled into the gaol. Hilde explained in the secret message to her father:

> I can understand how Hitler came to power, with the help of workers whom he rescued from despair by finding jobs for them. I can understand, though less easily, how many intellectuals came to accept him, although in his book he had stated exactly what his aims were.
>
> What I cannot understand is how these educated people did not turn against him when he began persecuting the Jews; and after he had extended the borders of Germany by taking in Austria and regions in the east. I know that at the end you were no longer in agreement with him. But what I do not understand is why you did not break with him in 1940.

There was no ducking the child's search for answers. She was entitled to frankness. Speer thought and rethought every sentence before committing his reply to paper. It took him two weeks to write one of the most important letters of his life. He told Hilde:

> What you are really asking me is how an intelligent man was able to go along with Hitler. Let me begin my answer by a confession which is most difficult to make. In my case there is just no excuse. The fault is mine, and expiation there must be. It is not enough, confronted by the enormity of these crimes, to plead that one simply obeyed orders, ignoring the rest.
>
> The fact of having accepted Hitler's orders means that I have to share responsibility. I feel myself responsible for everything that took place at this time — even things I knew nothing of, or was not directly concerned with. Let me assure

you that I knew nothing of all the horrors, and that fact was accepted by the judges. But there is scant satisfaction in asking oneself what one ought to have known, what one could have found out, if one had wished to know.

I am one of the few taking the view today that the Nuremberg trial, despite its defects, was necessary. The judgement which came to me counts as something towards the price of my redemption. I am satisfied and content with my sentence and imprisonment. I regard my destiny as though it had been fixed by a court of God, judging not only illegalities, but recognizing that these were a relatively small part of the total profound fault, which was marked by an easy acceptance of things on my part.

In the drama of Sophocles, Oedipus is cruelly punished by Providence for having killed his father and then marrying his mother, not knowing who she was. Any modern tribunal would acquit him. But the moral ideas of the Greeks decreed that he had to endure severe punishment and torment.

Without being able to explain why, exactly, I find this quite right. I must say at this point how much I have been helped in applying this to my own case. My comrades have fulminated against their destiny — whether unmerited or not is not for me to say — and in their protests they have suffered grave nervous strain, whereas I, to the general astonishment, have stayed fit, precisely because I see in my fate here a profounder significance. When I am released I shall be liberated from my guilt. I shall truly have expiated it.

That is all very well, you may say, from an egotistical viewpoint, but what about us, your children, who on your account have suffered so much? That is precisely the weak point of the whole affair. I have so far made no attempt to tell you of what I count myself guilty: first the persecution of the Jews, to which one must add the persecution, too, of the men opposing Hitler; and then the unleashing of a horrible war. At Nuremberg I did not try to disavow my guilt, and actually did not wish to make a final plea on my own behalf. But for you the important question I must try to answer is, 'How can an intelligent man, as I see myself to be, take the wrong turning in life so completely as I did?'

I was not active in politics because politics did not interest me. Until 1933 I was merely one among three or four million other members, merely paying my membership contribution — apart from the help I gave as an architect, in the reconstruction of Party buildings. I knew some very intelligent Jews living in Mannheim who were aware that I had joined the Party, and one of them, to my great astonishment, told me that but for its anti-Semitism he would have nothing against joining the Nazi Party himself.

One did not take terribly seriously all the exaggerations, thinking that in time, as often happens, things would sort themselves out and so become more palatable. If Hitler had said in 1933 that some years later he would set fire to synagogues, persecute the Jews, lead Germany to war and kill off his political enemies, he would have lost most of his followers at one go, and, I think, myself included. When in 1939 I clearly understood that Hitler's foreign policy aims were leading to war, and that he hated the Jews and was persecuting them, I was in many respects his prisoner.

Sometimes in the life of a people collective suggestion shows its effect. Let us not forget the sorcerers who were burned in the Middle Ages, and the terror during the French Revolution. Man is full of bad instincts, which he tries to suppress. But if the barriers once give way, then something dreadful is unleashed.

Some few individuals escape the common folly, but when it is all over, and one regains awareness, the world takes its head in its hands and asks: 'How did I come to do it?'

Then for me personally there was one factor making for the exclusion of all criticism, if I had wished to express any. You must realize that at the age of thirty-two, in my capacity as an architect, I had the most splendid assignments of which I could dream. Hitler said to your mother one day that her husband could design buildings the like of which had not been seen for two thousand years. One would have had to be morally very stoical to reject such a prospect. But I was not at all like that. As I have already told you, I did not believe in any God, and that would have been the only possible counterbalance.

There was one enormous fault, one which I shared with others. It had become a habit to do one's job without occupying oneself with what the neighbours were doing. By that I wish to say that I did not think it had anything to do with me when somebody else said all the Jews ought to be wiped out. Clearly I said nothing of this kind, neither did I think like that. I never showed any anti-Semitism myself, and stayed calm. The fact that I helped many Jews is no excuse. On the contrary, it aggravates the moral fault. More than once I have put to myself the question what I would have done if I had felt myself responsible for what Hitler did in other spheres of activity. Unfortunately, if I am to stay sincere, the answer would be negative. My position as an architect and the magnificent projects on which I was engaged became indispensable to me. I swallowed all the rest, never giving it a thought.

In the spring of 1944, as you know, I had a long illness and thanks to this I rid myself of part at least of the influence Hitler had over me. Then, too, there was a reason that goes far beyond the inexplicable. Hitler had exercised a strong domination on those in close contact with him — partly because of his persuasive power, which had something of the hypnotic about it, and partly by reason of his amiability and high office. You will understand me when I cite as an example your talking to Mr McCloy [US Military Governor and High Commissioner in Germany 1949-52]. His high position was right away a reason for your allowing yourself to be influenced by him.

The first consequence of my becoming detached from Hitler led to my resignation as minister. I stayed in only because my friends asked me to stay. You have already read what I did after that. It went quite far, and cannot be understood except in the light of the exceptional circumstances in which we lived. I am a peaceful man by nature.

But even this period, well known to the Allies, cannot serve me as an excuse. I did not really become roused until I knew that Hitler wanted to take all the German people down with him into the abyss. Practically all that I did amounted to a struggle against that. It was not directed against him because of the persecution of the Jews and the unleashing of the dreadful war. That did not concern me. I continued to persuade myself for a long time. I did not begin to move actively against him until the day he attacked my own sphere of activity — until he showed that he wished to destroy industrial centres in France, Belgium and Holland.

Speer knew that any attempt to send the letter to Hilde through official channels would have resulted in it being stopped because of the strictly enforced rule forbidding family letters to include politics; but this was one letter that *had* to reach his family. He had it smuggled out to Hilde.

17: THE EIGHTH MAN OF SPANDAU

According to official four-Power records, there were only seven major war criminals occupying Spandau gaol. There was, in fact, an eighth inmate; Hitler's ghost haunted the prison. He never left the seven alone, nor stopped dominating their lives, constantly intruding into their thoughts, conversations, recollections, recriminations. Six drab, once important men repeatedly turned on the Führer who had led them to their brief spasm of triumph. Most sought to transfer their guilt to the man whom they continued to claim was solely responsible, who issued orders they had to obey.

The seventh, Rudolf Hess, still believed his Führer was right and maintained unrepentant Hitlerism, anti-Semitism, and hatred of all who had opposed Nazi Germany.

'Hitler chose a voluntary death because he could not submit to the jurisdiction of judges who had no right to try him,' Hess declaimed. 'The spectacle would have been intolerable because he was one of the most significant personalities in the history of the world.'

Although not as fulsome in praise of the Führer as Hess, Hitler's creed remained a living thing for Dönitz. He confessed to having reservations about the Führer and admitted faults, but Dönitz considered drastic criticism of Hitler treason. Possibly loyalty to past authority was bound up with the fact that it was via this authority that the mantle of succession to the presidency of the Third Reich had been bestowed upon him. Even in Spandau, Dönitz asserted to his six companions: 'Never forget that I am the legal Head of State in the Third

Reich, and my orders are therefore still binding upon you — even in here.'

Neurath tended to side with Dönitz. So did Raeder, although he was no Dönitz lover. Schirach could not make up his mind; Funk usually agreed with Speer; whilst Hess remained airily indifferent, except when defending Hitler's qualities.

The ironic aspect of Hess's blind worship of his Führer was, as Speer pointed out: 'Whenever Hitler ranted and raved about treason and treachery, he usually complained, "This all began with that idiot, Rudolf Hess." Hitler would then couple Hess's defection with the 20 July Stauffenberg conspiracy, which was, of course, an utterly different affair.'

Funk's journalistic mind offered the shrewdest observations on their erstwhile leader: 'The Third Reich was based more upon Hitler's personal fascination than on the appeal and realities of the Party's ideals.'

Agreeing, Schirach, who used to laud Hitler poetically as 'this genius grazing the stars', ventured: 'The Third Reich was founded more on his personal charisma than upon the appeal of an idea. The identification of Hitler with the State was complete. The State was so indissolubly bound up with him that, when he died, so did the State.'

Another of his poetic dedications to the Führer had proclaimed: 'I was but a leaf in limitless space, Now you are my home and my tree'; but now Schirach admitted: 'Hitler was obsessed with fantasies and new scientific discoveries — as long as they suited his own ideas.'

Funk, the servile nonentity who had played such a key role in interesting business leaders in Nazism in the early 1930s, by temptingly promising the destruction of organized labour, also said:

'Hitler was an inveterate actor who was always conscious of being "on stage", and behaved accordingly. Look how fond he was of drifting into endless monologues. Fortunately, he occasionally fell asleep smack in the middle of some of his own tedious outpourings, whilst everyone present gossiped on in whispers, hoping he would wake up in time for dinner.

'At the beginning of a conversation he appeared not to listen, let alone understand, and could stay silent for ages, as if in some weird trance. Suddenly he'd explode into a shrill harangue with his raucous one-sided arguments getting faster and louder until he was thundering away at us as if he were addressing an audience of thousands. The unstoppable torrent of words could last from ten minutes to an hour, and then peter out — as though his batteries had run dry. Only when he'd spent himself was there a chance for anyone to risk making a counterpoint, and then he could become surprisingly hesitant and ask for time to think things over.

'He was a rotten businessman, totally ignorant of commerce and economics. When we mobilized our economy for war, he nearly strangled business with forms. Official communications made up more than half of a German manufacturer's entire correspondence. Even before that period it was bad enough. Our export trade involved 40,000 separate daily transactions, yet for a solitary transaction as many as forty different forms had to be completed. We disillusioned business-and money-men who had welcomed our regime by burying them under mountains of red tape.'

Uncharacteristically, the usually mild-mannered Neurath said scathingly: 'He was a dangerous, obstinate amateur. Like so many self-taught individuals, he hadn't the slightest inkling of the importance of properly utilizing specialist knowledge, yet chose to bear a massive volume of crucial decision-making. To make matters worse, he disliked changing a view once he had expressed it — even if it was obviously wrong. He was dangerously innocent regarding so many things. He had naïve ideas about the English mentality. I had to point out repeatedly that the methods he had adopted during his rise to power were unsuited to win English sympathies.

'He really knew so little about his enemies and, still worse, didn't really want to be told. He preferred his own uninformed ideas and so-called inspirations, which utterly underestimated others. England he labelled "Our enemy Number One", yet he hoped to reach some convenient arrangement with England to enable him to conquer countries with impunity. Early in the war he was absolutely positive that the West was too feeble and decadent to wage effective war, and later he longed for a break in the alliance between the Western Powers and Russia. At the start of our invasion of Russia he calculated on them collapsing within a few weeks. For years he and Stalin reviled each other as arch enemies, yet he never recognized how closely his policies paralleled Stalin's policies.'

In *Mein Kampf*, Hitler wrote:

> It must never be forgotten that the present rulers of Russia are blood-stained criminals, that here we have the dregs of humanity which overran a great State, degraded and extirpated millions of educated people out of sheer blood-lust, and that for years they have ruled with such a savage tyranny as was never known before. It must not be forgotten that these rulers belong to a people in whom the most bestial cruelty is allied with a capacity for artful mendacity and which believes itself today more than ever called to impose its sanguinary despotism on the rest of the world. One does not form an alliance with a partner whose only aim is the destruction of his fellow-partner. Above all, one does not enter into alliances with people for whom no treaty is sacred ... the

representatives of lies, deception, thievery, plunder and robbery.

That *Mein Kampf* attack on despotic Russian tyranny became a prophetically tailor-made description for the Third Reich Hitler fashioned.

'Hitler totally lost touch with public opinion,' Neurath asserted.

Defensively, Speer said: 'In the years before the war he was a restless human dynamo, but from around 1942 he began ageing terrifyingly fast. He started to appear senile at fifty-five.'

Neurath insisted: 'He progressively devoted less and less time to public affairs and left others to carry on however they liked in the spheres that they had grabbed for themselves. He was more occupied with you, Herr Speer, and your grandiose projects — particularly the beautification of Berlin.'

'That's true,' conceded Speer, 'but he loved to design or amend my drawings, even retouch my scale models. He wanted Berlin rebuilt as a tribute to his glory. He always maintained that he became a politician against his will, and that basically he was an architect.'

Neurath admitted that throughout his years as a Minister he seldom met Hitler, except at official functions, and avoided building a close personal relationship with him. He never became one of the cronies who joined in the Führer's intimate late-night sessions, and was similarly ill at ease with other members of the Nazi hierarchy. Hitler considered Neurath valuable, but unimaginative.

'He was undoubtedly a human powerhouse during one period of his career,' Neurath agreed, 'but he was essentially lazy, and intractable even when too lazy to deal with matters efficiently himself. He was incapable of fully analysing problems or applying himself to regular duties. In this respect he was completely the opposite to Mussolini, who thoroughly enjoyed his job, and especially studying and annotating reports.'

Funk focused on another aspect of Hitler's personality: 'One of his favourite pastimes was laughing at the expense of others — which is why he liked so many of my jokes — but in fact he was humourless.'

That brilliant word-spinner, Goebbels, also knew how to keep him entertained with anecdotes, usually scandalous. Apart from wanting to amuse Hitler, Funk often used his story-telling to inform the Führer of events that would sooner or later reach his ears. Experience showed that whoever implanted with Hitler a specific version of an affair achieved the best impact. In consequence, jokes were often deliberately linked to real occurrences so that he was kept well informed under the guise of foolery, and rarely realized the extent to which his opinions were manipulated in this manner. Göring, Goebbels, Bormann and Funk were particularly skilled in the technique of cunningly influencing the Führer.

Funk explained: 'If, for example, anyone was praised too excessively within his hearing it often had the effect of causing their demotion in Hitler's eternally suspicious eyes, which were forever looking over his shoulder for the over-ambitious.'

'I had to keep that particular trait of his in mind when he asked for my opinion on leadership qualities,' Speer said. 'The indications were that he was about to name his successor, so I tactfully spoke well of people, but avoided overpraising.'

Dönitz repeatedly derided Speer in Spandau for the Berlin bunker discussion with Hitler regarding who might be best suited to undertake the Reich presidency after his death. 'You got me into all my trouble,' he complained to Speer. 'You were the one who finally convinced the Führer that I was the one to follow him.'

According to Funk, there were three Hitlers: 'The first was a pallid man with a jumbled complexion and vague ice-blue eyes that were constantly lost in dreams. This gave him an absent air — the disturbed face of a medium, or sleepwalker. He was, in fact, an *Abendmensch* [a night man who comes alive only from dusk]. He used to say: "I always get my most creative ideas late at night", which is undoubtedly why he hated working in the mornings and preferred a very late breakfast.

'The second Hitler was animated, fired by almost uncontrollable passions, who often displayed psychosomatic and hysterical symptoms. His nostrils would twitch, his eyes ceaselessly dart about. He overflowed with violence, lusting for domination or the destruction of opponents, driven by cynical boldness and a fierce energy. Prepared, even without provocation, to pull the whole world down around him. The face of this Hitler was that of a morbid, unbalanced, "possessed" character who alternated between states of intense excitement and deep depression.

'The third Hitler was almost a country bumpkin: dull, vulgar, easily amused, laughing uproariously as he slapped his thigh. This Hitler's face was undistinguished, uncultured, but with the ill-digested culture of the self-taught; this Führer let his imagination feed on every kind of element. Here was the notorious hypochondriac, ever concerned about his pulse rate, his potency, and getting fat, who used to say: "Imagine me with a pot-belly. It would mean political ruin." It was also the Führer who maintained: "A highly intelligent man should take a primitive stupid woman. Imagine if, on top of everything else, I had a woman who interfered with my work!"

'Whilst on the subject of his sex life,' Funk added, 'I don't think I ever saw him completely relaxed and human — not even with Eva Braun. He seldom revealed inner feelings. Whenever anyone tried to get too close, he erected a barrier. Even with his Eva he always retained a gulf between the Führer and the simple girl.'

Hess made a rare interruption: 'There was only a certain point of familiarity you could reach with him — even for me. Beyond that point you could not go.'

Hitler and Hess shared a characteristic: whenever things went badly they conveniently escaped into another mental world. Ascetic-looking Hess deliberately accentuated the creation of an eccentric appearance, relishing the role of a martyr. Hitler did the same.

'There was something missing in Hitler,' said Speer. 'You felt that at the core of this being there was just a deadness. He needed people's applause like a drug. I'm sure he was religious, yet I never saw him pray. But he never disclaimed his Roman Catholicism, called on God in practically every speech, avoided blasphemy, and sometimes claimed Jesus Christ for the Aryan race.'

Schirach's poetically inspired sense of the dramatic prompted him to introduce a musical theme into the assessments: 'Hitler "lived" Wagner's work, believing himself to be a Wagnerian hero. He was Lohengrin, Siegfried, and especially Parsifal, who cured the bleeding wound on the side of Amfortas and restored its magic to the Holy Grail.'

'He was a cold-blooded realist who was answerable for all the evil committed because he was aware of every move his collaborators made,' according to Neurath. 'And also a chronic liar and hypocrite who while signing treaties was already thinking of how to wriggle out of them. I remember sizing him up, when we first met in 1932, as a medium-height, ill-dressed, rather common-looking man who seemed also to be shy. The only remarkable things about him were his eyes, burning with unquenchable fire, and the voice, which had an extraordinary persuasive quality.'

That early radical Hitler fast became middle class and lulled into security, but his authority remained intact because he sustained the Third Reich like the ash or fir tree of German mythology that holds up the world. If he fell, the world he had built would also fall, and those who served him realized this.

Neurath continued: 'I warned him that anti-Semitism was irresponsible and ill advised, but he was intransigent. It was useless to discuss the Jewish issue with him, for he had a passion here upon which no reason could prevail. He raged against America, Britain, and the Jews, who he said were to blame for the air raids.'

The spirit of Hitler in Spandau gaol must have smiled at these reminiscences, recalling Neurath's docile compliance with racial terror. For whilst deploring the effects of the violent persecution of Jews on foreign policy, Neurath nevertheless publicly welcomed regulations to 'clean up' German public morals and claimed in a speech that the anti-Semitic decrees were an 'absolute necessity, cleansing our public life'. In April 1933, even as he appealed to President Hindenburg to help restrain Party excesses against individual Jews, he joined in the sponsorship of a series of decrees limiting the number of Jews in the universities and professions. He meekly swallowed Hitler's race hatred as a fact of life he could not resist.

'Nobody demonstrated the stupidity of the "pure race" theory of dominant Nordic characteristics more than Hitler and Goebbels, who weren't in the least Nordic,' protested

Funk. 'We Germans are largely a mixture of aborigines and foreigners — mainly from Swedish, Baltic, and Slavic regions.'

Hess hated Jews. With Hitler, Gürtner, Minister of Justice, and Frick, Minister of the Interior, he had signed the Nuremberg Laws of September 1935, which led to the appalling persecutions and atrocities. He now suggested: 'As regards the "Jewish problem", I think Jews were well advised to enter "protective camps". It was up to them to make their lives as nice as possible to their own taste, within the camps.'

Then, blinding himself to realities as always, he stubbornly declared: 'I still deny absolutely the truth of reports on Gestapo methods, which were spread as propaganda and invented by other powers.'

He conveniently forgot that he had not been as certain that the concentration camp stories were fabrications when he was a prisoner in Britain. In statements written during this period in his own neat, slanting handwriting, partly in English, partly in German, he promised: 'When I return to Germany I shall cause an investigation to be made about the facts that are related.'

Reports of the Gestapo torture camps plainly disturbed Hess; in a note he wrote in 1945, he asked to be permitted to view captured film records of the camps. The request read:

> I gather from the Press that films are available of concentration camps in Germany, now occupied by British and American troops, in which atrocities took place. I should greatly value a chance of seeing these films.

Was this innocence, or merely curiosity about the captured film evidence?

On the same theme Raeder commented: 'When there were reports, or even rumours, of ruthless measures on the part of the National Socialist Party or the Gestapo, Hitler's behaviour and observations always deliberately gave the impression that such things had not been ordered by him, but by someone else.'

'For anyone to make such a claim would indicate utter ignorance of the nature of the Führer's Germany,' Speer interrupted. 'We all knew that nothing of any consequence happened without his knowledge.'

Raeder was unable to resist the over-used stock war criminal's defence: 'It was only towards the end, and in particular during the Nuremberg trials, that I first heard of the atrocities committed in the concentration camps.

'Hitler was so obsessed with the need for secrecy, often insisting on it to an extent bordering on absurdity. He called it the "patriotic duty of silence". That's why he had placards on the walls of Gestapo offices warning: "You must know nothing except what concerns your service. Whatever you learn you must keep to yourself." Those secrecy measures enabled him to veil secretly perpetrated brutalities. Atrocities could be committed with the confidence that nobody dared expose them.'

In 1939, just prior to the outbreak of the war, Hitler had signed a directive that decreed:

> No one must have any knowledge of secret affairs that are outside his own province.
>
> No one is to be given more information than is strictly necessary for carrying out his task.
>
> No one must be informed of the obligations incumbent upon him earlier than is necessary.
>
> No one is to pass on to subordinate services more than is necessary of the orders essential to carrying out a task and before it becomes necessary.

One Gestapo officer was shot for telling a brother officer in another Gestapo department about the work on which he was engaged.

When war came, Raeder and the Commander-in-Chief of Army were both raised to the rank of Cabinet Minister, but neither ever attended a Cabinet meeting. Hitler loved upstaging aristocratic professional fighting men or ordering them about like lowly NCOs. The mistrustful Führer revelled in sabotaging prestige or destroying the reputations of even close associates.

Dönitz recalled: He never lost an ingrained distrust of officers. His ex-corporal's inferiority complex had remained within him since World War I. He was never truly at ease with generals and admirals and referred to the old breed as *Die Oberschicht* ("the upper crust"). He was particularly nervous about the army. I remember him saying: "My army is reactionary, my navy Christian, and my air force National Socialist." He was more confident about the Luftwaffe because it had been fashioned by Göring, substantially using new cadres recruited from the Party's ranks. But he knew that the army was still deeply monarchist and that even the Kaiser's birthday was still celebrated by many old soldiers.

Hitler was convinced that his military judgements and iron nerves were superior to those of his generals and admirals. He boasted: "All I know is that unprecedented strong nerves and unprecedented resolution are necessary if a leader is to survive in times such as these and make decisions that concern our very existence. Any other man in my place would have been unable to do what I have done; his nerves wouldn't have been strong enough."

'He was fascinated by maps, knew how to read them, and often stood for hours studying large-scale situation maps. He was so confident of his war strategy abilities that he made decisions completely without regard to technical foundations. Absorbing only what suited him from analysis information with which he was supplied, he largely ignored it because the grand design was supposed to be borne solely within his head. As a result, decisions were often made in a vacuum.

'Nevertheless, the great successes achieved by Hitler, and a feeling of happiness such as the country had never before experienced, seemed justification enough to accept what he did. But when, in spite of all the idealism, the honest endeavour, and boundless sacrifices made by the great mass of the German people, the ultimate result was irreparable misfortune, then *Führerprinzip* [the principle of dictatorship] as a political principle must be false. False because human nature evidently is incapable of making good use of the power that the principle confers, without succumbing to temptations of the abuse of power, which is inherent in it.'

Dönitz, who often compared Hitler with Napoleon, could not resist injecting some measure of acclaim for Hitler's Germany; but possibly this apparent loyalty to past authority was bound up with the fact that via this authority the mantle of succession to the presidency of the Reich had been bestowed upon him. Hitler would not have been as generous in praising the contribution of his generals and admirals to Third Reich achievements. Until his dying day he remained contemptuous of the Prussian officer class, who accepted with barely a murmur all his officially condoned mass murders.

Confirming the Führer's detestation of 'top brass', Raeder said: 'He was constantly berating and insulting General Staff officers. "You always want to retreat and surrender ground without reason!" he would shout. "You deliberately lie to me about situations in order to force me into authorizing retreats!" He was ignorant of the complicated factors that had to be taken into account when making advances, and refused to admit his failures.

'I never knew him personally nor had anything to do with him until 2 February 1933, when I met him at the house of General von Hammerstein, who was then Commander-in-Chief of the Army.'

Raeder said to Neurath: 'You were Foreign Minister then and arrived with Hitler at von Hammerstein's house.' They both recalled how Hitler cunningly kept associates to their own spheres, confining his observations to specific points at issue. In this manner he avoided the risk of coming up against a united front.

'He systematically isolated people within their own field of operations, and was a master of bluff,' Raeder went on. 'He was by nature a suspicious man and sensed immediately when anyone approached him with concealed doubts. On the other hand, he didn't always appreciate brutal frankness. There was a certain danger in being too often in his company. He had a way of influencing even sceptics, but the tremendous facility with which he expressed himself became less impressive in time, particularly if you were often with him, although you could never be quite sure that you really knew what he was aiming at. I gradually came to the conclusion that he always leaned towards extreme solutions, but as far as possible deliberately concealed this tendency.

'It was impossible for me to persuade him to do anything against Göring's wishes, for Göring had succeeded in dazzling him with an attractive picture of the power and greatness of the Luftwaffe as an independent weapon. What made the situation more difficult was that Hitler had a tendency to play off one disputing party against the other in the belief that in this way more could be obtained than by smooth co-operation.

He did this in connection with the struggle of the three arms of the services for labour power and raw materials.'

Funk offered another revealing insight: 'Hitler was obsessed by a vision he'd had that his career was destined to be brief — ten years at the most — which is why he was so impatient for lightning success, at any price.'

'He was after world domination, not only mastery of Europe,' said Speer. 'Domination of Europe was only a step on the way to his final goal. After the fall of France, he was confident that a campaign against Russia would be child's play. He was convinced that he was Providence's favourite.'

Dönitz had conferred with Hitler frequently during the war's final stage, and thought he looked anything but Providence's special son. He recalled: 'Every time we met, he seemed to have fallen more and more apart. His head seemed to be withdrawn into his shoulders, and he was like a man with the world on his back. He continually complained of a loss of his sense of balance, and his fast-failing eyesight flinched from sunlight. Week by week, he aged incredibly and shook like an old man with palsy. Almost overnight he seemed empty; more shadow than substance.'

'He didn't realize the war was lost. Wouldn't face the fact. Wouldn't admit it,' said Speer, who also visited Hitler several times in the Berlin bunker. 'When in 1945 I sent him a written report that we were down to only two weeks' supply of coal, and that through the loss of Silesia I could supply only a quarter of the coal and one-sixth of the steel we had been producing in the previous year, he refused to see me alone because, he said, I always had something unpleasant to say to him. He didn't want to hear me repeat to him the first sentence I had written in my report. It was: "The war is lost."

'Finally,' continued Speer, 'he said to me: "If the war is lost, the nation will also perish. This fate is inevitable. There is no necessity to take into consideration the basis that the people will need to continue a most primitive existence. On the contrary, it will be better to destroy these things ourselves because this nation will have proved to be the weaker one and the future will belong to the stronger eastern nation [Russia]. Besides, those who will remain after the battle are only the inferior ones, for the good ones have been killed."'

Schirach, though still retaining a literary touch, revised his thinking about the Führer: 'Like the picture of Dorian Gray, Hitler's image changed terribly. The later Hitler would not have recognized himself in the portrait of the early Hitler, had the picture not changed with him. Like Dorian Gray, Hitler hated this picture. That is why he was determined to destroy himself and to drive his country and every man, woman and child to destruction. Had he, in the final moments of his life, had the power to extinguish all living things at the same time, I believe he would have done it, if only to destroy the dreadful picture that he presented to mankind.

'Look how fanatical he was about orders and orderliness. There had to be order for everything. He demanded, and expected, absolute obedience to orders. His vanity allowed no room for opposition; and whenever someone unexpectedly entered his room, that same vanity made him speedily remove the spectacles he used for reading. He didn't like to be seen wearing them. When my wife and I once caught him with them on, he remarked embarrassedly: "You see, I need glasses, I am getting old, which is why I prefer to wage a war at fifty rather than at sixty."

'I should have taken more notice of the shrewd assessment made by my American cousin Helen. When she visited us from

Philadelphia, she warned: "I think you're completely mad. As a greeting you use the name of a man who has bats in the belfry and turns great men out of the country because they belong to another race. You want to frighten the world." She was right. The truth is that we saw in Hitler only what we let ourselves see.'

Neurath concluded: 'We who over-praised him have a lot to answer for. If we hadn't, he wouldn't have come to believe he was a genius in all things. To think that people used to say that the more people die for Hitler the more immortal he will be!'

Hess, however, who seldom commented at all when his Führer was debated, rounded off discussion of the eighth inmate of Spandau gaol with unstinted adulation. 'The figure of Adolf Hitler will stand like a beacon over the centuries,' he insisted.

18: THE QUALITY OF MERCY

'I won't forget Spandau,' Dr Konrad Adenauer, West Germany's Chancellor, assured Baron von Neurath's daughter, Winifred, before leaving for Washington to visit President Eisenhower. Nor did he. Although Adenauer's greatest service to his country lay in the fact that he and his associates restored the moral worth of Germany in the eyes of the free world, he still spoke up for the Spandau seven. They were one item debated at the President and Chancellor's White House meeting that did not appear on the official agenda; but they were discussed.

Adenauer remembered again when, less than a year later, at a Berlin meeting of the four-Powers' Foreign Ministers in January 1954, he repeated his request for a complete reconsideration of the custody of the seven prisoners. He got as far as receiving private indications from the United States, Britain, and France of willingness to reconsider the cases, but there were still influential opponents saying: 'Should anyone undo or reverse the sentences of the Nuremberg International Court, a court that shouldered full world responsibility for meting out justice to criminals of the Hitler war?'

Condemning Adenauer's request, the Soviets notified him that they would never agree to grant clemency to the seven, but a few months later did agree to a further easing of conditions within the gaol. Changes in regulations included consent for a prisoner's removal to a hospital near the prison under the jurisdiction of one of the four-Powers, if he required complicated treatment or major surgery; and that, on the death of a prisoner, the body would be buried inside the gaol with religious rites and in the presence of the prisoner's closest relatives, and these relatives would subsequently be allowed opportunities to visit the grave. Western proposals had also covered other modifications of the gaol's regime in matters such as visits by persons other than relatives, letters, and the right of inmates to talk to each other, all of which were accepted by the Soviet representative without objection.

The sole point on which there was difference of opinion was the question of burial. The Soviet Union vetoed the suggestion of a quiet burial outside the gaol, on the grounds that it might lead to disturbances. Such a successful outcome of four-Power talks was almost unprecedented in Allied dealings with the Russians in Germany. The Soviet representative, with an unfamiliarly business-like approach to the whole question, showed a desire to co-operate.

Chancellor Adenauer said that, whilst not condoning the Nazis in Spandau, public opinion in the country was increasingly concerned with the fate of the seven. Right-wing newspapers and right-wing political parties were already pushing for an amnesty for all war criminals.

Protests about the punishment of war criminals — especially the Spandau seven — were high on the list of resolutions of German veteran associations and favourite subjects of editorials in West German newspapers. To a very high proportion of Germans, there were no war criminals because people refused to acknowledge the legality of Allied courts. The press habitually referred to 'so-called war criminals'.

The 'Free the Spandau Seven' campaign was unequalled. No possible pressure angle was ignored by families, friends, and underground Nazi sympathizers. One cannot blame wives and children for trying to get their menfolk out of gaol, whatever the crimes, but the motives of many others fighting to free the seven were often less laudable.

The Three Allied Commissioners in Western Germany were frequently petitioned and none more so than François-Poncet, the French representative, one-time Ambassador in Berlin and long-standing friend of Neurath's daughter and Raeder's wife. Winifred von Mackensen had also been friendly with the late Sir Nevile Henderson, Britain's Ambassador to Germany when war was declared, so she approached British High Commissioner Sir Ivone Kirkpatrick, a former colleague of Henderson. Their brief discussion of Spandau was conducted with strict formality.

'Couldn't you try to speak in England or do something for my father?' Frau von Mackensen asked. Kirkpatrick told her that nothing could be done; but the Neurath family never stopped trying. The Baroness recruited the assistance of Countess Attolico, whose husband had been Italian Ambassador to both Berlin and Moscow. His wife wrote to Molotov about the Baron, using the diplomatic bag to ensure the letter reaching the Kremlin. She thought she might get somewhere because she had been extremely popular in Moscow, but she was not popular enough to persuade the Russians to forget Nuremberg.

The Baroness then asked her close friend the Countess of Stauffenberg to try and help. The Countess, mother of Colonel Stauffenberg, leader of the bomb plot attempt on Hitler's life, had also been a friend of Britain's Queen Mary during the Württemberg days. The Countess was so anxious that her letter to the Queen should not go astray that she arranged for it to be carried by hand to Switzerland, where it was passed to another courier who took it personally to London and Queen Mary at Marlborough House. The Kings of Sweden and Denmark, both of whom the Neuraths knew well, were also asked to intervene in any way they could for the Baron.

When President Truman was in office, Princess Ysenburg of Bavaria, in close touch with Washington circles, delivered a letter from the Neuraths to the President. Then, when Eisenhower was voted into the White House, he was asked to contact Malenkov with a view to securing the release of Neurath, Raeder and Dönitz as it was thought that the Soviet Union, having granted an amnesty to war prisoners, might now be more amenable. No avenue was overlooked by relatives and friends of the seven to get them out before their legal time.

'Forgive and forget' campaigners received their greatest supportive boost in January 1951 from Britain's Sir Ivone Kirkpatrick and subsequently, to a lesser degree, from John McCloy, the US High Commissioner. Overnight, London and Washington were startled by a sudden realization of the extent of power that had been handed to these two men — enough power to override the carefully balanced judgements of Nuremberg.

The awakening started at a luncheon at the British Press Club in Berlin, during which Kirkpatrick, who was guest of honour, agreed to answer off-the-cuff questions from British, American, French, Swiss, German and Soviet correspondents. An American correspondent asked him whether he was aware of the enormous pressure being exercised for a revision of the sentences passed on former Admirals Raeder and Dönitz. Dealing first with the general question of war criminals, the High Commissioner replied that he thought everyone in the room would agree that there was a need for peace in the world and that we should all strive for peace. He then exploded the first bombshell by saying:

'If we are agreed on striving for peace, then we should agree that *hatred and revenge are bad counsellors.*' (My italics.)

He explained that he was engaged in a review of the sentences of war criminals confined at Werl Prison under his jurisdiction. There were some 240 of these prisoners and he hoped to complete his review of their cases within a few months. He knew that John McCloy was engaged in a similar review of the sentences of those confined at Landsberg Prison in the US zone. He further confirmed that he and his colleagues had received an appeal from the Senate of Kiel University on behalf of Grand Admiral Raeder, who was an honorary doctor of the university. Exploding his second bombshell, Kirkpatrick said:

'I personally would be prepared to review also the sentences against the prisoners confined in Spandau in a manner similar to the review now being made in Western zones. This was a matter which required four-Power decision, and I propose to discuss with my colleagues the specific appeal which we have received for Raeder.'

'Would you be prepared to review the case of Hess, whom you know so well?' another correspondent asked. (Mention of his familiarity with Hess was a reference to Kirkpatrick's having been one of the team of Hess's interrogators in England.)

That question launched the High Commissioner's final bombshell: 'There is no one whose case I personally would not be prepared to review.' He concluded by revealing that the appeal made on behalf of Raeder was already under consideration by the Law Committee of the Allied High Commission.

When Kirkpatrick's answers made international headlines, for the first time the full extent of the campaigns for a more merciful treatment of the imprisoned Nazis was revealed. Questions were raised in the Senate and House of Representatives in Washington, in the House of Commons and House of Lords in London, and in the French Assembly in Paris. Thousands of protests poured in to all three Governments — from ordinary individuals, trade unions, and other organizations. Characteristic of the attacks were two received at the Foreign Office in London. One, addressed to Foreign Secretary Ernest Bevin, came from the Honourable Ewan S. Montagu, CBE, KC, President of the Anglo-Jewish Association. During World War II, Ewan Montagu was one of the key intelligence specialists responsible for devising the legendary ruse that later became known as 'The Man Who Never Was'. (This ploy, which successfully fooled Germany, was based on laying a false invasion trail with the aid of a dead body carrying misleading documents. The corpse was deliberately washed ashore for discovery by German spies in the Mediterranean.)

On 2 February 1951 Montagu wrote to Ernest Bevin:

> The indictment of the major war criminals was intended to establish a new principle of international law — namely that crimes against humanity were not to be left unpunished because they had been committed by the heads and leaders of a State. The Nuremberg and other trials were intended also to indicate the principle that large-scale murder is still murder.
>
> The Council of the Association fully appreciated that mitigating circumstances may induce the exercise of the prerogative of mercy in individual cases, but it is seriously concerned that suggestions can be made that 'changed circumstances' or political considerations may have made less reprehensible the murder of hundreds of thousands of innocent people and other scarcely less odious crimes. To countenance any such view must seriously undermine the rule

of law and encourage those elements in Germany which have consistently refused to acknowledge the criminality of the Nazi regime.

Montagu's reference to 'changed circumstances' and political considerations being underlying factors behind the softening of attitudes towards war criminals was due to awareness of the increasing demand in Germany for at least a review of the sentences passed on all war criminals, with possibly complete amnesty. There was extensive resentment within that country that war crime trials had ever been held; and it was constantly intimated that, as a condition of Germany's entry into Western Defence, some gesture of recognition and reconciliation should be made by the High Commissioners in favour of an immediate review or even release of war criminals. In plain language, it was political blackmail, and it nearly succeeded. It might well have done if Kirkpatrick had not let the cat out too soon — before he had put into effect decisions that were, at the time,, his prerogative to take without consulting Whitehall.

More ominous than public outrage over indications of interference with the verdicts of the war crimes courts was the private reaction of judges and prosecutors who had been involved with the trials. They were deeply incensed that judicially balanced decisions, reached after full due process of law, could be overturned at the whim of Government servants in possession of too much influence. Three Nuremberg Tribunal judges privately voiced their anger. From his Washington home Judge Francis Biddle wrote to Nuremberg prosecutor Sir Hartley Shawcross asking that he challenge the policy in his capacity as Britain's Attorney General. The President of the Nuremberg Tribunal, Judge Sir Geoffrey Lawrence, and Judge Sir Norman Birkett, also immediately contacted Shawcross. As a result, on 26 January 1951,

Shawcross sent the following written advice to Prime Minister Clement Attlee:

> I see that the Foreign Secretary is to be asked a question in the House of Commons in regard to statements which Sir Ivone Kirkpatrick is alleged to have made in Germany to the effect that he was engaged in a review of the sentences imposed on the surviving chief German war criminals, including those sentenced by the Nuremberg Tribunal and 'there was not now one war criminal in custody whose sentence he personally would not be prepared to review'. He is alleged to have added 'hatred and revenge are bad counsellors. On political and humane grounds it is incumbent that we should review their cases.'
>
> I think I should tell you that this alleged statement has caused many of us considerable concern. So far as concerns the Nuremberg Tribunal, I do not understand that the Judges have been consulted and I have no reason to think that the English Judges would approve of any review of the sentences imposed at the present time. I have received a letter from Francis Biddle, who was the American Judge, expressing the view that before any decision of the kind indicated by Kirkpatrick is taken, he thinks the Judges should be consulted and, as I understand, it is certainly the practice in this country to consult the Trial Judge when any question arises of remitting part of a determinate sentence.
>
> Expressing my own view, which I think would be shared by all the Judges and with which Maxwell Fyfe is in agreement, I would have felt that this was certainly not the moment at which to interfere with the Nuremberg sentences. The facts that our relationship with the Russians have gravely deteriorated and that they and others appear to be ready to commit crimes similar to those for which the Nuremberg Defendants were sentenced, seem to me, on the contrary, to be reasons why we should emphasize the validity and continued effectiveness of the rule of international law as laid

down at Nuremberg and make it abundantly clear to those who disregard the Nuremberg warning that similar breaches of the law will not be treated leniently. Moreover, Kirkpatrick's reference to hatred and revenge seems to me to be a most unfortunate reflection on the establishment and conduct of the Nuremberg Tribunal and on the other Courts which dealt with war criminals. The original sentences were not imposed on the grounds of bitterness or revenge and, with the exception of Hess who was convicted only of conspiracy to prepare, initiate, and wage aggressive war and of war crimes against peace, all the surviving Defendants were convicted of war crimes and some of them of crimes against humanity, in other words, of murder on a large scale.

So far as concerns prisoners who were convicted at subsequent trials, the case in which I am most interested is that of Von Manstein. Rumours appeared in the newspapers in November that the possibility of his release was being considered and I wrote to the Foreign Secretary on the 22nd November in regard to the matter. He replied to me on the 5th December that he was assured by the High Commissioner that he had no intention of considering Von Manstein's release. I have, however, reason to believe that in fact consideration is now being given to the possibility of making some remission in Von Manstein's sentence and Kirkpatrick's alleged statement that there is no war criminal whose sentence he would not be prepared to review is indeed a public confirmation of the information which I have. As you will remember, all sorts of obstacles were put in the way of Von Manstein's trial in the first instance. It was only in 1949 that the trial took place, and after what everyone agrees was a most careful and fair investigation, he was sentenced.

I do not know whether his health has deteriorated since then but ill health, even if it exists, is not necessarily a ground for releasing a man from prison. Many criminals have died in prison before.

So far as concerns the Nuremberg criminals, they cannot, of course, be released without Russian consent. The Russians had a legitimate interest in the case of some of the other war criminals who were alleged to have committed crimes in the Eastern territories. It seems to me that this is a most unfortunate moment at which to state publicly that it is contemplated that the sentences imposed on these Nazis, so justly hated by Communist and non-Communist alike in Eastern Europe, are to be reconsidered. It provides the Russians with effective propaganda to use against us and I believe it shocks considerable feeling in this country.

I am sorry to trouble you about the matter but I write to you owing to the Foreign Secretary's illness.

Hartley Shawcross

The following week, on 31 January 1951, a very worried Shawcross wrote yet again to the Prime Minister:

I hope you will not think that I am taking a legalistic view about this matter. As one of the chief actors in it, I am, of course, concerned that the proceedings of the Nuremberg Tribunal should not be compromised in any way, or, as Birkett [Sir Norman Birkett, the second British judge on the Nuremberg Tribunal] has put it to me, that currency should be given to the idea that the sentences were too severe thus indicating that an element of revenge entered into them. My real concern is, however, rather a political one. Whilst I do not question the policy of German re-armament, the Communists and other opponents of it have, of course, been making great play with the use of the phrase, re-armament of the Nazis. If at the very time that German re-armament is under consideration, steps are taken to review and remit sentences which were passed on military leaders who were notorious Nazis and whose crimes merit little sympathy, a more sinister complexion can be put by our critics on the proposals for German re-armament. From what I know of the feeling in this country and in France, I feel that the proposed review of the war criminals' sentences at this moment will cause widespread misunderstanding and that it will provide most useful propaganda for the Cominform.

The Governments of Britain, the United States and France were almost overwhelmed by the appalling effect that apparent solicitude for top-ranking Nazis had upon the general public, and especially on those who had suffered so much from the actions of these men. A member of the French Assembly said:

> If we extend more leniency to those devils it would be equivalent to condoning and excusing their infamy. They should be removed to the criminal settlements of Devil's Island. The law of forgiveness doesn't apply to war criminals, and the law of resentment is both ethical and just.

Closing ranks around Kirkpatrick and rallying to his defence, some Foreign Office departmental heads submitted a report to the Cabinet that largely sought to justify his stance. Dated 1 February 1951, the report stated:

> Whilst we must not allow ourselves to be deflected from doing what is just and right, it is, nevertheless, a fact that we have a strong interest in mitigating public resentment in Germany. It is now our declared object, and that of US and French Governments, to bring the Federal Republic into full political and economic co-operation with the West, and discussions are already in progress with the view of enabling Germany to contribute to Western defence. When a factor of serious importance emerges which hinders the implementation of this new policy towards Germany, it is incumbent on the High Commission and His Majesty's Government to take this factor into consideration and to give it due political weight. The German attitude to war crimes has

been recognized as such a factor and an important one by both the UK and US High Commissioners in Germany. It is therefore desirable that nothing should be left undone which places the question of war crimes in its true light in Germany and ensures that no reasonable cause for complaint can remain.

The British Government was compelled to reassure Members of Parliament and the House of Lords that there was no intention of altering the sentences of the major war criminals held in Spandau. The outcry stifled the moves to free the seven at such an early stage of their imprisonment. Although there was no suggestion that either Kirkpatrick or US High Commissioner McCloy intended to cast any reflection on the courts that had passed the original verdicts and they genuinely felt their reviews would be dispassionate, their actions were nevertheless undoubtedly inspired by considerations of what they thought would be good for Germany. Insufficient account appeared to have been taken by them of how such actions would be interpreted internationally. Great pains were taken afterwards to make it clear publicly that a review of sentences did not necessarily mean alteration of sentences, and that it was right for sentences to be reviewed from time to time, as was customary in civilized states. It was emphasized that review did not mean automatic reduction, and that the issue was unconnected with German rearmament. The latter contention was, in fact, at variance with internal secret records at the Foreign Office in London, and at the State Department in Washington. These verify how much concern for improving relations with the new Federal German Government influenced reviews.

Two brief letters were sent to the Foreign Office during February 1951 from the Attorney General's chambers at the

Royal Courts of Justice in London. They initiated a complete change of British, American, and French policy towards the war crime sentences. The first letter, from Sir Hartley Shawcross, was dated 2 February:

> If proceedings of contempt of court were available in respect of the Nuremberg Tribunal, I would have thought that the reference to hatred and revenge in direct association with the Nuremberg Court would have been a ground on which I might have felt obliged to take action. Certainly the two British Judges take a very poor view of the matter and the observation is, in addition, a direct reflection on Lord Simon, who was a party to the original arrangements to establish the Court, on Maxwell Fyfe, who took a lead part both in the establishment of the Court and in the conduct of the case, and on myself, who was the chief prosecutor for the United Kingdom.
>
> It is to be observed that notwithstanding the remarkable clemency shown by the Americans towards a number of war criminals, they have decided to execute Dr Ohlendorf, Blobel, and one or two others who commanded and formed part of Einsatz Gruppe D., the SS Task Force that operated under the command of Von Manstein and in respect of whose genocide activities Von Manstein himself was found guilty on the grave count of knowingly allowing them to take place.[13]
>
> Newspaper reports say that Von Manstein is the first name for consideration on Sir Ivone Kirkpatrick's list of those

---

[13] *Einsatzgruppen* (Extermination Squads), led by the SS Elite Guard, were typical of the most inhuman and degrading aspect of the whole Nazi spectacle. They were one of the main instruments of the extermination policy, and the Nuremberg Tribunal found that the squads were responsible for the murder of 2,000,000 people. The political and racial character of most of their victims, who included women and children, belied any pretence that the wholesale executions were military and bore any relation to military security, as was claimed in many cases.

whose sentences he would now be willing to consider 'in view of the changed circumstances' although what real change has taken place since the sentence on Von Manstein was imposed I am not sure.

Shawcross's follow-up letter, dated 8 February, warned:

> I am exceedingly doubtful whether it is constitutionally desirable to delegate to an official power of exercising clemency towards criminals sentenced by the King's Courts. It really has grave political implications for which Ministers should be responsible. I do not know whether the nature of the delegation is such that the High Commissioner is invested with complete discretion for which the Foreign Secretary would not feel obliged to answer in the House.

Repercussions continued, but mostly out of public hearing. Also on 8 February, Sir Ivone Kirkpatrick wrote the first of two letters on the dispute to Kenneth Younger, MP, Minister of State at the Foreign Office:

> Dear Younger,
>
> I have had your message about war crimes. I have the impression from some of the papers I have received from the Foreign Office that it may not be completely recognized in London that a clear distinction must be made between my functions as representative of His Majesty's Government and the quasi-judicial functions which have been specially delegated to me personally by the Secretary of State in the matter of persons sentenced by British Courts in Germany.
>
> These powers have been delegated to me in writing, and I have been told that this is a personal responsibility which I must not devolve on anyone. Now I fully recognize the public interest attached to the whole question of war criminals and the desire of Ministers that nothing should be done in this

field except under their direction and instructions. But I feel that in these circumstances Ministers should take the personal responsibility for the decisions in theory as well as in practice.

After careful consideration I have come to the conclusion that I must ask to be relieved of all responsibility in respect of war criminals in Werl and Spandau. But I realize that this might cause inconvenience and I shall not therefore put forward a formal request to this effect until I have had an opportunity of discussing the matter with you in London next week.

Yours ever,

Ivone Kirkpatrick

On 12 February Prime Minister Attlee made a special statement in Parliament on the subject. The following week a 'personal and confidential' message received by Kirkpatrick from London advised:

The Minister of State has asked me to transmit to you for your information and guidance the following extract from a paper on war criminals which he is submitting to the Cabinet:-

'I have drawn the attention of Sir I. Kirkpatrick to the danger of expressing, even on a personal basis, controversial opinions on matters on which no authoritative guidance has been obtained from HM Government. I have also reminded him that British and Allied opinion is at present highly sensitive on all questions relating to the possible revival in Germany of militarism and Nazism and that this public feeling must be taken into account no less than German opinion in framing official policy.'

I may add that the following paragraph is also included in the paper:-

'In conclusion I trust that my colleagues will agree that our High Commissioner in Germany should have reasonable freedom to make speeches and give Press Conferences in

Germany. His position, and that of his United States and French colleagues, is very different from that of an Ambassador in a normal country — he forms in fact a considerable part of the actual Government of Germany and it is in that capacity that it is right and proper that he should from time to time explain HM Government's policy in respect of Germany, for the execution of which he is responsible.'

A few days after the Prime Minister's Parliamentary statement on the controversy, Kirkpatrick formally asked to be relieved of all responsibilities in regard to war criminals in Spandau and Werl prisons. He wished to be relieved not merely of the powers of clemency but also of the duties concerning conditions in the prisons and the care of the prisoners. He explained:

> Since it is plain to me that any measures I may feel bound in conscience to take to regulate the conditions of imprisonment are liable to misinterpretation, I must ask to be relieved of this responsibility also. I suggest that the Secretary of State should assume it and act under the advice of Home Office penologists.

Little more than a week later the Foreign Office recommended that the Power of Clemency should be withdrawn from High Commissioners in Germany and Austria and exercised in future by the Secretary of State for Foreign Affairs. It was felt that it would be better if jurisdiction over war criminals was moved back to Whitehall. It was considered too dangerous an issue to remain at the discretion of individual civil servants or politicians. A memorandum on the subject considered by the Cabinet stated:

At the time when we (somewhat unwittingly) gave the High Commissioner unrestricted powers, it was not necessary for us, or at any rate we did not trouble, to provide him with a directive or terms of reference to guide him in exercising the Power of Clemency. Now that we are asking the High Commissioner to prepare recommendations for the Secretary of State, the question arises whether we ought to provide him with a clear directive, and if so, in what terms.

It was realized that, if a clear-cut frame of reference was not provided, High Commissioners could come close to re-trying war crime cases — a procedure that would be utterly unacceptable to Governments. A total rethink of the question was urgently necessary.

At the 12 February 1951 meeting of Britain's Cabinet, a Paper on war criminals, drafted by Minister of State Kenneth Younger, declared that the Cabinet:

(a) Were inclined to the view that the duty of reviewing the sentences of war criminals should not continue to be delegated to the High Commissioner, or that he should at any rate be expected to seek the Foreign Secretary's guidance on the more important cases; and accordingly 'invited the Minister of State to submit proposals on the manner in which responsibility for reviewing the sentences of German war criminals should be exercised in future'; and

(b) Invited the Minister of State to arrange for His Majesty's Ambassador in Washington to ask the State Department to ensure that the United Kingdom Government had an opportunity of making representations in regard to any proposed remission of sentences on German war criminals held in the United States Zone of Germany.

The Cabinet document — detailing the background to the

problems, commencing with by whom the power of clemency was to be exercised — stated:

> When the power of clemency was originally delegated to Sir Ivone Kirkpatrick's predecessor, intention was that the power should be exercised on a consultative basis; the nature of the delegation contemplated was indicated in the following minute by one of the Legal Advisers which was written at that time.
>
> The process of confirming the sentence of a Military Court is a judicial one and Ministers ought not to give instructions to the confirming authority. But in any subsequent review of sentences, the High Commissioner is not exercising a purely judicial function. It would be proper for him to take into account, and he does take into account, considerations of policy and humanity, and that being so, there would, in my view, be no objection if the Secretary of State were to issue either general instructions as to the considerations to be taken into account in reviewing all sentences, or specific instructions on a particular case. The delegation of powers merely authorizes the High Commissioner to exercise certain functions. It is not, and was not intended to be, an exhaustive delegation of all the Secretary of State's powers to the High Commissioner.
>
> However, owing to a misunderstanding, no limitation of the power of clemency was prescribed either to General Robertson or to Sir Ivone Kirkpatrick. They were, therefore, entitled to assume that they had entire discretion in the matter and they acted accordingly.
>
> There must be a clear-cut final authority in the matter.
>
> The grounds on which sentences passed by the courts or tribunals in such cases may be reduced or amnestied are roughly three, namely:-

(a) Doubt whether the conviction was legally justified, as a result of revaluation of the evidence, or new evidence becoming available;
(b) The ill-health of the prisoner;
(c) A change in public opinion since the time the sentence was imposed.

Ground (b) is not likely to raise political complications of any kind. Ground (a) is also unlikely to cause serious political difficulty, unless the number of cases should, contrary to present expectations, prove to be large. The real difficulty arises over the third consideration. In the case of war criminals the question is complicated because there are two public opinions to be considered, British opinion and German opinion. The High Commissioner may be in the best position to gauge German public opinion but he is not in a position to assess British public opinion. Moreover, the weight which should be given to German public opinion where it conflicts with British public opinion, and the balancing of the two, is not a decision which it seems to me to be right to place upon the High Commissioner. It is because this third class of case is likely to be the most common, and is certainly the class which is likely to cause the most political feeling, that it is considered that the Secretary of State himself should exercise the power of clemency.

On what basis the power should be exercised
The method recommended is that preparatory work should be done in the first place in Germany by the High Commissioner's staff and by the High Commissioner himself; the resulting recommendation based on all those factors which he and his staff are competent to appreciate will be transmitted to the Secretary of State. The recommendation will be considered in so far as it is based on legal considerations by the Foreign Office Legal Adviser, while at the same time an assessment will be made in the Foreign Office of the different factors of British and German public

opinion. In occasional difficult or awkward cases the Foreign Secretary will wish to consult with one or more of his colleagues, for instance, the Attorney-General or the Lord Chancellor, where legal questions are concerned; if the difficulty arises on other grounds, he may for example wish to call for independent medical advice, while if he foresees political complications he might consult the Lord President or the Prime Minister.

As regards the grounds on which the High Commissioner will base his recommendations to the Foreign Secretary, the Foreign Office is preparing a Directive in consultation with the Legal Adviser in Germany. In coming to his own final decision, however, the Secretary of State cannot act solely on the basis of a formal directive, since no such document prepared in advance can provide for the widely varying problems which arise in the exercise of the power of clemency.

How best co-ordination with United States and French policies can be secured

Do not recommend that we should address any reproaches to the Americans over their action in regard to the Landsberg prisoners, first, on the general principle that it is a bad thing to stir up muddy water, and second, on the ground that the Americans might consider themselves entitled to reply that in informing us (as they did) of their intention to institute a review based on certain principles, they had fulfilled their obligations under the Charter of the Allied High Commission.[14]

---

[14] This referred to the section of the Charter of the Allied High Commission concerning purely individual responsibilities of High Commissioners. Each High Commissioner was responsible to his Government; nevertheless, so far as possible, he was expected to co-ordinate general policies with those of the other High Commissioners and exercise these powers in accordance with tripartite legislation or policies.

We are entitled to draw the attention of the Government of the United States to the co-ordination called for in this agreement, to the complete lack, as yet, of any tripartite legislation or agreed policies, and to say that in present circumstances we consider such co-ordination more than ever desirable. There is also the question of the extent to which the disposition of war criminals is a matter suitable for attention under the new phase of our relations with the Federal Government, involving placing the occupation on a basis akin to a treaty. We should ask the United States Government (and, at the same time, the French) to join with us in instructing our High Commissioners to provide their Governments with a report and recommendations by a fixed date covering all aspects of the war criminals problem.

What is to be said in Parliament
For the present all we need to tell the House of Commons is that the power of clemency has been withdrawn from the High Commissioner and will, in future, be exercised by the Foreign Secretary. Prefer to avoid disclosing to the House of Commons the exact manner in which it is proposed that the power of clemency should be exercised, or the nature of the directive to the High Commissioner. In the first place, these matters can provoke a great deal of argument which had best be avoided. In the second place, it is not considered appropriate that the power of clemency, which derives from the Royal Prerogative and is to be exercised in a personal capacity, should be defined and debated in public.

After considering the draft Cabinet Paper on war criminals, Sir Hartley Shawcross wrote to the Minister of State Kenneth Younger:

In exercising the power of clemency, general questions of policy can have but a limited effect. The nature of the offence of which an accused person stands convicted can hardly be affected by subsequent policy unless, indeed, policy went to the extent of treating such an offence as no longer criminal. If, for instance, the act of rape were relegated from the category of a criminal offence to that of a field sport, this might justify a review of sentences imposed for rape. Again, if, as a matter of general policy, imprisonment were no longer thought to be a suitable punishment for a particular class of offence, this matter might be reflected by the exercise of clemency towards those sentenced to terms of imprisonment for that offence, but the extent to which regard is had to questions of general policy is a matter to be watched with caution; each case should be dealt with upon its merits.

(2) I would reject any question of reviewing the decision, whether or not a conviction was legally justified, as a result of what your paper euphemistically describes as 'revaluation of the evidence'. If new evidence becomes available which tends to throw a completely different light upon the matter, the whole evidence should no doubt be reviewed in that light, but I think it would be strongly objectionable to revalue the evidence upon which the Court had acted, the Court's decision having already been confirmed and reviewed by the appropriate authority and again reviewed by the Committee under General Wade. One really must have some finality in regard to the merits of the conviction in a particular case and I suggest that finality has already been reached and that it would be quite intolerable that different minds should seek to arrive at different conclusions in regard to what had already been settled according to law.

I agree that one of the factors to be taken into account in the exercise of clemency is the ill health of the prisoner. Here, the Foreign Office would do well to be guided by the Home Office practice. Prisoners have died in prisons before now and it does not shock me that some war criminals should meet this fate.

The question of how far a change in public opinion since the sentence was imposed should influence the exercise of clemency in particular cases is one of some difficulty but I must say I view with great misgiving the general tone of your paper in this respect. Unless it is to be said that the Courts which impose these sentences and authorities who subsequently review them, including General Wade, were inspired by 'hatred and revenge' (as, indeed, one report of the speech by Sir Ivone Kirkpatrick suggested), I cannot see that supposed changes in public opinion can have much to do with the matter. One should certainly start any review of sentence on the assumption that the sentence imposed by the Court, as subsequently confirmed and reviewed, was a just and proper sentence and that the tribunal best fitted to assess the appropriate sentence was the Court which tried the case and saw and heard the witnesses and the convict. If there is any substantial body of German opinion which is really anxious about the welfare of the Nazi war criminals, it is unfortunate, but I suggest again, as I suggested in my Cabinet Paper, that the proper line is not to bow to this opinion, if indeed it exists, but to do our utmost to destroy it. There is no reason whatever, as far as I know, to think that opinion in this country is in the least inclined to condone the acts of the Nazi war criminals or to think that they have become white because the Communists have committed similar offences.

Were it necessary to review particular cases because of new evidence, I suggest that legal advice should be sought either from the Judge Advocate General (who had a responsibility in respect of the War Crimes Courts) or from the Law Officers. It seems to me that it would be quite unfair to put this burden on the Foreign Office Legal Advisers, experts though they are on questions of international law. These are matters which should be looked at against the background of experience in the ordinary criminal courts, for the offences of which these men were convicted were ordinary crimes. I should say also that in cases where legal problems arise about which the Foreign Secretary wishes to consult, the normal course should be for the Government's Legal Advisers, that is to say, the Law Officers, to be brought in.

Shawcross went on to refer to the general unfortunate impression created on the public mind by Sir Ivone Kirkpatrick's statements on the subject, and John McCloy's extensive releases of war criminals in the American zone. He pointed out that the truth was that the public had hitherto known very little about these releases. Had it been given all the information about the many cases in which the decisions of the courts had been departed from, questions might well have arisen in regard to them. Shawcross concluded:

> Broadly speaking, therefore, as you will see, my feeling is that our attitude towards this question should really be stiffened up. I am not sure whether you will have time to include in your paper some reference to my view. If not, perhaps a convenient course would be for me to put in a paper myself.
> I am sending a copy of this letter to the Lord Chancellor.
> Yours sincerely,
>
> Hartley Shawcross

Replying to criticisms of the Nuremberg trial, the Attorney-General said that in the absence of an international criminal court — and the question of constituting one was being canvassed before the United Nations — any enforcement of criminal laws of war was almost inevitably by the victorious Power. The procedure had been fair, and evidence more than adequate to prove the facts. Criticism that soldiers were punished simply for obeying orders was wholly wrong. If, in any other war, any officers of ours did the things that Keitel and Jodl and Raeder had done, they would fully deserve the same punishment. The idea that a soldier must always obey orders, and that, if he did not, someone else would, was monstrous. A soldier was bound only to obey a lawful order. There was no such thing as a duty of absolute obedience; that would mean absolute tyranny. Staff officers enjoyed no special privileges entitling them to immunity from the ordinary laws of the land.

Shawcross also placed on record with the Cabinet the following document:

Secret

War Criminals
Memorandum by the Attorney-General
The Minister of State has been good enough to show me his paper on War Criminals in draft so that I might have an opportunity of submitting my comments on it to my colleagues. I desire to do so.

(1) I must say that in recent months I have found the Foreign Office approach to the subject of War Criminals, as exemplified by the present paper and the one which preceded it, a little disquieting. I could wish that in the last five years, the Foreign Office had devoted as much active consideration to the education of public opinion in Germany, and particularly in the schools and universities, on the true principles underlying the Nuremberg judgement and the facts (so fully documented from German sources) on which it was based as they have recently directed it, if not to the condonation of the war crimes, at least to the exercise of clemency towards the offenders. I fear that we are in danger here of bowing before those very elements in public opinion, namely Fascism here, and the old nationalism and militarism in Germany, to which we should be most firmly opposed.

(2) I am entirely in favour of seeking to influence and co-ordinate our policy in regard to War Criminals with the Americans — and I would add, with the French. It now appears reasonably clear that we neglected an ample opportunity to represent our views on the deplorable

American decision to release Von Krupp. I have no comment to make on the procedure to be adopted but I hope we shall succeed in avoiding any repetition of such incidents. In connection with the co-ordination of our policy with the Americans, I think I may tell my colleagues that Mr Justice Jackson, who was American Prosecutor at Nuremberg, has recently written privately as follows:

'...I do not think the United States could have handed the Kremlin a better propaganda issue certainly in those countries which the Nazis occupied than in the release of Krupp. This is not a sudden change. The change here began when Mr Stimson's influence left the Department and Mr Secretary Royal came in. It has proceeded rather insidiously ever since. I could give you many instances of the change in attitude which now comes to the surface in these concrete acts... This country is so worked up about Communism at the present time that the public temper identifies as friend of the United States anyone who is a foe of Stalin. It figures the Nazis were his foes, entirely forgetting that they did not hesitate to become his allies when they thought they would gain by it. General Eisenhower has pretty effectively stopped the movement which was in full swing virtually to rearm them. I hope a saner outlook will arrive here but at the moment the scene is rather depressing. The Spring will probably turn the tide one way or the other. I hope to God we will regain our senses.'

(3) I agree also that the power of clemency should be withdrawn from the High Commissioner and vested in the Secretary of State. I do not dissent from the general opinion which was expressed by a Foreign Office Legal Adviser as to the exercise of this power. It is unfortunate that his opinion had not been conveyed to Sir Ivone Kirkpatrick. Had it been, he would not have laboured under the misapprehension, disclosed by the Lord Chancellor, that he was discharging some high judicial function in which he was independent of the Government and answerable only to his own conscience.

(4) But whilst questions of public policy must certainly affect the exercise of clemency in particular cases it is important that it should not be influenced by the clamour of particular sections of public opinion. Broadly, I suggest that the Secretary of State should act on the same principles as those which would guide the Home Department in the case of ordinary criminals. In particular:

(a) There should be no question of doubt whether the conviction was legally justified (as the Foreign Office paper suggests) nor any 'revaluation' of the evidence. If really significant new evidence turns up, no doubt the whole matter should be reviewed by lawyers in the light of it. But in the absence of new evidence there should be no further 'revaluation' of the evidence. These cases were confirmed in the first instance and have been reviewed more than once, in the last instance by the Board under Major General Wade. There really must be finality in this process and it would be intolerable if there were a perpetual process of revaluing the evidence in order to whittle down the conclusions to which it had led. These cases can now only be approached on the assumption that the convictions were legally valid and must be allowed to stand.

(b) No doubt, humanitarian considerations, such as ill health, would be matters to be taken into consideration in deciding whether or not to exercise clemency. It is, however, not uncommon for prisoners to be ill and even to die in prison.

(c) I would view with great jealousy the exercise of clemency on the ground that public opinion had changed. This seems to me to substitute political expediency for principle. It must be remembered that the cases in point now are all ones where the prisoners were convicted of ordinary war crimes, stigmatized as criminal by the Hague Conventions, International or Municipal law before the war and corresponding to grave crimes under our law. We are not now dealing with the crimes against peace or crimes against humanity which aroused some controversy in the Nuremberg

Trial. The crimes for which these men were convicted are as reprehensible now as when they were enacted before the war or when the prisoners were convicted. The only change in public opinion can be one which regards the Nazis with less dislike. But this would afford no ground for extending clemency to war criminals. Here again any review should proceed on the basis that prima facie at least the Court which saw the criminals and the witnesses is better qualified to fix a correct sentence than individuals without experience of criminal justice sitting in the comfortable detachment of Government Departments.

(4) I suggest also that the Foreign Office should follow the practice of the Home Department in regard to reviews of sentence. Long sentences are not under a constant and perpetual process of review. They are, as I understand, brought forward every four years. In view of the fact that Major General Wade's review has only recently been completed, no fresh review would seem called for until some considerable time has elapsed.

(5) Where legal questions are concerned, especially if they involve the so-called 're-valuation' of evidence, it would hardly be fair to the Foreign Office Legal Advisers to impose the burden upon them. They would be the first to disclaim any special knowledge of the rules of evidence, of trial procedure or of the criminal law. These were Military Courts. The Judge Advocate General is the most obvious person to advise on legal matters arising from their decisions but in special cases the Law Officers might be brought in.

(6) I deprecate the form of answer which it is proposed to give in reply to the suggested Parliamentary Question and suggest that it invites trouble. There is remarkably little information about the cases in which, and the reasons for which, clemency has been exercised. I should certainly not care to commit myself to unqualified approval of the action taken in the case of the twenty-seven prisoners who, as I understand, benefited from clemency under the powers

delegated to the High Commissioner although clemency had not been recommended by Major General Wade. In any event, it does not seem to be desirable to invite the suggestion of 'white-washing' which the draft answer would no doubt provoke.

The Solicitor-General has seen this paper and agrees with it.

HWS

21st March 1951

King George VI was informed by the Cabinet that in future the power of clemency in respect of German war criminals would be exercised by him on advice tendered by the Secretary of State for Foreign Affairs. Hitherto, the Crown had not been directly concerned with the question because a Royal Warrant of June 1945 gave the Secretary of State for War authority to exercise clemency in such cases. This authority was delegated to the Commander-in-Chief, Germany, and subsequently transferred to the Secretary of State for Foreign Affairs. A similar delegation to the UK High Commissioner in Germany followed. The King was advised that, in consequence of withdrawal of the power from the High Commissioner, it was now reverting to the Crown.

Years later Kirkpatrick admitted that, during the whole of his service in Germany as British High Commissioner, the contentious issue that weighed heaviest on him had been the problem of war criminals. As for his reference to hatred and revenge being bad counsellors, he insisted he had meant that sentiments of hatred and revenge should not inspire refusal to make a review.

The seven attempted, through innumerable legal manoeuvres, to get their cases reheard by de-Nazification tribunals with the aim of achieving a second chance before a possibly more lenient court.

Funk and the others were told that no German tribunals had authority to re-examine their cases; but US High Commissioner McCloy indicated a willingness to do so. The tidal wave of international resentment caused by the general review of war crime sentences also threatened McCloy, who firmly defended the administration of de-Nazification.[15]

Disclosing the fate of many top former Nazis, McCloy claimed that the occupying powers had performed 'major surgical operations to remove the evil of the Nazi regime from the German body', and added: 'A serious effort has been made to punish the guilty, but it cannot be denied that some guilty persons have escaped punishment and detention.' Admitting that many Nazis were back in public service and in industry, he gave the following details of the twenty-four most important Nazi Cabinet Ministers and other top leaders: 'Six have been executed; six are still serving sentences up to life, and eight have either died or committed suicide. The fate of one is obscure, and three are at liberty.' The one whose fate was obscure was Martin Bormann, generally presumed to have died during the fall of Berlin, although his body was never found.

Two distinct camps battled over the future of convicted war criminals. One, whose ranks included the Nuremberg judges and prosecutors of the United States, Britain and France, resolutely opposed any review of sentences that could be taken

---

[15] The de-Nazification court system was intended to bring to punishment every Nazi criminal or sympathizer from top to bottom of the German social structure. Devised by the four occupation Powers, it dealt with 'the arrest and punishment of war criminals, Nazis and militarists, and the internment, control and surveillance of potentially dangerous Germans'. The system divided offenders into five categories and specific penalties, and it also provided for ex-Nazis in higher categories to be downgraded for good behaviour and eventually exonerated.

as casting doubts on the justice of the original trials and verdicts. The second camp, pressing for 'softer attitudes', insisted that considerations of international policies were legitimately applicable in assessing political advantages that might be gained through a modification of sentences. The latter group had significantly influential backing from within the foreign affairs Ministries of the three Western Powers. The fight largely came down to one of the judiciary versus the politically motivated, who were striving to overturn judgements in their anxiety to curry favour with political and public opinion that was changing. The judiciary accused the 'judgement meddlers' of having politically convenient short memories for the long knives with which the Spandau seven, and other war criminals, had murderously and mercilessly hacked their way to power, committing immeasurable crimes against humanity to further their ambitions.

19: THE GOLDEN DILEMMA

A storm was raging around Sir Ivone Kirkpatrick and John McCloy because of their attitudes towards the war crimes sentences. Meanwhile, a petition from Neurath's lawyer, Dr Fischinger, who had already conferred with McCloy earlier in the year, arrived on Kirkpatrick's desk for submission to the Government in London. After referring to the latest medical reports on Neurath, it went on:

> I do not wish to consider the question whether or not the sentence passed by the International Military Tribunal in the case of von Neurath will be justified by history in the future. In a memorandum, entitled 'Are there reasons for an act of mercy for Freiherr von Neurath?' which was submitted to your predecessor, I have already attempted to explain that we now have evidence which shows that in the year 1938 Herr von Neurath was replaced as minister for foreign affairs by the obedient Herr von Ribbentrop *for the very reason* that Herr von Neurath was opposed to Hitler's war policy and did all he could to preserve the peace; that furthermore Herr von Neurath only accepted the position as Reichsprotektor in Bohemia and Moravia at the urgent advice of members of the resistance movement who were in the German foreign office and foreign diplomats *in order to* preserve the peace.
>
> The so-called 'Heidelberger Kreis Deutscher Volkerrechtler' (Heidelberg circle of German experts for international law) has recently turned its attention to the treatment of prisoners in Spandau. It was stated that the methods of penal treatment in Spandau are not in accordance with the rules internationally recognized by civilized nations. In comparison the penal

treatment in Landsberg and Werls is very much more humane.[16]

Permit me to call attention to the parallel case of Marshal Pétain: according to my information, Mme Pétain was given permission to take care of her husband during the day and to live very near him. Frau von Neurath on the other hand is in constant anxiety and uncertainty. Due to the fact that her property is still blocked, she can afford the trip from her home to Berlin only very rarely.

The statement that it would be difficult if not impossible to obtain Russia's consent to Herr von Neurath's release is not convincing. If it really may be assumed — and I am indeed presuming that it may be — that it is an offence against internationally recognized principles of penal treatment to subject an old man who is seriously ill, and *incapable of enduring imprisonment*, to an unusually strict enforcement of punishment, then the three Western Powers who are sharing in the prison administration in Spandau, cannot — especially in view of the principles of law established in Nürnberg — maintain these conditions without themselves incurring grave guilt. In such a case it should be possible to find in the name of justice ways and means of solving the matter without Russia's consent.

According to the London Statute the Control Council was authorized to permit alleviations in prison or a premature release from prison as an act of grace. The Control Council no longer exists. In all other matters the three Western powers have taken steps without Russia's consent. The penal treatment in Spandau has been the only exception. Anyone who desires to uphold the rights of the individual as for

---

[16] The Heidelberg Kreis — a group consisting of senior judges, university professors, and a number of lawyers — were frequently approached to intervene in respect of the Spandau sentences. Finally, in the summer of 1951, they sent delegations to the Allied High Commissioners, and a different delegation visited each Commissioner.

instance the UNO did in the General Declaration of the Rights of Man on December 10, 1948, must, before it is too late, do all in his power for the rights of an old man who is incapable of enduring imprisonment and who has the misfortune of serving a sentence in the prison of Spandau. I beg you to understand these frank words.

Possibly, as his lawyer claimed, Neurath *did* travel the road described by one war crime defendant as the 'ridge between obedience and rebellion', yet the main impression, and the most disappointing, was that he continued to consider that what he did was right because he was doing it under orders and for his country. This exaltation of orders was more disturbing as an attitude than as a defence. Defendant after defendant, high and low, put forward this defence at Nuremberg and other courts. There was always some superior, right up to Hitler, to use as an excuse for accepting orders. No one, apparently, was expected to think or have any standards of official or personal performance except the thoughts and standards laid down by one man. This defence chant of 'superior orders' persisted long after the war. Wives, lawyers, and others campaigning for the Spandau seven continually submitted this point in petitions for remission of sentences. As far as they were concerned, in a nation of sixty million people there was only one man, or less than a handful of men, responsible for everything that happened. So as long as there was an order that trickled down from the top, they maintained that everyone in the wash of it was entitled to enjoy a bath of immunity.

The bare fact was that, with most of them, willingness must have entered into their actions. There had to be ready co-operation. Without it Hitler could never have kept control. No solitary man could have made an entire nation goose-step to his will.

Shortly after receipt of Neurath's petition by the High Commissioners, he was again at the centre of controversy. About to reach their golden wedding anniversary, the Baron and Baroness asked whether they could be granted a relaxation of prison restrictions to permit them to mark the occasion.

The request from Neurath's lawyer for the grant of special facilities for the golden wedding, which fell on 30 May, was received by US High Commissioner John McCloy. McCloy first spoke to French High Commissioner André François-Poncet, who said he did not object to granting the facilities requested. A message was sent to Sir Ivone Kirkpatrick, seeking his approval. As May was Britain's month in Spandau, it would be up to the British Governor to make the arrangements. McCloy advised Kirkpatrick that Neurath's son was coming specially from the Argentine to see his parents and that the High Commissioners had been asked to permit him and other members of the family to hold a family gathering in a room at the gaol without supervision. They were also asked to permit a German priest to celebrate the customary golden wedding ceremony and to allow the members of the family to eat a meal together. Finally, Neurath's lawyer requested that the Baron be given the possibility of discussing with his relatives the terms of his own will, and that a notary be admitted to the prison so that the necessary formalities could be completed.

Both McCloy and François-Poncet were prepared to consent to everything, but Kirkpatrick cautioned:

> I do not think it would be prudent to grant all these requests. I am advised that from the point of penal administration it is not desirable to allow interviews without supervision or to allow entertainment of visitors at a meal. I would be agreeable

to authorizing the British Governor to agree with his French and United States colleagues, for joint submission to the Russian Governor, a proposal for authorizing a supervised visit of five persons, with facilities for the religious ceremony.

At a special meeting of the four Prison Directors held on 28 May 1951, the Soviet Director refused to agree to a special visit to Neurath of five persons including the prisoner's wife, son and daughter, and vetoed the holding of a traditional golden wedding religious celebration by a German priest, giving as reasons:

> The Statutes of the Prison not only do not permit consideration of such a question but directly prohibit German clergy from holding religious services in the Prison. The Governors should be able to recall an incident which occurred very recently, as at the 257th meeting of the Prison Governors they took a unanimous decision to refuse the request of a German clergyman, Bishop Dibelius, and the question of a religious service on the occasion of a Golden Wedding Anniversary of the prisoner can only be discussed in the light of holding this service by a non-German clergyman.

The four Directors finally agreed: (1) Neurath's wife and *either* son *or* daughter could visit him for fifteen minutes on 30 May or any subsequent date, this visit to be counted as one against the prisoner's yearly allotment; (2) the prisoner (without any relatives) could attend a special service conducted by the prison chaplain on the date of the visit; fellow prisoners would be allowed to attend the service. The Soviet Director also refused to permit a legal representative to visit Neurath in order to draft a will.

As shrewd as she was in organizing tactics, Neurath's daughter, Winifred von Mackensen, weakened her own efforts on occasions by deliberately spreading false stories concerning conditions. She supplied Bishop Würm with material for letters he wrote to many eminent international personages, seeking to enlist aid for the Spandau inmates. The Bishop referred to 'damp cells' and prisoners 'given water soup with potato peelings and four slices of dry bread twice a day' as meals during the Russian months.

The Foreign Office demanded a full report on the allegations from Le Cornu, the British Governor of the prison, who even the prisoners considered to be fair-minded and humane. Le Cornu's report advised:

> The statement that 'nobody else (other than immediate family) is allowed to correspond with them,' is incorrect. No restriction whatsoever exists as to from whom a prisoner may receive a letter, provided that the basic rule as regards receiving one letter per month is adhered to and that the letter is passed by the censor.
>
> *Russian month*
> That part relating to food is an exaggeration, and the food during the last Russian month was adequate and good. Previous to this Russian months had not compared favourably with those of the Americans, French or ourselves, but at no time have I noticed any resemblance whatsoever to 'starvation diet'.
>
> The statement regarding prisoners being taken into the open air seldom is incorrect. Prison regulations permit of exercise for fifteen minutes A.M. and P.M., and I agree that when the Russian team is on duty they are not always as good as they should be about this question, but it is counter-balanced by the fact that the team following the Russian team during the following 'shift' invariably make it their first duty to take the prisoners out. The only work available for prisoners is in the garden and, provided the US, French, or

British teams are on duty during the 0800 hours to 1600 hours shift and the weather is reasonable, prisoners are in the open air daily from 0900 hours to 1230 hours and again from 1400 hours to 1600 hours. Taking into consideration the whole question of the prisoners going into the open air, I consider that during the Spring, Summer and Autumn there is no ground for complaint whatsoever, but that during the Winter the question is one obviously governed by the weather.

The statement that prisoners are under searchlight every half-hour is incorrect. The US, French and British Directors, some considerable time back, issued orders to their teams that switching on of lights for the purpose of security was to be reduced to an absolute minimum and this, to my knowledge, has been carried out by the three nations in question. During a Russian shift the lights are certainly switched on more frequently but I think it will be appreciated that it is impossible to do very much about this. A new system of lighting was installed a month or so back which gives a much more diffused light and an all-round improvement has undoubtedly been effected.

Visits are not limited to next of kin and prisoners may be visited by whom they like (security of course affecting this). Regulations state that a prisoner may get a visit of fifteen minutes every second month. Part of the grille in the visitors' room has now been removed and the only nation that takes down every word of the conversation during a visit is the Russians, though on one occasion I have known the French to do it.

There is no question of the prisoner [referring to Neurath] 'being so bent by rheumatism that he is unable to walk', and the statement that the cell is 'moist' is completely wrong. The floor is of cement covered by linoleum but at no time have I seen any signs of dampness and at no time have I had any complaints from either the prisoner under discussion or any of the other prisoners. A dentist is always available to visit the prison at very short notice and has very frequently done so, and the suggestion of a prisoner not being able to get proper dental treatment is completely nonsensical.

Treatment of prisoners during the Russian months differs in no way to that appertaining during the US, French and British months except possibly that prior to the last Russian month, as already pointed out, the food was not *quite* up to standard.

Taking the memorandum as a whole, the statements made therein are, if not entirely incorrect, very grossly exaggerated.

Stubbornly attempting to brand Le Cornu's report as a lie, Frau von Mackensen went on to make further complaints; but separate inquiries, independent of Le Cornu, totally supported his version. Usually the most subtle of all the campaigning Spandau relatives, Frau von Mackensen undermined her own case by overplaying her hand.

For additional confirmation of the entire situation, another exceptional measure was taken. Lionel Fox, Chairman of His Majesty's Prison Commissioners and therefore the senior authority on penal institutions, was asked to inspect Spandau and Werl prisons. In May 1951 he made the following report:

General Considerations
It is usual for penal codes to provide for different types of punishment involving deprivation of liberty. The Court decides which is the appropriate type of punishment and pronounces it as such, and it does so in the knowledge that its sentence will be carried out in accordance with the legal code for the execution of such a sentence.

A sentence of imprisonment is a simple deprivation of liberty, except in so far as the method of executing such a sentence is regulated by the penal code of the country concerned.

In considering the actual conditions in which sentences are being served by these prisoners in Spandau and Werl, I felt bound to address my mind to the question — what must the Courts which passed the sentences be assumed to have intended? Did they intend a simple deprivation of liberty, or something more? And if more, on what basis did they intend the sentences to be executed?

There is, so far as I am able to judge on the information I have obtained, no ground for assuming any intention to pass a sentence corresponding with the conceptions of 'hard labour'.

I would add that I had an informal conversation with Lord Justice Birkett, and I believe that if he were consulted he would express a similar view.

Spandau Regulations

It is not possible to draw up a code of prison treatment applicable only to these seven men which can be either rational or humane — for I regard it as a form of inhumanity in itself to condemn a handful of men to spend together, in these conditions, what for most of them may be the rest of their natural lives. If my conclusions in paragraph 1 are correct, this condition is based on a fortuitous circumstance and is not inherent either in their offences or their sentences.

Another exceptional feature of the regulations, again due to the unique conditions of this prison, is their preoccupation with security and the possibility of suicide. The greater part of the fantastically expensive security machinery in force is wholly unnecessary from the point of view of any normal prison administration. While this adds to the repressive effect of the prison as a whole, it also affects the treatment of the prisoners directly in various ways, e.g. allowing only a spoon to eat with and inspection 'at frequent intervals throughout the night'. The latter provision led to a complaint to me by one prisoner that he was deprived of sleep by the light being constantly turned on. The provision that cells should be 'thoroughly searched at least twice daily' must also have an irritating and repressive effect on the occupants. I understood also that provision of suitable work and leisure occupations was limited by these considerations.

As I have indicated above, I am not in a position to say how these regulations compare in detail with the German code of 1943. I can, however, state that in general they appear to be, in several respects, out of accord with general international practice in executing a sentence of simple imprisonment and, so far as I can say from admittedly superficial observation and inquiry, with contemporary German practice in the British zone at least. In particular I note —

(a) certain provisions which are specifically repressive and defamatory in intention,

(b) the twice repeated provision that 'prisoners shall not talk or communicate with each other or others unless specially authorized by the Governorate',

(c) the provision for solitude in isolated cells except for work, religious services, and walks.

(d) Regulation 17, dealing with punitive powers, which contravenes nearly every internationally accepted principle. Although no doubt these powers are not used in practice their mere existence constitutes a scandal.

Conditions in Spandau Prison

I was shown round the prison by the British Governor, attended by the other three Governors and a Russian interpreter. So far as I am aware I saw all parts of the prison used by or in connection with the prisoners. I saw all the prisoners at work in the garden, and spoke with each of them. Afterwards I had a talk with the English and French Governors, the American having being called away, and the Russian not wishing, although invited, to participate.

I found it difficult to reconcile the actual regime in force, at all points, with the regulations. I gather that in the absence of a higher authority a good deal of elasticity has of necessity developed in the interpretation of the regulations, so that in certain respects practice is more defensible than precept. On the other hand there are certain things which could be permitted even within the terms of the regulations, as I interpret them, and ought to be, but are not permitted. I was informed that such improvement as practice shows over precept is due to continued pressure by the British and American Governors against continued opposition by the Russian, with the French occupying an equivocal position. I was further given to understand that of late the Russian Governor has been much more co-operative. The impression I carried away was that the process of improving conditions had been carried out as far as it could be expected to go without the direction of higher authority: any further pressure might result in a reaction in favour of 'the pure milk of the word'. It may be significant in this connection that the Russian Governor of Berlin had visited (I believe for the first time) shortly before I paid my visit: whether he had heard that I was to visit is conjectural.

On the material level I could find no cause for complaint. The cell-block was newly painted and pleasant in appearance; the cells were of reasonable size, well lighted, heated, and ventilated, with adequate bedding and furniture. The prisoners had photographs and small personal belongings. Their clothing was adequate; they were allowed their own overcoats, and special cupboards had been provided outside the cells for these and their working clothes. So far as I could judge the dietary was adequate and reasonably varied, though I was unable to judge the standard of cooking and service by personal observation. The medical services appeared to be good, though I would here make one qualification. The special treatment of these prisoners as compared with their colleagues in Werl Prison required that, whereas prisoners have been released from Werl to undergo specialized medical or dental treatment, in Spandau even a major operation must be performed in what seemed to me most unsuitable conditions (this happened to the prisoner Funk).

Work — Regulation 9 provides that 'in principle there shall be work every day except Sundays and general German holidays'. Practice here falls a good deal short of principle. In the ordinary course the only work provided is attention to a piece of ground on which flowers and vegetables are cultivated. The prisoners were engaged in this occupation when I saw them. The atmosphere was more one of a mental hospital than a prison or any place where work means work. Most of them were just fiddling about with their tools, occasionally pausing to wander vaguely to and fro. Admitted this was as much as could be expected of five of them, though Speer and von Schirach are active men and could do a useful job. What I feel bound to emphasize is that this is the *only* provision made for work. During many months of the year it must be too cold or wet for the sick old men to be outside, or the ground must be unfit for cultivation. But there is nothing else to do. Certainly they have themselves repainted their cell-block; and made a good job of it, but that is done now. I could get no convincing answer to my question why an indoor work-room was not provided. The regulations indeed seem to require it, since they say that there shall be work each day and that the work shall be communal.

I regard it as wholly wrong and inhumane to keep men confined for a long period of years with no adequate means of employment.

Leisure — The position here is more satisfactory, but could be improved. The library service is excellent, and the prisoner Speer told me how much it is appreciated. They are also allowed writing materials and may, if I understand correctly, write what they like except personal memoirs, though I understood also that the prisoners in Werl are allowed to write personal memoirs.

Two improvements could be made within the terms of the regulations, of which the first seems to me desirable, the second essential —

(1) Regulation 14 gives the Governorate discretion to allow the prisoners to have 'other occupations', which in the context means other than reading library books. Under this they have been allowed writing materials, and in Speer's cell I found pencil drawings and plans and designs of an architectural character. But I was informed that no other forms of recreation (e.g. painting, puzzles and problems, chess-boards, hobbies) would be allowed. The only reason I could gather was the suicide-security complex.

(2) One of the worst features of the situation of these men is that they are allowed absolutely no means of contact with, or knowledge of, the stream of thought and events in the world outside their prison. The only newspaper they may see is the religious periodical *Die Wirsche*. There is no radio in the prison. This is not so at Werl, nor in any other penal system within my knowledge for men serving sentences of this length. There is nothing in the regulations that I can interpret as prohibiting this, and the admission of *Die Wirsche* supports this view. Even if objection can be found to daily newspapers, they might at least be allowed to obtain serious periodicals — whatever may be the German equivalent of such publications as *The Spectator* or *The New Statesman*, and specialized journals dealing with any particular interests they may have.

Conversation and Association — I have already drawn attention to the Rule of Silence prescribed by the regulations. It is fortunate indeed that this is not enforced, though so long as it exists there is always the danger that it may be. I cross-examined the English and French Governors closely on this, and both agreed that it would be correct to say that conversation between the prisoners, though forbidden in principle, was virtually unrestricted in practice.

Nevertheless, I am strongly of opinion that these prisoners ought, like their colleagues at Werl, to be provided with a sitting-room where, for a limited period in the evenings at least, they may if they wish talk together or play chess or similar games. I understand that except when employed in the garden they are locked in their cells. This situation, over so long a period of years, must have such effects on body and mind that it could properly be described as inhumane. I would go further and suggest that they might take their meals, or some of them, in common: this practice is now usual for long-sentence men of good behaviour in all progressive penal systems.

Letters and Visits — This was the one question about which all the prisoners who had complaints did complain. They wanted more letters and longer visits. They may now, according to the regulations, write and receive a letter once in four weeks and have a visit once in two months: the length of the visit is fifteen minutes. The Governorate has discretion to allow additional letters 'in exceptional cases' and to extend the length of a visit, and from the information given me this discretion is freely exercised. I am not able to say how far this standard conforms with general practice, but I understand that in German practice a prisoner may have a letter and a visit every four weeks: in England and at least some other European countries he would have a letter once a fortnight and a visit once a month.

The only point at which the regulation is open to criticism as being unduly harsh is the short period of the visit, though as I have said this seems to be freely modified in practice. By good contemporary standards, I should suggest one letter a fortnight each way, and one visit a month of not less than thirty minutes.

Shaving — I noted one small but characteristic point. For no good reason, shaving is allowed only twice a week. This is not conducive to self-respect, and I think the prisoners should be shaved every day.

Attitude of the prisoners — I spoke with each of the prisoners through the British Governor, German being the only language permitted. Each of them was asked whether he had anything he wished to say to me, and they did not appear to be under any sense of restriction in what they said. The complaints made were however few. Principally they spoke of letters and visits. Dönitz (or possibly Raeder) complained that the paper he was allowed for writing was given only 20 sheets at a time, and then removed. Funk complained bitterly of being deprived of sleep by the turning on of lights in the night.

I thought that all but Speer and von Schirach, the two youngest, looked markedly affected by their imprisonment. Speer was the only one who still seemed to retain the spark of life and humanity. Dönitz spoke with some force and a bitter undertone. Funk, a pathetic and very sick old man, worked himself into a state of violent indignation about the treatment accorded to one in his state of health. The attitude of the others was apathetic. The five older men were aged much beyond their years.

Conclusions on Spandau Prison
I cannot satisfy myself as to the legal basis of the regulations in force. Subject to correction on the questions of law and fact, I am of the opinion that the regulations, and the practice followed under the regulations, include features which are contrary to accepted international practice and to the Standard Minimum Rules for the Treatment of Prisoners approved by the League of Nations in 1933. I am of the opinion that the following features in particular ought not to be tolerated by His Majesty's Government, as a responsible Power, if there is in the existing situation any means of correcting them:

(1) The failure to provide adequate means of employment.

(2) The failure to provide knowledge of outside events.

(3) The regulations dealing with punishment.

(4) The absence of any provision for association except at work.

While I have also suggested certain other desirable changes, e.g. as to leisure occupations, better facilities for letters and visits, and shaving, I consider that with the changes suggested the system at Spandau, assuming that it must be maintained as a separate prison, would not be open to criticism as inhumane or contrary to good international practice in the treatment of long-sentence prisoners.

When Stalin died in March 1953, the seven prisoners speculated whether the reshuffle at the Kremlin would affect their future.

'Change is not necessarily reform,' Neurath warned.

Berlin's Mayor, Ernst Reuter, had for months been pointing to signs of growing weakness in the Soviet regime. He immediately advocated that the West should grab the opportunity presented by Stalin's successor, Malenkov, who had offered a 'peaceful solution to all outstanding conflicts'.

'That could include us,' Funk said. 'Reuter has even asked President Eisenhower to meet Malenkov in Berlin.'

A few months later, as the seven stepped out into the prison garden on the morning of 18 June 1953, Funk, unable to contain himself any longer, exploded with the news that had just reached him. 'There's an uprising in East Berlin!' he almost shouted.

Neurath and Dönitz became as excited as Funk and could not understand why Schirach, Speer, Raeder, and Hess did not react as they had to the news.

'Aren't you interested in your country anymore?' Dönitz asked scathingly as the four continued labouring in the garden as if nothing extraordinary had just occurred outside the prison walls.

'It all started because overworked, undernourished East Berliners were ordered to work even harder,' Funk explained. 'Workers on building sites on the Stalinallee stopped work yesterday in protest and marched to Alexanderplatz, where they were reinforced by workers from other sites. It developed into a march by a crowd of some 5,000, on the Government buildings in Leipzigerstraße. The demonstration suddenly became a revolt, and a general strike was called for today. This could change things for all of Germany, and for us,' he added hopefully.

About 100,000 marched through East Berlin's streets. Marchers tried to avoid provoking intervention, but the Volkspolizei — in effect the East German army — opened fire; Russian tanks appeared everywhere, firing on groups of people who tried to stop them by throwing stones into the tracks. Police barracks were set ablaze, but the protesters never stood a chance.

East German Ministers requested Soviet aid, and the Russian commandant proclaimed a state of emergency and imposed a curfew. Within hours the Soviet Army was in control; the border was closed, patrolled with tanks and armoured cars. Nobody knew how many were killed in East Berlin.

For months after the uprising the Spandau seven nervously anticipated possible side effects. Following success in quelling the revolt, it was feared that the Russians might also be tempted to flex their muscles again within the gaol by seeking to reimpose harsher treatment. But tensions gradually eased, and the following year brought a major switch in Soviet policy towards the prisoners.

For years Russia had set her face against even minor measures aimed at slightly easing the regime at Spandau. Then, in the spring of 1954, she unexpectedly consented to a number of such changes. In November of that year the Soviet Government showed yet again how blandly it was prepared to go back on its own long-standing policy — if it suited. A letter sent by the Soviet High Commissioner for Germany, Pushkin, to the French High Commissioner, François-Poncet, announced;

> In connexion with the illness and advanced age of Konstantin von Neurath, who was sentenced to 15 years' imprisonment by the international military tribunal and is serving this sentence in the allied prison at Spandau, I have been instructed to submit the proposal for the premature release of Neurath for discussion by the High Commissioners of France, the United Kingdom and the United States.
>
> I am further instructed to notify you that the Government of the Czechoslovak Republic is agreeable to the submission of this proposal for discussion by the High Commissioners of the four-Powers, and to the possible decision on Neurath's premature release. I have sent the same letter to the United Kingdom High Commissioner, Sir Frederick Hoyer Millar, and the United States High Commissioner, Mr J. B. Conant.

The proposal, which the Russians realized only too well would meet with Western approval on humanitarian grounds, was regarded as a political stroke aimed at impressing West German nationalists. It was in line with the steady release of German prisoners of war and the general Soviet propaganda tune that true sovereignty could be found under Soviet patronage. In view of past battles over even comparatively insignificant suggested concessions for Spandau gaol, genuine Russian humanitarian motives seemed remote in Neurath's case. Because Neurath, then eighty-one, was convicted of war crimes committed while he was 'Reich Protector' in Prague, Czech approval was included in the letter from Soviet High Commissioner Pushkin.

On 4 November 1954 Erich Raeder rushed out of the library into the corridor shouting: 'Read this!' Suddenly, controlling his excitement and lowering his voice to prevent Neurath hearing, he read from a copy of *Die Welt* newspaper he was clutching. The item was an uncensored Associated Press report that Soviet High Commissioner Pushkin had recommended Neurath's release because of age and ill health.

The six prisoners and the guards were ordered not to let Neurath see the newspaper until he had been given a sedative. Seeming to take the news calmly, Neurath remarked: 'I won't believe any such reports until I am standing on the other side of the prison gate.'

Hess dismissed the story and claimed: 'It's just a propaganda lie. I know the Communists' tactics!'

The Baroness and her daughter had only just returned home from their bimonthly journey to the gaol, unaware that, virtually while they were there, the Soviet authorities were proposing Neurath's immediate release. On 5 November, Winifred von Mackensen received a telegram asking her to report to Spandau the following morning at 11 a.m. She was not told why.

For years the Allies had tried to free the ailing Neurath ahead of his time. Now the Russians, who had previously blocked every move, had relented, pompously indicating that this was done 'as a humanitarian act from the hearts of the Soviet leaders'.

The next morning the Russians cleared Neurath's locker of clothes and books. 'What right have they to do this?' he demanded angrily. Without warning, he was summoned for his weekend bath. Led by an American guard, he shuffled slowly away and disappeared through the iron door at the end of the corridor.

'He's gone,' guard Charles Pease said quietly. The remaining six inmates were visibly affected. Shaking his head, Hess kept repeating: 'I didn't really think it was possible.'

After the bath, Neurath was handed a fresh suit — prison attire, but minus a number — and, a few moments later, given his gold watch, the only personal possession he had carried into the gaol in 1947. He did not know that his daughter was waiting for him in the visiting room.

When Winifred von Mackensen overheard two of the prison staff complaining about their inability to remove the number 3 from her father's overcoat, she inquired: 'May I take my father with me now?'

He was not given any official release papers, but was informed that no restrictions would be imposed on his freedom.

Father and daughter walked out of the building arm in arm. He had been nine years and six months in gaol.

Bouquets of flowers were sent to his Berlin hotel in Kurfürstendamm, including one from the Federal Government, whose personal representative in Berlin, Herr Vockel, also put his official car at Neurath's disposal. A few hours later, still wearing his Spandau suit, he appeared for press cameras at the hotel. Winifred von Mackensen explained that he was too ill to stand questioning: 'All he wants to do now is go home.' When a reporter asked whether her father would be applying for a pension as a former Foreign Minister, she said: 'I presume he will get that without asking.'

At the airfield, the Baron was taken straight on to the aircraft and not subjected to the normal checks. This procedure, presumably adopted on account of his health, was normally applicable only to members or guests of the Government.

He returned to his estate near Stuttgart to a welcome of chiming church bells and offerings of flower-garlands from villagers. Tears streamed down his face as he embraced his seventy-nine-year-old wife and his brother, Wilhelm.

Professor Heuss, the President of the Federal Republic, acknowledged as one of the most decent and liberal of the new Germans, wrote in a letter to Neurath on his release:

> The martyrdom of these years has come to an end for you. I am happy that you are now restored to your family and to your Württemberg home, with which you always remained linked, and that our cares and thoughts must no longer be troubled by a bitter imagination. I can only wish that your naturally strong disposition will soon recover from the consequences of the harsh years, and that, restored to your familiar surroundings, you will find peace of mind too. Please greet from me Frau von Mackensen, who in these days, if with such bitter delay, will certainly have received with a glad heart the crowning of the efforts for her father. With best regards to you and your family.

Martyr or criminal? Possibly only a weakling, but weakness can make a man both. The decision of the four-Powers to free him was not greeted in Germany as an act of mercy but as one of belated justice. The touch of personal warmth in Professor Heuss's letter was perhaps understandable, because, like Neurath, the President was a Württemberger. But the word 'martyrdom' made the letter far more than a purely humane and personal greeting. The President was too intelligent a man not to appreciate that 'martyrdom' is more than a distressing experience; it implies sacrifice for a cause.

Chancellor Konrad Adenauer, who claimed that he had supported efforts to free Neurath solely on humane grounds, said to the Baron in a telegram:

> The news that freedom has been restored to you after long hard years has sincerely gladdened me. I express to you, your wife, and your children my heartiest congratulations and

coupled with my best wishes for the restoration of your health.'

There was criticism in some German quarters for the President's and the Chancellor's sympathetic messages to the Baron. The Socialist newspaper *Nacht Depesche* asked: 'Was it a martyrdom and not a punishment? Either von Neurath was a war criminal, as the verdict states, or he was not and the court was merely a farce run by avengers.'

The manner in which Neurath and other war criminals were acquitted in the eyes of so many German people gave an ugly warning that admiration for the policies of the Nazis had not died. Adulation lavished on the Baron by the Federal President and Chancellor was discouraging to hopes that Germany's greatest desire was to wipe out the evil past, and encouragement to neo-Nazi reactionary elements anxious to impede their country's evolution as a democratic State. Britain and other Western Powers were basing their future strategy on trust in a rearmed Germany. The public reception Neurath received meant that alliance with West Germany, to which the West was committed, needed to be tempered with vigilance; for this man, now called a martyr, was no helpless simpleton. He was one of the foundation stones upon which the scaffolds, gas chambers, and crematoria of Nazism were erected. He knew what it was all about, understood what was being done. His role in the Hitler story was clearly defined at Nuremberg, when it was declared:

> He cast the pearls of his diplomatic experience before Hitler; guided Nazi diplomacy ... and was prepared to be the instrument of the Führer's policy so long as it added to the Reich.

20: ORDERS ARE ORDERS

'We U-boat men cannot and will not believe that the former Admirals Erich Raeder and Karl Doenitz must stay behind prison walls in Spandau,' Eberhard Godt, last commander of Germany's U-boat fleet, shouted to some 3,000 submarine shipmates who served in World War II. The thousands of ex-servicemen attending the rally roared approval of the call for the early release of their Spandau comrades.

Dönitz's lawyer, Dr Otto Kranzbühler, was endeavouring to advance his client's official freedom date by more than a year: to May 1955 instead of October 1956. This fresh approach was shrewdly timed to coincide with the termination of the official occupation of Western Germany on 5 May 1955, when the Allied Kommandatura would remain the governing authority in Berlin, retaining certain rights, powers, and responsibilities in the city. In particular, the Berlin police stayed under the command of the Allied authorities, who also had the right to take such emergency measures as were 'necessary to fulfil their international obligations, ensure public order, and maintain the status and security of the city'. The Occupation Powers became the allies of the Federal Republic. Their status did not change in Berlin, although they committed themselves to 'consult with the Federal Republic in regard to the exercise of their rights relating to Berlin'.

Dönitz and his lawyer thought that any significant shift of control in Berlin — particularly with the Federal Republic being given a louder voice in the city's affairs — might provide an opening for changing attitudes towards Spandau. Kranzbühler submitted to the Federal Government that, as

Dönitz had been arrested by British troops on 23 May 1945, time spent in custody before trial should be taken into account. The Bonn Foreign Office agreed; so did several right-wing newspapers, the Association of Returned Prisoners of War, and prominent members of the Free Democratic Party. Kranzbühler petitioned the three Ambassadors of the United States, France, and Britain, and Soviet High Commissioner Pushkin.

Sentences of the Nuremberg Tribunal were deemed to run from the day they were imposed.

Most of the war criminals gaoled in the British zone were ex-members of the armed forces. The demand for a reduction of sentences or for amnesty was also therefore put forward as a means of restoring the 'honour of the German soldier', and linked with the question of Germany's entry into Western defence. Nobody was more vociferous than Dönitz in charging that verdicts against many former members of the German Army and Navy maligned the German military and naval professions as a whole, despite the fact that the unquestioning exaltation of 'superior orders' as an absolution was totally rejected at Nuremberg. When Chancellor Adenauer raised with Sir Ivone Kirkpatrick the same defence as a mitigating point on behalf of Dönitz and Raeder, the British Commissioner answered:

> People are wrong in thinking that the prisoners are men who can justifiably claim merely to have executed military orders and to have committed acts which were only subsequently described as crimes by allied law.
>
> In the slave labour camps and concentration camps the brutality shown to inmates was indescribable. On this point I can only say that every decent German would be rightly

indignant and would demand punishment if a German treated one single dog as these millions of human beings were treated.

All these actions were crimes under the moral law and under the law of every civilized country. The question then arises whether a plea of acting under superior orders can be regarded as a complete defence. On this point it is interesting to observe that German courts conducting war crime trials do not regard this plea as absolving defendants from guilt. The German Government's treatment of Commandos during the war seems to me to dispose effectively of the argument put forward by some Germans that war criminals who were carrying out orders cannot justly be held responsible for their crimes. The theory of individual responsibility applies to all, victors and vanquished.

John McCloy's reaction was:

The sentences rendered at Nuremberg against members of the military profession were based on charges of excesses beyond anything which could possibly be justified on the grounds of military security. The individuals in question were convicted for directing or participating in savage measures of reprisal and oppression against civilian populations far exceeding the limits of international law or accepted military tradition. Whenever the heat of battle or true military considerations could persuasively be pleaded, a conscious effort was made to moderate sentences. In reaching my conclusions, I recognized, as did the courts and the Clemency Board, the bitter character of partisan warfare on certain of the fronts. But with every allowance for these considerations there still remain excesses which cannot be rationalized or excused. Where sentences have been imposed upon former officers, they have, of course, been based on individual responsibility and participation. These sentences reflect upon the individuals concerned, not upon the honour of the German military profession.

> With every disposition to grant consideration because officers are impelled to take measures calculated to protect their country and their command, there still remains, in these cases, an area of real guilt which, whatever his nationality, a professional soldier sensitive of his responsibilities cannot countenance.
>
> Much has been said about the honour of the German soldier and of the German officer. The suggestion has been made that condemnation of individual officers is a reflection on the German military profession as a whole. To condemn those who were not faithful to their professional obligations is not to condemn the whole profession any more than to condemn the doctors and lawyers who participated in the medical experiments and in the administration of people's courts under the Nazis is to condemn the medical and legal professions as a whole.

The plain fact was that the association of officers of the highest rank with Nazi 'liquidations' was closer than generally admitted, and their personal conduct in this connection placed them beyond military justification.

Petitions stressing the 'orders are orders' angle were also frequently submitted for the other five Spandau prisoners. On Albert Speer's behalf, it was stated that the armies of slaves he controlled as Minister of Production were simply allocated to him by Governmental authorities, and conditions under which the labour was confined and worked were directed entirely by concentration camp commanders in the case of civilians, and by the army in the case of war prisoners. However, enforced employment was illegal for civilians and contrary to the Hague Convention for prisoners of war. Furthermore, there is no doubt that this labour was inhumanly treated, constantly subjected to corporal punishment and other cruelties.

At no time did men like Admiral Dönitz and Field Marshal von Manstein — the sailor and soldier whom officers were taught to look up to as models of German officer virtue — show remorse for anything but their defeat. On the contrary, they went out of their way to brand as traitors the survivors of the genuine opposition to Hitler. They suffered no revolt of conscience against the immorality and infamy of Hitler's war.

Otto Kranzbühler, whose legal brilliance at Nuremberg saved Dönitz from many more years in gaol, was unable to achieve any remission of sentence in spite of persuasive fresh pleadings. The four-Powers rejected all the arguments.

In anticipation of years ahead requiring greater understanding of the handling of long-term inmates, it was decided to bring to Spandau staff with professional experience of such problems. During February 1955 the first American professional guard arrived. He had worked in an institution for mentally sick prisoners.

By the time spring and summer months of 1955 came round, Raeder had become too frail to continue enjoying work in the garden. He had to be content to sit on a garden stool twice daily, staring into space, no doubt absorbed by memories and regrets.

In June more professional guards arrived from United States prisons and demonstrated their efficient know-how in dealing with the psychological stresses of long-term inmates. The new Soviet Director was also persuaded to authorize two-hour garden working periods for both mornings and afternoons.

The Federal Government pressed again for Raeder's freedom. Early in August three identical letters were received by the Soviet Government from the three Western Powers. The letters pointed out that, as with Neurath, Raeder's age and medical condition were felt to warrant his release. On 24

September, again making the running, the Soviets decided to concede this point. The Spandau Directors met two days later and, after visiting Raeder's cell, the British doctor took him to the medical room, ostensibly for a further examination. Prisoner No. 4 never returned.

Raeder on Hitler's left taken at Kiel during a wartime inspection. General Blomberg is on Hitler's right.

Few passers-by outside the gaol recognized the seventy-nine-year-old man in a crumpled black suit who limped through the prison gates, supported by his wife and two walking sticks, as the former Commander-in-Chief of the German Navy. Clutching the bunch of roses brought by his wife, he was helped into a car, then driven to a Berlin hospital to pay a brief visit to an old friend. That afternoon he flew to Hanover, where a number of former naval and fleet air arm officers employed at the airport shook his hand. A car drove him from the airport to his home in the little Westphalian town of Lippstadt, where he was met quietly by a large crowd. Flowers and telegrams from many well-wishers awaited him at his apartment. The Free Democrats, second largest Party in the West German Government, telegraphed congratulations: 'We are happy over your return home and wish you a quick convalescence.'

The Spandau Prison Governors issued a statement declaring: 'The Governments of France, the Soviet Union, the United Kingdom and the United States of America decided to release Erich Raeder from Spandau prison on September 26 on account of his advanced age and the state of his health.'

Asked if he had any political ambitions, Raeder replied angrily: 'For God's sake no!' His wife interposed sarcastically: 'He only wants to be Emperor of China'; and Raeder: 'Trying to go into politics would just about complete my misfortunes. I never thought I would leave Spandau prison alive. I accustomed myself to the idea that I would end my life there.'

Determined to avoid further public attention, Konstantin von Neurath stayed quietly on his estate and seldom discussed the past. When his daughter suggested that he could dictate to her material for a book on his life, he declined, saying: 'I am afraid that it wouldn't be so helpful. I could only say how sad it was that I fell for all of Hitler's lies.'

With that excuse, the Baron was not even being honest with his own daughter. His reluctance to re-examine past actions and motives was undoubtedly prompted more by the uncomfortable thought of having to reassess himself in the process. It was not only Hitler's lies that he had fallen for; it was his own lies, to himself.

France's High Commissioner in Germany, François-Poncet, in whose joint charge Neurath was in Spandau, knew him better than any of his Allied colleagues did. François-Poncet had served as French Ambassador in Berlin throughout the Baron's term at the Wilhelmstraße Foreign Ministry, from 1931 to 1938; he was Ambassador to Italy 1938–40, was arrested by the Gestapo in 1943, and liberated by the Allies in 1945. He was thereafter appointed President of the French Red Cross, President of the Permanent Commission of the International Red Cross, then French Commissioner to the Allied High Commission in Germany from 1949 until he left the post in 1955. From many years of close association with the Baron, he recalled Neurath as possessing:

> Experience, common sense, and composure. He was level-headed, moderate and sensible. Unfortunately his virtues were marred by serious defects. He lacked frankness, was crafty, something of a liar, and a clumsy liar at that for he would get flustered as he lied... A weak character, wanting in moral courage. He would yield to pressure and was no doubt conscious of doing so. He was prepared to perform or condone acts he himself condemned so as to avoid the obloquy of slackness or cowardice. Also he was lazy.

For Christmas 1954 and 1955 Neurath sent greetings from his home to the remaining Spandau occupants via the prison chaplain. Then, almost sixteen months after his release, on 14 August 1956, a severe bout of asthma overtaxed his heart. Two days later a French guard informed Funk, Dönitz, Speer, Schirach, and Hess: 'Le Numero Trois est mort.' The aristocrat and war criminal whom Germany and the world had left behind had died in his country home at the age of eighty-three.

On 17 August his former Foreign Minister colleague Franz von Papen, who was acquitted at Nuremberg, laid a wreath bearing his and Rudolf Hess's names on the grave where Neurath was buried in the family plot. One newspaper obituary — in the *Deutsche Zeitung* — noted: 'There is no reason to doubt Neurath's human virtues and his personal abhorrence of Hitler's criminal policies. But this statesman's shield can never be washed entirely clean.'

Neurath's guilt was that, despite his declared hatred of Nazi methods, by collaborating and descending to their level he brought war crime retribution on himself. The Baron's favourite poem was recited at the funeral:

> Think and be quiet
> Feel more than you show
> Bow down before God
> And you stay your own master.

For ten years Karl Dönitz and Albert Speer had fought a non-stop battle in Spandau. The Grand Admiral could not forgive Hitler's architect and production wizard for admitting guilt at Nuremberg.

'It was dishonourable and disloyal to Hitler and to Germany,' Dönitz said bitterly.

On 30 September 1956 Dönitz was about to become the first of the Spandau seven to complete his sentence. On his last day in gaol, Funk and Schirach stuck close to him in the garden, hanging on to his every word. Talking big, he promised to use his lawyer and 'influential contacts among the Allies' to get the rest of them out.

'Don't forget I am still legally entitled to be regarded as Head of the German State,' he boasted imperiously, 'because the Führer's arrangement has never been formally revoked.'

In confirmation of this often repeated claim, he pointed out that Germany's extreme rightists had also declared that, as the

Third Reich had never been legally extinguished, his appointment as Hitler's successor was still valid. Dönitz was well aware that he had retained many admirers among the country's incorrigible nationalists, both young and old.

Hess and Speer kept their customary distance from the Admiral during that last day. Suddenly Dönitz approached Speer, but it was not for a reconciliation. 'What did I have to do with politics?' he complained. 'But for you, Hitler would never have had the idea of making me Chief of State. All my men have commands again, but look at me! Like a criminal. My career is wrecked.'

Speer counter-attacked: 'For ten years here you have slandered, disparaged, and ostracized me. This war killed millions of people. Millions more were murdered in the camps. All of us here were part of the regime, but your ten years here perturb you more than the fifty million dead.'

Both later calmed down, and Dönitz asked for a sedative to steady his nerves. Before they were locked into their cells again, he took leave of the others. Hess said: 'All the best, and rest up your nerves.'

Dönitz went over to Speer to say *auf Wiedersehen*. They shook hands and Speer wished him good luck.

The Russians did not want to give him his clothes until midnight, the exact moment when his sentence expired. When Western Prison Directors reminded the Soviets that this would mean he would still be in gaol after midnight, thereby imposing illegal detention, they agreed to hand him the clothing five minutes before midnight.

Because of reports received by the police of a 'Dönitz Movement' alleged to exist to re-establish him politically, special security measures were prepared to deal with demonstrations that might occur on his release. President of the Navy League Rear-Admiral Heye, who had commanded frogmen and naval saboteurs in the latter part of the war, appealed to the German Navy to refrain from turning Dönitz's release into a political jamboree.

Dönitz's wife, Inge, who had been in Berlin several days to finalize arrangements, said: 'He is about to be born again, into a new world.'

The large crowd outside the gaol included an army of press correspondents, TV crews and photographers. When a limousine with two passengers emerged from the prison gates a few minutes after midnight, the press and crowd surged mistakenly towards it, permitting Dönitz and his wife, who were following in a taxi, to get away seconds later. West Berlin police, out in strength, deliberately prevented photographers from recording the scene for reasons best known to their commander, and impeded reporters from taking up the pursuit. Protesting to the Western Allies concerning what they described as police brutality against photographers, the Board of Governors of the West Berlin Foreign Press Association said batons were used, several photographers' cameras were smashed, and reporters were almost run down by official vehicles to stop them chasing Dönitz. Clearly someone in authority considered that the man who became titular head of the Third Reich on 1 May 1945 still warranted VIP police protection on being released from gaol on 1 October 1956.

The Dönitz taxi headed straight for the Berlin suburb of Zehlendorf and the villa of his old naval comrade Commander Horst Else. Offered a glass of wine, Dönitz said he had not touched alcohol for eleven years — which was not true — sipped only half a glass, and went to bed.

He declined to say whether he regarded himself as still Führer and Chancellor of the Reich. The West German

Government, treating him as a retired officer, was to pay him a normal admiral's pension.

Grim and unsmiling, with an occasional nervous twitch of his face and hands, his shabby blue-grey suit and prison boots the only reminders of the years of captivity just ended, Dönitz said:

> Do not forget that until yesterday I was in prison. In a cage. Place yourself in the position of a man who has been separated from the outside world for eleven and a half years. I'm not in a position to pass any judgements. I have no opinion about the situation existing outside, therefore it would be foolish of me if I said anything or criticized anything, so it is my task now to be silent and to fit myself into the world again. I want to be silent today and I shall be silent in the future.

From Berlin he flew with his wife to the city of Düsseldorf to spend a few days with his lawyer, Otto Kranzbühler; then he returned to his ground-floor apartment in a house outside Hamburg, two miles from Iron Chancellor Bismarck's grave. This became the retirement home of the man who had masterminded the submarine campaign that destroyed about fifteen million tons of Allied and neutral shipping, with a loss of tens of thousands of lives — the man they called the 'Weekend Führer' because he was Head of State for only a few days before Germany surrendered.

Although, on being freed from Spandau, Dönitz had said he intended to remain silent, he did not. Nothing came of his boast that somehow he would get Speer, Schirach, and Hess a remission of sentence, nor of his post-Spandau ambitions for himself. Those prepared to restore him as Führer chose the wrong horse, for he found it hard to adjust to the new Germany and outmanoeuvre the many skilful rivals able to outpace him politically. The beaten Admiral was compelled to settle for endeavouring to re-establish himself with a book on his naval career, but it had little impact.

Seven years after his release Dönitz was invited to lecture to three hundred pupils at a high school in the town of Geesthacht. He was asked to talk about naval and military problems of World War II, about the Nuremberg trials, and his imprisonment. The lecture had been arranged by a former Christian Democrat member of the Land Parliament of Schleswig-Holstein.

During the ninety-minute lecture, Dönitz defended Germany's war against Poland and the unrestricted U-boat tactics; asserted that the Nazi invasion of Poland was justified because Hitler had no cause to expect Britain to declare war on Germany; defended submarine 'total warfare' on the basis that the Baltic Sea 'would otherwise have become an English lake'. For justification of Hitler's invasion of Norway he used a parable: 'If one housewife makes her way into a bakery ahead of another housewife, this is not a punishable offence' — referring to the notorious rumour that a full-scale British invasion of Norway would have occurred if Hitler had not stepped in first. This story is still propagated through a number of German history books.

For imprisonment in Spandau, Dönitz blamed Stalin, although in fact he was condemned for authorizing unrestricted attacks almost exclusively against Western shipping in the Atlantic. This educated guess was in some respects accurate, however, because, as official documents referred to earlier in this book reveal, it was Stalin who insisted on a trial instead of agreeing to major war criminals being shot out of hand.

Dönitz's school lecture was warmly applauded by the pupils, a response that many of the boys' parents regarded as more disturbing than the Admiral's views. But within three years he had changed his mind about one thing: in a 1966 interview published in *Christ und Welt*, he confessed that, in so far as crimes against humanity were concerned, the basic principle underlying the Nuremberg trial was 'an understandable effort at purification and, as such, better than no effort at all'. So at least some chink of light seemed to have burst through to the former Führer by the time he reached his mid-seventies.

At sixty-six, Funk looked like a man in his eighties. His diabetes had got worse, but he deliberately poured a bowl full of sugar into his coffee the night before a urine sample was to be obtained from him for testing. He wanted the diabetes to show up worse than it was and risked harming himself in the hope that it might yet speed his release. The tactics finally began to work. The self-poisoning took effect and he was bedridden with bladder inflammation and a swollen liver.

Possibly in an effort to make a favourable impression, during the past year the wily Funk had apparently taken to studying books on Soviet history, East German newspapers, and even Russian conversation phrase-books. Furthermore, he casually claimed to have had Russian ancestors.

Grinning at Schirach, he said: 'Maybe I've finally discovered the secret of how to win friends and influence Russians — by learning to speak their language a little.'

The West German Foreign Minister, Heinrich von Bretano, pressed for the ailing Funk's release. Bretano also advocated freedom for Speer, but on totally different grounds.

Hess's case was also considered again from a purely health viewpoint. During April 1957 the long list of psychiatrists who had sought to fathom his mind grew even longer: three more checked and tested him. Specialists still seemed to be wondering whether there was sufficient medical justification for converting yesterday's sins into current emotional ills. They discovered, as others had over the years, that chronically vague Hess had an amazingly detailed recall of the past when it suited him or when he was caught off guard. The latest French and two American psychiatrists concurred unanimously that, although Hess was prone to what they termed 'hysterical disturbances', he was remarkably fit for his age and his general condition did not warrant transfer to a mental institution or hospital.

On 14 May 1957, Frau Funk was asked by the gaol authorities to come to Berlin. No reason was given.

The four prisoners were in the garden when a Russian warder asked Funk to follow him. He was taken first to his cell, then on to the medical room where he was given a sedative and told he was to be freed immediately. His clothes were ready for him in the visiting room, and his wife was outside in a car in the yard. A communiqué from the four-Powers stated that he had been set free because of age and ill health.

Funk, whose utterances during the war had reflected unbounded confidence in the future of Nazi Germany, had to exchange his sumptuous Reichsbank suite with its gilded handcarved baroque-style furniture, fabulous Gobelins and handstamped leather-covered walls, for a sparse cell in Spandau. His gourmet office meals used to be served by liveried footmen.

Funk was driven away from Spandau to live only another three years in obscurity in Düsseldorf.

21: AND THEN THERE WERE THREE

The grim fortress-exterior of the gaol aroused visions of Dr Manette in the Bastille, of the prisoner of Chillon in his dank dungeon, and of the Count of Monte Cristo scraping his way through to freedom through two eternal decades. Those were fictional characters, however. Rudolf Hess, Albert Speer, and Baldur von Schirach — Spandau's remaining inmates — were real, justly tried and sentenced. The trials that had sent them to prison were more than trials of individual defendants for individual crimes. They were group-trials of men who, while participating separately, were engaged in a vast criminal enterprise against international laws and humanity. No decent-minded person would excuse or wash away one drop of the blood in which the Hitler gang will forever be steeped. Hess, Speer and Schirach might have been executed in 1946 along with some of their partners in infamy. Instead, they were buried alive in prison.

Had the United States, Britain and France been the only nations involved, it would all have ended long ago, through either a remission of sentences or transfer to other general prisons. The question was whether the four-Power gaolers should display moral superiority by extending to the three men the mercy they had denied to others, and the humanity they had once rejected.

When Hess, Speer, and Schirach were the only ones left in Spandau, negotiations were again initiated to close the gaol. A compromise was proposed between continued confinement and the grant of unrestricted freedom. It was suggested that if complete freedom was unachievable by international agreement then some arrangement should be reached by which the three could regain liberty by being placed on parole under open arrest, with a duty to report periodically to the authorities. Supervision could be gradually relaxed until, almost imperceptibly, it would cease to be enforced at all. It was felt that the civilized world would agree that the justice seen to be done years ago should be tempered with mercy, with the remaining long and 'life' sentences remitted in favour of well-behaved captives.

Since the release of her father, Winifred von Mackensen was no longer at the forefront of the fight to free Spandau prisoners; and the political manoeuvring of Luise Funk, Inge Dönitz and Erika Raeder similarly ended with the return of their husbands. Nevertheless, the battle for the remaining three never let up for an instant. Families, lawyers and politicians continued pulling every possible string to get them out ahead of their allotted time. James B. Conant took over as US High Commissioner from John McCloy, and he was not prepared to bend with changes in political and public attitudes. He insisted: 'They were justly sentenced gangsters.' Explaining that criminality had been the Hitler style from earliest Nazi days, Conant expounded:

'One of the most significant factors in Hitler's success was the plain gangsterism of his followers. The strong-arm methods of Hitler's thugs became increasingly bolder. Hitler aimed to control the streets by terror, and often did. Civil authorities proved powerless in many instances. Street fighting between Communists and Nazis became frequent and bloody occurrences.

'The regular police — following the lead of the democratic politicians — virtually abdicated, while retaining their nominal positions, and the various private armies brawled and killed at will, while they stood by. They stood by most steadfastly when the Nazis were winning.'

Speer remarked philosophically: 'Prison would be harder to bear if we always felt on the verge of being free.'

'They'll never trust us, or Germany, again unless German people destroy the legend that we are a country congenitally devoted to acts of aggression,' Schirach ventured. 'Even Anthony Eden said Hitler didn't want a second world war, but deliberately created situations that he must have realized would inevitably lead to its outbreak.'

Two months after Funk's departure from the gaol, an historic moment occurred that was to affect the three's chances of freedom. The European Economic Community, the 'Common Market', was born in July 1957. At first the Kremlin sneered at the giant concept, and the Moscow Institute for World Economy and International Relations forecast that the Community would never change the nature of European capitalism. (Five years later the same institute changed its mind.) But as the Community dream became reality, Soviet Premier Nikita Khrushchev, recognizing it as a formidable barrier to Soviet ambitions of further European expansion, decided that if the West was pushed out of Berlin, Europe's future could be settled on Russia's terms. So in November 1958 Hess, Speer, and Schirach found themselves in the midst of another Berlin tug-of-war. The Kremlin created the crisis by charging that the status of West Berlin threatened Soviet security and peace.[17]

---

[17] On 4 August 1950 the Berlin City Assembly passed a constitution defining its special position under technical three-Power control. Under German constitutional law Berlin is a *Land* of the Federal Republic, but this law was suspended by three-Power reservations. Nevertheless West Berlin sent representatives to the Bundestag (Lower House) and Bundesrat (Upper House) in Bonn, although

During the worst periods of Cold War, prevailing tensions outside and inside Spandau created a state of affairs in which almost all the ingredients of a real war were present, apart from the sound of guns and the sight of blood.

Explaining the news to Hess, Schirach said: 'Moscow has threatened that if, within six months, the three Western Powers haven't settled the problem, they'll let the East Germans act any way they like in respect of land, water and air communications affecting the city, and end all contact with the West. You know what that almost certainly means: a repeat of the blockade. Before Khrushchev decided to challenge the West again, he must have weighed the risk not only of limited local war but also of nuclear war.'

A December 1958 public petition appealing for Speer's release was monumentally mistimed, coming as it did hard on renewed Soviet Berlin threats. More than two thousand of Speer's home-town neighbours in Heidelberg petitioned the four Heads of State, but Spandau's inmates were once again embroiled in Berlin diplomacy. All three Western commandants decided that it would be advisable to 'show the flag' regularly at the gaol to demonstrate to the Soviet authorities that they would not allow any attempts to manipulate the prison's regulations and its prisoners as political pawns in the Berlin chess game. The American, British and French commandants began to make a habit of frequently inspecting the gaol and talking to each of the prisoners, to the obvious exasperation of the gaol's Soviet Director, who was always present. The Kremlin got the message and was careful not to precipitate any Spandau crisis.

---

these representatives had no vote in the plenary sessions of either House. To be valid in West Berlin, Federal law had to be specially adopted there.

During the following year, Moscow manoeuvred for an East-West meeting of Heads of State to discuss Berlin. Soviet officials started to hint to Western diplomats that it might now be advisable to release Hess, Speer and Schirach, or place them under German supervision. This, it was indicated, could become necessary if Russia was to carry out its threat to withdraw completely its forces from Berlin and hand over its powers to the East Germans. The Soviet Embassy in Bonn even suggested that the Nazis' fate could become the responsibility of the Red Cross. The USSR had previously refused to permit the Red Cross organization any access to the gaol.

Meanwhile Hess had increasingly been having bouts of stomach clutching and moaning, apparently writhing in agony on the floor of his cell. Investigations finally produced a surprise cause. Medical officers were certain he had deliberately been swallowing laundry detergent to bring on cramps. In plain old soldiers' language, he was 'swinging the lead'. An order was issued ruling that he could use washing and cleaning materials only under supervision. Hess switched tactics; one November 1959 morning a French warder found him lying on a blood-drenched bed with a slashed wrist. The duty medical officer, who was making the rounds at the time, stitched the wrist wound.

'I wanted to end my life,' Hess told him.

He had used a lens from his spectacles to cut the wrist, but doctors, warders and Directors were unanimous that the 'suicide' was planned to ensure that it would not prove fatal. Hess was well aware of the warders' regular rounds and realized that the medical officer would be conveniently in the vicinity at the time. He was nevertheless given a further medical going over and declared 'normal in all respects'. From then on he was supplied with plastic lens spectacles.

Schirach's word for Hess's attitude in prison was 'oysterization'. When asked questions he did not want to answer, Hess would retire into his shell. 'I would sum him up as aloof and inscrutable, with a strong fanatical streak that would be produced whenever the occasion required it,' said Schirach. 'In a sense he seemed to consider himself a sort of adopted son of Hitler. He was never inclined to be talkative, and in conversation didn't convey the impression of great ability, but people who knew him best would have agreed that first impressions were deceptive. He certainly wielded in Germany more influence than was generally believed.'

Even though Speer did not get close to Hess, or come to terms with Schirach and his ideas, the three found themselves becoming increasingly dependent on each other. They made a habit of walking together in the garden every day, weather permitting.

After years of convincing himself that drugs were injected into food to control the victims, Hess admitted to his companions: 'I've stopped thinking that my food is doctored to give me stomach cramps and other symptoms. After all, I can take any of the food that is on the table for all of us.'

A couple of months later, in June, the Spandau three heard that Funk had died, aged sixty-nine; and in mid-November Raeder also died. Their restored freedom had been very short. Raeder had written memoirs that pointedly avoided reminiscences of the Spandau years. Like the man himself, the account of his life was dull. He wrote:

'I always believed it would come to a controversy with Great Britain. It is the tragedy of my life that the development took a different course.'

Two momentous events in 1961 had traumatic repercussions within Spandau Prison: the trial of Adolf Eichmann and the building of the Berlin Wall.

Hess, Speer and Schirach had heard of the kidnapping by Israeli agents in South America of the infamous Eichmann. When his trial opened in Jerusalem in April 1961 each of them warned their families that trial evidence would undoubtedly refocus world attention on war crime atrocities to such an extent that pressure for early remission of their sentences would be futile for a long time to come.

They had heard that West Germany's Ambassador in Moscow had notified Bonn that there was scant chance of Speer or Schirach being freed before completion of their sentences.

'As newspapers swamp the public with stories of the activities of Eichmann and his gangs of anti-Semitic "experts", and also of his alcoholic friend Kaltenbrunner, there will be few people left still prepared to openly support mercy for us,' Schirach remarked gloomily to Hess.[18] 'People reading the gory details of the "emigration" of Jews from the occupied countries, which Eichmann initiated, and of his death camp convoys, will be in no mood to listen to our appeals for clemency.'[19]

---

[18] Dr Ernest Kaltenbrunner, former head of the Austrian SS and one of Himmler's top aides, was tried and convicted at Nuremberg. He was hanged on 16 October 1946, together with Foreign Minister Ribbentrop and the Jew-baiter Streicher.

[19] Eichmann's power over the Jews became absolute after the decree signed by Martin Bormann on 1 July 1943 depriving Jews of recourse to ordinary tribunals and placing them under the jurisdiction of the Gestapo. He was hanged by the Israelis in June 1962, his body cremated and the ashes thrown into the sea.

As if mentally dismissing Schirach's references to Eichmann's organization of mass murder, Hess's sole comment was: 'He managed to stay free for almost nine years in South America and worked in the Mercedes-Benz factory there.'

Seated beside Hess under a walnut tree in the prison garden, Schirach reminisced about Eichmann: 'You were a prisoner in England when Eichmann "planning lunches" at his Kurfürstendamm offices became a daily ritual. Himmler was present whenever possible. Between dessert and brandy they used to debate the results of concentration camp medical experiments and the average human intakes of gas chambers.

'Kaltenbrunner was a regular guest at the lunch table. Looking at that ugly, vulgar, vast hulk of a man, one would never believe that he was an intellectual and a former lawyer. He enjoyed visiting camps and watching people being gassed.

When the Führer and Himmler gave Eichmann the job of completing the "final solution of the Jewish problem", Eichmann and Kaltenbrunner were in constant contact. It was almost laughable how Kaltenbrunner always used to ask solicitously about the health of Eichmann's family, then the pair of them would issue orders authorizing the killing of thousands in the camps.'

Chain-smoking Kaltenbrunner was a veteran Austrian Nazi who had joined one of the first groups of National Socialist students whilst he was studying law at university. He was nearly seven feet tall. His delicate, nicotine-stained hands contrasted surprisingly with his massive physique and coarse, duel-scarred face.

Joining Hess and Schirach in the garden and hearing the conversation topic, Speer commented: 'I have absolutely nothing to say for myself when a name like Eichmann's is mentioned. I shall never be able to get over having served in a leading position of a regime whose true energies were devoted to an extermination programme.'

On the hot summer Sunday of 13 August 1961 the whole gaol was agog with news. Berlin was being divided and sealed off. Three days later erection began of the Berlin Wall, under the supervision of armed contingents. Concrete posts sunk into the streets were draped with barbed wire; the complete closure of the Eastern sector had begun. The wall's construction amounted to the final incorporation of East Berlin into the German Democratic Republic: a situation whose equivalent had never been permitted to develop in the Western half of the city.

The Russian Director of Spandau and the three Western Directors were not the only antagonists within the prison. The relationship between Schirach and Speer deteriorated to such an extent during this period that they barely exchanged a word. Evidence in the Eichmann trial aroused revulsion and guilt in Speer, which prompted constant self-recrimination. Schirach loftily declared this was unwarranted. The increasing hopelessness of the fight to curtail their sentences, as well as the threat posed by the Berlin Wall itself, heightened the strain on the three prisoners. Speer was further incensed by Schirach saying: 'We were not responsible for Hitler being a pathological anti-Semite.'

Speer retorted angrily: 'We were guilty of accepting as a matter of course Hitler's hatred of the Jews. It doesn't matter how much or how little we knew of the horrors perpetrated. As senior Ministers, we were party to them. No justification and no apologies are adequate.'

Speer never bothered to argue the issue with fanatical Hess, but could not tolerate the so-called sensitive Schirach's hypocritical stance. Schirach, who was not as effeminate as he often let himself appear to be, defended his role in the Nazi Party throughout his Spandau years, and until the day he died.

Speer kept in closer touch with the outside world from spring of 1962, after a pocket Japanese transistor radio was smuggled in to him. Using an earphone hidden under his cap, this was the first time in seventeen years he had been able to listen to the radio. It was from one of the news bulletins that he heard of a placard and pamphlet campaign in several Bavarian towns calling for the release of Hess. Written in six languages, placards announced: 'Free Rudolf Hess, the man who tried in 1941 to end World War II and who is still in prison twenty years later.' Speer informed Hess about the campaign, without revealing the source of his information.

Hess began to play up again; this time his teeth were the focus of dispute. He refused to allow the British dentist to extract his last six teeth. Appealing to the Directors, he maintained that no operation should be performed on a prisoner without the prisoner's consent. The Directors concurred. Other opinions were requested. French and Soviet dentists also advised the removal of the surviving teeth. Hess had only one more card to play; he asked for an American opinion, and got it. After further X-rays of the six teeth the American dentist decided they could be saved.

In December 1963 Schirach began limping badly. X-ray examination revealed blood pressure problems. He was given four-hourly check-ups, and injections to prevent blood clots. As soon as news of his illness reached his family it was passed on to West German politician Thomas Dehler, who immediately petitioned Soviet Premier Khrushchev for Schirach's release. 'Herr Dehler made the request "for humanitarian reasons",' a spokesman for the Free Democratic

Party said. A former chairman of the Free Democratic Party, Dehler was Minister of Justice for several years, and in 1963 vice-president of the Bundestag, the lower house of Parliament. He advised the Ambassadors of the United States, Britain, and France of the telegram he had sent to Moscow. Khrushchev ignored it.

Apart from Speer's illicit transistor radio, the Spandau three were far better informed on international matters beyond their cell walls than they had been since Nuremberg. From 1964 their families were again allowed to send books on virtually any subject, although books containing references to events of the years 1933-45 were still barred.

At the end of April 1964 Hess heard from his wife that she had just lost the latest stage of her ten-year fight to have him legally regarded as a prisoner of war, so that she could claim a maintenance allowance. On 23 April a court decided that he was not entitled to be classified as a war prisoner. Under the law, dependants of men who were still prisoners of war after March 1945 could receive a special maintenance allowance. The law was introduced to help the families of men still in Russian camps. Ilse Hess maintained that her husband's flight to Scotland in 1941 was made at the instigation of the Führer, despite previous statements to the contrary. She further claimed he should be considered a prisoner of war because he wore his uniform when he was first imprisoned in Britain after landing there. Totally rejecting the submissions, the court said a man was not necessarily a soldier because he wore a uniform.

A few months later, November brought a momentous day in Hess's imprisonment years — the longest any of the Spandau seven had served. For the first time since his Nuremberg trial, he asked to see his lawyer. 'I want to see Dr Seidl from

Munich,' he informed the Soviet Director of the gaol, who was in control at the time. 'It is time I made my will.'

A Russian telegram brought Dr Alfred Seidl hurrying to Berlin. To his surprise, he was not confronted with an ailing client. Hess's hair was grey, but Seidl thought he looked well.

'Although I feel perfectly fit, I simply felt it was time to make a will.'

'There is no real necessity for a will,' Seidl advised. 'Under German inheritance laws your family inherit automatically anything you leave.'

Turning to the question of appeals on his behalf, Hess said: 'I do not wish you to press that I be released as an act of clemency. I could not accept that. You must fight on the basis that I was convicted illegally. I should not have been condemned for preparing aggressive war in 1939. In such a case, Sir Anthony Eden and the French Prime Minister Guy Mollet should also have been condemned for the attack on Egypt at the time of Suez.'

The thirty-minute talk that took place in the presence of an official witness became more personal when Dr Seidl asked: 'Why do you not receive your family?'

'I do not wish to upset myself or them with the sadness of greeting and farewell,' Hess replied. 'I talk with Schirach and Speer and notice that after they have had visits they are left in a state of collapse. For myself I do not wish to undergo such an experience.'

Discussing health, Hess assured his lawyer that he considered himself to be reasonably fit, apart from some circulation trouble in his legs.

As Dr Seidl was about to leave, Hess again emphasized that he did not wish to be freed on a clemency basis. Then, reminding his lawyer that Speer and Schirach could well be released the following year, he added: 'I hardly think I shall be kept alone in the most expensive prison in the world. In fact I look forward to being pardoned.'

Ilse Hess was not so optimistic. 'The final glimmer of hope of Spandau being wound up altogether will come when Speer and Schirach are released,' she said. 'We have done everything in our power. Only the Federal Government can manage to bring the former Allies to a conference table for a talk about the prison, but it behaves with extreme passivity; only words of consolation. I have not the slightest illusion about the success of efforts to bring the fate of my husband before public opinion; nor do I fully accept reports that the Russians are no longer interested in keeping the remaining prisoners of Spandau in captivity and would respond to an initiative by the Bonn Government.

'I was advised that I should allow my husband to be declared of unsound mind. Then, perhaps, he might be released. I would never do such a thing. It would mean stabbing him in the back. It would be a hard blow to his self-respect. He is mentally completely sound.'

Dr Seidl agreed. Following his visit with Hess, he said: 'He is not mad.'

Two months later, as Schirach and Hess were walking together in the garden, Schirach complained of stabbing flashes and spots before his right eye whenever his right foot met the ground. Hess called a warder across. Schirach was led to his cell; the duty medical officer was summoned. The cell was darkened and an eye-patch was provided for Schirach's right eye. The following morning ophthalmoscopic examination confirmed that two-thirds of the retina was almost completely detached. The right eye was virtually blind. He was immediately transferred to the prison infirmary, where both eyes were covered and he was made to lie with body elevated and head lowered, angled slightly to the right. He was told to remain still and permitted to sit up only for meals.

At an emergency meeting of all the gaol's medical officers the Western doctors recommended immediate transfer to hospital. The Russians wanted the operation performed within the gaol. The Allies refused, pointing out that the prison's medical facilities were inadequate for such delicate surgery. The Russians gave in and the now white-haired Schirach was sent to the British Military Hospital, where an attempt was made to stitch the retina back into place. When he returned to the prison infirmary several weeks later he was still almost blind in the eye; doctors were concerned that if the left eye became affected he could be totally blind. He could scarcely see even light with the right eye.

His general condition was further complicated by the onset during February 1965 of thrombosis in the left leg. This responded to treatment, but his sight continued to deteriorate.

Returning to gaol, Schirach was supplied with a low chair to enable him to sit with feet up on the bed. Suppressing animosity and feelings of contempt towards him, Speer requested to be allowed to read to him for thirty minutes every morning. In the afternoons Hess was permitted to visit Schirach's cell for the same period of time. Schirach was granted longer garden exercise periods and practised walking in the garden and cell with his eyes completely shut, saying:

'I want to be prepared for the worst.'

Convinced that his father would become completely blind, his twenty-nine-year-old lawyer son Klaus asked to be allowed to call in the best possible specialist help. In particular he wanted Professor Meyer-Schwikerath, of Essen, who had developed laser-beam techniques to weld detached retinas.

'Only a doctor from one of the four-Powers can examine a Nazi war criminal,' the prison's Soviet Director insisted, but the American eye surgeon warned: 'It could already be too late. In Berlin only the Germans are equipped for such an operation.' The Soviet authorities still refused to authorize a German doctor being called in.

US Prison Director Colonel Eugene Bird, who assumed his post towards the end of 1964, threatened the co-Directors: 'This man could be going blind. If he's not allowed out of the prison we will force him out under guard.' Soviet Director Lazarov stormed from the conference room. Bird followed, to warn: 'We are not going to bear the responsibility that through lack of guts or character we allowed this man to go blind.'

Lazarov undertook to report to his headquarters and return immediately with an answer. He did not. He suffered a thrombosis attack. His Chief Warder replaced him and advised that he had secured consent for Schirach to be treated by the German professor in hospital.

There were already indications of the imminence of similar retina detachment in the left eye. The operation, performed in May, was successful, however. As he lay in bed, Schirach confessed to Corporal Graham Lazenby from Yorkshire, one of the military police who guarded him in hospital: 'I firmly believed that what Hitler stood for and promised to do was right. I found I was wrong about this and now recognize the Nazi creed for what it was — a horrible thing. There is no excuse for what we did.'

While confined to bed, Schirach liked Corporal Lazenby to stand by the room's barred window, study the street below and describe what he could see. During months in hospital he often asked about the latest Beatles hits and even nicknamed his British guards 'Beatles'. To sustain friendly relationships with the guards he talked endlessly of his family and inquired about theirs. He also pointedly repeated from time to time regrets for his Nazi past. Nevertheless, one morning, whilst admitting to one of the hospital guards, Corporal Terry Hollingsbee, that his punishment was justified, he could not resist adding: 'Undoubtedly we would have done the same to Lord Baden Powell, my equivalent in Britain, had we won the war.'

For six months the German eye specialist was allowed to check progress regularly. Schirach needed a cane to help his mobility. When, at the close of a medical examination, he gratefully clasped his doctor's hand, the strictly forbidden handshake was reported to the Soviet Director, who demanded punishment for the breach of regulations. Schirach was told that his next authorized letter home was now cancelled as a penalty for the handshake.

Schirach's months of near blindness defused the tensions that had persisted for so long between him and Speer. It was difficult to continue to detest and ignore a man verging on losing his sight, especially after having volunteered to read to him daily. On 1 January 1966, the final year of their sentence, the reconciled pair trudged round the garden together discussing the remaining months ahead.

'I feel like the contents of a champagne bottle waiting to escape,' Schirach said with suppressed excitement. 'I'm employing every possible distraction to act like a wired cork on me and prevent me from bubbling over until I'm released. Our debt to some of the past and present staff here is enormous. They, our letters home, and visits from family are largely responsible for the fact that we're still sane. None of our appeals for clemency got anywhere, but at least having hopes helped keep us going.'

After a thoughtful silence Speer commented: 'All these years I have had the feeling of walking on unstable ground. I have never been able to do more than guess what I intended honestly and what hypocritically.'

As their final Spandau time passed, Schirach and Speer became increasingly nervous and short-tempered to the point of rudeness to staff. Normally such behaviour would have automatically resulted in punishment and a temporary withdrawal of privileges; but understanding the inmates' stress, the Prison Directors agreed to ease the enforcement of punishment regulations.

On 10 May, Hess would not leave his cell, refused to eat, and sat staring at a wall. Nothing and no one could alter his mood or extract any explanation from him.

'It's all phoney!' Schirach yelled from his cell, as always infuriated by Hess's attention-getting ploys.

One of the staff remembered that the date was the twenty-fifth anniversary of the flight to Scotland. Hess had been a prisoner ever since.

'He feels like Napoleon, even if only on St Helena,' commented Schirach.

As the Spandau three spent the final September days working, and walking in the garden, Schirach became almost inseparable from Hess. He advised him to continue conveying the impression of insanity. Speer later counselled against this, warning that such tactics would throw a shadow on everything he had ever done.

The day of freedom approached. Of the two men soon to be released, one was fifty-nine, bowed, partially blind, and certainly broken; the second was sixty-one, upright, mentally alert, and of steely determination. The Germany they had last seen twenty years before had been gasping for life, battered into unconsciousness, scavenging dustbins for food scraps, afraid of the future. What they were about to witness on their first day of liberty could make them think that Germany had finally, in fact, won the war.

Schirach, who had transported 50,000 children from Nazi-occupied territories to forced labour camps, who had replaced Christian crosses with swastikas and announced 'God's command is to stand together and fight for Adolf Hitler and the German Fatherland. If you do that you will be fulfilling My will', had arranged a secret Bavarian hideout to complete memoirs he had been illicitly writing in gaol. This man, who wrote a special brand of hate into children's books, now aimed to live the life of a recluse and spend retirement playing with his grandchildren. He had no possible role in reborn Germany.

Speer, on the other hand — whom Hitler had called a genius — intended to carve his career anew both as architect and author.

Speer was returning to the family villa in Heidelberg where, in the current telephone book, his name had reappeared: 'Albert Speer, architect, 50 Schloß Wolfbrunnen-Way: 26895.' He considered himself fortunate to have survived and to be given a second chance. For on receiving his twenty years' imprisonment, he had commented with grim humour: 'It would be laughable if I were to protest against the sentence.' Remarkably, he was now about to emerge from prison with relatively undamaged morale and mental power. Would he be the one to become a focal personality for the rebirth of German nationalism? He was certainly the most suitable of the seven for such a purpose.

'I hope to find outside the spirit of a country that has turned its back on the Nazi past,' he told Schirach.

The day before their release, Schirach and Speer strolled in the garden with Hess. Speer calculated that the imaginary round-the-world walking tour he had undertaken over the years had covered 31,936 kilometres. Both Schirach and Speer realized that it was impossible to imagine the feelings of seventy-two-year-old Hess as they took their farewell walk. They aimlessly discussed the weather. Schirach related an anecdote about his granddaughter Viktoria, then suddenly said encouragingly to Hess: 'You may not remain here long after we've gone. Don't forget that Raeder, Funk and Neurath were all released before their time.'

Hess listened quietly, but Schirach observed that his words had failed to penetrate the resignation. Schirach could see he was a broken man, but knew he was not mentally unsound. All four Governors of the prison also agreed he was sane, but to a duty warder Schirach remarked anxiously: 'Once he's alone, he might well go mad as he endures the heaviest punishment that exists, and to which he was not condemned: lifelong solitary confinement. No man can stand that.'

On 30 September, the last day, Speer, Schirach and Hess took advantage of the garden as usual; but on returning to the cell block, Hess informed warders that he wished to be left alone and would be taking a strong sedative. After shaking hands with Schirach and Speer he disappeared into his cell, calling to the warder to put the light out. The request was granted — though it was only five o'clock, and under Spandau regulations lights out was at 6.45 p.m.

Speer attempted to speak to him at supper time. Hess waved him away and was not seen again by either of his fellow prisoners.

A coming-out reception was expected, but arrangements outside the prison broke down as thousands of Berliners swarmed into the area. The police, who had not anticipated such a large crowd, decided to permit them to line the road running past the gates — the route cars from the prison were scheduled to take when they drove out. British military police on duty at the main entrance refused to accept bouquets for Schirach and Speer. As the time approached for their departure, the carefully prepared security collapsed into a shambles as sightseers joked, jostled, and sang.

Just prior to 11.30 P.M. Schirach and Speer changed into the fresh set of clothes they had been given. Speer was even issued the old ski jacket in which he had reached the gaol. At 11.30 they were led before the four Prison Directors. The British Director, Ralph Banfield, in charge of the gaol that month, completed the release formalities, handing over the few possessions taken from them on their arrival twenty years before.

At 11.45 the prison gates opened to allow two cars to enter: one with Speer's wife Margarete and lawyer Dr Flaeschner, the other with Schirach's sons Klaus and Richard. Whenever Margarete Speer had previously attended the gaol she had felt as if she was being conducted into a mausoleum to visit someone who was not fully dead, yet somehow not alive.

At a minute to midnight the four Directors accompanied the two prisoners to the outer door, where their relatives were waiting. Speer and Schirach shook hands, wished each other well, parted, and went to their respective cars.

At the stroke of twelve the giant main gates swung open. Floodlights mounted on platforms erected opposite the gaol stabbed through the darkness, bathing the scene in glaring light. A battery of camera bulbs flashed, and cheers rose from sections of the crowd of 6,000 as the two black Mercedes shot out of the steel gates. Both were accompanied by police escort cars. Speer's car was instructed to leave first.

The two ex-prisoners, pale but smiling, waved to noisy gesticulating Berliners who had waited for hours for a glimpse of these former architects of Hitler's Third Reich. Seated on the back seat with his wife, Speer produced a little gold watch from a trouser pocket and gave it to her, claiming he had assembled it in the prison workshop. She disbelieved him, and was right, because Dr Flaeschner had slipped it to him in the car. It had all been arranged during an earlier visit by the lawyer to the gaol. In the second car Schirach, with a patch over his blind eye, was beside his son Klaus.

Speer went straight to the fashionable Gerhus Hotel, in the Grünwald suburb, once the home of Nazi VIPs in the heyday of the Third Reich. Schirach spent the night at the Berlin Hilton, had a champagne-and-oysters party, and sent a message of thanks to doctors and nurses at the British Military Hospital who had helped save his sight.

At a midnight press conference in his hotel, Speer expressed thanks for the treatment he had received at the prison. Declining to discuss the mental state of Hess, he declared that during the final three days Hess had shown a 'normal reaction' to the inevitable strain of watching the other two prisoners preparing to leave. Facing a battery of microphones, and speaking in German, French and English, Speer added:

'I think that you have been not quite correct in your reporting of conditions in Spandau Prison. The beginning of the imprisonment was, of course, in Stalin's time. But Stalin is no longer here. Since his death so much has changed. We are — excuse me, I must say we were — treated correctly and properly the whole time. Food was ample. I have no complaints.'

The following morning both men left the city by air: Schirach, accompanied by his sons Robert, Richard and Klaus in a fourteen-seater aircraft chartered by *Stern* magazine, which had bought his story; and Speer and his wife aboard a normal Pan-Am flight. A small crowd at the Tempelhof airport cheered when he arrived shortly before 7 A.M. after a sightseeing drive through the British and American sectors of the city he had not looked at for over twenty years.

At his departure and on his arrival in Hanover Speer received top-level treatment. His daughter Hilde clutched a bunch of celebration carnations sent to her by West Berlin's Mayor, Willy Brandt. Mayor Brandt was afterwards criticized for the gesture. At Hanover airport, after an official had assured waiting crowds that 'not even the West German President' would be transported directly from the tarmac, a convoy of private cars picked up the party at the aircraft and took them through a side exit.

In London the Foreign Office confirmed that Britain, France and the United States had made 'certain proposals' to the Soviet Union concerning conditions for Hess's future imprisonment, and the Soviets had indicated willingness to discuss them. The proposals were that Hess should be moved to a hospital. The USSR appeared to prefer the establishment of a hospital-type wing within Spandau Prison itself, to preserve the four-Power principle and, of course, retain its foothold in West Berlin.

So Speer and Schirach were gone. Now the last remaining inmate in the vast gaol, Hess was scheduled to spend the rest of his life there, or in some other prison.

22: AND THEN THERE WAS ONE

Only one of the cells intended to house altogether six hundred inmates was occupied. Duty rosters of sixty soldiers commanded by a colonel; teams of civilian warders from four different countries; four Prison Directors; four army medical officers; cooks, scullions, waiters, porters and others: the immense Spandau staff-list was now all for one man — Rudolf Hess. When he had arrived there, some of his guards had not yet been born. Over the long years the gaol had developed into a unique institution with its own traditions.

A month prior to the release of Speer and Schirach, the US State Department made a proposal to the Soviet Union, Britain and France on ways of reducing the costs of operating the prison when only one prisoner remained. It was suggested that fresh arrangements should be made to house Hess and that the expensive gaol should then be handed back to the Germans.

After several weeks of procrastination, virtually as Speer and Schirach were about to drive out of the main gates, the Russians agreed to talks. Three choices were considered. One was to continue the current-style imprisonment until death overtook seventy-two-year-old Hess. The second possibility involved his removal to a smaller establishment such as transfer to a wing of the prison's hospital within the gaol compound, but there was no suggestion of moving him out of Berlin. The third choice called for freeing him and thereby completing this phase of the war.

Soviet attitudes on the Spandau issue were fundamentally the same as those with which the Western Allies had to deal in the larger issue of international relations. However, the case of

Hess involved something far more than a passion that crime should be expiated in full. There were two well-understood reasons for the Russian stance. The first was that the USSR had neither forgotten nor forgiven those who invaded its land in 1941. Although Hess was already a British prisoner at the time, he shared the Hitler Government's collective responsibility. The Russians consequently felt no charity towards him, and watched unmoved as his life ticked away in Spandau. As far as the Soviet Union was concerned, his mission to Britain was aimed at bringing that nation into the war on the Third Reich's side, against Russia. Because of this they maintained that Hess must have known Hitler was about to rape their country.

The Soviets' second reason for opposing his release was the prison's West Berlin location and the fact that it was one of the last examples of working four-Power co-operation. Since most of the highly expensive operation was paid for by West Berliners, this did not displease the Russians.

The official Soviet account of Hess's flight to Scotland in 1941 — six weeks before Germany's invasion of the USSR — may also hold a clue to Kremlin policy. The Soviet version of the motivation behind the flight, published nineteen years after it occurred, contained four major errors of fact. It implied that Hess was invited to Britain by Winston Churchill's Government. The text alleged that Hess was 'expected', that the RAF was ordered to let his aircraft fly in unhindered, and that two fighter planes were placed on stand-by for its emergency protection. To suggest that Churchill's Government was contemplating a deal with Hitler was not only false and insulting to the British people; it also showed that the Russians, having made a pact with Hitler to divide Poland between them, were afraid other countries might follow their example.

Lord James Douglas-Hamilton, second son of the Duke of Hamilton — whom Hess had wanted to contact — was posted to guard duties at Spandau Prison while serving as an army officer in Germany.

In 1967 an organization called the Society for the Release of Rudolf Hess was founded. Its aim was to influence the responsible powers of custody by enlightening the general public internationally, as well as to take direct measures to secure his release. Chairman of the Society was former West German Federal Minister of Justice Dr E. Bucker. The Society recruited hundreds of distinguished names all over the world to support its aims. Special newspapers, newsletters and books, solely devoted to Hess and largely seeking to exonerate him from war crimes, were distributed in several languages. Substantial funds were raised from undisclosed sources to finance this massive propaganda onslaught. 'Freedom for Hess' voices grew ever louder.

Meanwhile, from the instant of Speer and Schirach's departure, the prison's Directors stepped up the round-the-clock surveillance of their remaining charge, especially during the night. No chances could be taken that Hess's loneliness or depression might lead to his suicide.

Ten days later, Hess's lawyer, Dr Alfred Seidl, was granted a visit to advise him that he had petitioned the four Heads of State concerned, requesting a review of his case.

'I do not wish you to base pleas on my behalf on mental grounds,' Hess warned him.

To avoid laying themselves open to any justifiable complaints of dietary maltreatment, the Directors ordered that he was to be provided with basically the same meals as they ate themselves.

Night after night Hess was supplied the 'sleeping injection' he demanded. 'They give me a very strong sedative,' he informed his wife. It was distilled water. He was knocked out every night by pure suggestion. Both Hitler and Hess were chronic hypochondriacs, forever swallowing pills and potions for practically everything. They were constantly into 'health diets', but most of what 'ailed' them was psychosomatic, usually hysterical.

His only prison garden companions now were the birds whom he regularly fed with crumbs obtained from the kitchen. He disliked crows. Berlin possessed many bird colonies. One of the largest — Nebelkraeke carrion crows — nests in Poland, spends the summer in Russia, and winters in Berlin.

Spandau's solitary prisoner became the focal point of a series of international attempts to free him. All were repulsed by the Soviets. The West German authorities were footing a bill for some 850,000 Deutschmarks a year towards keeping Hess in Spandau; understandably, they were unhappy about the cost. His son, Wolf, came to Britain to launch a campaign on behalf of his father; he said:

'Perhaps it is all hopeless. I just know it is my duty to do everything I can.'

Wolf was only three when his father left Germany and had not seen him since, because Hess considered it beneath his dignity to receive his family in prison. Elaborating on this, Wolf explained: 'I fully understand. He is a proud man and says that parting would be more difficult than the meeting. It would be more than a meeting. It would be getting to know each other. What would I do if it was too much for my father and he broke down? I wouldn't know what to do or say. I'd start stammering and it would be stupid, embarrassing, and womanly.'

Of 518 German Parliamentary representatives approached by Wolf Hess, only 53 agreed to support the 'Free Hess' campaign. Many were unwilling to risk being labelled neo-Nazis.

In France, in 1968, it was said that what went on in Spandau prison was contrary to the demands of French law, which forbade holding a prisoner in solitary confinement for more than a year. French jurists said that the fate of Hess had gone far beyond the intention of those who had sentenced him at Nuremberg.

Persistence began to achieve results. Support for the French jurists' attitude was even obtained by Wolf Hess from the President of the Tribunal that had sentenced his father. Lord Justice Lawrence, who had assumed the title of Lord Trevethin and Oaksey, wrote to him in January 1968: 'I have on several occasions expressed my opinion that Rudolf Hess should be released. I will once more express these feelings to the appropriate authorities and hope very much that it may be of some avail.'

During November 1969 prisoner No. 7 suddenly stopped eating. His weight fell alarmingly. All he did was stay in bed and moan. The duty Soviet medical officer asked the British doctor, Lt.-Col. D. D. O'Brien, to join him immediately in the cell block for a consultation. Both examined Hess and diagnosed an intestinal blockage requiring hospital investigation.

'Treat me here,' the prisoner pleaded. Only when it was pointed out that Spandau's medical facilities were inadequate for the thorough investigation needed did he agree to be transferred to the British Military Hospital. It was the first time he had been outside the gaol since 1947, and soldiers were on constant guard at the door of his hospital security suite.

X-rays confirmed a perforated ulcer, but revealed that the ulcer had already sealed itself. Frau Hess and their son Wolf were notified and were anxious to visit. When advised of this by the Prison Directors, rigidly adhering to his policy, prisoner No. 7 answered:

'No visitors!'

Convinced he was about to die, he kept repeating: 'It will be all over for me soon', but he suddenly began to gain weight.

The Russians, allowing for any eventuality, requested a rediscussion of burial arrangements. It was reaffirmed by all four-Powers that, in the event of his death, the body would be cremated and interred outside Berlin. At one stage of the discussions the Western Allies opposed a Soviet proposal for the ashes to be buried within the gaol grounds. The idea was resisted vehemently to prevent the Soviets gaining a right to guard or regularly supervise the grave, thereby creating an excuse for the retention of such a foothold in West Berlin.

Further barium meal tests on Hess, however, indicated that he was on the mend. Then, and revelling in the sensation it caused, he wrote an extraordinary letter to the Directors:

> I request the visit of my wife and son, if possible. As it will be the first visit for 28 years, I ask that at the beginning there should be no witnesses in the room. The talk that I will have with my wife could be recorded on a tape recorder, or a hole could be cut into the wall so that anybody could see that I will not put any writing or anything like that into the hands of my family. Also I will promise that I will not stretch out my hand to them. My family will promise the same thing.
>
> I beg you to realize that von Schirach and Speer within 20 years had a great number of family visits, but for me it will be the first one. It will lessen the psychological tension with my family very much if I can get this permission. I ask you,

realizing it is my first visit, and that it will only last for half an hour, so please let us eat a Christmas dinner together.

It will not matter at all to me if direct witnesses are there at this dinner. I intend to be silent about all these privileges as far as my family are concerned. I won't tell them.

Rudolf Hess

He had already been a prisoner for twenty-eight years. Suddenly, without fellow prisoners to converse with, overpowering loneliness proved too much for him to hold out any longer against seeing his family.

The Directors were delighted. Personal family contact offered the best safety valve against suicidal dangers. They agreed on the visit taking place in a room adjacent to his own, and arranged for a table to be positioned between him and his wife and son, who were to be allowed to see him together for thirty minutes. The request to be permitted Christmas dinner with them was vetoed. Wolf Hess made a written application to be allowed a sixty-minute stay instead of the allotted thirty, and also asked whether he could talk to his father in the presence of only his doctor. Both requests were denied.

On 26 December 1969, after an absence of 28 years, 6 months and 25 days, Ilse Hess and their thirty-two-year-old son, Wolf Rüdiger, an engineer and airport designer, arrived. Spandau's four Directors were present for the occasion. First there were official formalities to complete. Mother and son were each handed a copy of the nine-point visiting regulations and requested to sign a printed undertaking to respect them.

Wolf Hess immediately objected to Rule 8, which forbade any disclosure to the press of details of the visit.

'If you do not sign there will be no visit,' the Soviet Director warned, and for once all four Directors were in total unison.

'And if you reveal details about your father's health and your stay with him, we will prohibit future visits,' the Soviet Director added.

'I will publicize your impossible behaviour!' Wolf Hess protested angrily; but he realized that he and his sixty-nine-year-old mother were faced with the decision to comply or jeopardize further visits. They signed.

After being cautioned again that handshaking and embraces were strictly forbidden, an adjoining glass-panelled door was opened to reveal the prisoner in pyjamas and dressing gown, already seated at the table. As wife and son entered, he shot up and in traditional German style cried: 'I kiss your hand, Ilse!'

Wolf Hess grabbed his mother's hand to stop her offering it to be kissed. Handshaking and embracing were classified as dangerous because they offered opportunities of passing poison phials or pills.

'We mustn't shake hands, but how are you?' were Wolf Hess's first words to the father he had not seen since he was an infant. Then, after an awkward significant pause, he asked: 'How did it all happen, Papi?'

Hess reacted by nervously babbling about his medical symptoms, but the Directors were very conscious that the question from a son deprived of his father for so long was equally applicable to so much else in the Hess saga. He discussed illness and his son's work. Thirty minutes soon passed. Before leaving, it was arranged that one of them would visit again the following month, only days away.

After the ordeal, a puzzled Ilse Hess asked Dr O'Brien outside the room: 'Why did he ask for this visit?'

She was convinced it was because he had discovered that he was suffering from cancer and had not long to live.

'He hasn't got cancer,' Dr O'Brien assured her.

Ilse Hess handed over some packages — Christmas gifts — and left.

Hess said to one of the Directors in his room: 'I'm sorry I waited so long.'

He had refused all those years because, apart from fearing his own emotions, he considered it would be demeaning for Adolf Hitler's former deputy to be seen in gaol.

'The reunion was unnerving,' Wolf Hess commented afterwards. 'For me it was practically becoming acquainted with my father. My mother was also shocked.'

In January, Hess's seventy-year-old sister, Frau Gretl Rauch, who had not seen him for thirty years, came with Ilse Hess. Gretl Rauch saw him first, whilst Ilse Hess was informed that an eminent British neurologist had just flown from London to examine her husband and had pronounced him to be in excellent condition for a man of his age. There were often as many as fifteen people present when Hess was questioned by psychiatrists. The Russians insisted on doctors speaking in English, even if the doctors spoke German. Then an interpreter translated into German, which was in turn translated by other interpreters into Russian, English and French.

Following publication in Christmas 1969 newspapers of the news of his transfer to hospital, a letter from Lord Shawcross appeared in *The Times* on 2 January 1970. It read:

> I have, on other occasions, given my personal opinion (for a Chief Prosecutor for the United Kingdom at the Nuremberg Trial of the major war criminals, I have long since been *functus officio*) that the continued imprisonment of Rudolf Hess serves no useful purpose whatsoever.
>
> His life sentence by the International Military Tribunal at Nuremberg was, in comparison with others, by no means a

lenient one. I suspect that all of us on the Western side took it for granted that it would be subject to the sort of commutation recognized in civilized systems of criminal justice and would not literally be for life...

I still believe that the merciful are blessed.

Wolf Hess swiftly attempted to consolidate the impact of this letter by flying to London again to recruit further allies. He approached Airey Neave, MP, who had been a war prisoner of the Germans and was the Nuremberg Tribunal officer who served indictments on the leading Nazi war criminals, including Hess. Airey Neave took Wolf Hess to George Thomson, who held the post of Chancellor of the Duchy of Lancaster, at the Foreign Office. Thomson promised that Britain, the United States and France would continue to press the Soviet Union to consent to Hess's release. Neave also organized a Parliamentary Motion backed by 190 Members. The Motion tabled in the House of Commons stated:

> That this House, reaffirming its detestation of Nazism and remembering its countless victims and their relatives and friends who mourn them, recognizes that Rudolf Hess is an old and sick life prisoner, and urges Her Majesty's Government to continue their efforts to secure his release on compassionate grounds.

It was considered that he should receive greater care in what were felt could be the closing months of his life. Hess, however, lived on to outlast all his fellow prisoners.

Airey Neave explained: 'I never defended Hess as a Nazi, but with friends in the United States Congress and the French Parliament, I organized a campaign for his early release.

'I had the impression that the Russians were worried and concerned at suggestions that they were inhumane in this case.

I realized that many said he was lucky to escape being hanged. He was a leading Nazi and responsible for setting up the Nazi regime of repression in Germany and Austria, and also for the so-called Nuremberg laws restricting the rights of Jews. For this, in my opinion, he deserved the sentence he received. But when the sentence was announced, I think the three Western Powers had in mind a review of the sentence after some years. On the other hand, we have to remember that there are many countries where a life sentence means "life" and the Russians looked at it in that light.'[20]

Many well-intentioned and equally distinguished international personalities joined Neave and Lord Shawcross in voicing disquiet at Hess's continued solitary confinement. Lord Oaksey — who, as Lord Justice Lawrence, presided over the Nuremberg Tribunal — further commented: 'I think that in view of his age and ill health he should be released. I don't see that he can do much harm now.' Concern was undoubtedly heightened by persistent unsubstantiated stories of 'fast deteriorating health', and 'insanity' — misleading rumours that only top-secret Spandau medical records could have speedily dispelled.

---

[20] Airey Neave, who ended the war as a lieutenant colonel and was awarded the DSO, MC, Croix de Guerre, and other foreign decorations, escaped from Colditz, the German prisoner-of-war camp for hard-line escapers. Later he joined MI9, the secret service responsible for organizing escape routes for captured Allied servicemen. After the war he was an officer of the British War Crimes Executive and, as a barrister, also acted as adviser to Hess, Göring, and other leading Nazis during the early days of their imprisonment. One of his tasks was to inform prisoners of their rights, and he was also responsible for finding lawyers for them. He was assassinated by a terrorist's car bomb within the precincts of the House of Commons.

Newspapers were bombarded by sympathetic letters portraying Hess as someone who had abandoned Hitler when 'he saw the light', and who could not have been aware of the most horrific Nazi brutalities. Misguided letter-writers overlooked the fact that the appalling Dachau concentration camp had existed in 1933, and that the sickest sick jokes current in Germany during that period were about Dachau. As the *Guardian* newspaper's authoritative former Berlin correspondent, Terence Prittie, pointed out:

> As a racialist crank, Hess must inevitably have known what was being prepared for the Jews and what was already being done to them. As a founder member of the Nazi Party and the head of the Party Chancery, he was morally and materially responsible.

Although Prittie conceded that humanitarian reasons could justify early release, he warned:

> Humanity should not become mixed up with foolish, sickly sentiment. One can only be disgusted by appeals on Hess's behalf based on the thought that the worst things of all were done by the Nazis after Hess had flown to Scotland. One might as well try to argue the case for a strangler, because he did not torture his victim before putting him to death.

Ilse Hess clearly showed where Hess's sentiments still lay. She wrote a book entitled *Between London and Moscow*, which included an account of her and her husband's friends celebrating Hitler's birthdays since his death.

The overriding question was whether the Western Allies ought to risk the consequences of a deliberate breach of four-Power agreements, and perhaps another confrontation over Berlin and its millions of decent citizens, for the sake of Rudolf

Hess. Fear of a new Berlin blockade indisputably lay behind the reluctance of the three Western Powers to disregard the Soviet Government and free him, despite growing public pressure calling for such a drastic step.

The three Western Powers were convinced that Hess had paid his penalty to the full. Many were sure that clemency would not mean that Nazi crimes were being forgotten. But in March 1970, in the House of Lords, Lord Chalfont, Minister of State at the Foreign Office, announced that to release Hess without Russian consent 'would mean breaking solemn international obligations, and we would not contemplate this'. So during March he was returned to prison after fourteen weeks' absence in hospital. On medical advice, conditions were altered. Instead of the old cell, he was switched to the room previously used as the chapel, and it was agreed that his diet should no longer vary as each nation took its monthly turn of administering the gaol. His hospital bed, with adjustable controls for elevating his head and feet, was substituted for the old bed. Also brought from the hospital was the adjustable table that swung over the bed for reading and writing.

As the new cell did not possess its own toilet, it was necessary for him to use the one in the adjoining cell, so authorization was given for his cell door to remain permanently unlocked. He was also now allowed to switch his light on or off as he pleased, but not off before 6.45 p.m. Instead of the old light-flashing procedure, a blue-tinted light was installed that sufficiently illuminated his bed at night for warders to check without disturbing him. His permitted garden exercise periods in the morning and afternoon could be extended if he undertook light gardening work.

Being, in fact, two cells knocked into one, the new room had two barred windows. Even an electric water-heater was provided to enable him to make instant coffee whenever he felt like it.

Ilse Hess carried a large bunch of spring flowers as a birthday token for her husband when she arrived for her April 1970 visit. When she emerged, she was still holding the flowers. She was not allowed to give them to him. Regulations governing gifts remained strict, but otherwise Hess's gaol existence completely altered on his return from hospital. The general routine was as follows.

Morning exercises on rising. Toilet and washroom with authorization to shave himself with an electric razor. He was allowed a knife to cut bread at breakfast, although watched throughout by a warder. After breakfast, the food trolley was pushed by him with used crockery to the corridor door where a warder took charge of it. At 10.30 A.M. he was accompanied to the garden, where after walking around it several times he settled on a garden chair to read the book he had brought. On returning to his cell an hour later he was searched to check whether he retained any gardening tool or sharp stone with which he might injure himself. His cell was searched regularly during the garden outings.

Following an after-lunch nap he went into the garden again. When the evening meal was over, he could visit the library or write a letter until 10 P.M. when, having inserted ear-plugs, he would sleep soundly after a 'sedative injection' (sterilized water) or 'sleeping pills' (sugar pills), which effectively knocked him out.

'That is all it took to make him sleep like a baby,' said Joannes Boon, a Dutch prison medical orderly and former prisoner of war in Germany. Boon, who married a Berlin girl and established a small food store and bar close to the gaol, had been an orderly at Spandau since 1946. He probably had more contact with Hess than almost anyone else did, and commented:

'I have seen enough to know, without a shadow of doubt, that Hess was in no way insane. He simply cut off, whenever he wished, by pulling a shutter down in his mind.'

On Saturdays he bathed and received his weekly letter, already scrutinized by the censor. In turn, he handed in the letter he had written. Once weekly the French military padre visited him for an hour. An American warder's report stated:

> Hess always posed the same problems. He abhorred exercise, studiously avoided work, and at times accepted punishment rather than go out into the garden. Spoke excellent French to French warders, and English fairly well. Over the years, attended chapel service only once.

In September 1973 consultants at the British Military Hospital in Berlin undertook the most comprehensive medical examination ever carried out on him. Among the examining specialists was a Dr Hugh Thomas, who was posted to the hospital in 1972 as Consultant on General Surgery. By chance Dr Thomas happened to be a specialist in gunshot wounds — an expertise acquired in Belfast. Although Hess's medical history logged wounds he was said to have received in World War I, Dr Thomas was surprised to find no trace of them, and was certain that the man he had examined had not been shot in the chest then or at any other time. Possibly, he thought, Hess never had been wounded as claimed. Even if a rifle bullet passes between ribs without touching them, the shock of its passage leaves visible damage on both ribs nearest its path; and if the bullet damages a lung, one long-term effect is a clearly visible track. Yet in none of the X-rays were there any signs of damage.

Dr Thomas did not report these significant facts at the time, but whenever the opportunity arose, which was infrequent, he continued to investigate and consider all the implications. Years were to pass before he officially declared his findings and his suspicions that the Rudolf Hess in Spandau gaol was either a fake or a chronic liar. Such accusations could never surprise the Soviet warders, who had always labelled Hess a faker, whilst the prison's British staff maintained that there was fundamentally nothing wrong with him that a kick in the pants would not cure.

Meanwhile freedom campaigners continued to disseminate stories depicting a frail, seriously ailing Hess approaching death. Largely due to these reports, in April 1974 West Germany's President Heinemann made a fresh appeal to the Heads of State of the United States, Britain and France to use their influence to end the Spandau story. Dr Heinemann's plea, made privately, represented something of a new departure; because while many West German individuals, including Churchmen and victims of Nazi persecution, backed the campaign, successive Bonn Governments kept officially silent, not wishing to appear pro-Hess or pro-Nazi. Nobody could accuse Heinemann of Nazi sympathies. His record of anti-Nazism and devotion to Protestant standards of morality and justice was unflawed.

A few months later, in August 1974, Hess was informed that Baldur von Schirach had died while on holiday in the wine-growing village of Kroev. Schirach had never attempted to contact Hess again following his release, and had lived with his son Klaus in Munich. He left three sons and a daughter. With his death at the age of sixty-seven, only Speer and Hess now survived of the Spandau seven.

On the night of 20 October 1975, Lord James Douglas-Hamilton, MP, the Duke of Hamilton's son, told the House of Commons:

> It is no part of my case to suggest that Hess was other than a dedicated fanatical and ruthless Nazi Party leader. The case for clemency in 1975 does not rest on any alleged innocence during the Night of the Long Knives, or, indeed, on any claim to ignorance of the impending attack on Russia. All the evidence would suggest that he was fully implicated in both episodes, as well as in many of Hitler's crimes.
>
> The present situation gives rise to a number of questions. Is Hess a danger to anybody at this stage? All the evidence suggests that he is not, and I suggest that if he were released, after the initial burst of publicity he would fade into the background in the same way as Raeder and Dönitz did. Second, does it serve any useful purpose to keep him in Spandau prison guarded by a large number of soldiers? It would seem that, far from serving any useful purpose, it imposes on the soldiers a dull and denigrating duty.

The Minister of State for Foreign and Commonwealth Affairs, Roy Hattersley, replied:

> The hon. Member for Edinburgh, West, is to be congratulated on having raised this subject tonight, and also on having set the scene for his call for Government action and for describing the Government's attitude so clearly. There are some things about Rudolf Hess that we do not know and perhaps never will. We do not know why he flew to Scotland on 10th May 1941. Perhaps he did not know exactly himself, but for the rest of the war he was imprisoned. When the war ended he, with other Nazis, was tried in Nuremberg in 1945 and he appeared before an international military tribunal which the Allies had established.

The Government have tonight been asked to make a specific and categorical statement of our position as to his continued imprisonment, so let me leave the House in no doubt whatever. It is the Government's belief, for reasons of compassion, that Hess should be released and released now. Were it within our power we should release him tomorrow. It is, however, my gloomy duty to tell the House that whilst we believe, for reasons of compassion — and I emphasize that because I want neither to dispute nor agree with the contentions that there are reasons for releasing him as for keeping him prisoner — that he should be released at the first opportunity, that is not within our power, if we are to maintain our international obligations and keep faith with our international treaties.

The view that he should be released is not held simply by the Government of Great Britain. Two of the other parties to the quadripartite agreements — France and the United States — have joined with Britain in urging clemency on the fourth party to the agreement, the Soviet Union. Whilst on occasion we have done it together, there have been numerous other occasions on which Great Britain has made individual approaches. I assure the noble Lord that we shall draw the attention of the Russian Ambassador to tonight's debate.

When we last made approaches to the Soviet Union we were told that Hess would become the focal point of a resurgent Nazi spirit and organization. We were told that as Deputy Führer he had borne special responsibility for the deaths of many millions of citizens of the Soviet Union, and that Russian public opinion would neither understand nor tolerate his release.

Belief in the necessity to release Hess for humanitarian reasons is not held simply by the Government in which I serve. It was held by the previous Government and the Government before that.

The Nuremberg Tribunal, established by formal agreement between the Governments, was something to which we were formally committed in international law. The charter of that military tribunal clearly states that it is the responsibility of the Control Council for Germany — the Four-Powers — to reduce or alter sentences. The Four-Powers act by quadripartite agreement in a number of things. They acted in that way when Spandau Prison was chosen, and they did so in drawing up regulations to govern the way in which prisoners live in that prison. The techniques and methods by which prisoners should be guarded have all changed since the original sentences and incarceration.

There is a little more to it than the obligation that I hold dear that the British Government should observe their international responsibilities. In Berlin the whole Western position depends on the success of and respect for the Four-Power agreements, agreements similar to those which concern Spandau Prison and the incarceration of Rudolf Hess. The three Western Powers have always respected the agreements governing Berlin scrupulously. We have regarded it as right and expedient to maintain the strong legal position so that there was never a legitimate reason for the Soviet Union to interfere in the government of what were the sectors of that city controlled by France, the United States and Great Britain. I believe that to begin unilaterally unravelling the quadripartite agreements now would lead to serious dangers and possible repercussions in Berlin. Her Majesty's Government could not act unilaterally in the matter and we do not believe that, were we to attempt to do so or contemplate doing so, we would be supported by the Governments of France or the United States.

I do not believe that we can make a unilateral declaration on the grounds of incapacity or sickness. The noble Lord suggested that Rudolf Hess was in less than good health, but I am advised that his health is remarkably good for a man of 81 years who has been imprisoned for 34 years. I believe that it would be a breach of an international obligation were we to pretend that matters of health required him to leave prison to return to his family. In the past when he has gone into hospital for necessary and proper medical treatment we have been scrupulous in ensuring that the obligations we have to the other Powers have been observed and that they knew he was leaving prison whilst treatment took place. What we can do is to make a further approach to the Government of the Soviet Union. That we shall do, and we shall make it in the spirit of the declaration that I have tried to make tonight — namely, in the most positive and unequivocal terms. I believe that Hess should now be released from Spandau Prison.

Two days after the debate, Cyril D. Townsend, MP, one of the prime movers of the British Parliamentary pressure group working for Hess's release, wrote to Minister of Defence Roy Mason. Townsend again suggested the withdrawal of British troops from Spandau guard duties, but this time proposing that such duties should become the full responsibility of the highly competent civilian warders at the gaol.

The pressure group's leader, Cyril Townsend, emphasized: 'It is no part of our case to suggest that Hess is other than a dedicated Nazi Party leader, and I believe he was correctly sentenced at Nuremberg, but we consider that he should be allowed to die in peace.'

Rudolf Hess lived on, and so did the legend that many people strived to maintain around him. In 1976 the Muenz und Kunst publishing house in Munich offered for sale medals bearing Hess's likeness. The gold medal cost 390 Deutschmarks (about £80); the silver, 180 Deutschmarks.

One morning in February 1977, when the French were in charge of the gaol, warders caught Hess slashing his wrists with a knife. He had already made several deep wounds and only prompt action prevented more serious self-inflicted injury. The authorities did not notify his family of the suicide attempt, but

Hess mentioned it to his son when he arrived for one of the regular monthly visits three days later.

'Why did you do it?' Wolf asked his father.

'Because I was so depressed,' was the reply. 'Is it surprising considering that I have been alone in this prison for more than ten years, and when I read of others convicted to life imprisonment but released after fifteen years?'

The prison administrators rejected Wolf Hess's demand for his father to be taken immediately to a civilian hospital for treatment by a German specialist. He requested this because his father had also complained of severe stomach pains and alleged that he was being given inadequate medical treatment. The stomach pains were psychosomatic; the accusation of poor medical attention was grossly untrue. Although Wolf Hess understandably always fought for his father, he was scrupulously careful never to say anything implying that his father's sins should be condoned or forgotten; nor was there any reason to suppose that this caution was merely prompted by tactical expedience.

Hess was taken to the British Military Hospital in Berlin for yet another thorough check-up, but returned to the gaol the same afternoon, since his condition was not such as to warrant hospitalization.

The Parliamentary group then sought to submit the case to the European Commission for Human Rights, but were informed that it would not constitute an admissible petition under the provisions of the European Convention on Human Rights for a number of reasons. They were advised that the real difficulty was that Hess's life sentence was imposed by an *international* military tribunal; consequently any remission of sentence would be dependent on the agreement of the four-Powers.

Although he had never shown the slightest interest in gaol chapel services, other than enjoying Walther Funk's dexterity at the organ, Hess was glad of the continuing weekly visit by the prison chaplain. At least it offered someone to talk to for a while. In his own warped way, he was religious. He admitted to the existence of a force called God, although it was a God who was uninterested in such trivialities as human beings. After his imprisonment Hess was convinced that it was the Devil and not God who held power on this earth, although he hoped that God would someday come, 'conquer Lucifer and bring peace to tortured humanity'.

He eagerly looked forward to his weekly conversation with the chaplain but was in no way interested in rehabilitation. Throughout the Spandau years he remained a steadfast Nazi and anti-Semite. Incredibly, despite the USSR's notorious repression of religion, including religious observance by its remaining Jews, he insisted: 'The rule of Bolshevism is the rule of the Jew.'

In the early days of captivity Hess's letters home were full of 'unquenchable optimism', discussing reunions and plans for the future. Now, as plea after plea on his behalf was dismissed, he commented: 'I have had to learn to stretch the thread of hope that reaches out towards the day of liberty — to stretch it more and more.' As he became enveloped in what he described as a 'shell of melancholy', he wrote to his wife: 'My *real* thoughts are shared with nobody nowadays. They pursue their way inside.' This man of intense blind loyalties confessed in another letter that he was always 'in favour of drastic solutions. One must be possessed by *something*. It doesn't matter what, as long as you are *possessed*.'

Utter commitment to Hitler and Nazi ideologies was echoed in another letter to his wife. Despite all that had happened to him, he could write:

> Very few people have been privileged, as we were, to participate from the very beginning in the growth of a unique personality [Hitler] through joy and sorrow, hope and trouble, love and hate and all the manifestations of greatness — and further, in all the little indications of human weakness, without which a man is not truly worthy of love.

The French suddenly changed their minds about the disposal of Hess's body in the event of his death in Spandau. Although they had signed a four-Power agreement on the issue, which had taken an interminable time to conclude, they decided that they did not want him cremated after all, nor his ashes given to his family. The French Government wanted the whole matter discussed anew, although the gaol's French Director disagreed with his country's change of policy.

Church dignitaries in West Germany, Britain, the United States and France concerned themselves persistently with the case. Replying to a May 1978 letter from the Right Reverend Lord Bishop of Bath and Wells, a letter from 10 Downing Street explained:

> 5 June 1978
>
> Dear Bishop,
>
> I fully share your concern at the unyielding attitude of the Soviet Government to Hess's imprisonment. As you know, the Western Allies have repeatedly pressed the Soviet Union to agree to Hess's release but with absolutely no success.
>
> Like you, I do not believe in giving up easily. I can assure you that we shall not relax our pressure on the Soviet Government to take a more reasonable view. But I frankly do

not think it would help if I were to take up your suggestion of making a public statement on the case myself. I shall keep the idea in mind, in case there is an opportunity to include a reference to Hess in some more general comment about Soviet policy; but for the moment I think it better that any statements on the subject by members of the Government should come in response to questions and representations from others.

Governmental pressure on the Soviet Union can make little impact unless it is seen to have the backing of Western public opinion. The efforts of the All Party Freedom for Rudolf Hess Campaign are especially valuable in this connexion; and I wish you and other members of your Committee success in your determination to demonstrate the continued strength of public concern in the West on this humanitarian issue.

Yours sincerely,

Jim Callaghan

In September 1978 the Minister of State at the Foreign Office, Frank Judd, decided to go to Spandau gaol to make a personal study of conditions. The surprise visit by a British Minister caused some anxiety among the Americans and French, but curiously not among the Russians. Judd was amazed by what he saw. It was not at all as he expected. Given a guided tour by the Director in charge, he saw the suite of rooms Hess occupied, comprising a bedroom, dining room, and a well-stocked library. The Director informed the Minister that Hess had made himself an authority on the Moon and corresponded with Cape Kennedy on the subject.

Prisoner No. 7 was allowed access to all the prison grounds, and a summer house had just been erected in the garden for his use. Two chefs catered for him. He chose menus at the start of each week, and ate like a horse. On the day Judd was there he was eating lobster.

The Russians refused to permit him to read or see anything about the Nazi period; but he had a radio, had been issued a colour TV set, and could select programmes he wished to view at the commencement of each week. He was not allowed to watch or listen to news bulletins. Guards switched off the set when news or any other barred programmes came on. He received daily newspapers, but forbidden items were cut out before he was allowed to read them. He could study German football results, but was kept ignorant of political events. He had collected an extensive gramophone record library and played records particularly loudly when visited by the priest, to whom he had suddenly taken an intense dislike.

Talking to Hess, Judd found him astonishingly well for a man of his age and very much on the ball. His main complaint was the trouble he was having with one of his legs, which he claimed was making it difficult to maintain firm balance. The Minister had a fleeting impression that in a curious way Hess had to some extent turned the tables on the Allied Powers. He seemed to see himself as a key individual around whom a large staff and ceremonial had evolved.

Prior to his departure for Berlin it had been suggested that it might be worth pressing for Hess to be transferred and kept in a special security ward in the British Military Hospital in the city. But following inspection of the gaol Judd concluded that such a ward would almost certainly be worse for Hess than his current extraordinary conditions in Spandau. He found Hess to be 'a very lively old man' and reported that the basic case for securing his release was made even stronger after having seen the incredible circumstances of his Spandau quarters and life. As a result, on returning to London, Judd advised the Soviet Ambassador that visiting Spandau had confirmed that the Russians were kicking into their own goal; the very nature of his solitary confinement in the prison made Hess appear to be far more important than he now was in reality.

Confirmation that the elaborate Spandau paraphernalia inflated Hess's view of his own stature was underlined by one of his gaol comments: 'Fulfilment of great tasks entails great suffering. I can achieve Germany's salvation if I regain my freedom.'

The Russians maintained that no punishment could ever repay the price of Hess's past evils. 'We are keeping a symbol alive, not an individual,' the Soviets' London Ambassador insisted. Since the world was still hunting down and punishing war criminals, 'Why then should we let Hess go free and continue against others?'

The Kremlin admitted that it was concerned over the revival of interest in Nazism in the West, and added that if Hess were freed he could provide a figurehead if not an effective leader.

'Look how the Nazis and Vichy French used a frail old shell of a man like Marshal Petain as a figurehead,' the Moscow line continued. 'Just imagine what a time they would have, all those Nazi sympathizers, and what a triumph it would be for them if Hess was freed. If Hess were no longer demonstrably Fascist, if he first renounced Nazism and showed his repentance, returning to the outside world just as he is, an old man who wishes to live his last years quietly in freedom, the danger of reaction would be obviated.'

Unfortunately for Hess, he gave no indication of repentance. Neo-Nazis were among the most vocal clamouring for his release, which was less than helpful to those fighting on his behalf on purely humanitarian grounds. Airey Neave, MP, who — with colleagues from all political Parties in the House of Commons — had led the British campaign for eleven years, said:

I think it wrong of the Russians to refuse clemency to a man of his age. It is wrong for the Governments of the United States, Great Britain and France to acquiesce in Soviet cruelty. I have supported Frau Hess and her son Wolf in their efforts to mitigate this harsh treatment but I do not forget the words of the Tribunal. The judgement of the Nuremberg Tribunal in 1946 of Rudolf Hess was right. No one was closer to Hitler in his early days. He was Hitler's shadow for twenty years, and none knew better than him how determined Hitler was to achieve his ambitions, and by what means.

Since 1973 Dr Hugh Thomas, Consultant on General Surgery to the British Military Hospital in Berlin, had been searching for every scrap of evidence appertaining to Rudolf Hess's past medical history, and particularly pre-war records. In autumn 1978 Dr Thomas met Ilse Hess and asked her about her husband's World War I wounds. She is said to have confirmed that he bore scars on the front and back of his body from infantry days. Dr Thomas accepted the statement as corroboration of a startling theory that the lone inmate of Spandau gaol was not the real Rudolf Hess, although he admitted that Ilse Hess's apparent ignorance of what he believed to be a Hess impostor was puzzling.

Thomas reported his findings. He claimed that, because there were no apparent signs of scars on the body, the man in Spandau could not be Hess, since on 8 August 1917 Hess was said to have been shot through the left lung. These allegations were taken sufficiently seriously for Foreign Office Minister Sir Ian Gilmour to indicate that the British Government was studying Dr Thomas's report with a view to deciding whether any further steps were called for. These would have necessarily involved the other Powers equally responsible for Hess.

It was possible that Hugh Thomas's medical findings could have a bearing on the true extent of Hess's World War I record, if it was established that he had exaggerated the war wounds. If Thomas was right, there would have had to have been an incredible conspiracy; Ilse Hess and her son never doubted the identity or handwriting of the man in the Spandau cell — nor did Speer, Neurath, Schirach and the other prisoners, all of whom had had intimate discussions with Hess concerning matters of which only the genuine Rudolf Hess could have been aware. Yet Thomas's report maintained: 'As his records and his wife testify, the real Hess was shot through the chest by a rifle bullet in 1917. Prisoner No. 7 has never been shot. Any experienced surgeon would see this at once.

'There is undoubtedly a difference between records of his history in World War I and the torso of the man in Spandau.' Thomas's report concluded: 'The torso cannot lie'; but war records can. Rudolf Hess would not be the first soldier to prove to be a line-shooter about 'wounds'. If he had lied about injuries in the first place, Dr Thomas's otherwise impressively researched theory amounted to nothing.

The absence of wound scars was borne out by other doctors. Dr J. Gibson Graham, who saw Hess after he landed in Scotland in 1941, agreed that there were no major scars on the prisoner's chest. 'There was certainly nothing to notice,' he said. Dr Ben Hurewitz, a New York physician who examined him when he was brought to Nuremberg in 1945, confirmed that there was no sign of damage by a rifle bullet. All such statements, however, were significant only if Hess was ever, in fact, shot.

Reacting sharply to the suggestion that the man in Spandau was not her husband, Ilse Hess said of Dr Thomas: 'Dieser

Kerl hat nicht all Tassen im Schrank.' (Translated politely: 'This fellow hasn't got all his cups in the cupboard.')

Frau Hess further described the claim as 'ridiculous and preposterous'; nevertheless, with her son, she called for an independent inquiry. Wolf Hess said that he did not doubt Thomas's professional honesty. He could only think that the doctor had been misled because of 'insufficient possibilities of medical examination'. He proposed that an independent commission should investigate the claim.

Speer confirmed that he, too, was convinced that the Spandau prisoner was Rudolf Hess and not an impostor. 'We spent many hundreds of hours together in conversation, exchanging the most intimate knowledge about the Nazi regime,' Speer explained. 'Not even a computer brain could have learned by heart all the secret details about Hitler that only someone like Hess could have known.' After his release from gaol, although unable to correspond directly with Spandau, Speer kept in touch with Ilse and Wolf Hess to ascertain Rudolf Hess's general condition.

During one of her visits to the gaol Ilse Hess informed her husband of Dr Thomas's suspicions. Laughing, he assured her:

'The old lung bullet wounds are still there.'

Frau Hess commented: 'Does anyone really believe that there is a human being who, for the sake of mystery — even if the Secret Service persisted — would, until his death, be willing to lead such a life?'[21]

When Ilse Hess visited her husband at the gaol on 29 December 1978 he said that during that very morning he had suddenly lost his sight almost fully and was convinced that this had been due to some form of stroke. He admitted he had not told the prison authorities of this because he was afraid her

---

[21] Written in a personal note to Jack Fishman

visit might have consequently been cancelled at the last moment. Ilse Hess immediately informed the Directors. He was moved the same day to the British Military Hospital.

When his son Wolf spent an hour with him at the hospital on 3 January he obtained his father's views on his physical condition, which Wolf Hess afterwards discussed with the hospital's head physician. He learned that a US Forces' neurologist and a British medical officer had checked and confirmed that his father had suffered a slight stroke.

During this visit Rudolf Hess told his son: 'The American physician gave me a routine examination on 28 December without any extraordinary findings resulting. But during the afternoon of that day I had a splitting headache and when I got up the following morning my right eye had grown absolutely blind and the perceptive range of my left eye was restricted by a fourth.' (The vision of his right eye had already been affected increasingly by a cataract for some years.)

'My heart is definitely bad. After a slow walk of only twenty minutes in the garden I am entirely exhausted and need sleep. I also get exhausted after only short mental concentration, and I get pain in the region of my heart. My right leg frequently fails me at the knee joint, causing me to fall when I am walking, and I can no longer climb stairs without assistance.

'I have a lot of trouble with my bladder and need to urinate frequently during the night. I suffer attacks from gastrospasms and enterospasms, accompanied by violent pain, on the average four times during twenty-four hours. I need to wear a truss for a hernia in my abdomen, and even coughing causes problems in this respect. I have a permanent cough.

'For years I have had fluid congestion in my feet, rising as far as my calves. The overall state of my health is so poor that I am certain my days are numbered now.'

On the evening of his son's visit Rudolf Hess was considered well enough to be transferred back to the prison. Two days later his son presented to the senior physician of the British Military Hospital a series of questions prepared for him by German consultants. The frank and detailed medical replies he received assured him that his father's blood pressure, pulse rate, and bronchial condition were no cause for concern. His appetite and digestion were good, and no diet was necessary; however, he adhered to light fare. The functioning of his liver and kidneys was normal. All blood tests and the results of an electrocardiogram were normal. He had been subject to prostate enlargement for many years and urinary infection several times, but in view of his age an operation was ruled out. He undoubtedly had a congestion problem in his legs but there were no indications of thrombosis.

Wolf Hess's work as an airport designer took him to Jeddah immediately after that Berlin visit, but on 13 January 1979 he wrote the following letter to Professor Dr E. Kolb, Dean of the Faculty of Medicine of the Technical University of Munich:

> Dear Professor Kolb,
> *Re: Rudolf HESS*
> In view of the alarming deterioration of my father's physical condition since the date of the stroke he recently had I feel bound to approach you with the following request.
> Please find enclosed a 'Report relating to Rudolf Hess's physical condition', which is based on the facts that have become known to me. The Hess family would feel very grateful to you if you in your faculty could effect an expert opinion by the competent specialized colleagues on my father's situation.
> I am well aware of the fact that the basis for such an opinion is more than restricted. The allied custodial powers, however, stubbornly refuse up to this day to permit any

examination of my father by a physician whom the family trusts; to say nothing of a transfer to a West German hospital.

I cannot imagine that a man in my father's physical condition can be called fit for imprisonment if the standards generally accepted in civilized countries are applied.

I wish to emphasize that my request does not originate from a distrust of the efficiency or sense of duty of the attending physician. I cannot help suspecting, however, that the overall circumstances under which my father is imprisoned allow neither a factual diagnostic work nor such medical care as is nowadays feasible.

Trusting that I will not meet with a refusal.

I remain, yours very sincerely,

W. R. Hess

The document accompanying that letter began:

1. *Preliminary remarks*
The following particulars have been compiled by Dipl Ing [Certified Engineer] Wolf Rüdiger Hess, Rudolf Hess's only child. They are based on general knowledge of the family, statements of Rudolf Hess himself, as well as statements of the head physician of the British Military Hospital, Berlin. It should be emphasized that Wolf Rüdiger Hess has no knowledge of medicine. The talks with the head physician of the British Military Hospital took place in English, which W. R. Hess speaks fluently. The head physician's statements were literally noted down to a large extent, the medical technical terms were taken from dictation by the head physician. All particulars have been rendered to the best of W. R. Hess's knowledge and belief.

2. *Personal data of Rudolf Hess*
Born in Alexandria, Egypt, on 26 April 1894 as eldest of 3 children. Height: 182 cm. Weight: 75 to 78 kg (estimated). General appearance: lean.

Detained without any interruption since 10 May 1941, including detention as only prisoner in a 600-man prison since 1 October 1966. Prior to his detention on 10 May 1941 healthy and sporting. No sicknesses worth mentioning, except for occasional gastrospasms. About sickness or complaints since 10 May 1941 — exclusive of the exceptions mentioned hereinafter — nothing is known because the custodial powers observe strict secrecy and, during visits made by members of the family, talks on the physical condition are normally prohibited.

Exceptions:

(a) Breakthrough of a duodenal ulcer on 20 November 1969 with subsequent in-patient treatment in the British Military Hospital from 22 November 1969 to 13 March 1970.

(b) Prostatic troubles — according to Rudolf Hess's own statements since 1970.

(c) Swelling of the legs — according to Rudolf Hess's own statements since 1970.

Rudolf Hess has never smoked, had drunk spirits before his detention only very temperately and none at all since 10 May 1941. In all those years of his detention he deliberately trained his body, made rounds of about one and half hours in the prison garden every day and under any weather conditions, and, moreover, practised gymnastics.

The food — at least during the last 15 years — can be called normal. For the last 8 years, during 9 months of the year (US, British and French guarding), Rudolf Hess has been allowed to present his own requests for food which, without exception, concern light fare.

Wolf Hess went on to describe general living conditions and some of the regulations at the gaol, then presented his father's view of his own health. This was followed by the senior hospital physician's findings.

A copy of Wolf Hess's letter to the distinguished German medical specialists, and the accompanying reports, reached the Foreign and Commonwealth Office in London. Commenting on them in official correspondence, Minister of State Frank Judd declared on 2 April 1979:

> I agree that on the basis of the information which Hess gave his son it might be concluded that he is in no fit state to remain in prison.
>
> While it is only natural that a man of nearly 85 should suffer from ailments which induce discomfort or worse and certainly no one can guarantee that his health will not suddenly deteriorate, the regular medical reports we receive from Berlin suggest that Hess's general health remains at least reasonable for a man of his age and his mind is alert and lucid.
>
> I therefore see no present cause for alarm. The constant medical care he receives is of a high standard. He is given a thorough examination at least once a week, and if circumstances warrant it, more frequently. Although quadripartite agreement is needed before he can be transferred to the British Military Hospital, the Russians do not withhold such agreement, as is shown by the fact that in recent months he has twice been transferred to hospital. Before he can be taken back to Spandau, doctors of all Four-Powers must agree that he is in a fit state to leave the hospital. And we have the strong impression that, if the medical reasons do not compel him to be in hospital, he prefers to remain in the familiar environment of Spandau.

On 27 September 1979 Ilse Hess received the following letter from Spandau Prison:

> Dear Mrs Hess,
> I am writing in confidence to confirm my telephone call of Friday 21 September.

As you know, your husband was admitted to the British Military Hospital on 4 September for Routine Medical Tests. A senior urological specialist from the United Kingdom examined your husband on 8 September.

The specialist considered that, because of his prostate condition, your husband was now at severe risk of renewed urinary infection (which could lead to septicaemia) or complete retention of urine, and that treatment now while his general health was good would be preferable to treatment in an emergency. The specialist therefore recommended that your husband should be advised to have an immediate operation. The four senior prison medical officers agreed that the operation should be carried out subject to your husband's consent.

However, when the position was explained to him, he declined the operation. He was therefore returned to Spandau Prison on September 10.

Sincerely,

G. T. P. Marshall,
British Governor, Chairman

On his mother's behalf on 3 October, Wolf Hess sent the following reply addressed to the Administration of the Allied Military Prison, Berlin:

Dear Sirs,

In response to your letter of September 27, 1979, which was addressed to my mother, I hereby, confirming and supplementing the oral statements I have already made in the Allied Military Prison on October 2, 1979, give the following information on behalf of the family.

From your above-mentioned letter and the telephone conversation connected therewith my mother had with your Governor Mr Marshall on September 21, 1979, it can be gathered that you wish to induce the family to persuade my father to consent to an operation on his prostate.

In connection with the visit I paid to the Allied Military Prison on October 2, 1979, you have forbidden my father to inform me of the reasons why he has declined an operation. Further, it can be gathered from remarks my father made on the occasion of my visit and from the fact of the non-arrival of one of the periodical weekly letters of my father in the period concerned that you have withheld a letter my father addressed to the family in which my father explained in writing the reasons why he declined the said operation.

Finally you have failed as yet to give the family any detailed information of my father's state of health or to disclose any particulars about the kind of operation which is intended to be performed anyhow. As everybody knows, there are several kinds of prostate operation, depending on the character of the findings. Under the prevailing circumstances it is, to put it mildly, an exacting demand to expect the family to give any advice whatever as to the operation. The family is also obliged to strongly refuse to be saddled, as it has been tried, with the responsibility of saying 'yes' or 'no' to an operation.

Therefore I apply for:

1. Delivery as a loan of the complete test report including radiographs, laboratory findings, uroflowmetry, etc, connected with my father's examination which was performed between September 4 and 10, 1979.
2. Delivery as a loan of all further medical test reports, etc, covering the period since July 1947 inasmuch as they might be relevant to my father's present state of health.
3. Transmission of an autograph letter of my father disclosing the reasons why he declines the said operation.

The family will discuss the material requested for with physicians of our confidence and will decide thereafter what advice as to an operation we can give my father.

As an alternative of the three above-mentioned points I apply for:

4. The permission for three physicians of the family's confidence to inspect such medical material as specified in points 1. and 2. hereof in the Allied Military Prison and/or the British Military Hospital in Solicitor Dr Alfred Seidl's and my presence.
5. The permission for the three aforesaid physicians to talk to my father and to perform an examination of my father if this is deemed necessary by the three physicians.
6. The permission for the three physicians to talk to the senior medical officers for the four-powers.

I beg you to immediately respond to all applications I have made herein since according to your letter of September 27, 1979, acute danger of my father's life has to be assumed.

Finally I apply for:

7. Notification of my father of the present letter.

Yours faithfully,

W. R. Hess

The French were in charge of the gaol when the foregoing letter was received. It was answered in French, on 12 October. Translated, the reply from the French Director in charge, M. H. Planet, read:

> The Governors have taken note of your letter of 3 October 1979 which contains some statements and requests that are unacceptable. It is not their intention to comment on them here in detail.
>
> However, they are prepared to organize a meeting between yourself alone, or accompanied by Madame Ilse Hess, with the doctors of the Four-Powers who are the competent authorities caring for the prisoner's health.
>
> Following the meeting, you would be authorized to make a new visit with your father.

> I should be grateful if you would inform me of your reply in good time so that practical arrangements can then be taken.

A week later Wolf Hess informed the prison administrators that he was 'amazed and astonished' that they should classify his assertions and requests as unacceptable. Repeating his previous demands he indicated that he was unable to respond to the offer to meet the four prison doctors until 'clear answers to my applications' had been given. Pointing out that due to emotional stress his mother would prefer not to attend the suggested consultation, he asked whether their lawyer, Dr Alfred Seidl, could represent her. Finally he requested that Professor Dr Egbert Schmiedt, Director of the Urological Clinic and Policlinic of the Ludwig Maximilian's University of Munich, should be admitted to the consultation as an additional physician.

On 31 October the Directors notified Wolf Hess that the offer for him alone, or accompanied by his mother, would remain valid, but that no one else could be substituted for them. Hess reacted by adhering to his original requirements, including authority to bring a German physician of his family's choice. The authorities would not concede this. As Ilse Hess and her son decided not to see the doctors of the four-Powers unless they got their own way, the situation reached stalemate and the operation was abandoned. The authorities considered that in view of the fact that Rudolf Hess had been provided with the highest standard of medical attention throughout his Spandau years, it was impertinent for the prisoner's family to cast doubts on the integrity of all the medical officers and specialists who attended him.

Acting for Hess, Dr Seidl took legal action in December 1979 to ensure that the Bonn Government presented his client's case to the International Court in The Hague. He filed a motion to that effect with the Federal Administration Court in Berlin. This was the court of last instance after the failure of previous attempts to have the matter submitted to the United Nations and the European Court in Strasbourg. Dr Seidl stressed that his client had not been convicted of war crimes against humanity by the Nuremberg Tribunal, but for co-operating in the preparation of an aggressive war, an offence previously unknown in international law.

In earlier hearings, courts had granted the Bonn Government discretion on which grounds to plead for Hess's release. This time Dr Seidl hoped that the Berlin court would decide that the Federal German Government would be empowered to argue for freedom on legal as well as humanitarian grounds. This fresh tactic got no further than previous efforts.

Also during December 1979 Britain's Foreign Secretary, Lord Carrington, wrote to his Soviet counterpart, Andrei Gromyko, urging a change of heart towards Hess by the Kremlin. The appeal was ignored on the grounds that in Soviet eyes Hess was not a person; he represented Nazi Germany and the crimes that Hitler committed. He was, to the Soviets, a surrogate Hitler. To let him go seemed like an act of forgiveness and forgetting, for which they were not ready. They were, as ever, quick to remind the Western Allies that not only had they suffered under the Nazis to an extent that has never been fully understood in the West, but they also continued to regard Germany as a potential danger. They paid close attention to the activities of small neo-Nazi groups that never stopped defending Hitler; noted the tendency among fairly respectable right-wing politicians to talk more of German losses than German war crimes; and above all felt that they still needed a residual or potential German threat to keep the

Warsaw Pact together and invoke, in difficult times, the spirit of the 'great patriotic war'.

This combination of genuine feeling and political expediency lay at the root of the USSR's unwillingness to release Hess. The three Western Allies were reluctant to disturb the delicate balance of four-Power arrangements in Berlin, so Hess had to continue to bear the burden of the history he personified; and since he had shown no signs of repentance, he commanded limited sympathy. The main motivation prompting most of the pressure for his release was the feeling that, if the Western world was to be true to its own values, it would put the human being Hess before Hess the symbol of Nazism.

Voices opposed to Hess's being freed pointed out that it might be useful for those concerned with compassion and humanity to recall all the inhuman decrees that Hess had signed, and all the Hitler-worshipping speeches he had made up to 1941 when he flew to Scotland. Hess, it was recalled, had recommended the strengthening of the Waffen SS in Poland because, as he said, 'through their intensive National Socialist training in racial problems, the Waffen SS must be looked upon as particularly well qualified for employment in the occupied eastern territories'.

The significance of this had been spelled out in a letter from the Reich Ministry of Justice to the Chief of the Reich Chancellery dated 17 April 1941, concerning special penal laws for Jews and Poles in those occupied eastern territories:

> The suggestions of the Deputy Führer [Hess] have been taken into consideration to a far-reaching extent ... any Pole or Jew in the eastern territory can in future be prosecuted, and any kind of punishment inflicted upon him for any attitude or action which is considered punishable... In accordance with the opinion of the Deputy of the Führer, I started from the

> supposition that the Pole is less susceptible to the infliction of ordinary imprisonment... Under these new kinds of punishment prisoners are to be lodged outside prisons, in camps, and are to be forced to do the heaviest and hardest labour.

That was how Hess had opened the gates to Auschwitz, Treblinka, Maydanke, and the rest of the death camps.

To those who cried, 'Shouldn't we set Hess free from his life sentence? Hasn't he paid enough?' others replied, 'How much is enough?'

On 2 September 1981 a warder informed Hess that he had just become the sole survivor of the seven. Albert Speer had died in London. Speer, who was seventy-six, had come to Britain to record an interview for a BBC television documentary about Hitler's plans to plunder the art treasures of Europe and store them in a museum to be built in Austria. After spending the morning on the set at the BBC Television Centre, he returned to his hotel, collapsed, and died in hospital a few hours later. He was the only one of the freed six who stayed in touch with the Hess family after his release from gaol.

Political aspects of the Hess case were constantly confused with merciful arguments in his favour. On 1 December 1981 the US Department of State explained in a letter answering yet another representation for America to take unilateral action and release Hess in defiance of Soviet opposition:

> Hess is in prison under Four-Power arrangements, the same as those which serve as the legal basis for the Allied presence in Berlin and, hence, help guarantee the security of the city and the two million inhabitants of the Western sectors.
>
> In terms of principle, it is wrong to violate deliberately any international agreement. In political/military terms, it would not be in the interests of the United States to violate

agreements with the Soviets in Berlin. To help maintain our position there, 110 miles behind the Iron Curtain, we must hold the Soviets accountable for the strict implementation of all of the Four-Power arrangements. Should we set Hess free under the conditions suggested, our ability to hold the Soviets to these agreements would not be strengthened. The United States Government favors the release of Hess and will continue, together with the UK, France and the Federal Republic of Germany, to seek to obtain Soviet agreement.

Hess's personality increased the complications because he was an extremist who took his ideals to lengths that usually owed little to reality, and his utter devotion to Hitler remained undiminished throughout his Spandau years. Despite all the horrors and catastrophes brought about by his beloved Führer, he still maintained that Hitler's image was untarnished and sought to camouflage his own guilt and failure by inflating his sense of pride and dignity to heroic proportions. Despite the misguided futility of his flight to Scotland, he always insisted it was 'the greatest achievement of my life'.

He was labelled 'demented, half-mad, schizophrenic, totally insane, a frail harmless old man', but outlived his six Spandau companions. The most exhaustive medical case history ever compiled in respect of one person completely rejected any question of insanity.

Hess was not mad. He was simply a fanatic — a Nazi fanatic.

Because of frequent stimulated amnesia, malingering, and the personality he deliberately sought to present, his continued imprisonment aroused extraordinary and widespread compassion, yet of his years as a Nazi leader he once ventured:

> Even if I could, I would not want to erase this period of time from my existence. I am happy to know that I have done my duty to my people, my duty as a German, as a National

Socialist, as a loyal follower of my Führer. I do not regret anything.

Hess was convinced he was destined to become Germany's new Führer. Outline details on the formation of a revised Nazi Government were found in his Nuremberg cell. He intended issuing them when he eventually 'took over Government'. From prison he wrote to his wife:

> My fate is bound up with absolutely sure conviction that for me there yet awaits a great mission. I have so much evidence of this mission. To doubt it would be the same as doubting that tomorrow the sun will not rise.

He was confident that the German people would back him as Führer. In one ranting speech during his trial, he had cried out:

> I was permitted to work for many years of my life under the greatest son my country has brought forth in its thousand-year history. If I were to begin all over again, I would act just as I have acted even if I knew that in the end I should meet a fiery death at the stake!

Although his life didn't finish at a fiery stake, he nevertheless achieved a spectacular exit when, on 17 August 1987, the 93-year-old unrepentant Nazi's suicide ended his dream of leading a revival of National Socialism.

For forty years, the Allies had spent millions of pounds to prevent him taking his own life in captivity, as both Göring and Himmler had succeeded in doing. Twenty-four hours after the announcement of his death, an official statement issued on behalf of the four-powers responsible for the jail admitted that he had hanged himself by tying one end of a lamp flex, which he had wound round his neck, to a window frame in a prison summerhouse, and jumped from a chair. The other end of the flex was attached to a reading lamp. He had always taken a brief rest in the summerhouse when out on his daily strolls in the prison garden, and the lamp was there to help him read a book if he wanted to. It was never thought for a moment that he would ever use the flex for any other purpose.

The official statement explained: 'All available evidence — including results of a full autopsy and investigations by the Special Branch of the Royal Military Police — indicates that Hess used an electrical extension cord to hang himself and that the cause of death was asphyxiation.'

He also left a suicide note, dated 27 July, written on the back of a letter to his family, and this appeared to support the authorities' version of events.

To avoid neo-Nazis using his funeral and grave for propaganda purposes, he was buried in secret in an unmarked grave plot — three days before his scheduled funeral. A few hours later, his son Wolf suffered a brain haemorrhage, but recovered.

As for the fortress-gaol itself, the Soviets wanted it preserved as a monument to the evils of Fascism, but British authorities had other ideas. They indicated that they intended to demolish it totally.

Year in and year out, Rudolf Hess had slavishly repeated to his six fellow Spandau prisoners: 'The Führer was always right and always will be right.'

After his long, punishing loneliness as the gaol's solitary inmate, one of the Directors asked Hess whether, if he had his time over again, he would do the same. He answered: 'Yes, I believe I would travel the same route and end up here, in Spandau Prison.'

23: SUMMING UP

The punishment of the Spandau seven was far more than retaliation. The Allies did not seek to avenge injustice with new injustice. Justice is much greater than a collection of verdicts. It is the basis of freedom; so free men and women are entitled to be assured that the Powers that govern the world will be strong enough to repress outrageous evil and punish men who commit outrageous crimes against humanity, as did the Spandau seven.

Criminal guilt is personal. Mere membership of a criminal organization is in itself no crime. The crime consists in membership linked with knowledge of crimes defined, or with personal implication in such acts. The Nuremberg Tribunal decided that a criminal organization is analogous to a criminal conspiracy, and Hess, Speer, Schirach, Neurath, Funk, Dönitz and Raeder paid for their part in the Hitler Conspiracy. Even enemies are entitled to justice, and the seven received it.

In an address to the American Society of International Law, Justice Robert H. Jackson challenged:

> If aggression is so wrong that international law calls upon our youth to die in remote parts of the world to stop it, these innocents have, I submit, a moral right to ask, 'What will you do about those persons guilty of it?'

The most significant thing about the Nuremberg trial was that it happened. For the first time in history the judicial process was brought to bear against those who had offended the conscience of humanity by committing acts of military aggression and related crimes. Benign, balding Lord Justice

Lawrence dominated Nuremberg for a year. To everyone he was the embodiment of the principle of a fair trial. He had been a judge of the High Court of Justice in Britain since 1932, and a Lord Justice of Appeal since 1945. As President of the Tribunal he, more than anyone else, deeply impressed all the defendants because of his evident impeccable sense of justice.

Sir Geoffrey Lawrence, who after World War II became Lord Trevethin and Oaksey, never wrote his autobiography or any book dealing with his Nuremberg experiences. But at various times he did set down afterthoughts about the Tribunal and war criminals. It is therefore appropriate that this great man's subsequent reflections on the subject, extracted from his personal papers, should sum up the significance of the sentences served by the seven men in Spandau gaol, and what the symbol of this unique war crimes prison stood for. The Rt Hon Lord Oaksey noted:

> After the surrender of Germany, the discovery of the conditions in the concentration camps there and in the occupied territories were so appalling that the civilized world stood aghast. There were also many other dreadful crimes known to the Allied Governments and to some individuals, but not by any means to the majority of ordinary persons. The United States, the Soviet Union and Great Britain had already declared their intention of punishing the crimes Germany had committed.
>
> There were, I suppose, three possible courses; to let the atrocities which had been committed go unpunished, to put the perpetrators to death by executive action, or to try them. Which was it to be?
>
> There were many people in England in 1945 who doubted if there ought to be a trial and if British judges ought to take part in it. Their view was, I think, either that the victorious powers had no right to punish the vanquished at all, or that it

was an executive right which had nothing to do with the administration of law and that it would only bring the administration of law and particularly British justice into disrepute if British judges took part in such a trial. Such views are, I think, based upon the idea that International Law, backed as it is by no force, is so uncertain and so fluid that it affords no safe foundation for a criminal trial.

Whether a trial was necessary at all, and whether the jurisdiction conferred upon the Tribunal was valid according to international law were questions considered again long after Nuremberg.

What would have happened if Great Britain and the United States had refused to participate in any form of punishment? Would they have done any good by refusing to act with their Allies? It was inevitable then, it seems to me, that punishment should be meted out, and, if so, it surely was right that it should be after a trial which was intended at any rate to be fair. In all probability, if there had been no trial, all the major war criminals who were tried at Nuremberg would have been executed and the Tribunal at least did not think that that was just.

It will be remembered that after the first World War alleged criminals were handed over to be tried by Germany, and what a farce that was! The majority got off and such sentences as were inflicted were derisory and were soon remitted.

The fundamental purpose of the Trial was not only punishment of those who were guilty but the establishment of the supremacy of international law over national law and the proof of the actual facts, in order to bring home to the German people, and the peoples of the world, the depths of infamy to which the pursuit of total war had brought Germany. Had it not been for the long drawn out and elaborate Trial, the production of German documents, the authenticity of which could not and was not denied, and the actual evidence of several of the worst criminals themselves, no one would have believed what the Germans did. It would have all been ascribed to Allied propaganda. Would anyone have believed, had it not been proved by the evidence and the documents, that the Germans in September 1939 ordered the Polish intelligentsia, the nobility and the clergy to be killed out of hand; that actually before making war on the Soviet Union they ordered all Commissars to be killed on capture; that they ordered that the Jews and other prisoners should be gassed if unable to work; and that in accordance with these inhuman orders many millions of human beings had been butchered? One frequently meets ignorant or prejudiced people who do not believe it still. But the major war criminals at Nuremberg did not deny it and one would think that no German in the future will have the face to deny it. It was suggested by some of the defendants that they were ignorant of the conditions in the concentration camps and of the most brutal atrocities, and it is possible that some of them were, but it seemed to the Tribunal incredible that the substance of these conditions was unknown to many of the defendants, and there was and can be no dispute that the principal defendants were parties to them or some of them.

I would ask you was it possible to let such atrocities go unpunished? Could France, Russia, Holland, Belgium, Norway, Czechoslovakia, Poland or Yugoslavia be expected to consent to such a course? We, in England, must remember that though we have suffered we have not suffered as they did. We were not neutrals, we had no pact with Germany: we were not bombed without a declaration of war: we were not invaded: our people were not deported to work as slaves: few, if any, of our nationals were shot as hostages, and few were, I think, in concentration camps.

The other principal object of the Trial, as it appears to me, was to bring home to Germany and to the world that a nation cannot with impunity resort to total warfare in defiance of international law and laws of war which have been recognized as part of international law since the Middle Ages.

One must remember that international law grows by custom, agreement and precedent and not by the action of an international legislature, and no greater international step has been taken in the history of the world than was taken on August 8, 1945.

Unless in some way war can be prevented and International Law takes its place, what future is there for the world?

The conscience of the world has called for some system of International Law for centuries, but the fact that there is no International Legislature and no International armed force to enforce its law has made the world grow accustomed to war as though it were a right to which any nation can have recourse without incurring any blame. But just as individuals under primitive conditions came in the course of time to recognize the necessity of obeying some form of law, so the nations have in a primitive and undeveloped way come to recognize that there are certain obligations which even sovereign nations must observe, and that if they do not, other nations, if they have the power, will punish infraction by the guilty individuals.

Such obligations have come into existence by custom and agreement and so an undeveloped International Law has come into existence. Laws of war at any rate have been recognized since the fourteenth century and were to some extent crystallized in the Hague Conventions of 1899 and 1907. But still this law was not fully developed, and sometimes as in the 1914 war not observed by the Germans.

Directly the 1914 war was over Hitler began to form his Nazi party with the avowed intention of putting an end to the Treaties of Versailles and St Germain which had set up as sovereign states, Austria, Hungary, Czechoslovakia, Poland and Yugoslavia. The most important question of International Law raised by the Nuremberg trial was whether it was an international crime to plan and make an aggressive war in pursuance of his policy.

From 1923 to 1928 the League of Nations, which had been set up by the Treaty of Versailles, had, by resolutions and agreements, expressly condemned aggressive war as an international crime, and in 1928 the Kellogg-Briand Pact was agreed to by sixty-three nations, including Germany, condemning and solemnly agreeing to renounce war as an instrument of national policy.

After the war, by the Charter of August 8th, 1945, the four great nations of Russia, USA, France and Great Britain, who were in occupation of the whole of Germany and Austria and to whom Admiral Dönitz, Hitler's successor as Führer, had surrendered, laid it down that aggressive war was a crime and that the planners of the recent war should be tried as the major war criminals.

The trial was held under this Charter and it seems to me, who had nothing to do with its framing, that it was a great achievement of legal diplomacy to have secured agreement to it.

It is apparent now, more than ever, that it is a matter of the highest international importance that such an assertion of international jurisdiction should have been made by the Four Great Powers with the adherence of so many States and with the silent acquiescence and recognition of the rest of the civilized world. Whatever view may be taken now or in the future of the trial itself, the agreement in the Charter laying down what, in the opinion of these Nations, constituted International Crimes will always be a factor of the utmost importance.

The Charter also provided that the Tribunal might declare any group or organization of which the prisoners were members, and in connection with which any act of which an individual prisoner might be convicted, a criminal organization, and where an organization was declared criminal any member might be tried for membership by a national military or occupation Court.

It was argued that this provision was novel and unjustifiable, but the Tribunal took the view that the provision, like the creation of the Tribunal itself, was a matter of procedure, and that just as it has been the practice of nations to set up courts for the trial of war crimes and to invest those courts with jurisdiction and to regulate their procedure, so it was competent to create a novel form of procedure in order to deal with the great number of prisoners possibly implicated in the crimes of these organizations.

The Tribunal set up a Commission which heard a great number of witnesses for these organizations and examined thousands of affidavits, and the Tribunal after considering this evidence, and hearing further evidence, declared some of the organizations criminal but in the case of others — notably the General Staff and High Command — refused to make the declaration asked for by the prosecution. The Tribunal limited its declaration to those 'who became or remained members of the organization with knowledge that it was being used for the commission of acts declared criminal by Art. 6 of the Charter or who were personally implicated as members of the organizations in the commission of such crimes.

The difficulty of accepting the view that in International Law aggressive war is a crime, in the minds of some people, is that it denies the right of nations to make war as they decide, and it is sometimes said that whatever may have been agreed to in the Charter or decided at Nuremberg, the nations will always take the chance of making a war which may be aggressive, confident in their ability to win and, having won, perhaps to declare that the beaten nation was the aggressor. That is, of course, in accord with Hitler's principle. It was he who said:

'The victor shall not be asked later on whether we were telling the truth or not. In starting and making a war, not the right is what matters, but victory.'

The danger that a law will not be observed is, of course, especially inherent in a law which has no force behind it and, until there is an International Police Force, such a danger will always exist. But can anyone deny that International Law has existed in an undeveloped form since the Middle Ages and that its mere existence has had a great moral and actual effect?

The fact that International Law may limit the free action of states is no more an objection than that national laws may limit the freedom of individuals. The world can no more tolerate another aggressive war than a state can tolerate anarchy. Must not nations be compelled to observe rules of good faith and conduct which for centuries have been imposed by national laws upon, and observed by, individuals?

The arguments of these critics are really argument against any punishment at all. But whether a trial is held or not a victorious nation will always be able justly or unjustly to punish the vanquished, either with or without trial.

The fact that it may be difficult to decide when a war is aggressive is no argument against setting up some legal standard. In municipal law there is the same difficulty of distinguishing between assault and self-defence. The only question is whether in the International field you want the matter to be decided by law or by power.

The dictatorship of Hitler was, of course, pleaded as a defence to every atrocity, but such a plea is simply a denial of the existence of International Law. It makes no difference whether sovereign power is vested in a dictator or in a parliament; unless the orders of either are to be controlled by the Law of Nations there is no security for the nations of the world. It is true of course that a German faced by the orders of Hitler may have been in a position of personal danger, but in matters of life and death anyone can be placed in such positions. If you see a woman or child being beaten to death, is it consistent with your duty to remain passive? Moreover the Charter provided that the defence of superior orders might be considered in mitigation.

The Nazi regime was one of the mightiest efforts in history to achieve domination over the whole world. Hitler, with complete disregard for the sanctity of life, freedom, or truth, tried to fashion the German race into the most powerful weapon of war the world has ever seen and, after the war had begun, to enslave all the other nations who fell before him. He asserted, and it may have been the fact, that in the middle of the war two hundred and twenty-five millions of people were working for Germany. If it was true it shows what the United Nations achieved in production and in the field.

The result of his ruthless dictatorship produced for his people acute conflicts of loyalty — loyalty to their Führer, loyalty to International Law and the engagements entered into by their country, and loyalty to their own moral sense. For I would not for a moment suggest that there were no Germans who opposed Hitler. Many of them, no doubt, gave their lives in the concentration camps for their beliefs and their principles. But the majority, when commanded by him to perpetrate the most terrible atrocities, did not refuse and the defence of the men we tried at Nuremberg was, as a rule, that they had sworn to obey the Führer and could not disobey.

It is this conflict of loyalties which causes to some people in this country the greatest difficulty in accepting the decision of the Tribunal. But if you consider the matter you will, I think, see that to assert that a national sovereign can issue any orders he chooses is in reality a denial of any law based upon the moral sense and a denial of the existence of International Law. Hitler, you will remember, issued orders that the Polish intelligentsia, nobility and clergy, and Russian Commissars should be exterminated and that officers who had escaped from prisoner of war camps, as their duty was, should be shot in cold blood. Anyone receiving such an order, whether a soldier or a civilian, must have known that it was murder and not a legitimate act of war, and so pressed by this feeling were the Generals who were tried at Nuremberg that they admitted that they were overborne by Hitler and protested that they tried to circumvent his more brutal orders. But although they made this defence, none of them ever made any real effort to resign, there was no document produced which referred to any offer to resign and it was evident that they continued to carry out his murderous orders to the end.

It has been felt, I think, by some soldiers and sailors that strategic planning of war is their duty and that the fact that the war which ensues may be held to be aggressive is not their concern. There is of course in some cases much force in this, and it was for this reason among others that the Tribunal refused to declare the General Staff and High Command a criminal organization. But the Generals who were condemned at Nuremberg were, in the opinion of the Tribunal, not mere soldiers who had planned a war which when it was waged was aggressive, but soldiers who combined political activities with their soldierly duties, who knew full well the aggressive nature of the wars they planned and who in addition were parties to a series of the most appalling war crimes the world has ever known, persisted in up to the very last day of a war which lasted six years.

The trial was not only important in so far as it established the law, but in establishing, as it undoubtedly did, the facts. From their own mouths and from their own documents so laboriously created and so carefully preserved, the history of German aggression and German brutality was proved and can never be denied. As the defendant Frank said at the trial, 'Thousands of years will pass and this guilt of Germany will not be erased.'

It may seem that it is unchivalrous to remind the world of guilt. But one must remember how after the 1914 war was over she began at once to deny her war guilt and to plan her next war of revenge.

England is always inclined, it seems to me, to be too generous or too casual and too undisciplined in dealing with her conquered foes.

There are I venture to think lessons to be learnt in the realm of morals from the conflict between International and National Law. Just as International Law should have supremacy over national law, so the law of God, the law of right and wrong, or of conscience, or whatever you choose to call it, should have supremacy over both. National laws are backed by force, but they are not necessarily just. They may be the expression of the tyranny of the majority in a democracy, just as the laws of Hitler were the expression of the tyranny of a dictator. But in a democracy we are in larger measure, at any rate, responsible for our national laws, and both in their framing and carrying them out we should be guided by our conscience. Do not allow your judgement to be affected too much by the judgement of others. The individual can no doubt at times get inspiration from a number: *esprit de corps* can be communicated. But it is derived from the individual. Advance can only come from the advance of individuals. Let us never then lose the sense of our individual responsibility for our judgements and for our actions, and, by a firm adherence to principle, we shall make our influence felt.

We may think that our individual influence is insignificant; but who can tell how far the influence of a great act or a great decision of an unknown individual will carry? Conflicts between what you believe to be right, and what the law permits, occur in the lives of most of us just as conflicts occurred in the lives of German soldiers between the orders of Hitler and International Law.

It is argued by critics of the Trial that in future no statesman or general will be safe. The arguments of these critics are really arguments against any punishment at all, but whether a trial is held or not, a victorious nation will always be able justly or unjustly to punish the vanquished either with or without trial. The fact that it may be difficult to decide when a war is aggressive is no argument against setting up some legal standard. The only question is whether you want the matter to be decided by law or by power.

Look back at the past. Have we not emerged within our own knowledge of history from barbarism, and how much further if one could but penetrate to the secrets of the ice age?

> Men who are educated should discipline themselves. Positive law backed by compelling force should not be necessary for them and cannot be their only guide. When educated men have learned to discipline themselves there will be less and less necessity for national laws and less and less necessity for force to back them. There is indeed no need for law in an educated family. When education and understanding have spread through the family of nations there may be no need for International Law.

Those were the post-Nuremberg thoughts of Lord Oaksey, President of the Tribunal that confined the seven in Spandau gaol. It was not for a single lapse that they were condemned, but for acquiescing year after year in the brutal and obviously criminal orders of Hitler.

There is great danger in denouncing the Nuremberg and Tokyo war crimes trials, for denunciation plays into the hands of reactionary political elements. If we cannot trust the honourable intentions and processes of the men who conducted the trials, then we can trust nothing. Although defendant after defendant sought sanctuary behind the camouflage of 'superior orders' and the domestic laws that governed the fundamentally lawless Nazi regime, no law can be called upon to defend mass murders, enslavement, and the cruel treatment of millions of people. If such blind philosophies are to be negated and there is to be a world of law and justice, then those in authority must always be answerable for their acts. Murder, pillage and enslavement are against the law everywhere and have been for at least this century. Law requires accountability for violators.

Nuremberg signified that law remains at all times supreme over everyone, including leaders of States and all who follow them. Individuals, from the highest to the lowest, must be answerable to society, so tomorrow's world should never forget what yesterday's world did. The Spandau seven were leaders of a regime and a conspiracy that set out to stab the free world in the back. The sentences passed on them constituted a giant step towards world recognition of the moral and political justice of international law. Although razed to the ground by bulldozers soon after Hess's death, the forbidding Berlin gaol, and its final seven inmates, must be remembered. We cannot afford more long knives and short memories.

AUTHOR'S NOTES AND ACKNOWLEDGEMENTS

Although for this book, as for all others that I have written, I have done my own research, I am deeply indebted to many people and institutions for generous co-operation.

Understandably, as the story has been investigated, collated, and written over a period of more than thirty years, thanks are due to a vast list of personalities and authorities all over the world; but it is impossible for me to identify those still subject to security restrictions who, mainly because of the intimidatory effects of the Official Secrets Act, must remain anonymous. It is difficult to acknowledge their assistance publicly without implying that they may have indiscreetly revealed to me matters likely to endanger security. Due to this impediment, it was neither feasible nor advisable to include detailed notes on all sources, nor page-by-page references. Nevertheless, the origins of a substantial proportion of documents and letters incorporated in the text are self-evident. Moreover, as I explained in Chapter 1, conversations and comments by the prisoners were derived from their letters from the gaol — authorized and smuggled — as well as from my personal discussions and correspondence with their families, associates, and legal advisers. Quotes from them also came from unauthorized correspondence and interviews that I conducted with the seven through intermediaries, and in some cases directly with the prisoners themselves after they were released.

My thanks are also due to many members of the Spandau Prison staff — officers and men of all nationalities — and the staff at the British Military Hospital in Berlin, none of whom I can name, since their collaboration with me could lay them open to prosecution.

In all my dealings with the war criminals concerned, their families, and friends, I did my utmost to maintain a balanced and objective view. I wanted the seven men's place in history to be determined largely by their own actions and words, and on the basis of evidence provided by people of the highest international authority and repute.

I must express my appreciation for co-operation, and the use of personal correspondence or other evidence, to:

Viscountess Astor; Nuremberg trial Judge Francis J. Biddle; former Mayor of West Berlin and Chancellor of the Federal German Republic, Willy Brandt; officials of the Berlin Senat; former US High Commissioner in Germany, James Bryant Conant; General Lucius D. Clay; Minister of State at the Bonn Foreign Office, Dr Peter Corterier; Grand Admiral Karl Dönitz and his wife Inge; Hans Erhard, former Minister-President of Bavaria; former French Ambassador André François-Poncet; Walther Funk and his wife Luise.

I am particularly grateful to the Lord Chancellor, Lord Hailsham, for his fulsome comments on war criminals; to Lord James Douglas-Hamilton, MP; to Miss K. J. Himsworth of the Western European Department of the Foreign and Commonwealth Office; to the three members of the Hess family — Rudolf Hess, Ilse Hess, and their son, Wolf Rüdiger Hess; and to the Holdsworth Club and Faculty of Law at Birmingham University.

I acknowledge the valuable comments provided by Justice Robert H. Jackson, who was the US Chief Counsel at Nuremberg, and Frank Judd, former Minister of State at the Foreign Office in London. Yet another of the Nuremberg prosecuting team to whom I am indebted is the Earl of

Kilmuir (formerly Sir David Maxwell Fyfe), as I also am to one of the most brilliant defenders at the trials — Dr Otto Kranzbühler. Sir Ivone Kirkpatrick's records were of immense importance. The eminent German lawyer Klefisch and Dr Dieter Kastrup of the Bonn Foreign Office were also helpful. I was grateful for the frank information and guidance given to me by Albert Speer's very knowledgeable former personal secretary, Frau Annemarie Kempf, and by Hans Rechenberg, Walther Funk's former aide.

I acknowledge material from John J. McCloy, who for so many years was Sir Ivone Kirkpatrick's American opposite number in directing the rebirth of Germany; from Baron von Neurath's daughter, Frau Winifred von Mackensen; and the perceptive comments of Baron Moss and Francois de Menthon, former French Minister of Justice and French prosecutor at Nuremberg.

Baron Konstantin von Neurath and his wife both personally made significant contributions to the book; as also did the late Airey Neave, MP. I must also thank the President of the Nuremberg Tribunal, Lord Trevethin and Oaksey (formerly Lord Justice Lawrence), and his widow, Marjorie, Lady Oaksey, who so kindly offered me a recorded tape made by her husband shortly before his death and permitted me to quote extensively from his papers. Comments from Judge John J. Parker, of the United States, further enhanced my legal dossier on the subject.

I am indebted to Grand Admiral Erich Raeder and his wife Erika; to Lady Robertson of Oakridge, widow of General Sir Brian Robertson, who became Baron Robertson of Oakridge; and to Rudolf Hess's lawyer, Dr Alfred Seidl.

The Rt Hon Lord Shawcross, GBE, QC, was most helpful; as were Albert Speer, his wife Margerete, and daughter Hilde

Schramm-Speer; also Baldur von Schirach and Henriette von Schirach, who was exceptionally forthright about her husband.

United States Nuremberg prosecutor Brigadier-General W. Telford Taylor (Professor of Law at Columbia University), and Professor A. N. Trainin of the Institute of Law of the USSR Academy of Sciences, made outstanding legal contributions; Cyril Townsend, MP, provided important Parliamentary material; and the controversial surgeon Dr Hugh Thomas, frankly debated his findings with me.

The last of my alphabetically grouped acknowledgements is for my late good friend, Evelyn Walkden, MP.

I would also like to thank several former newspaper colleagues of mine, in particular: *Sunday Times* Berlin correspondent Antony Terry; Ian Fleming, who used to be my newspaper group's Foreign Editor and became James Bond's creator; ex-Intelligence and Political Warfare specialist Frank Lynder; and *Sunday Times* Diplomatic correspondent Nicholas Carroll. I am also indebted to Terence Prittie, former Berlin correspondent of the *Guardian*; *Daily Express* Berlin correspondent Colin Lawson; *Daily Mail* correspondent Ian Macdonald, and the Editor of the BBC *Listener* magazine.

My wife, Lilian, whose French is far better than mine, was of great help in dealing with documents, letters, and other material I obtained from France, or in French from Germany. As a journalist's wife she understood why I needed to be secretive even with her regarding the identities of so many of my Spandau informants and information sources in Germany.

I am also indebted to the Controller of the Public Record Office in London for leave to quote extensively from British official files, which remain Crown copyright, and to M. J. Callow and F. B. Sedgwick-Jell at the Foreign and

Commonwealth Office Library for their unfailing assistance in doublechecking innumerable facts.

I was privileged to have obtained access to some of the records of the Legal Committee of the Allied Kommandatura, the governing body of the Occupying Powers in Berlin, and also of the Office of Military Government, US, known as OMGUS.

Further acknowledgements and thanks are due for the cooperation of French Foreign Office sources in Paris, and the following United States authorities in Washington: the Department of State; the Office of the Assistant Secretary of Defense; the National Archives and Records Service, Modern Military Branch, and the General Archives Division; the Central Intelligence Agency. In London I appreciated the helpfulness of Joseph Gaffey of the American Embassy.

This book cannot claim to be the entire story of Spandau Prison and its seven inmates. To achieve this, one would require day-by-day diaries from all the seven, which do not exist, and years of daily minutes and reports on every aspect of the gaol as recorded by all four-Powers — again unavailable documentation. But the book does present the fullest comprehensive picture ever obtained from official and unauthorized sources, covering the internal and external affairs and crises of the Allied Prison, Spandau, since its inception.

BIBLIOGRAPHY

Andrus, Burton C., *The Infamous of Nuremberg* (Leslie Frewin, 1969).

Arnold-Foster, Mark, *The Siege of Berlin* (Collins, 1979).

Bird, Eugene K., with Demond Zwar, *The Loneliest Man in the World* (Seeker & Warburg, 1974).

Brandt, Willy, *My Road to Berlin* (Peter Davies, 1960).

Brandt, Willy, *The Ordeal of Coexistence* (Harvard University Press, 1963).

Charles, Max, *Berlin Blockade* (Allan Wingate, 1959).

Clay, General Lucius D., *The Papers of General Lucius D. Clay* (Indiana University Press, 1974).

Davison, W. Phillips, *The Berlin Blockade* (Princeton University Press, 1958).

Deacon, Richard, *A History of British Secret Service* (Muller, 1969).

Dönitz, Karl, *Ten Years and Twenty Days* (Weidenfeld & Nicolson, 1969).

Gilbert, G. M., *Nuremberg Diary* (Eyre & Spottiswoode, 1948).

Hamilton, James Douglas, *Motive for a Mission* (Mainstream, 1979).

Harris, Whitney R., *Tyranny on Trial* (Southern Methodist University Press, 1954).

Heinemann, John Louis, *Hitler's First Foreign Minister* (Berkeley: University of California Press, 1979).

Hess, Ilse, *Prisoner of Peace* (Britons, 1954).

Kilmuir, the Earl of, *Political Adventure* (Weidenfeld & Nicolson, and the Trustees of the Kilmuir Literary Trust, 1964).

Kirkpatrick, Sir Ivone, *The Inner Circle* (Macmillan, 1959).

McCloy, John Jay, *The Atlantic Alliance* (Carnegie-Mellon University, 1969).
Mander, John, *The Eagle and the Bear* (Barrie & Rockcliff, 1959).
Neave, Airey, *Nuremberg* (Hodder & Stoughton, 1978).
Raeder, Erich, *Struggle for the Sea* (Kimber, 1947).
Rees, J. R., *The Case of Rudolf Hess* (Heinemann, 1947).
Schirach, Henriette von, *The Price of Glory* (Muller, 1960).
Smith, Bradley F., *Reaching for Judgement at Nuremberg* (André Deutsch, 1977).
Speer, Albert, *Inside the Third Reich* (Weidenfeld & Nicolson, 1970).
Speer, Albert, *Spandau: The Secret Diaries* (Collins, 1976).
Speier, Hans, *Divided Berlin* (Praeger and the Rand Corp., 1960).
Telford Taylor, W., *Nuremberg and Vietnam* (Quadrangle, 1970).
Thomas, Dr Hugh, *The Murder of Rudolf Hess* (Hodder & Stoughton, 1979).
Vishinsky, A. J., *The Soviets* (Institute of Law of the USSR Academy of Science, 1943).

Photographs illustrating this book were obtained from the personal family albums of the seven prisoners, or are the copyright of Jack Fishman or United Press International.

A NOTE TO THE READER

If you have enjoyed this book enough to leave a review on **Amazon** and **Goodreads**, then we would be truly grateful.
Sapere Books

Sapere Books is an exciting new publisher of brilliant fiction and popular history.

To find out more about our latest releases and our monthly bargain books visit our website: **saperebooks.com**

www.ingramcontent.com/pod-product-compliance
Lightning Source LLC
Chambersburg PA
CBHW050058170426
43198CB00014B/2381